Ludovic Kennedy was born in Edinburgh and educated at Eton and Christ Church, Oxford. Since 1955 he has been well known on British television — first as a newscaster, then as presenter and interviewer on programmes such as *This Week, Panorama, Tonight, 24 Hours, Midweek* and *Did You See?* The maker of many successful documentaries, including *Battleship Bismarck* and *Great Railway Journeys of the World,* he has also written a number of naval books and travel anthologies, as well as four books on miscarriages of justice. The latest of these, *The Airman and the Carpenter,* was published by Collins in 1985.

By the same author:

Naval
Sub-Lieutenant: A Personal Record of the War at Sea
Nelson's Band of Brothers (*republished as* Nelson's Captains)
Pursuit: The Chase and Sinking of the *Bismarck*
Menace: The Life and Death of the *Tirpitz*

Crime and the Law
10 Rillington Place
The Trial of Stephen Ward
A Presumption of Innocence
The Portland Spy Case
Wicked Beyond Belief
The Airman and the Carpenter

Travel and Diaries
One Man's Meat
Very Lovely People

Play
Murder Story

Anthologies
A Book of Railway Journeys
A Book of Sea Journeys
A Book of Air Journeys

ON MY WAY TO
THE CLUB

*

The Autobiography of

LUDOVIC KENNEDY

FONTANA/Collins

First published by William Collins 1989
First issued in Fontana Paperbacks 1990
9 8 7 6 5 4

Printed and bound in Great Britain by
HarperCollins Publishers Ltd, Glasgow

for
Morar and Katherine

Whenever I see Mr Ludovic Kennedy in a television studio, he gives me the impression that he has been good enough to drop by to see if he can lend a hand while on his way to the club.

Television critic

ILLUSTRATIONS

My father as Commander, 1916
Aged two with my mother
On the Culloden Stone
With Crummy Carter
Highfield School Football Eleven, 1931
Shooting at Landverk with my father
The young Bob Boothby
The Fourth of June at Eton
The flight to Le Touquet (Maurice Buxton)
Eton leaving photograph
My father before sailing on his last voyage
HMS *Rawalpindi* in action
    (painting by Norman Wilkinson)
With Spider Wilson
HMS *Tartar*
The raid on the Lofoten Islands, 1941
    (Ludovic Kennedy)
Admiral Gunther Lütjens and his staff officers
Bismarck at anchor near Bergen
    (Imperial War Museum)
The end of HMS *Mashona* (Ludovic Kennedy)
Ship's company, HMS *Tartar*
As ADC to the Governor of Newfoundland

Moira Shearer (Vivienne, London)
Moira as Odile in *Swan Lake*
Moira with Massine in *The Red Shoes*
Moira as the Aristocrat in *Mam'zelle Angot*
    (Vivienne, London)
Moira with Frederick Ashton in *Façade*
    (Sadler's Wells Ballet)
With best man Bill Richmond
Hampton Court, 25 February 1950
Margot Fonteyn and Moira at Ailsa's
    christening (Baron/Camera Press)

9

The family at Piers Place, Amersham
Rachel, 1988 (Tom Hustler)
Fiona, 1986
Ailsa, 1971 (Dudley Harris)
Alastair, 1986
As a newscaster with ITN, 1956
With Richard Dimbleby (Keystone)
With Lord Mountbatten
With Admiral Dönitz
Filming in the gold bullion vault of the
    Bank of England
The Rochdale by-election, 1958 (*Daily Mail*)
With Jo Grimond (cartoon by Emwood)
The Timothy Evans Committee outside
    10 Rillington Place (BBC Hulton)
With Bryan Magee
With Anna Hauptmann

FOREWORD

The question I was most often asked when writing these memoirs was: Did you keep diaries? The answer was Very rarely, except for ten years of schooldays when hundreds of entries said things like, 'Rained a.m. Played ping-pong with Pemberton minor p.m. Had Toad-in-the-Hole for supper. Yippee! Did stamp album after.' A few preserved letters, a few scribbled notes, some press cuttings and several transcripts of programmes have been of help, but mostly what I have written about has been what I wanted to write about: memories of relationships and events that have remained lodged with me over the years.

I trust that my accounts of investigations into miscarriages of criminal justice will not be considered disproportionate to the rest; they have been a central feature of my later life. Sometimes I have been asked whether in cases I have investigated I have ever been convinced of the complainant's guilt. The answer is no, because I have never pursued cases where I have been uncertain about guilt or innocence. In those cases I have written about, my initial instincts that the person in question was not guilty have been fully confirmed by subsequent investigations. It should however be emphasized that, contrary to popular belief, cases of guilty men proclaiming their innocence and *continuing to do so with evidence to back it up* are so rare as to be almost non-existent.

I would only add that in my method of investigation I have always followed the wise words of Julian Symons who said in one of his books that events at a trial are seen from a distorted perspective in that we have to work backwards from the crime, considering the evidence bearing on it. But in life one thing follows another and, says Symons, if we work forward from a natural starting-point, this evidence can wear a very different appearance. My starting-point has always been a presumption of innocence, and in all my cases I have found a narrative story based on that presumption to be far more convincing than a continued assumption of guilt.

My grateful thanks to (titles and/or ranks omitted) Robert Kee and Mark Bonham-Carter for reading the text in manuscript and suggesting various improvements; for information and advice to Brian Batsford, Joseph Beltrami, Wilfrid Bourne, British Broadcasting Corporation, David Brown, Maurice Buxton, Anne Carey, Simon Carey, Christopher Collins, Geoffrey Cox, Maurice Cranston, Carl Davies, Celia Euman, Nicholas Fairbairn, The Jockey Club, Francis King, John McCluskey, Robin Orr, Graham Owen, Mary Pain, Bridget Plowden, Royal Norwegian Embassy, George Scott, Scottish Rugby Union, Linda Smith, Society of Authors, Alexander Stockton, Norman Swallow, Hugh Wilson, John Yarborough; to my editors Ariane Goodman and Carol O'Brien for their support and patience over three years and, more recently, to Amanda McCardie and Ron Clark; to my secretary Joyce Turnbull for all she has done for me over the past 23 years; and to Annie Davies for her usual impeccable typing.

Ludovic Kennedy
September 1988

PART ONE

CONTENTS

List of illustrations   page 9
Foreword   11

PART ONE

1 The Family   15
2 Early Days   34
3 Eton   52
4 The Flight to Le Touquet   74
5 Death of My Father   87
6 HMS *Tartar*   103
7 The Pursuit of the *Bismarck* 122
8 Convoy to North Russia   138
9 Newfoundland   150
10 The Invasion of Europe   165
11 Oxford, Ashridge and *The Red Shoes* 173

PART TWO

12 To America with the Ballet   199
13 Hollywood   215
14 The Rochdale By-Election   230
15 *Panorama*   256

16	10 Rillington Place	274
17	The Trial of Stephen Ward	290
18	Scotland and the Meehan Case	302
19	Admiral Dönitz and the German Navy	327
20	Cardinal Hume, Albert Speer and the Queen Mother	343
21	The Luton Post Office Murder	358
22	The Lindbergh Baby Kidnapping Case	384
23	Reflections on Television and the Almighty	402
	Index	415

1

The Family

Alf Garnett, the right-wing working-class hero of the popular television series *Till Death Us Do Part* was, in one episode, looking at the television screen.

'There's that Ludovic Kennedy,' he muttered to his wife. '*Bloody Russian Mick!*'

In fact both names are Scottish, though it's true that some Kennedys who couldn't make it in Scotland crossed the sea to Ireland; and that those who couldn't make it there sailed on, with better luck, to Massachusetts. The Ludovic stems from the Roman Ludovicus and is the equivalent of Ludwig, Luigi, Louis, Lewis. Our lot came from the south of Ayrshire, and were prominent in Scottish history from earliest times. James IV of Scotland made the Lord Kennedy of the day the first Earl of Cassillis; three hundred years later William IV made the twelfth Earl of Cassillis the first Marquis of Ailsa. His brother Robert was my twice-great-grandfather. They lived in a stunning Adam house called Culzean on the cliffs opposite Ailsa Craig, which today is the most visited of all Scottish National Trust properties. The Kennedy crest is a smiling dolphin on a bar, and the family motto '*Avise le Fin*' – 'Consider the End' – which I can't say I've done until recently.

Robert begat John who begat my great-uncle William who became an admiral, and my grandfather, Edward, who became a rolling stone. Great-uncle William, bluff and bearded, wrote three books, *Hurrah for the Life of a Sailor, Sport in the Navy and Naval Yarns,* and *Sport, Travel and Adventure.* They are all entertaining in a gung-ho sort of way, depicting not only the rigours of life in the mid-nineteenth-century Navy (in 1852, as a midshipman, he witnessed a boat's crew being given forty-eight lashes for drunkenness), but the effortless superiority with which the British ruling classes looked on Kipling's lesser breeds. Returning up the Yangtse from delivering despatches during the 1856 war with China, he spotted some tame ducks in a paddy field. Without a thought for their owner, 'I landed and blazed into the crowd till all the ammunition was expended, when we gathered up the slain amounting to 180 – sufficient to supply the squadron.'

On another occasion he accepted the hospitality of an Arab chieftain in a village near Zanzibar. 'We passed a peaceful night, disturbed only by the barking of a dog. However I soon settled him with a rifle ball.' Next day, finding himself surrounded by noisy, smelly natives (they had what he called "the *bouquet d'Afrique*") 'I ordered one of the boat's crew to disperse them by charging into the midst of the crowd with a 4lb piece of pork tied to a string. The natives, who abhor pork, fled in all directions.' He killed birds, beasts and fish wherever he could: wild bulls in the Galapagos Islands; a swan, an ostrich, two armadilloes and a flamingo in Patagonia; tigers and pea-fowl, pigs and peacocks in India; sheep in the Falkland Islands; ducks and deer, trout and salmon everywhere. He writes with gusto and a good ear for an anecdote, and in his long, cheerful and often destructive life, I guess that little troubled him.

On his retirement he bought for a song a gem of a sporting lodge called Landverk in the middle of Sweden. The lodge, situated close to where a river spills out of a huge lake, is an eight-mile journey by motorboat from the main line railway station at Ånn. In the river and the lake were trout and char so large and numerous that you had to put back those under a pound, and in the woods and marshes and on islands dotted about the lake were tree grouse called *ryper* and ducks of every description. Uncle Will having only a daughter (Aunt Alice), it was my father's hope that he would leave Landverk to him. I think he would have done so had not Aunt Alice, late in life, married Uncle George – a grave disappointment to my father, who took the view that Uncle George was an opportunist who had married Aunt Alice for her money. Although Uncle George was generous in his invitations, my father understandably resented having to depend on them when previously he had had the run of the place and could more or less come and go as he pleased. I remember Uncle George well. He had a round, red face like a cheese and was a great smiler and chuckler. Later he invited us to Landverk, as I shall recall.

Great-uncle Will's younger brother Ted, my father's father, died a few years before I was born. He seems to have been interested only in country pursuits and in writing, and had just enough of a private income not to have to take up gainful employment. In his youth he was a strikingly handsome man, with a long, lean body, strong, aquiline features, and hair that curled profusely above the ears; later photographs show him in baggy tweeds, the curls as thick as ever, and usually with a dog at his side.

Sent by his father to make his fortune in the City and finding it not to his liking, he took passage to Australia where, after being conned out of some of his money by a property speculator, he joined the Black Police of Queensland. Their job, under the direction of white officers, was to keep law and order among their often murderous fellow Aborigines: this meant days of trekking and camping in the open, which suited my grandfather's temperament, as well as offering opportunities for rod and gun. On his return to England he wrote a book about his experiences, and later dashed off a couple of novels with Queensland settings. In one of these a character expressed doubts about the Nicene Creed, which shocked my grandmother dreadfully.

For the rest of his life my grandfather lived first at a house in Wales and later in the village of Farringdon in Hampshire. At both he shot and fished, studied the local wildlife, took part in amateur theatricals, and wrote articles for the newspapers. But he was a loner by nature, and increasingly cherished his annual summer visits to Norway and Sweden. Here, for five months a year, he wandered about with rod, gun and knapsack, occasionally staying in comfort as when visiting his brother at Landverk, but more often sleeping in farmers' barns or mountain huts, subsisting on what he killed and cooked over a wood fire, and in some places having the free run of waters which today are beyond the reach of any but the very rich. He wrote another book, *Thirty Seasons in Scandinavia*, and also kept a huge (3 by 2 feet) and fascinating family album; a hodge-podge of sepia photographs, amateur theatrical cast lists, game records, letters to the Editor, maps, menus and charming watercolours – of English and Scandinavian landscapes by himself, of clippers under sail and warships of Nelson's time by Uncle Will.

I remember his widow, my grandmother, and the house in Farringdon well. Deanyers it was called; a rambling Edwardian building with a drawing-room full of Victorian bric-a-brac and glass cases of brightly coloured stuffed birds which my grandfather had brought back from Queensland. There was a lawn outside the drawing-room where we played tennis, and beyond it a ha-ha, giving on to open countryside. When I was seven or eight I used to walk across that field and others beyond it, but I was always careful to keep the house in view. When I felt I had gone far enough, I would look at other fields still stretching into the distance and think, as explorers have always done – What lies beyond? Today, looking at the sky, I sometimes think the same.

I called my grandmother Granno. She was a formidable old lady with a small, round, remarkably unlined face, and was always dressed from neck to toe in black. Her silvery hair was scraped back into a bun and she had an odd habit of purring like a cat, which I suppose was due to some asthmatic condition. She called a handkerchief a 'pocket-aty'. These were the days – even for modest households – of cooks-general and house parlour maids, and every morning before breakfast six or seven of them would troop into the dining-room for family prayers: while we knelt Granno, between purrs, would give us the Lord's Prayer and the General Thanksgiving and perhaps a few lines from a psalm. Her only daughter, my Aunt Moggie, a cheerful soul who had trouble with her Rs, was living with her at this time, her own husband having been killed in the war. I think Moggie was fond of me, as I was of her, for she never nagged. She had a little sitting-room of her own, up a narrow staircase that led nowhere else, and I always felt privileged when she invited me there to tea.

My memories of Deanyers, more than of any other house I know, are memories of smells: the smell of flour from Atkinson's flour mill across the lane; the smell of cow dung and cow parsley in the lane; the sweet smell of apples stored in the stable loft; the smell of wood-smoke from Aunt Moggie's sitting-room fire; and the sour yet surprisingly appetizing smell of the hot mash with which Aunt Moggie allowed me to feed her hens.

My other vivid memory of Deanyers is that of the airship R.101 passing overhead, and of my waving long and hysterically at it in the hope that someone might see me and wave back. It was my first attempt to win public recognition.

My father, who adored his own father, often spoke of his happy childhood in Wales and at Deanyers, learning from him to excel at shooting, fishing and hunting, activities which were to give him much pleasure throughout his life. From an early age, and no doubt inspired by Uncle Will, he was bent on entering

18

the Navy – undeterred by wretched ill health in his early years; chronic asthma which he succeeded in keeping from the medical entrance board, and later recurring bouts of enteritis and Maltese fever. He was lucky not to have been invalided out. Convalescing from one illness in Biarritz in 1893 he found Mr Gladstone sitting on the pier wrapped in a shawl and later heard him reading the lesson in the English church.

In 1900 he went to China as a lieutenant in the *Barfleur*, and was given command of the ship's pinnace in the fighting between the Boxer rebels and the allies. On two occasions he put ashore a landing party of bluejackets commanded by his future commander-in-chief in the Grand Fleet, David Beatty, then a young commander. Beatty's dash did not impress him. 'He does not lack pluck but is very hasty. Both the attacks he has organized have proved failures, and we have had to retire with a loss of life we can ill afford at present.' Later he would become a Jellicoe rather than a Beatty man.

In 1905 he became a term officer at the naval college at Osborne in the Isle of Wight, in charge of a group of young cadets. From accounts of his contemporaries and from letters sent to me after his death he would appear to have been an outstanding officer, and when his time was up, he was asked to stay on to oversee the first year of the young Prince Edward. He accepted unwillingly, for he had been expecting to return to sea, and as the Prince already had his own term officer, he found time heavy on his hands. But he accompanied the Prince during his sea-training week on board the college's attendant destroyer, supervised his exams, and afterwards wrote: 'Having now got to know him fairly well, I like him. He has a pleasant though nervous manner, is not over-intelligent and finds more difficulty than the other cadets in picking up the work on board. Never having been at school, he is at a disadvantage; he is most sensitive and is much disturbed if he thinks he has annoyed anybody.'

The years rolled on, and in 1916 my father found himself commander of the battlecruiser *New Zealand* based at Rosyth as part of the Grand Fleet under Admiral Beatty. In 1918 he was appointed captain, first of the minelayer *Angora* and then of the light cruiser *Cassandra*, also based at Rosyth.

Engagements between units of the Grand Fleet and the German High Seas Fleet during the First World War occurred but rarely, and both spent much harbour time awaiting events. For some

Grand Fleet officers the boredom of weekends passed swinging round an anchor in the Firth of Forth was relieved by invitations from local people. Among those who held Sunday afternoon tea and tennis parties was a Writer to the Signet called Nevill Dundas who lived in a large house called Redhall out at Colinton with his wife Cecil and two daughters; their son Henry, a brilliant boy who had been captain of the Oppidans at Eton and had won a scholarship to Christ Church, was away fighting in France. A family relation called Philip Warre, a friend and fellow officer of my father, was a frequent guest at the tennis parties, and on one visit to Redhall he took my father with him. There my father met other Dundas relations: Cecil's sister Mabel, wife of Sir Robert ('Tom') Boothby, general manager of Scottish Provident and an amateur composer, and their only child Bob; her other sister Ethel, wife of Sir Ludovic Grant, Professor of Public and International Law at Edinburgh University, and their only child Rosalind. And before long my father and Rosalind fell in love.

At this time my father was thirty-nine and my mother twenty-five. She was a large, comely girl with a mass of dark brown hair tied usually in a bun, and of a lively and curious disposition which – like her unpunctuality – remained with her all her life. In a brief memoir she wrote just before she died, she spoke of her happy childhood, said that she had been as devoted to her two parents as they had been to each other, but that she was insufferably rude to her mother which she always afterwards regretted. She said too (and this is revealing) that she always wished she had been a boy, and once at the hairdresser's when her nanny wasn't looking, she had the woman attending to her cut off her curls. Her education had been informal, dispensed by a succession of governesses and later at a *pension* in Freiburg in Germany. She was, and remained, extremely sociable, enjoying dancing, golf, tennis, skating, bicycling, sporting weekends in country houses, summer holidays at North Berwick and Nairn. She also had a passion for amateur theatricals, and her scrap-books are full of programmes of sketches and playlets and mono-logues in which she and her circle of friends took part. These included her first cousins Henry and Anne Dundas and Bob Boothby. With all three she was very close, particularly Henry, with whom she used to talk privately in Scots.

The choice by this spirited and gregarious girl of my dear

father, a man nearly fifteen years older than herself, austere, conventional, unsophisticated, wholly unintellectual and with little income outside his naval pay (for in the course of his wanderings his own father had accumulated nothing) was perhaps surprising; but it was not one which in the long run she ever regretted. She first thought he was going to propose when she visited his ship for lunch; but the nearest he got to it, after showing her some mines, was to exclaim, 'I say, Miss Grant, what jolly shoes you are wearing!' He did propose in Edinburgh a few days later. She asked for time to think it over, then early one morning telegraphed his ship: 'THE ANSWER IS YES. COME TO BELGRAVE CRESCENT THIS AFTERNOON. ROSALIND.' She had assumed that this would be passed direct to *Cassandra*, but in fact the ship was lying far down the Forth and the message had to be signalled by light through a succession of other ships from the signal station at South Queensferry – so that most of the Grand Fleet knew that my mother was going to marry my father before my father did.

They were married at Nairn in September 1918. Philip Warre was best man and the two Dundas girls and another Grant cousin bridesmaids. My mother had always loved a funeral dirge Tom Boothby had composed for her father's beloved Airedale, Blarney, and asked if he could adapt the words and music for a wedding; this he did and it was sung by a family friend, with Tom at the organ, during the signing of the register. After the wedding they left for a week's honeymoon at Loch Morar on the west coast, and liked it so much they agreed to call their first daughter Morar if ever they should have one. Some years later they did, and when they told Philip Warre about it, he said he was glad they hadn't gone to Rhum, Eigg, or Muck.

After her honeymoon my mother had a sad homecoming, for at Waverley Station she was met by my grandfather with the news that her cousin Henry, a captain at twenty with an MC and Bar, had been killed in action in France. My mother, who adored him, was much distressed, for the war was almost at an end. On 21 November Admiral Beatty took the Grand Fleet including the *Cassandra* into the North Sea to escort into the Firth of Forth the surrendered German Fleet. A month later my father and *Cassandra* were on a mission in the Baltic when the ship struck an unswept mine and sank, fortunately with very few casualties.

Early in 1919 my father was given command of another ship, the light cruiser *Constance*, with orders to join the North American and West Indies station, based at Bermuda. My mother, who found she was pregnant just before he sailed, remained at Belgrave Crescent, where, on 3 November, I was born. A cable announcing the event reached my father in Bermuda as he was about to embark in his admiral's barge for a dinner-party. Many years later the admiral's daughter, who had been fifteen at the time, wrote to me: 'I have never seen any man so completely transported by joy and excitement. He was almost speechless and clasped my hand all the way across.'

Although by birth a Lowlands Scot, my father and his father had become too anglicized to have any feelings of roots there. But the Grants were Highlanders who had always lived in Scotland, and although Anglo-Scottish in her lifestyle, my mother felt an attachment to Scotland and, when in the south, a longing for it which my two sisters and I have both inherited. Her father's family came from a place called Dalvey, now no more, in Elgin; and in 1688 James Grant of Dalvey, Solicitor General for Scotland, accepted the offer of a Nova Scotia baronetcy. (In return for the baronetcy, he was supposed to go and settle in Nova Scotia, but seems to have ducked out of it.)

So began a line of Grants of Dalvey of whom very little is known, for unlike the Kennedys they seem not to have written books or to have been much engaged in public life. Indeed the only relic I inherited from the early Grants was a huge oil painting of Sir Alexander, the seventh baronet, in full eighteenth-century Highland dress, which I have since given to the present baronet, Sir Patrick Grant who, appropriately enough, runs a bagpipe factory in Glasgow. My sister Morar tells me that she thinks it was Sir Alexander's heir Sir Robert who was responsible for losing a very great deal of the family money which, as the reader will come to see, has been a distressing and recurring family failing. However he seems to have partly retrieved his position by marrying a Miss Battelle from the West Indies, whose family had made a fortune in the slave trade.

By the end of the nineteenth century the Grants had settled in Edinburgh where my great-grandfather, Sir Alexander, was Principal of Edinburgh University. He married Susan Ferrier, grand-daughter of John Wilson, alias Christopher North, the rumbustious essayist and literary critic of the early *Blackwood's Magazine*, scourge of Keats, Coleridge and Tennyson, and whose splendid portrait by Sir John Watson Gordon hangs in my study today. Susan's great-aunt, also Susan Ferrier, was the Scottish novelist so much admired by Sir Walter Scott; and Scott's biographer Lockhart tells of her tact when Scott, in ailing health, used to lose track of whatever story he happened to be telling her. 'Miss Ferrier, pretending to be deaf, and to have missed some part of what he said, would ask him to repeat an early part of the story so that he could pick up the thread again.' So Christopher North and Susan Ferrier join Great-uncle Will and my rolling stone Kennedy grandfather to form a rather rum quartet of literary forbears.

Indeed the contrast between my two grandfathers was no less marked, for Sir Ludovic (whom I called Grandad) was as much a public figure as Ted Kennedy had been a private one; and whereas Ted was lean and clean shaven, Grandad was big and burly with a white Bruce Bairnsfather moustache. Like his father, he was a classical scholar (Fettes, Balliol, Faculty of Advocates) and at the age of only twenty-eight was appointed Professor of Public Law in his father's university; a post he held until his retirement thirty-two years later. According to Lord Rosebery he was the best after-dinner speaker in Scotland. He was also a fine golfer, playing for Oxford against Cambridge three years in a row, and becoming captain of the Royal and Ancient in 1911. When he was seventy and I was thirteen we used to play level and make quite a match of it. In 1906 he was chosen as that year's President of the Edinburgh Sir Walter Scott Club, in which office sixty-two years later I was proud to follow him.

My early memories of him and of the tall house in Belgrave Crescent are of the happiest, for I was the son he never had. 'My dearest old cocky!' he used to address me, and there were few requests I made of him that he did not grant. Allowed to watch him dress in the mornings, I was fascinated by the things on his dressing-table – a very long shoehorn, an instrument for lacing boots, two ivory hairbrushes marked 'L.J.G.', a tortoiseshell stud-box and rows of silver topped bottles. Hand in hand we would go down the two long staircases to a dining-room decorated with targes, where the food came rumbling up on a lift from the kitchen and every day without variation my grandfather carved himself a plate of cold ham to be accompanied by a lightly boiled egg. Sometimes bits of egg got stranded on his moustache which filled me with wonder and awe, for it seemed entirely to change his personality.

For elevenses I would visit the kitchen to importune Bessie the cook for a spoonful of black treacle and, if she wasn't too busy, a hand at cards at which (she told me quite recently) I often cheated. In the afternoon I might play clock golf with my grandfather in the crescent gardens or, if the weather was fine, take a book to the back garden. Here was buried the dog Blarney, my grandfather's constant companion at home and university. Once he had bitten two German maids engaged by my grandmother, so that during the war, when anything German was unpopular, my grandfather had inscribed on his tombstone: 'He bit Germans'. Sometimes as a special treat my grandfather might take me on a tram ride to the Leith docks to see the ships, for ships and sea voyages had already fired my imagination. I loved the Edinburgh trams, the yellow slatted wooden seats, the whine and rattle as they gathered speed, the driver's low-pitched bell to shoo people out of the way. I was intrigued too by the exotic-sounding destinations which they and some of the corporation buses displayed: Portobello and Balerno, Ratho, Joppa and Bo'ness. Ours was the Granton tram which knew when it reached the North British Hotel to go left down the Leith Walk and not straight on to Portobello or right up the South Bridge – though just *how* it knew I never discovered. At the docks my grandfather would grease the palm of some loitering tar to show us round his vessel, and there I encountered for the first time the powerful, indefinable smell of ships, a blend of paint and polish and filtered air, ropes and fuel oil and the salty sea, for me a lifelong psychological aphrodisiac. Here I would peer down alleyways and through scuttles, visit cabins and wireless rooms and galleys that spoke of worlds elsewhere. And when I had had my fill we took the tram home, stopping off at Alfresco's in the Leith Walk for a banana split or a knickerbocker glory.

In the winter, in the early evenings, I would watch Stevenson's Leerie come down the street, lighting the gas lamps with a long, thin rod. Then my grandmother's maid Helen, in black taffeta with white cap and pinny, and feet pointing outwards like a ballet dancer, came in to draw the curtains and lay the tea. And what a tea! Two silver teapots, one for China and one for Indian tea, and a silver kettle resting on a flame from a spirit lamp; toast and a honeycomb of heather honey; treacle scones, drop scones, ordinary scones, oatcakes, shortbread, gingerbread and butter— long pats for the salted butter, round for the unsalted – or was it the other way about? After tea we would play 'Old Maid' and when my grandfather found that he was holding the queen in question, he would clear his throat and tut-tut in a very marked way which (because I knew he would then try and pass it to me) made me quite hysterical with excitement.

On these visits, between the ages of say six and ten, my grandmother and my mother must have been at Belgrave Crescent too, but I do not remember a thing about them.

After a successful commission on the West Indies Station, during the latter part of which my mother and I had joined him in Bermuda, my father paid off the *Constance* and we all embarked in the liner *Melita* for home.

These were the days of post-war naval economies and on a visit to the Admiralty to inquire about employment, my father found the prospects bleak. 'Apparently very little doing for captains,' he wrote in his diary, 'and shall be on half pay in six weeks' time – a poor return after my services.' Next day the situation looked happier. He reported to the surgeon-general's department for a long-standing complaint which often left him in great pain and exhausted. 'Am given three months' sick leave, which means full pay and bright prospects.' But the pain grew worse and it wasn't until a major operation in Edinburgh for pruritus just before Christmas that he was finally cured.

The illness had had one blessing in that it had kept him on the active service list, and on 3 April he was ordered to report to Portsmouth with thirteen other captains for a special signals course. It was good to be back in uniform and see old friends again like Admiral Greatorex in the battlecruiser *Courageous*, and he found the course fascinating. 'We are shown many new wonders still in their infancy – they are experimenting on finding a submarine by means of wireless.' This of course was the beginning of Asdic, which was to play so vital a part in helping us defeat the U-boats twenty years later.

At this time the country was in industrial turmoil. On 1 April the coal miners had come out on strike, and it was feared that the railwaymen and transport workers would join them. The King had proclaimed a state of national emergency and a civilian defence corps was formed. 'Strike situation very grave,' my father wrote in his diary on 6 April. 'Weekend leave stopped and only allowed in 15-mile radius.' On the Saturday afternoon he was about to drive off the first tee of Haslar golf course when a message arrived to return to the base. Here he found that he and other captains on the course had been appointed to command battalions of Royal Fleet reservists to go into those areas of the country where the strike situation was gravest. They were not to break strikes but to prevent riots and protect property. My father's battalion of six hundred men and an active service half-battalion under a Captain Edwards were destined for Newport, Monmouthshire, the home of many of the reservists.

Within days he was drilling his battalion on the Pitt Street parade-ground. For the job allotted to them they were hardly promising material: none had more than five years' service, 90 per cent were trade unionists of whom 200 were miners, and more than half of whom were stokers without any field training. Furthermore they were organized along military, not naval, lines, a clumsy arrangement of which neither they nor their officers had had any previous experience. But my father, as always, saw the bright side. 'I have been given a splendid body of men and some thirty-five officers, all very keen to make a good show.' Just what form the show would take remained unclear. 'You will require No. 5 dress and second suit,' my father's orders ran, 'also underclothing for three weeks.'

The administrative arrangements for the battalion were bungled from the start. Instead of sending the men to Newport by day to allow them to settle in, they were embarked in two special trains leaving Portsmouth at midnight and 2 a.m. My father went in the first train. 'Cold night and little sleep.' They arrived at Newport at 4 a.m. where they marched through snow to billets which would house only half the battalion. An army officer drove my father round the town looking (unsuccessfully) for other billets until the second train arrived at 8 a.m. No arrangements had been made for the men's breakfast or dinner, so my father gave them leave to find their own with a promise of reimbursement later. He and the army officer spent the rest of the morning searching for proper billets and finally ended up at Stow Hill Municipal School where washing and cooking facilities were reported as being totally inadequate. There it was found that the men's bedding had been left behind in Portsmouth, so they had to sleep that night and several succeeding ones on the bare floor. My father and his officers were billeted in the King's Head Hotel which he called 'a dirty, smelly, tavern'. It was not the happiest start to what many thought, then and later, to be a thoroughly ill-conceived venture.

After this things gradually settled down, though when 250 men went down with diarrhoea caused by the wretched food, they suffered badly by there being only two lavatories. A routine was established whereby the men drilled in the mornings and played football in the afternoons. 'Great keenness and *esprit de corps* shown,' wrote my father in his diary, though with hindsight one does wonder whether this was wishful thinking. A lift to morale came with the commissioning of the battalion's colours, a white ensign with '2.RFR' in one quarter and the arms of Portsmouth in another. And my father's morale was raised further by a letter from Admiral Greatorex inviting him to be his flag-captain in the *Courageous*. This would not only ensure him further employment but, in the long run, mean probable promotion to flag rank.

The battalion's time in Newport might have continued without incident had not orders come through to shift billets from Stow Hill School (now needed for the children) to the government box factory. The authorities had no idea how bitterly this would be resented. Although hardly living in comfort at the school, the men had adapted to conditions there and were loath to be uprooted. The box factory was four miles outside the town in a very isolated position and, said my father, lacked any facilities for recreation.

This led some men to think they were being sent there as punishment – a belief strengthened by hearing that the place was surrounded by barbed wire. Further, they had been told before leaving Portsmouth to expect to be away three weeks; a change of billet after two weeks could only imply they were to be kept there longer. As trade unionists they still nursed a suspicion that they might yet be called on to break the strikes of fellow unionists, and many were afraid of their reception on returning to civilian life. Had the men belonged to an active service battalion, few of these considerations would have arisen.

The battalion arrived at the box factory in mid-morning, and having stowed their weapons and slung their hammocks (a euphemism for putting down mattresses), had time to contemplate the disagreeableness of their new surroundings before being promised a hot dinner at 12 noon. But noon came and went, and the hungry men (for since breakfasting at 7 they had marched four miles) grew not only increasingly hungry but increasingly bloody-minded. The hot dinners finally arrived at 1 p.m., and the men had hardly begun to tuck into them before the bugle sounded for 1.15 Assembly. This was the last straw; they reckoned they had been pushed around enough. Of the 600 men present, only the petty officers and about 100 men obeyed; the rest went on eating their dinners and began cheering. The bugle was sounded again and met with the same response. Platoon officers ordered the men to fall in but only a few obeyed. The commander then entered and ordered the men to muster in one of the mess-rooms where my father would address them.

Had my father been commanding regular sailors, he would (as he said later) have called up the active service half-battalion under Captain Edwards, surrounded the box factory, sought out ringleaders and arrested them. But he was dealing with men of a quite different type; men who in his view would have been more likely to have been inflamed than cowed by the approach of an armed force to quell them. It had been reported to him that extremists among them had been heard advocating burning the place down, and he knew that it would take no more than a match to set alight the millions of empty cartridge boxes stacked in the factory. He also knew of the men's justified grievances.

Having told them they had committed a very serious offence, he said he understood they had various complaints, and if each platoon would elect two representatives to outline them in a respectful manner, he would promise there would be no victimization. The battalion fell in and with the help of the officers elected the representatives. The grievances concerned poor food, insufficient leave and wretched washing and sleeping facilities. One man emphasized that as trade unionists, they would lay down their arms if called on to use them against their fellow workers – an assertion which was received by a hum of assent. My father asked the representatives if the battalion would fall in when General de Lisle was due to inspect them at evening quarters. One of them said, 'I can guarantee it – further that the men will follow you, sir, anywhere.' The promise was kept. When the general arrived, the commander reported to my father that the battalion was fallen in and ready for inspection.

A full-scale mutiny had been averted, but discontent still simmered, and while the officers patrolled that night with loaded revolvers, some of the extremists broke into a store and smashed things up while others wrote filthy things on the walls. 'The saddest day of my life,' my father wrote in his diary and when he reported the matter to Captain Edwards as senior officer and Edwards said that the battalion was now useless for any policing duties and must be returned to Portsmouth, my father could only agree. They left in two special trains the next morning.

In Portsmouth the men were split up among different ships and my father was ordered to take up quarters in the *Orion* as a guest of Admiral Phillimore, pending the findings of a board of inquiry. 'The heaviest blow that one can receive,' he wrote. 'The outcome cannot be seen yet.' A heavier one was to follow; on the day the board of inquiry first sat, his appointment as captain of the *Courageous* was gazetted, then temporarily cancelled.

The inquiry, under an Admiral Dent and two captains, lasted three and a half weeks and interviewed scores of witnesses. My father was incensed by Admiral Dent – 'His policy seems to be to catch out the officers with the result that instead of talking freely, they are afraid of incriminating themselves and say no more than is necessary.' He himself remained steadfast in his belief that he had done the right thing ('Had I attempted force in any form, the result would have been disastrous'). After a few days he was allowed ashore until 10 p.m. to see my mother and myself ('The beloved babe now able to walk unsupported and possessing quite a large vocabulary'). But he wasn't permitted to sleep ashore until two days before the inquiry ended.

On its conclusion he was granted leave which he spent at Deanyers; and there received a letter that he was to be court-martialled for not having brought the Newport insubordination to an end. Although this came as a shock, he must have realized that it was likely after so prolonged an inquiry and with so prejudiced a president; but he remained optimistic about the outcome and was delighted that his old friend Percy Noble (later Admiral Sir Percy Noble) had agreed to support him as accused's friend. 'Mean to have a d---d good fight' he wrote in his diary that night, and two days later in Portsmouth, 'Lunch at barracks, and meet many old acquaintances and gather that the whole Navy is in sympathy with me.' Another piece of encouraging news was that Admiral Greatorex had re-applied to have him appointed to the *Courageous*.

The court under the presidency of Admiral Sir Michael Hodges assembled on board Nelson's flagship HMS *Victory* at Portsmouth on 21 June 1921. 'Full of ginger,' my father wrote, 'Noble and I face the ordeal and are as happy as possible about the result.' The full charge was that he had been guilty of neglect to the prejudice of good order and naval discipline in that he did not take proper measures to suppress an outbreak of insubordination on 29 April; specifically that he had not attempted to identify the ringleaders, that he had not called on the senior naval officer for assistance, and that by asking the platoons to nominate representatives, he had deprived the officers and petty officers of their rightful authority. If the prosecutor had been hoping the battalion's officers would support these charges, he was to be disappointed. All of them agreed (because the protest had been spontaneous) that it had been impossible to identify ringleaders. One officer said it had not been necessary to call on outside help, another that outside help would have only aggravated the situation. As for the representatives, these had been chosen with the approval of the platoon commanders, and only after the rightful authority of the officers and petty officers had been exercised without effect. It was quite wrong, said Commander Gloag, to suggest that my father had shown any weakness; at all times his attitude to the men had been firm.

My father did not give evidence as such but read to the court a long statement, the gist of which was that he had fully considered the action he had taken and was satisfied that there was no alternative under the circumstances. 'There was a choice of two courses and an instantaneous decision was imperative. No fixed rules can be laid down for such a contingency. In view of the fact that order was restored owing to my action after the outbreak and was maintained so long as the battalion remained under my command, I submit that the charge against me falls to the ground.' He concluded on a note of which Nelson – the great innovator – himself might have approved. 'Through the ages, because men have in an emergency acted on their own initiative, and taken certain responsibilities which have not been supported by those in high office, they have suffered and have become landmarks for others following . . . In my case I chose that course which I considered right and for the best interests of the Navy and the country. The question of the support from the authorities naturally did not enter my mind or weigh with me; nor would it if I had to face the same responsibilities again today.'

But the day that had opened so bright with promise was to end in disillusion, for when the court re-assembled to announce its findings and my father entered the room, he saw the point and not the hilt of his sword facing him across the table. 'The word *Proved* simply knocks me flat. It's incredible, for we had cleared every point and straightened the case all round. My anger and indignation know no bounds, and as I look down on that court composed chiefly of grey-haired old gentlemen I would ask them, "Have you ever been in such a situation, and how would you have acted?".' Admiral Hodges pronounced the sentence of the court: that my father be reprimanded.

It seems to me, looking at the case as dispassionately as a son can sixty-five years after the event (and moreover as one who has had some experience of trials) that my father was in a no-win situation. He had restored obedience to orders very quickly. It is certain he could not have restored it any quicker by the use of force, and there was the very real danger there of the men resisting and possibly firing the factory. But what neither my father's way of doing things nor the use of force could have ameliorated was the men's bloody-mindedness caused by deeply-felt grievances of which the move to the box factory and the non-arrival of the hot dinners was the last straw; and it was this, as Captain Edwards at once saw, that thereafter rendered them useless as guardians of law and order.

The root cause of the affair was the failure of the authorities to recognize that the living conditions they had imposed on the reservists were intolerable; and it was they rather than my father who should have borne the brunt of any criticism. There was nothing to prevent the board of inquiry or the court-martial from stating this; but for Admirals Dent and Hodges and the other grey-haired gentlemen – some still no doubt hoping for promotion – to have done so would have been to show a moral courage that none of them possessed. As so often happens, a scapegoat was handy and my father happened to be it. A finding of guilt against him absolved them all.

During the next few days expressions and letters of sympathy reached my father from many quarters. 'I do believe the whole Navy is behind me,' he wrote, and, 'One's true friends shine out on these occasions.' It was not a case that made national headlines, but such press comments as there were were unanimous in support of him. 'During the trial,' said the *Portsmouth Evening News*, 'it became quite clear that instead of showing inefficiency Captain Kennedy handled a dangerous situation with great skill and tact. In our opinion he ought to have been acquitted and complimented instead of being convicted and reprimanded.' The magazine *John Bull* said that the incident could have been prevented by an Admiralty with brains while the man with the real brain had been censured. 'What about those whose negligence led to the trouble?' the paper asked. And the magazine *Truth* said, 'There is more at issue here than an act of monstrous injustice to an officer who has deserved the thanks of the country. If this sentence is to stand, it will go forth to the service that any officer who trusts to tact and personal influence in handling his men at a dangerous moment, instead of instantly delivering the knock-out blow, will do so at the risk of his own career . . . The sentence ought not to be allowed to stand.' Admiral Greatorex showed him great sympathy and said he still wanted him to command *Courageous*. But two weeks later word came from the Admiralty that, because of the findings of the court-martial, the appointment had now been officially cancelled. 'Feel more bitter than ever', my father wrote, 'at the whole of this absolute injustice.'

He and my mother went back to Deanyers where they bought a new 10 h.p. Singer car for £395 and motored to Scotland on indefinite leave. (His diary records that the cost of this trip, including forwarding of heavy luggage by train, petrol for 600 miles, a night's lodging for two at a Boroughbridge hotel and all meals *en route* was £10 8s 0d.) In November he was informed that he was to be appointed assistant to the Admiral Commanding Reserves and Coastguards at the Admiralty, and he took up the appointment early in 1922. But another round of post-war service cuts was about to be made, and the prospects for further employment for senior officers, even for those without a black mark on their service sheets, were not good. In July it was announced that 105 captains were going to be axed, and when my father's name did not appear on the list of the first fifty, he hoped he had escaped.

But his diary for 5 July told a different story: 'Arrived in office after lunch to find a large envelope addressed personally. I fear the worst as I find another inside marked Confidential. My service career is finished. All ambitions, all hopes, are in this one moment dashed to the ground. I did not truthfully expect it, but as other good people are similarly dealt with, why should I go free? Feel just crushed to pulp.'

He would remain in the Navy for another eight months and during this time his mind naturally turned to what he might do on retirement. His difficulty was that he had only ever had one ambition in life, to rise as far in his chosen profession as his talents would take him; how else to pass the time and earn a living had simply never occurred to him. The variety of jobs and other activities which his diary tells us he was considering is astonishing: Chief Constable of Hampshire, Keeper of Ports and Lighthouses in Egypt, captain of the South African training ship *General Botha*, a partnership in a Scottish shooting and fishing agency, a post on the Harbour Board, organizing the British Empire Exhibition, joining my Uncle Tom's firm Scottish Provident, investing in a soda water franchise and a palais de danse (he did invest £1000 – the equivalent of some £16,000 today – in some other enterprise and lost the lot).

His comments after his interview with the shooting and fishing agency are revealing. 'Fully decided I am not fitted for the job which requires years of experience and a good knowledge of the law . . . this is but another example of what I have always stated, that the naval officer's training is useless in nearly all civil employment.' Lacking the drive to learn a new trade or discipline and increasingly aware of his own limitations, he would in the end settle for the humblest of jobs, that of a Conservative Party constituency agent. He was not a Conservative – any more than he was a Christian – by intellectual conviction, rather by tradition and habit; but the job was basically one of organizing people and events which he felt his abilities were suited to.

On 28 February 1923 he cleared his desk in the Admiralty for the last time, and that night wrote in his diary:

'Tomorrow I become a retired officer. Now that the whole thing is over, I must confess I feel a deep sense of relief at being a free person. It has made it so much easier leaving a job like this, for which I have little tact and which lacks much interest, than leaving a ship at sea – the only real service. So goodbye to the past and welcome to the future to which I look forward enormously no matter what it may bring.'

But – and he would have laughed if told this at the time – a day would come when his future would be his past; when he would be reinstated as a captain in the Royal Navy, and blessed again with what he called 'the only real service', that of commanding a ship of war flying the White Ensign at sea.

2

Early Days

My father's first job as Conservative Party agent was in the constituency of mid-Bedfordshire, and in 1924 the three of us plus a small staff moved into 47 Shakespeare Road, Bedford.

I was five when we went to Bedford and twelve when we left. Had I been asked what I remembered of my time there, I would until recently have said very little, and then mostly small, pleasurable things: tobogganing on a field above the Kimbolton Road; reading *Modern Boy* and drinking fizzy lemonade while afloat on the boating pond; seeing my first film, *Ben Hur*, and ducking as the chariots came racing towards me; listening to Henry Hall and the BBC Dance Orchestra on the wireless; taking part in amateur dramatics my mother put on at the Corn Exchange. I recall too one midnight of acute pain and being bundled in blankets into the car, and driving through black empty Bedford to God knows where; finding myself lying on a long table and a white-coated man advancing with a black rubber object which he clamped to my face and told me to breathe deeply; and after the nausea and panic such a shuddering and juddering in my head that it seemed as if a steam-hammer was trying to split it wide open, a memory so painfully vivid that even after sixty years I shrink from recalling it. And a few days later they showed me a glass jar with a pink tadpole floating in it and told me it was my late appendix.

Yet the more I have thought about Bedford, the more I have managed to dredge up. And the child being father to the man, I have found myself recalling the genesis of traits, emotions, attitudes which have characterized my life. It was here for instance that I first became aware of a physical nervousness which was to dog me ever afterwards. To this day I cannot walk through a field of cows without keeping a weather eye on the fence, ready to vault over at the first sign of a friendly movement in my direction; and I admire more than I can say those who, to test themselves, go out of their way to court physical danger. At the Bedford swimming-baths my instructor supported me by a pole attached to a canvas belt; there were times I could hardly bring myself to go there, for fear the attachment would snap and I should drown.

Once, having pinched a sweet from a shop while my mother and the shop assistant were talking, I was haunted for days by the fear of a knock on the door. Two policemen (one was not enough) would put handcuffs on me while my mother and father watched with bowed heads. I would be taken straight to prison and flogged with a cat-o'-nine-tails. My school friends would send me to Coventry. I was too weighed down by guilt to eat the sweet, and too frightened of being caught attempting to return it. So one evening after dark I sidled into Shakespeare Road and dropped it down one of the drains.

But my most abiding fear, then and thereafter, was of my mother. My mother had some deep-rooted obstacle in her relationship with me, whether it was because she herself had always wanted to be a boy, and having been denied it was jealous of me for being one, or whether she resented the great affection her own father had for me, I do not know, and nor, I think, did she. To say that she did not love me is questionable, for who can assess the innermost feelings of another? But to say that she never gave any outward sign of loving me is to state no more than a fact. At the age of sixty-nine it may sound ridiculous to record that after babyhood (and for all I know during it) my mother never once showed me by a kiss or a cuddle the slightest vestige of physical affection, but that is how it was. Indeed on meeting and parting, on saying good-night and good-morning, she would put forward her own cheek for me to kiss, an act which as time went on filled me with physical revulsion and yet which (until her dying day) I had not the strength of mind to discontinue. When, later in life, I read of Freud's theory that a boy who has been truly loved by his mother never has self-doubts, I found an explanation for all my youthful agonies of indecision. Nor, I am sure, could my own son have the self-confidence he has without the affection that has always existed between him and his mother.

Physically and emotionally my mother dominated my life (and

35

sometimes my father's life too). She was, like her own father, big and burly, which helped her to project the masculine image she seemed to cherish. (She had three close women friends just like her, and when the four of them came down the road together in tweeds and brogues they were like a squadron of battleships in line abreast). She saw herself as a disciplinarian *par excellence* and would often say, 'All children should learn to obey *like that!*' – clapping her hands together. And if one failed to obey or was slow off the mark, she would lash out with her tongue: 'Did you not hear what I said? Then will you please do it *at once.*' She would brook no argument or opposition and on the rare occasions when I stood up to her, her right cheek would begin to twitch, and she would shout at me, 'Come here, Ludovic. *Immediately.* How *dare* you speak to me like that. If you don't say you're sorry at once, I shall speak to your father.' Twice at Bedford she got my father to beat me, an event which I think was as distressing for him as it was for me.

Sometimes she would take me to a grown-up family lunch-party and at some juncture would try and catch my eye from down the table. She would then wipe her cheek to indicate I had spinach on mine. At times, in a show of independence, I would wipe the wrong cheek and look away. This would result in more gesturing and grimacing, and if I ignored that too, there would be hell to pay on the way home. Smallish misdemeanours, like filling the bath too full or forgetting to post a letter or spilling ink on my trousers, always resulted in a flood of recrimination. 'You're so dashed *feckless*,' she used to say.

And she liked to dramatize too. I remember one occasion when I had mislaid a tie some relation had given me. We searched for it unsuccessfully everywhere. Then, weeks later, she called me. 'Will you come here please, Ludovic. I have something to show you.' I knew from the doom-laden tone of voice that something was up. I entered the room and there on a table lay the tie, crumpled, dirty, sodden, beyond all human repair. She looked at me, then at the tie, then at me again.

'Oh, Ludovic,' she said, and if the tie had been pure silk, she couldn't have sounded more devastated. 'Oh, Ludovic.' There was a very long pause in which I knew I was supposed to consider the full extent of my iniquity.

She let out a long sigh. 'I don't know what to say,' she said, and again she let the silence hang heavy.

After a bit, I said, 'Where did you find it?', which was what she wanted me to say.

'Where do you think I found it?'

'I don't know.'

'Just think.'

I thought, to no avail.

'You've no idea?'

'I just said so,' I said.

Her right cheek began twitching. 'Now don't be impertinent.' A final pause. 'Your father found it in the raspberry cage this morning.' I remembered then being sent to pick the last of the raspberries for a Sunday lunch and removing my tie because of the heat. My father could have brought me the tie himself, but that would have deprived my mother of her histrionics.

'And what do you have to say?'

I had nothing to say.

Then the hectoring started, what my mother called (on this and many other occasions) 'thrashing the whole thing out'. Thrashing the whole thing out could go on for hours, and was exhausting. It consisted principally of her posing rhetorical questions, for I soon learnt that to answer any would only prolong the ordeal. Was this a proper way to repay Aunt Susan's kindness in giving me such a lovely tie? Did I know that ties cost money, and Aunt Susan didn't have all that much money to throw about? What was she going to say to Aunt Susan if asked about the tie? Such utter fecklessness on my part, such total inability to look after my things, was becoming all too frequent. What about the other day when I had run my bike into a stationary car because I wasn't looking where I was going? Did I know that it was going to cost seven shillings and eightpence to repair? Was I aware that she and my father had to budget for every penny of expenditure, and where was this seven shillings and eightpence to come from? How did I think we would manage financially if anything happened to my father? Sometimes, when thrashing the whole thing out in a room where my father happened to be, he would at some juncture peer out from behind his paper and say, 'Oh, do leave it alone, Rozzie.' Then she would round on him. 'No, I will not leave it alone, and I'll tell you why,' and she would thrash things out with him for a bit, which at least took the heat off me.

My mother's domination was all-embracing. I hardly had a

thought I could call my own. The questions never ended. What had my friend Billy and I talked about on our bike ride? Exactly what lessons had I been taught that morning at school? I could not write a letter or receive one without my mother having to read it. And she had an almost obsessive interest in the welfare of my tiny organ which, for no apparent reason, she called 'Tiddly' or, sometimes, 'Tiddly-Widdly'. When I was very small, my mother bathed me on my nanny's day out, and I can't say I cared for it at all. It was a great relief when I was older to be allowed to bath myself. But hardly an evening passed without my mother inquiring, 'Did you give Tiddly a good wash?' – as though grubby knees and feet didn't matter so long as one had a sparkling tiddly. I sometimes wondered if she called my father's organ Tiddly – until one terrible day I saw it, a thing like an elephant's trunk peering out of thick jungle: whatever else it was, it could not by any stretch of the imagination be classed as tiddly.

My mother had quite a thing about hygiene, and exhorted me never to sit on a public lavatory seat without first spreading paper on it. This was easier said than done, for I found it almost impossible to complete the oval without one or more pieces of paper falling off, or in. The idea was to avoid picking up some fell disease left by the bum of another; though just what this disease was my mother never explained and to tell the truth I don't think she had any clear idea. On other occasions when taken short in the country I would sometimes piddle on old cowpats for the fun of boring holes in them and hearing the hollow sound they made, like the tearing of cardboard, or rain on tin or leather. When I told my mother about this, she was horrified. She had heard it said that the germs which made their homes in cowpats could swim up against the current and create havoc in the bladder. Although I later discovered she was talking nonsense, I never dared piddle on a cowpat again.

I have few memories of my father during the Bedford years for he was in his office all day and I was often asleep by the time he returned. But I was never not aware of him, and this was confirmed in a recent letter from my former nursemaid now living in Australia. 'What I remember most clearly about you at Bedford,' she wrote, 'was your writing a name in an exercise book on the nursery table over and over again. It wasn't your name but your father's. "Edward Coverley Kennedy" you wrote, and covered page after page with it.' This does not surprise me, for even *in absentia* (particularly *in absentia*) my father was the only true and good and certain thing in my life, and I found strength and magic in his name as some find strength and magic in the name of God.

Two other events which were to set a pattern for the future are etched in my mind. Once my mother took me to tea with a bachelor friend of hers called Mitchell-Innes. I do not remember the man himself, but rather two things my mother told me about him; that he was a socialist and a prison visitor. I found both bits of information mind-boggling. I had never met any socialists, but as my father worked for the Conservatives, I assumed they must be his enemies – so wasn't taking tea with this man an act of gross betrayal? Even so, I was intensely curious. What sort of person was a socialist? How did his views differ from those of my father?

Similarly with the prison visiting. I could never pass the grim walls of Bedford Jail without thinking of all the murderers and robbers locked up inside – creatures who constituted a race apart, whose wickedness was beyond the pale. Yet here was a man who far from rejecting them regularly consorted with them, and I felt both shocked and exhilarated by the boldness and originality of his thinking. I longed to ask Mitchell-Innes what these murderers and others were really like, what he and they talked about, but I didn't have an opportunity and in any case was far too shy. Looking back, however, I think it was my encounter with Mitchell-Innes which in a general way first set me on the road to two lifelong commitments: Liberalism and miscarriages of criminal justice.

And then there was Crummy Carter, the girl who lived next door and was eight when I was seven. One day Crummy said to me, 'If you come over to my house after breakfast tomorrow, I'll wipe your bottom for you.' It seemed to me then, and even more so now, an extraordinary thing to want to do. But I have seldom been able to deny myself the chance of a new experience, and I looked forward to the occasion with a mixture of excitement and trepidation. I remember clearly going over to Crummy's house in the morning, entering the downstairs loo with her and locking the door; after that, mercifully, I can remember nothing.

When I was eight and a bit I was sent to Highfield Preparatory School in Hampshire, an establishment of some one hundred boys set in spacious grounds on the outskirts of the village of

Liphook. Among my contemporaries there were Tony Chenevix-Trench who had lost his front teeth while sleep-walking and later became headmaster of Eton and Fettes, Anthony Storr, the psychiatrist and writer, and Robin Maugham the novelist. 'I *loathed* Highfield,' wrote Robin in his autobiography, and Anthony and I felt much the same.

The headmaster was a portly clergyman with pince-nez and watery blue eyes whom we called the Bug and whose principal pleasures in life seemed to be commissioning stained glass pictures of saints for the school chapel and administering the cane. Of the teaching staff I remember the assistant master Mr Sutcliffe, a dear little man who was the spitting image of Mr Punch; Mr Davies, a Welshman who had eyes like a gurnet and continually picked his nose; and Mr Merrick and Mr Rudge who were both poofters. Mr Merrick was a slim, quiet, bespectacled man, and I well remember the scandal surrounding his sudden departure. Apparently he had been inviting two or three boys to his room of an evening. A friend of Robin Maugham called Neal, not having been invited to these *soirées*, disliking Mr Merrick intensely and being of a jealous nature, peered through the chinks in Mr Merrick's curtains. Having seen what he saw (according to Robin), he informed the Bug, and Mr Merrick departed on the last train.

I never knew about Mr Rudge. He was a florid-faced man who had been a Cambridge rugger blue, had an evil-smelling pipe and a loud voice and once slapped my face in the corridor without any given reason. But Robin says that when he went to stay with Neal one holiday he found Mr Rudge staying there too, ostensibly as Neal's tutor, in reality as his lover. So far as I know, Mr Rudge was never rumbled.

Of the rest of the staff I remember Miss Philips, the school secretary, a cheerful, dotty, amiable wisp of a woman; Sister Gilbert, the fierce, craggy Matron who dished out Radio-Malt and Ainger's Emulsion after lunch and rapped you on the knuckles with a spoon if you were caught dodging it; and young Miss Hutchinson the assistant matron, whose ample breasts, bulging through the blue cotton of her uniform, used greatly to disturb me – she must be over eighty now if she is a day.

Of the other boys I remember little, and of that, little good: Woolley agreeing to be my friend and go on walks with me until a consignment of tuck arrived for Nesbit minor and then abandoning me for him; Potter and me reading in the long grass and he unexpectedly showing me his tiddly (nothing to write home about); Crump, captain of my dormitory and a fearful bully, holding weekly breath inspection tests for the discomfiture of poor Clutterbuck who suffered from permanent hally; Bartholomew at the age of eleven startling us all in the showers with a great raft of pubic hair; Bartholomew who had grander toys than anyone and never shared them.

I can write all this now with a certain detachment, but it was not like that at the time. My years at Highfield, as at Shakespeare Road, were characterized by feelings of the grossest inadequacy; for although I was out of my mother's daily orbit, a sense of inferiority was now firmly instilled in me. I craved love and acceptance and continued to crave them for years. For instance, when the teams for the school matches were posted on the notice-board on Friday evenings I – a solitary figure – would already be there, waiting to see if my name was on the list; if it wasn't, disappointment verging on despair; if it was, elation, proof that I was needed. During my first two years at Highfield I worshipped a red-headed older boy called Dunston and used to send him little anonymous notes. One said 'Hymn 147, Verse 2, last line', and if he looked that up, he would find the words 'the secret of his love'. Another said simply 'EVOL' – 'LOVE' the other way round. I think I would have died of embarrassment had Dunston ever got to know who had sent them.

There were happy times at Highfield too. I enjoyed playing cricket (one school team we played against included Christopher Robin), growing lettuces and radishes in my allotment and, above all, browsing in the library. Percy F. Westerman, P. G. Wodehouse, John Buchan and Kipling were my favourite authors, but what really took a hold on me were the bound war-time volumes of the *Illustrated London News*. Here were graphic illustrations of Admiral Keyes' attack on Zeebrugge, life in the trenches, Zeppelin raids on London, the battle of Jutland; unforgettable photographs too of Bulgarians hanging from gallows. It was in the library that I wrote my first novel. It was two thousand words long and called *The Happy Three*. The last line read: 'And there on the lawn in front of them was the face of King George V in tulips.' No one could say I was not an imaginative boy.

And yet my imagination was the undoing of me; for fears of one kind or another remained, and the worst was that of being beaten by the Bug. When I had committed some misdemeanour which was recognized as a beating offence and believed that the chill summons 'The Bug wants to see you on the private side' could not be long delayed, I would retire to the lavatories, lock myself into one of the cubicles like an animal retreating to its lair, sit on the seat and wait. Sometimes I would wait for what seemed hours, instinct with fear, listening to the water dripping down the walls and the cisterns whispering their secret messages, hearing doors open and shut, the rustle of paper, the shuffling of feet, the pulling of plugs. I cherished the hope that if I stayed out of sight long enough, my crime and therefore my punishment would be forgotten. Nearly always my fears proved groundless, and I would return exhausted to playroom or classroom.

On one occasion when summoned to the Bug's study, I gave him rather more than he bargained for. He had beaten me a few days earlier for some offence and this time, I thought, I was along for nothing worse than a pi-jaw. But after the pi-jaw the Bug said, 'Now bend over that sofa. You've got to be taught a lesson,' and he moved over to the golf-bag which housed his collection of canes. I knew then that I couldn't take it: I wasn't prepared for it, I didn't think I deserved it, and I was still sore from the last lot. I sat down on the sofa and gripped the arm. 'No!' I shouted at him. 'No, no, no!' The Bug was nonplussed: this was a novel situation. He tried to pull me to my feet but I slithered to the floor, clutching the arm of the sofa like a drowning tar. 'No!' I repeated, 'No!'

Seeing my determination the Bug had no recourse but to return the cane to the golf-bag. 'Get out!' he shouted. I went. But for me it was a hollow victory. When the school assembled for lunch that day the Bug said, 'Before I say Grace, I should tell you about a boy I had to deal with this morning. Instead of taking his medicine like a man he grovelled about on the floor making a disgraceful exhibition of himself. It was not something I wish to see again.'

Although the Bug hadn't mentioned my name, it didn't take long for the school to find out; and that night in the dormitory, taunted with cries of 'Who's a cowardy custard?', 'Cowardy Kennedy custard!', I sobbed myself to sleep.

My last term at Highfield I quite enjoyed, for, among other perks, I was captain of my dormitory. Early in the morning I invited into my bed a little red-haired boy called Fairey to tell me about his holidays in India. Nothing untoward happened (at least I *think* nothing untoward happened), but I found the warmth of him comforting. Two things occurred in the last week. There was a school concert in which I sang in a piping treble one of my father's favourite sea-shanties. 'We'll rant and we'll roar like true British sailors', I trilled, off-key and almost totally inaudible. The other thing was the Bug summoning all leavers to the music wing to tell us the facts of life. In a room called Mozart he apprised us of Tiddly's other function. Mulling it over afterwards with Potter and Pemberton, we all agreed it was the most disgusting thing we had ever heard.[1]

Twenty years later there came a postscript to the Highfield days. An invitation arrived from the Bug and his wife asking me to a party at a London hotel to mark the school's fiftieth anniversary. While I would not have gone out of my way to turn up at such a function, I found I was going to be in London that day and so, out of curiosity, accepted.

There must have been around a hundred people chattering away when I arrived. The Bug was holding court at the far end of the room, and though now in his mid-sixties, didn't look a day older than when I had last seen him. I could not say the same of my former chums. 'I say, Kennedy old man,' said a voice as I moved towards the bar, 'how are you keeping these days?' I turned and found myself looking at Bartholomew, or rather a poor shadow of what Bartholomew had been, for he was almost totally bald. Bartholomew bald! When I remembered what a fright his pubic hairs had given us in the showers twenty years before, it was as much as I could do not to burst out laughing. We asked each other what we were doing, and Bartholomew said he was married and selling life insurance. Looking at him, I didn't doubt it.

Presently I found myself on the edge of the Bug's circle. I caught his watery eye once or twice but he made no move to welcome me. So I went up to him.

'Hullo,' I said, 'I'm Kennedy.'

'Yes,' he said distantly, 'I know you are.'

---

[1] I visited Highfield recently for the first time in fifty-seven years. It has changed little in appearance, but now under new management and with an intake of girls it gives the impression of being a first-class school.

43

'Good gathering you've got here.'

'Yes,' he said, looking at a passing waiter, 'not bad.'

I was about to make a further effort at conversation when the Bug turned his back and started talking to someone else. I wondered what I had done wrong. Had I been too casual and should I have called him Sir? Not that it mattered but it did seem odd. Then I had a word with his wife, also his son, who had been in my class, and received the same treatment. It was puzzling.

I was on my way out of the place when I felt a hand on my arm. It was Miss Philips the secretary; dear, dotty Miss Philips with a wisp of hair over her eyes and a tippet of fur on her shoulder.

'Why, it's Ludovic, isn't it?' she said. 'But I mustn't call you that any more, must I? How very nice to see you, though. What do you think of the party?'

'I think it's a miracle of organization,' I said guardedly.

'Oh, do you really, Ludovic? I do think that's nice of you to say so. Of course it wasn't easy getting all the names and addresses. I got in a bit of a muddle, I don't mind telling you. Some people turned out to be dead.' She gave a little giggle. 'Still, it's not a bad response, is it?'

Well, I thought as I went into the street, at least there's one person glad to see me. I set off towards Soho where I was meeting a friend for dinner. The more I thought about the Bug's chilly reception, the more it puzzled me. It seemed so strange. It was when I was about half-way across Soho Square that the solution suddenly came to me. I stopped dead in my tracks, said 'Good God!' out loud and stared into the middle distance.

And what I saw there was not the traffic going round Soho Square but the harbour of Polyarnyy in north Russia in the middle of the war. My ship had just come to anchor after escorting from Iceland one of those nasty Russian convoys. It was cold and dark and snowing. We were having our first drinks for a fortnight when the mail arrived and among the mail, believe it or not, was an invitation from the Bug to the fortieth anniversary party. I still had my seaboots on when I read this, and the thing seemed so ludicrous I laughed out loud.

And because I could never remember the Bug without a touch of nausea and because the contrast between our present occupations was so marked and because (as I recall it) I was just a

44

tiny bit stewed, I sat down there and then and wrote the Bug a letter; and it went something like this:

My dear Bug,

I have received your invitation to the 40th anniversary party. I can think of nothing (including what I am doing at present) that I would rather do less. My days at Highfield do not bear remembering, and my only wish, if I survive this war, is to be spared seeing you, your dreadful family and even more dreadful school ever again . . . Believe me, my dear Bug, yours *very* sincerely . . .

The next morning, I remember, I made some sort of effort to get the letter back. But it had already left for England in another ship. A few days later the thing went out of my head.

It had not of course gone out of the Bug's head. And yet, I wondered, why on earth had he asked me a second time? And then I realized it was not he who had asked me, but Miss Philips; and that she, dear old thing, had forgotten to cross me off the list.

My mother's father used to take a house every year at Nairn on the Moray Firth for the month of August, and it was there, from the time I was four or five onwards, that my mother, father and myself (and later my two sisters Morar and Katherine, six and seven years younger than I) used to spend the summer holidays.

The house was called Tarland and was (and still is) on the sea front next to the Golf View Hotel. At the end of the garden was a parapet and below it a flight of steps leading to a bathing hut where we changed into swimming things before going on the beach. The hut was divided into two sections, and one day when I was about nine my friend Dick and I discovered a hole in the woodwork in the ladies' section. This gave us a ringside view of the contours of my cousin Cynthia who, at the age of fifteen, was extremely well endowed; and we could, I think, have spun it out a bit longer had not Dick, observing Cynthia drying herself vigorously (for the sea there, even in August, was none too warm) whispered 'Jellywobble! Jellywobble!', which sent us into such paroxysms of laughter as to reveal our presence and lead to an outraged Cynthia shouting at us through the woodwork to get lost.

I loved Tarland. It was a light, airy, happy house. I adored my grandfather, my mother was at her least obnoxious and Bessie the cook provided the most scrumptious meals. My favourite dish was chicken (or rabbit) cream, a sort of *quenelle* shaped like a castle pudding with a white sauce over it, which alas now seems to have become extinct; as has another of Bessie's delectable concoctions, a thing called queen of puddings, consisting mostly of meringue and strawberry jam. At breakfast there were hot, fresh baps, the doughy insides of which my grandmother would throw to the gulls. The melancholy and almost continual cries of the gulls are among my most vivid memories of Tarland.

Sometimes the Boothbys also took a house at Nairn. Indeed almost my first recollection of the place – I think I was five – is of hurling a wooden engine in a rage at my cousin Bob, then a blossoming MP. What sticks in my mind is that instead of admonishing me, which I expected, he picked up the engine and hurled it back – not the sort of reaction that I had been conditioned to expect. But then Bob was always something of a maverick. Years later I remember him telling me that the men's washroom at the Nairn golf club had a notice saying 'Gentlemen are requested not to scrub their balls in the sink', which I fully believed to be true – and passed on to others – until informed it was not.

For me Nairn was a time of firsts: hooking my first trout on a pond called Bury-lea-dam (and weeping when it got off); shooting my first rabbit among the rushes of Loch Loy (and believing for one dreadful moment I had nailed the family spaniel); being given my first set of golf clubs and struggling with them on the children's course where Willie Whitelaw and David Blair were the stars; smoking my first cigarette, a Woodbine, on a bicycle ride with my friend Alan Cameron, and throwing up soon after. There were other firsts too: boys' cricket matches on the green, and paper-chases at Fort Rose, and deep-sea fishing, and paddling or swimming in the sea every day when it was fine. Once on the beach I threw a stone at a crab a long way off, never thinking to hit it; but I did, and seeing the poor creature's broken shell I was filled with remorse and tried unsuccessfully to repair it. Nairn first introduced me to two of my favourite smells: those of a golf pro's shop with its pungent aroma of balls and bags, clubs, tees and shoes; and those of the stationer's – paper and pencils, crayons and calendars, birthday cards and india-rubber.

It was at Nairn too that I first encountered another formative influence. One day we went to nearby Culloden Moor for a picnic and I was photographed in my kilt standing on the Culloden Stone.

'What happened here?' I asked my mother.

'There was a famous battle,' she said.

'Who was it between?'

'The English and the Scots.'

'Who won?'

'The English.'

Then, because I seemed interested, my mother told me the story of Bonnie Prince Charlie, his landing in the Western Isles, the gathering of the clans and the victory at Prestonpans, the march on London; then at Derby, when there was already panic in the capital, the decision to turn back, culminating in the final defeat at Culloden and the Prince's escape, helped by Flora Macdonald, back to France.

I found it a thrilling story, but was deeply puzzled by one thing. I mulled it over for a bit, then asked my mother, 'Which are we?'

'How do you mean, which are we?'

'English or Scots?'

'Oh, Scots *of course*,' said my mother, rather rattily, as if there could be no question about it.

I was glad to know I was Scots, glad to be on the same side as Bonnie Prince Charlie and (later) Mary, Queen of Scots; glad to know I belonged to a country which I had already come to love more than anywhere in England, and my affection for which has lasted a lifetime.

But I have left to the end the most thrilling event of the holiday, and one to which I always looked keenly forward. This was the Navy's annual visit to Invergordon. Early one morning someone in the household would shout out, 'They're here!' and we all ran on to the lawn to see for ourselves. There in line ahead, ten miles away across the Moray Firth, standing out sharply against the high ground of the northern shore, and with their grey paintwork glinting in the morning sun, were the ships of the Home Fleet – battleships, battlecruisers, aircraft carriers, cruisers, destroyers, submarines, almost like toy ships, all slowly and sedately making their way into the Invergordon anchorage. There were so many that it took them all morning to pass in, and for most of that time, through binoculars and with the naked eye, and with my father at my elbow explaining the function of each type of ship, I watched transfixed.

One year my cup of happiness brimmed over when we all motored round to Invergordon to have tea with the navigator of the battleship *Nelson*, Peter Carey, who had married Anne Dundas. We drove on to the quayside to see that great grey armada spread out at anchor before us. A picket-boat from the *Nelson*, its crew holding aloft raised boathooks, and commanded by a young midshipman, came deftly alongside. We embarked, and with a surge of power which left one tingling all over, the boat weaved a path through the crowded waters to where, at the foot of the *Nelson*'s gangway, two sailors were waiting to help us out. Looking up, I could hardly believe the sheer bulk and height of her. As we stepped from the boat the midshipman saluted, and at the top of the gangway on the quarter-deck other officers followed suit and a man blew a whistle. Oh, it was magic. And after tea a sailor was detailed to take me round the ship: to the bridge, the charthouse, the wireless office, the engine room, and I thought I would faint with the beauty and strangeness and excitement of it all. I had tears in my eyes as the boat took us away; and as the midshipman saluted for the last time, I thought, I want to be you, I want to wear a uniform like yours, I want to command a boat like yours, to belong to a ship like yours, like you to be part and parcel of the Navy.

But when I told my father this, that after Highfield I would like to go to Dartmouth, his own recollection of the economies of only nine years earlier still rankled with him, and he would not allow it. 'Frankly,' he said, 'I don't think that as a career the prospects are yet good enough. Why don't you see what the position is when you're sixteen, and then, if you're still keen, you can consider special entry.'

That year of 1931 was to be the last of my grandfather's twenty consecutive years at Nairn. For (as I learnt much later) the old sweetheart, without telling a soul, had been quietly speculating on the stock exchange and in the course of several transactions had lost some £17,000 (the equivalent of about £300,000 today); and Augusts at Tarland with many guests and a large staff and much entertaining could no longer be afforded.

So the next summer holidays my mother and father took me to stay with Uncle George at Landverk (Aunt Alice, who had polio, stayed at home) and before we left my grandfather, no longer in Nairn but in Edinburgh, sent me a typically generous *bon voyage*: 'How I wish I was going to be on the pier to wave my hand to you as you sail away to Sweden ... I shall think of you every day and all day. I wish the enclosed "tip" were as big as the love that goes with it. Best of luck, dearest old man.'

We sailed from Newcastle to Bergen, then up the fjords in a coastal steamer to Trondheim, and from there by train across the Swedish border and down to Ånn. Never having been abroad before, I found the sights and sounds, customs and scenery of this new country intoxicating, and understood at once what had drawn my Kennedy grandfather to it. The voyage in the coastal steamer, the *Sigurd Jarl*, was a delight, a leisurely journey in which we called in at little ports like Ålesund and Flora, Molde and Kristiansund, to embark or disembark passengers and stores, for the boat was their only means of communication with the outside world. On deck in the cool, still evenings, as we threaded a path through narrow fjords where the cliffs rose sheer on either side or in more open waters where the islands were dotted with red and yellow farmhouses, some with their own private jetties, a passenger played Norwegian folk songs on a portable gramophone: 'Den Norske Fiskerman' and 'Hurralavet' were two of them, and my parents were so enamoured of the music that they bought a set of records at Bergen on the way home.

For a boy of my age who had been taught to swim and shoot and fish, Landverk was a paradise, a super Arthur Ransome-land of forest and water which invited exploration at every turn. There was an old sailing boat which my father rigged up, and in this we would sail across the lake to fish some remote stream that he remembered from the old days, or anchor in a sheltered bay in search of fat char. Another ploy was to sail to a distant island, shoot its woods and marshes for duck and *ryper*, then after a picnic lunch put on a spoon or minnow to troll for trout on the way home. Or we might go down to the river, fishing the Suck or Meadow pool where Great-uncle Will had once landed a thirteen-pounder and which, until the day we left, I was determined to better.

Shooting the woods on the mainland my father always took a compass. 'Quite easy to lose your bearings,' he said, 'and go round and round in circles. Know what to do if you haven't got a compass?' I said I didn't. 'Go on walking till you find a stream.

Follow it. Sooner or later you'll reach the sea.' What I was supposed to do on arriving at the sea wasn't clear, but as it was a good hundred miles away and I should have died of exposure and hunger long before then, I thought it better not to pursue the matter. My father was always coming out with these useful saws. 'Know what to do if your dog gets involved in a dog-fight?' he once said. 'No.' 'Shove a stick up its arse. If you can't find a stick, use your finger.' Thankfully I have never been faced with that situation: if I had, I think I would have let the dog work out its own destiny.

I have sometimes wondered why I was as devoted to my father as I was, for he could never bring himself to be on intimate terms with me (or anybody else) and, apart from sport, we really had very little in common. Although a Conservative Party agent, he was not interested in political issues as such, and art and literature seem largely to have passed him by. His favourite reading was the sort of book his Uncle Will and his father had written (sport and adventure in foreign parts) and his favourite poems were Kipling's 'If', Masefield's 'Cargoes' and 'Sea Fever' and almost anything by Harry Graham and Rear Admiral Ronald Hopwood ('Now these are the laws of the Navy/Unwritten and varied they be/And he who is wise will observe them/Going down in his ship to the sea'). He was very fond of doggerel, and 'The Fisher's Lament' ('Upon a river bank serene/A fisher sat where all was green') and 'Advice to a Young Shooter' ('Never, never let your gun/Pointed be at anyone') featured prominently in the down-stairs gents.

His diaries indicate that he enjoyed the theatre, though his standard favourable comment, 'a top-hole show', gave one little idea as to what he had seen. His critical views of people were equally circumscribed: I heard him call some 'a thoroughly live wire' and others 'absolute ullage' but there was not much in between. The only group of people he couldn't stand at all were crooners, who in those days used to sing *castrato*. 'I'd like to see that fellow in a whaler in the North Sea' was his reaction to an Al Bowlly vocal. He talked often and with affection of his own father and what he had learnt from him – and this must have included his habit of pronouncing laundry as larndry and launch as larnch. Like him he avoided London whenever he could, but one evening on his way to a naval dinner, he was accosted by an ageing tart. Being very long-sighted with an uncertain memory, he walked some way with her under the impression she was a friend of my mother. I have often debated whether, if I had ever had a satisfactory relationship with my mother, I would have loved my father so much. I think probably not. Yet for all its limitations it was a very real relationship. Unlike my mother, he was a man of the most equable temper: in all the time I knew him he never once showed anger. When he gave me praise, which was rare, I basked in the glow of it; when I caused him displeasure, I was inexpressibly sad.

Being out of doors so much at Landverk gave my mother fewer opportunities to nag, though I could hardly hope to escape the routine complaints about staying too long in the lavatory thus denying it to others, not sitting up at table, not being rivetted by the unutterably boring conversation of a woman guest placed next to me, not being ready to leave when everybody else was, not putting my wet trousers in the drying room, not saying good-night to Uncle George, etc, etc.

The only really major row we had concerned flies. Outdoors, mosquitoes, midges and clegs were a perpetual torment, indoors we were plagued by flies and bluebottles. One afternoon I went to my bedroom to find my mother had recently been there with a flit gun, and that the floor and all wooden surfaces were littered with the bodies of assorted flies, most of them dead but some still struggling for life and, it seemed to me, with a fair chance of survival. Surveying this scene of carnage, of the dead and walking wounded, I was shocked by what I regarded as an act of wanton cruelty. So I set about rectifying the situation, putting back on their feet those insects lying on their backs with legs clawing at the air, breathing new life on to those I thought might benefit.

In the middle of this act of mercy my mother came in.

'What *on earth* do you think you're doing, Ludovic?'

'Helping some of these flies get back on their feet,' I said truculently. 'Those you haven't already killed.'

Her right cheek began to twitch. After a bit she said, 'I don't know if I'm hearing right. I really don't. *Helping flies get back on their feet?* What *do* you mean?' I didn't answer. My mother said, 'I think we'd better sit down and thrash the whole thing out.'

So we had a good ten-minute thrash. Was I out of my mind? She was really beginning to think so. Did I not realize that flies were filthy things which laid millions of eggs, each one of which was a possible source of disease? Did I appreciate that by helping these flies back on their feet, as I chose to call it, I was increasing the risk of disease a thousandfold? (There was something wrong with her maths here, but I let it pass.) How did I suppose she and my father would feel if the whole house-party went down with diarrhoea as a result of what I had done? How would she be able to look Uncle George in the face? Was this a decent way of showing our gratitude to Uncle George for all his hospitality? And so on and so on.

At the end of it she handed me the flit gun and told me to despatch all those which still showed signs of life. I longed to say to her, Why don't you do it yourself, you old cow, but such a positive act of defiance was not, and never would be, in my make-up. But as I carried out her order, I felt like a murderer.

At the end of that holiday two things happened. My father exchanged the constituency of mid-Beds for that of South Bucks and bought a house in Farnham Common on the edge of the Burnham Beeches. And I went to Eton.

3

Eton

Eton was another country, the size, antiquity and general ambience of which I initially found quite unnerving. There were eleven hundred of us there, dressed like beetles in black tails, black top hat, black shoes, though a small elite at the top, known as Pop, were permitted a touch of colour – fancy waistcoats, sealing-wax on their top hats, flowers in their buttonholes. Prowess at games was reflected in a profusion of caps and scarves of so many colours and patterns that new boys were obliged to memorize them, then pass a test three weeks after their arrival. It was a more grown-up world than any I had yet experienced, and at first I found it difficult to cope with the ease and self-assurance of boys whose early flowering, unlike my own, had been allowed to develop unhampered.

My housemaster, Sam Slater, was in some ways even more alarming than the Bug – a large, bald man with large, horn-rimmed spectacles and a purple nose, who was rumoured (I believe falsely) to be in the habit of beating his boys with a cane on the bare bottom. House discipline was in the hands of a group of some five or six senior boys known as the Library. They had a room of their own at the top of the house where they had tea, read the newspapers and girlie magazines, played the gramophone and shouted for fags. They also had the power to beat. I wondered how long it would be before I fell foul of them.

It was not long. One of the more pleasant aspects of Eton life was that, unlike most other public schools, one had a bedroom-cum-study of one's own from the day one arrived. This contained a fireplace and grate for a coal fire (there was no central heating), a folding bed, a washstand (there was no running water), a desk, an ottoman (for cricket gear, etc), an easy chair and a bookshelf. On the walls boys hung pictures of whatever they fancied. Thorburn's game birds were always popular, as were prints of Peter Scott's ducks; others preferred photographs culled from movie magazines of Hollywood stars like Carole Lombard, Ginger Rogers, Constance Bennett. Here one slept and studied and, with one or two other boys, made up a mess for daily high tea, cooked by the boys' maid along the passage; scrambled eggs and sausage or bacon, or, if one's parents were sporty people, a pheasant or partridge in season.

One evening, four or five weeks after my arrival, I had gone to ask something of a boy in another room. When I returned, I found I had left the ottoman too close to the fire and the material on one side of it was badly singed, indeed smouldering, and the room beginning to fill with smoke. The matter was duly reported by the boys' maid. That evening, after we had all retired, there was a knock at my door, as I feared there might be. It was a member of the Library. 'Will you please dress and come and wait outside the Library.' The word 'dress' struck terror into me, for it was not included if the captain of the house was just going to give you a pi-jaw. It meant only one thing: you were going to be beaten. I took three pairs of pants from the drawer and put them all on.

Outside the Library I heard chattering, then a cane being swished twice. A voice said, 'Come in.' The five members of the Library were sitting on the club fender that fronted the fireplace, the captain of the house in the middle. He had a rose in his buttonhole, was wearing Pop clothes, holding a Pop cane. Had

I known that in twenty years' time he would commit suicide after being found embezzling clients' funds, I should have found him much less frightening.

'I expect you know why we've sent for you.'

'Yes.'

'What have you got to say about it?'

'Nothing really. I'm sorry.'

'Not much point in being sorry now. Damage is done.'

'Yes.'

'Bloody careless, wasn't it? You could have set the whole house on fire. In fact, damn near did.'

'Yes.'

'And you've got nothing to say about it?'

'No.'

'No. Well, we're going to have to teach you a lesson.' (Where had I heard that before?) 'But because you're a new boy, we'll give you a choice. Either you can take six of the best now, or go without a fire for the next month. Which is it to be?'

I pretended to give the matter considerable thought. In fact my mind was made up.

'I'll do without the fire,' I said.

Their faces showed disappointment.

'Very well,' said the captain of the house, 'you can go back to your room.'

I could congratulate myself how wisely I had chosen, for I didn't have to remain in my room all evening, I could (as we all did) visit friends in theirs. But when the time came to go to bed and I lay shivering in my woolly underwear between cold sheets, I prayed that soon, dear God, please soon, allow this cup of cravenness to pass from me.

In the event I was beaten several times during the next two years, happily without causing shame to myself or embarrassment to my fellows. But I have never ceased to feel other than revulsion for it, and even today I think that to ask a person to remain still while you rain blows on him by way of punishment is both obscene and pathetic; obscene because it is a form of violent assault, pathetic because of the victim's acquiescence, a denial of all his natural instincts for self-defence. When I consider the whole, long history of English school canings, unparalleled in any other civilized country, and hear voices even today calling for the return of the birch and the tawse, I think of what Goethe wrote to Eckermann: 'Distrust all those in whom the urge to punish is strong.'

Most boys at Eton retain their housemaster for their whole time there, but I had a record three. Six months after my arrival Sam Slater and three other Eton masters were killed climbing in the Alps. Everyone said it was a great tragedy. I said it myself. When people commiserated with me about Sam's death, I said, 'It's a great tragedy.' In those days I went along with the prevailing view. Yet far from thinking it a tragedy, I found it a blessed relief that another ogre figure had been lifted from my life.

His successor was a tall, thin, dark, dotty man called Fortescue who taught French and spent his holidays canoeing. He was too dotty to last. It was the custom of housemasters to visit boys in their rooms after prayers to see if there was anything they wanted to discuss. You could hear Fortescue coming a mile away because he wore leg-irons for some infirmity and came clanking down the corridor like a Viennese waltz. One evening, when I was already in bed, he sat down on the end of it. 'Everything all right?' he asked. 'Yes,' I said, 'fine.' He reached forward with one hand, grabbed hold of the bedclothes and pulled them back. Oh, Lord, I thought, here we go. But he meant no harm. Grabbing hold of one little toe, he proclaimed, 'This little piggy went to market. Heh, heh! Good-night.' And he clanked off down the passage to call on some other hapless lad.

After a year he was pulled out, and for my last three years I had dear Brian Whitfield, with a croaky voice because he had been gassed in the war, lover of classics and cricket, the most understanding of housemasters, the most tolerant of men. Once, inspecting a boy's ottoman, he found instead of cricket bat and pads, bottles of gin and tonic. 'How considerate of you,' he remarked as he withdrew them, 'to have brought me my leaving present so early.' And when he found me reading *And Quiet Flows the Don* and I said lamely that it was very educational, he took it with a quizzical smile and said, 'Don't you think Eton's giving you enough education as it is?'

My best friend in my house during most of my time there was Billy Cassels, a fat, easy-going Jewish boy whose father was a banker and whose mother was always painted an inch thick. In the war Billy was sent to fight in Burma which he must have hated, and was killed. His parents had a house in Englefield

Green and a flat in the Brompton Road where the curtains remained drawn all day. Here Billy and I would read *Razzle* (a magazine of jokes and drawings about tits and bums) and play jazz and smoke and be generally decadent. Billy and I messed with a boy called Twysden who walked on the balls of his feet like a yo-yo, and had once launched a hen from the circle of the Empire Cinema, Leicester Square.

Another boy I messed with during Fortescue's year was called Smith-Calthorpe; he put Brylcreem on his hair and pronounced the name of the English historian Macaulay as Makulay. He was a few months older than me and in the Easter holidays he invited me to his house on a river where his father had fishing. One afternoon, having failed to catch anything, we retired to the fishing hut for tea and sandwiches. After tea he said, 'I feel like a toss.' I didn't know what he meant, but a moment later he had unzipped his flies, pulled out a much swollen tiddly and begun rubbing it up and down. I was very green then and had no idea what he was up to. After a bit he gave a shout, and a jet of what looked like Gloy shot out of his tiddly and landed on the floor. It was like watching a conjuring trick.

'Bravo!' I said, for want of anything better.

'Can you do that?' asked Smith-Calthorpe, mopping.

'I don't think so,' I said, 'I've never tried.'

'Why not have a go now?' he said. 'I'll give you a hand.'

But neither Smith-Calthorpe's helping hand nor my own could do the trick.

'Never mind,' said Smith-Calthorpe, 'you'll come to it.'

It must have been about this time that I bought my first hat, a brown Trilby, and for a curious reason. Such was the general reverence for death in those days that whenever a funeral procession passed down a street, everyone on the pavement would stop in their tracks and as the coffin drew level, men would doff their hats. I wanted a hat so that I could doff it too, and people around would remark on it and say, see what a fine, upstanding boy that is over there, showing respect for the dead. When I told my parents I wanted a hat they said I wasn't old enough, but I persevered until they gave in. But typically, after that, I never came anywhere near doffing distance of a coffin, and before too long and thinking hats looked silly anyway, I sold mine for half a crown to Billy Cassels.

Like waving at the R.101 as a small boy, hoping that someone would see me and wave back, this thing about the hat was clearly another attempt to win recognition. I do not know whether this trait was born with me, or whether I acquired it as a consequence of the feelings of worthlessness induced by my mother; and if the former, whether, had my mother been more supportive, I might have achieved more (or less) than I have done. Who can tell? For some there is an imperative to shine, to prove themselves, and for me, I think, there was more than most.

For despite the many new interests and attractions of Eton, there was no denying that my feelings of inadequacy continued. The slightest snub, real or imagined, brought on a sense of hurt, frustration, despair. I'll show them, I said to myself, one day they'll take a different view. Sometimes, when I had plumbed the bottom, I hallucinated to the extent of imagining I was the Second Coming, a secret which I would reveal to a waiting world in my own good time. I saw myself in a white robe, riding through Eton on a donkey while all the boys and masters joined hands and bowed and shouted 'Hosannah!' and 'Hallelujah!' At other times, I would be called from the touchline to replace the injured captain of the first XV and score the winning try, or else, not knowing a note of music, be summoned to conduct the school orchestra in the presence of the King and Queen. I also spent a fair amount of time peering at myself in the mirror to make sure I looked all right: the frequent sight of a giant herpes on the upper lip did nothing to improve confidence.

On a practical level, concerned that my fellows might come to take the same baleful view of me as my mother, I did what I could to make myself socially agreeable. Fortunately, being blessed with fair powers of mimicry, an ability to improve on schoolboy stories as well as a readiness to listen to the chit-chat of others, I was seldom short of company. It was a different matter though with those in positions of authority and power like the provost and headmaster. These I longed to impress, to leave some trace by which they would remember me, but I had no idea how to go about it and in their presence became self-conscious and tongue-tied. Later in life I latched obsessionally on to the famous, almost anyone famous, not for anything I hoped they might give me (often I forgot ever having met them) but so they might know I existed.

Meanwhile my relationship with my mother worsened rather

than improved. This was because being now almost a man and expecting to be free of her, I found myself a prisoner still. She continued to treat me at fifteen much as she had treated me at ten. I was still asked (only out of interest, she stressed) whose handwriting was on the letter I had just received, still castigated for minor misdemeanours, still had to kiss her cheek on parting when my whole being revolted against it, was still obliged to sit down and thrash things out. And because I was powerless to break free of the stranglehold, my feelings towards her grew from acute discomfort in her presence to active hatred. I hated her so much and so continuously I used to pray for her death – though had she died all of a sudden, I shudder to think of the burden of guilt I would have borne. Once, in desperation, I tried to enlist the support of my father when he mildly rebuked me for something I had said to her. 'Don't you *understand*,' I said to him, almost in tears, 'I *hate* her. I really hate her.' It had taken an immense effort on my part to choke out this *cri de coeur* and I had hoped he would recognize and respond to it. I should have known, I suppose, that he was incapable of it, that his loyalty to her was paramount, indeed that his fear of a scene with her was almost as great as mine. So he looked at his feet for a long time, and said nothing; and the moment passed.

What made everything so much worse was that I seemed to be quite alone among my fellows in my feelings, or rather lack of them, for my mother. Other boys seemed fond of their mothers, and looked faintly surprised as well as embarrassed if I ever indicated, however marginally, how much I envied them. I also noticed with what reverence and respect mothers generally were regarded. When I read that Lord Nelson had claimed that after his mother's death he could never speak of her without tears coming to his eyes, I realized that he and I belonged to different worlds. I was the odd man out, and because of it, I took on the additional burden of believing that the situation must be due to some defect in me.

The consequence of all this stress and strain was that at the age of sixteen I developed a duodenal ulcer, which was something of a record in those days, and had to go off to a nursing home in Windsor for six weeks to be fed hourly on milk and *purée* of potato and jelly. Paradoxically, my being both horizontal and ill and therefore in no position to displease her brought out the best in my mother, for when she was in a congenial mood she could be excellent company and extremely funny. She visited me every other day, bringing books and magazines, helping me pass the time with crossword puzzles and paper games; at one game, Telegrams, where you wrote down a dozen random letters and composed a telegram from them to a relation or friend, she was particularly inventive and witty.

When at last I returned to Eton, I had to have light lunches in a private room in the school tuckshop instead of the usual boys' dinner. But the indigestion persisted. I seldom ventured far from base without a ready supply of Bisodol, and I had to cut short many an evening party because of unexpected attacks of acute nausea. And I was told that on medical grounds I should now abandon any thoughts of a special entry cadetship in the Royal Navy.

While this was disappointing in some ways, there was compensation in that the creative side of me was now beginning to emerge and point in other directions. With a sense of mounting excitement I was discovering a path that could lead to conquering my feelings of inadequacy, to proving to myself and to others that I had something original to offer after all. I first disclosed it in a letter to my Grant grandmother, with whom I was now on the closest terms. '*Absolutely* between you and me,' I wrote, 'I do frightfully want to write. I think that sooner or later I will acquire the ability, that I've got it in me and it only wants time to mature.'

When I later floated the idea to my father, it was not well received. 'You can write in your spare time,' he said, 'but what are you going to do for a job? And anyway, what do you want to write about?' And there was the rub, because I didn't yet know. But I reckoned it was a craft to be learned like any other, and made a start while at Eton by taking (secretly) a correspondence course with the London School of Journalism. From them I learned about the construction of an article or story, giving it a beginning, middle and end, choosing the concrete rather than the abstract, the active rather than the passive, opening vividly, closing memorably; and for them I wrote test pieces which they judged and sent back. The first fruits of this were quite modest. That winter I went skiing at Davos with Billy Cassels and visited a nightclub called *Chez Nous*. On return I wrote a cliché-ridden three-paragraph piece about the band there and sent it on to *Melody Maker*. Not only did they print it but they paid me 8s 5d. (or it may have been 5s 8d). I was over the moon.

Meanwhile the school itself offered opportunities for testing the water. I won a Holiday Task prize on Stevenson's *The Black Arrow*, also the junior English Literature prize and the junior Rosebery History and Birchall Citizenship prizes, and I came second in the annual school Poetry Prize two years running. One year the subject was the Coronation and my poem began 'The hour is early, people throng the streets/Some sing, some sleep and some are eating sweets', which I hoped would have won the approval of the London School of Journalism for opening vividly. And I might have come somewhere in the Declamation Prize had I not memorized the wrong passage from the Bible. It was then that I first discovered the joy of what was to become a regular feature of my life; the choosing of some voluntary project on which to work alone, studying and making notes on it, then writing about it. From *The Black Arrow* to *Can Europe Keep the Peace?* (the subject of the Birchall prize which I studied in a spare room in my father's office) through *10 Rillington Place* and *Pursuit* to these memoirs, this solitary occupation has given me greater satisfaction and a greater sense of achievement than anything else I have done.

At this time, as might be guessed from my contribution to *Melody Maker*, I had developed a great liking for jazz — one that has remained with me all my life. At home I would listen on the wireless to the 'big' bands (though no one called them that then) of the day — Henry Hall, Harry Roy, Roy Fox, Carroll Gibbons, Geraldo, Ambrose, Billy Cotton, Jack Payne, Ray Noble, Jack Hylton; while at Eton Billy Cassels and I would sometimes spend an hour in a booth of the music shop listening to recordings of (and buying when we could afford it) the great American bands — Benny Goodman, Duke Ellington, the Dorsey Brothers, Count Basie, Artie Shaw. When I was fifteen I saved up enough from birthday and Christmas presents to buy myself a drum kit — bass and snare drum, tom-tom, cowbell, Korean blocks and a couple of Zildjian cymbals; and in the holidays I would shut myself away in a back room and spend many a joyful afternoon accompanying the recordings of my favourite bands. Sometimes my mother, never one to miss an opportunity of adding to the repertoire of acts at her village hall variety shows, would enlist me to accompany the pianist; while at Eton with Mike

Farebrother on piano and Humphrey Lyttleton on trumpet we formed a trio to play in an empty school hall on Sunday evenings (you could tell even then that Humph was in a different class). My last half at Eton, I was invited to join the school orchestra to play the drum part in Ravel's *Bolero* at the school concert, a herculean task which meant alternating one phrase, *dum*-diddledy-*dum*-diddledy-*dum*-*dum* with another, *dum*-diddledy-*dum*-diddledy-diddledy-diddledy-*dum* for no less than 340 bars; and it was one hell of a job not to muddle them up.

I was therefore more than a little interested when I heard that a boy called Bill Agar, a year or so older than I, was going to give a talk on jazz on the wireless. I asked him how this had come about, and he said that he had sent what he had written to the BBC and to his surprise they had accepted it. I cannot now remember anything about the talk (except that Bill clearly knew his subject) but listening to a voice I knew speaking to thousands, perhaps millions of people, I was as much fired to be a broadcaster as I had been to become a naval officer by the midshipman in the *Nelson*'s picket-boat. Like the wish to write, I had no clear idea of what I wanted to say, but that in the course of time I would find both subject and opportunity, I had few doubts.

For one brief fertile period that year I combined jazz and writing by composing, in the style of the period, lyrics for jazz songs. *Dance with me* and *Emberglow* were perhaps a little below par, but I was rather proud of *No Admittance Except on Business*:

> No Admittance Except on Business,
> That's what the Notice said,
> Those were the words I read,
> But I got business to do.
>
> No Admittance Except on Business,
> Meaning you can't come in,
> But I'm just gonna begin
> A little bit of business with you.
>
> I gotta long-term contract,
> And my prospects sure are fine,
> Get out your fountain pen,
> And sign right here on the dotted line.

No Admittance Except on Business,
That's what they said to me,
But I walked right in, you see,
Cos I got business to do. Yeah!
A little bit of business with you.

I sent it to a firm of music publishers in the Charing Cross Road.
They told me they would fix up a composer to set the words to
music and publish the combined result in a song-sheet if I would
send them twelve guineas. Unfortunately (or perhaps fortunately)
I did not then have twelve guineas to spare (though I might add
that the rights are still free).

Concerned about my unabated interest in the creative arts, my
father sent me along to an organization called the National
Institute of Industrial Psychology which a neighbour had assured
him had given excellent advice as to what sort of career his
own son should follow. So I spent a day there doing ink-blot
tests and solving puzzles; and a few days later they sent their
report:

> . . . while his literary powers appear to be quite adequate
> to such tasks as the writing of reports, we would not regard
> them as unquestionably first-rate. We believe therefore that
> he would be wise to abandon his earlier ambition to enter
> journalism . . .
> Our recommendations for him then are firstly a post of
> a business, secretarial kind as in a merchanting firm or
> a transport organization. Secondly we would suggest the
> profession of a solicitor, and thirdly that of an accountant.

Perhaps they were right. I'd certainly have been a lot better off.

During my early years at Eton, I used to spend part of my
Christmas holidays with my grandparents in Edinburgh; and I
looked forward to these visits, both as affording some respite
from my mother, and for the delights that Edinburgh had to
offer: golf with my grandfather at Barnton and Muirfield; visits
to the pantomime to laugh at Tommy Lorne; tram rides to
Corstorphine and Colinton where lived the Boothbys and
Dundasses; and above all, I think, for the atmosphere of a
well-regulated house where no one raised his voice and Bessie's
delicious meals appeared at regular intervals.

Yet my most striking and lasting memory of that time originated in my grandfather's library; for I had discovered there, in a long, red row on the top shelf, a set of William Hodge's famous series, *Notable British Trials*. And every day after tea (having now outgrown 'Old Maid') I would mount to the top of the step-ladder and sit there for hours, utterly absorbed. One day it would be the trial of Dr Buck Ruxton, the Parsee dentist from Lancashire who had chopped up his children's nursemaid and thrown the pieces into Moffat Gorge, another that of the beautiful young Madeleine Smith, charged with murdering her lover, Pierre L'Angelier, with arsenic, on other days Bywaters and Thompson, Charles Peace, Dr Crippen, Steinie Morrison. I was a great romantic at this time, in some ways still am, and what fascinated me about the accounts of those trials were two things: on the one hand the wickedness, the sheer depravity of those charged and the truly dreadful things they had done; on the other the majesty, panoply, immaculacy, mystique of the law. I never doubted for a moment (who did?) in the integrity of those taking part nor in the correctness of the verdict; that policemen could be corrupt, that witnesses could perjure themselves, that judges could be biased were thoughts that then never even remotely occurred to me. And when each murder trial reached its apogee in the terrifying ceremony of the judge receiving the black cap and passing sentence of death, I thought things had come to their inevitable and proper conclusion. Here was wickedness punished, virtue applauded, justice done. If anyone had passed an unfavourable comment on British criminal justice to me in those days, I would have stoutly defended it: it was the finest in the world – everyone said so. An added bonus was that the chief editor of the series, William Roughhead, also lived in the Crescent and sometimes my grandfather invited him to tea. For me it was like meeting God.

Sadly, when I was fifteen, my grandfather died after a two-year illness following a prostate operation, and my grandmother moved into a ground floor flat two doors away. After this, instead of my visiting Edinburgh alone in the Christmas holidays, the whole family came north for a week or ten days to stay with the Boothbys at Beechwood; there would also be visits to Belgrave Crescent and to the Dundasses at Redhall.

The chatelaines of these three establishments were all daughters of Margaret Lancaster who was herself the daughter of John

Graham of Skelmorlie who had become rich from trading interests in India and, later, from Graham's port in Portugal. His son-in-law having died young, John Graham set up a trust fund of £100,000 for his granddaughters and appointed their husbands (my grandfather, Tom Boothby and Nevill Dundas) as trustees. The trustees never met, being content to leave the investments in the hands of solicitors (I think they may have thought it slightly improper to be seen taking too active an interest in monies from which they stood to gain), with the result that when at last they did come to take stock, a sum which, invested wisely, should have made their heirs and successors comfortably off had dwindled almost to nothing – another prime example of family financial incompetence.

Apart from all being smallish women, the sisters could hardly have been more different. My grandmother (whom I called Ga and my grandfather called Old Muckrake) was the most unorthodox, a free-thinker, Liberal, and Scottish devolutionist before such things were fashionable, a woman of markedly individual taste who not only enjoyed wearing bright red and emerald green dresses and shoes but had her doors and blinds in those colours too. When the monthly nurse arrived one evening to look after me, she saw nothing but a red glow emanating from the windows and, thinking she had come to a brothel, went off to double-check. Ga loathed cats which had a cunning way of seeking her company, and with me shared a deep distrust of cattle and horses. She also had a fund of (and good ear for) Edinburgh stories. Once at the Waverley station she overheard one woman on the platform saying goodbye to another: 'Well, ta-ta and cheery-bye. Give my love to Auntie *and tell you know whom* (pause) *you know what!*' (I have often wondered what it was.) One day in a snowstorm in Princes Street just before Christmas and weighed down with presents, she met a Morningside friend similarly burdened. 'Are there not times, Ethel,' shouted the friend against the roar of the traffic and as the snowflakes whirled about them, 'when you wished our dear Lord had never been born?' When Ga related this story to Mab Boothby and Cecil Dundas, they were both rather shocked.

After my grandfather's death, I developed a close relationship with my grandmother; for if I was the son my grandfather had never had, she was the mother that I had never had. In the six years of life that were left to her, I used to visit her whenever I could, and we corresponded frequently. She kept all my letters to her, and going through them the other day, I was touched to see on how many occasions I was writing to thank her for this present or that cheque. She was deeply interested in everything I did but never tried (as my mother did) to prise things from me I had no wish to impart; and as a result I confided in her in a way that was impossible with my mother.

The Boothbys lived in a delightful Adam house (now a private hospital) whose policies marched with the zoo, and one of the joys of staying there was the possibility of waking up in the morning to find (as I did once) a blue-bottomed baboon which had escaped from its quarters during the night, quietly grazing on the lawn; and sounds of baying, trumpeting, and honking interspersed with manic shrieks drifted over the fence all day. There was a well-run walled kitchen garden in the charge of a Mr Macgregor who for years I thought must be *the* Mr Macgregor of Beatrix Potter's *Peter Rabbit*. Tom Boothby was a tall, bald man of quiet charm who always gave me £1 when it was time to go. This was the cue for my mother to put on her act of looking stunned and murmuring sepulchrally '*Oh, Tom*', as if he had just slipped me a couple of grand.

Aunt Mab was like a round ball of fluff whom I remember mostly in a lavender-coloured tweed skirt, carrying a chiffon lavender handkerchief, and wearing thick pebble glasses. But she had a great zest for life and laughter and was a truly wonderful listener. 'No!' she would say with seemingly genuine interest when one had imparted some faintly boring piece of informa-tion, '*Not really? Oh!*' Before lunch she would retire to what she called her boudoir (a little box of a room between the drawing-room and the library) and through the closed door you could hear her saying, 'This is Pink Carnation speaking. I want half a crown each way on Have A Go in the two-thirty at Hay-dock and five shillings to win on Plumgarnet in the three-o'clock . . .'

It was always worth being in the hall when the dishevelled, Falstaffian figure of her son Bob, then Conservative MP for East Aberdeenshire and making headlines for his opposition to Hitler, arrived off the night train. 'Bob,' said this tiny woman to this large and no longer young man, 'you haven't shaved, your shirt is filthy, and you're smelling of whisky. Go straight upstairs at once and have a bath and change before you dare come down to breakfast.' And the gravelly voice which could hold the House of Commons (and later radio and television audiences) in thrall would say meekly, 'Very good, mother,' and trot on up. I have seen her of an evening snatch a glass into which Bob was pouring whisky and say to him, 'That's *far* too strong. Pour half of it back.' And he did.

Bob and my mother were very close, being first cousins without siblings. Bob brought with him a whiff of the cosmopolitan world which was light years away from that of a Conservative Party agent or even the general manager of an Edinburgh financial institution; a world which encompassed Winston Churchill and Noël Coward, the Savoy Grill, golf at Le Touquet, Diana and Duff Cooper, Lloyd George and Thomas Beecham, Wagner at Bayreuth, the tables at Monte Carlo, White's Club; and at Beechwood and elsewhere he would hold forth for hours to an enraptured audience on the latest London political and social gossip. In the south he would often see and telephone my mother. 'Bob says there'll be no war', 'Bob says Baldwin's going to the country', she would tell people for days afterwards, as though God had spoken.

My own relationship with him was somewhat ambivalent, for although my mother was always urging me to call on him when in London, I never found I had much to say; moreover, having inherited his mother's curiosity as well as his father's charm, he had a habit of digging things out of me I would rather have left unsaid. He was, I think, one of the funniest men I have ever known, though often coarse in the extreme. When I was having a drink with him in the House of Lords one evening, he pointed to an elderly, dozing peer and said in a loud voice, 'That's Lord Bootle. His wife divorced him for rogering the butler. (*Pause*) Found them tucked up together. (*Pause*) Turned out he'd rogered the previous butler too. (*Pause*) Seems that only butlers gave him satisfaction. (*Pause*) To look at him, you wouldn't think he had it in him.' He was always coming out with stories like this, and you never knew whether to believe all of it, some of it, or none of it.

As he was such an outstanding egoist, many of his stories concerned himself and these also were grossly exaggerated, if not invented. A typical Bob story concerned his audience with Hitler. 'He greeted me with "Heil, Hitler!" and raised his arm, so I responded with "Heil, Boothby!" and raised mine' (a fantasy which of course he would have *liked* to have happened).[1] From

Eton days on, he was homosexual as well as heterosexual, not always correct in money matters (he resigned as a Minister for not having declared to the House a personal interest in frozen, wartime Czech assets, and he was awarded £40,000 libel damages against a newspaper which had alleged that he *was* homosexual) and to my certain knowledge he fathered at least three children by the wives of other men (two by one woman, one by another). I once told him to his face that he was a shit of the first order, at which he rubbed his hands, gave a deep chuckle and said, 'Well, a *bit*. Not *entirely*'; yet he was also politically brilliant, very generous and companionable, and of irresistible charm. I fell out with him in later years but became reconciled shortly before his death, by which time his huge frame had shrivelled to the size of a nut (in the House of Lords' smoking room I failed to recognize him). He kept his mordant wit to the end. A week or two before he died aged eighty-six, he wrote to me: 'There should be voluntary euthanasia from seventy-five, and at eighty-five it should be compulsory.'

I didn't visit Redhall and the Dundasses as often as Beechwood and Belgrave Crescent but I remember visits to old Nanny-Noo who had once been my mother's nurse and now lived in retirement on the top floor; playing billiard fives on a table in the basement; and fishing for trout in the Water of Leith which ran through the grounds. Nevill Dundas (who rarely stepped outside without a hat) seemed more serious than Tom Boothby, and Cecil too had a *gravitas* about her that was missing from her sisters. I do not think that either of them had ever recovered from the death of their brilliant and adored son Henry, and what he might have achieved had he lived.

[1] I am obliged to my cousin Simon Carey for telling me the origins of this claim. In his autobiography, *Memories*, Maurice Bowra, the former Warden of Wadham College, Oxford, writes of a meeting he and friends had with Hitler before he came to power: '. . . we were summoned to Hitler's presence in his hotel. There were some six of us, and as we came into the room, Hitler raised his hand in the Nazi salute, and we did nothing in return. This was soon expanded by the English Press into a story that he had said, "Heil, Hitler!" and that I replied, "Heil, Bowra!". The story brought me nothing but credit, but it was not true.' Bob was a close friend of Maurice Bowra and clearly adapted this story as though it had happened to him.

Since this book was first published, Mr Richard Usborne has informed me that he has looked into a variety of claims of similar encounters with Hitler and found none to be true. 'In no circumstance would or did Hitler ever emit that greeting . . . Alan Bullock and Hugh Trevor-Roper both confirmed this.'

Cecil was a very moral woman. She could never bring herself to use the word 'breast', preferring 'chest', so that there were times when you didn't know which she was talking about. Once she looked at me earnestly and said, 'I hear Eton is *a sink* of iniquity' which made me wonder if she knew about Smith-Calthorpe. She was also a woman of fierce commitments. Because of Henry she used to sell poppies in Princes Street before Armistice Day, and she was liable to savage those who spurned her wares. 'Call yourself a man of God,' she shouted at a clergyman who was hoping to slip by unnoticed, 'when you won't even buy a poppy for the sake of those who died in the war!' To another who ignored her she said, 'You revolting old man, I hope you get run over by the next tram,' and chased him into the gutter. She was also prone to telling her chauffeur to stop the car while she got out and belaboured some cart-driver for what she considered ill-treatment of his horse. 'I'll run you in, you brute,' she'd say, and sometimes did. Once in Princes Street she accosted a man who was dragging his dog along the pavement. 'Your dog wants to do Bigs,' she shouted at him, 'and you won't let him. I hope some day when you want to do Bigs, somebody will prevent you.' And when a young woman pedestrian in a brightly coloured mackintosh crossed against the lights, causing the chauffeur to brake sharply, she lowered the window and shouted after her, '*You yellow ass!*' But these outbursts were entirely without malice, and the moment they were over she gave a winning, half-embarrassed smile, as though to show awareness of (though not contrition for) her lack of restraint.

For me those Christmasses at Beechwood were happy ones. There would be a day over driven pheasants at Uncle Tom's shoot in East Lothian, an evening at the panto with Tommy Lorne's successor, the diminutive and equally funny Dave Willis ('*I'm* a Tyrolean/No' a *big* yun/Just a *wee* yun'), afternoons at the cinema or the funfair in the Waverley market, or playing Bob's Noël Coward records on the gramophone. And then at midnight on New Year's Eve in true Scots fashion, we assembled on the top of the steps outside the front door; and facing the now darkened Pentland hills, and with all the creatures next door tucked up for the night and their voices stilled, we listened to the chimes from Big Ben booming out on the wireless. And we ate shortbread and drank whisky, while in slow melodious tones Uncle Tom read us part of *In Memoriam*:

Ring out, wild bells, to the wild sky,
The flying cloud, the frosty light:
The year is dying in the night;
Ring out, wild bells, and let him die.

Ring out the old, ring in the new,
Ring, happy bells, across the snow:
The year is going, let him go;
Ring out the false, ring in the true.

Ring out the grief that saps the mind,
For those that here we see no more;
Ring out the feud of rich and poor,
Ring in redress to all mankind.

For an old romantic like myself, it was too much: every year I heard it, I blubbed; indeed still can.

After Nairn and the death of my grandfather, my parents had to look elsewhere for a place for summer holidays; and they found it in a delightful farmhouse which they took for several years before the war in the Hebridean island of Islay. The journey there took three days and for me the best part was exchanging the dull, lowland country between Edinburgh and Glasgow for the sweep and scale of the Highlands; huge bare hills on either side, blue lochs fringed with green reeds, a skyful of sailing clouds, grandeur, emptiness, space. *I will lift up mine eyes to the hills from whence cometh my help*, said the psalmist, and always in that country I have found it to be so.

But the journey was not without its hazards. To the west of Arrochar, at the end of Loch Lomond, is a mini-mountain called Rest-and-be-Thankful which the family car, because of the gradients of those days, was always reluctant to scale. Half way up, a jet of steam would start rising from beneath the bonnet and my mother would cry 'She's boiling!' (my mother had adopted my father's habit of referring to cars as if they were ships). Then I would be dispatched to the nearest inhabited dwelling (often a fair step off) to fetch water. Once this happened three times, and my mother became worried that we would miss the boat. 'Is she going to make it?' she inquired anxiously as we inched towards the summit, and my father said yes she was (and she did). From West Loch Tarbert the steamer took us by way of the little island of Gigha with its tropical gardens either to Port Ellen on the south side of Islay, or to Port Askaig on the east.

For me Islay has always had a kind of magic, though I find it hard to describe: I think it lies in the variety of its landscape and vistas, a blend unlike that of any other Hebridean island, of wildness and tameness, hilly moorland and rich farmland, tall cliffs, rocky inlets, yellow sands, distilleries and lighthouses, charming sea villages like Port Charlotte and Bowmore, distant views of Colonsay and Mull, the coast of Ulster, the Mull of Kintyre. Most of the island then was owned by two men; in the north John Morrison MP, later Lord Margadale; in the south Talbot Clifton, whose widow dedicated her book of memoirs 'To God for Talbot'.

There was a fair-size burn running near the farmhouse, unproductive in good weather, though after a spate my father and I would spend all day there and come back with a salmon or grilse and half a dozen sea trout. He also rented a parcel of moor, first on the cliffs of the Mull of Oa looking out over the Atlantic, later further up the coast on the Rhinns of Islay, and here I shot my first grouse, partridge, snipe. There was picnicking by trout lochs and on the seashore, sea fishing in Loch Indaal, a day in Jura climbing the twin Paps, and golf at Machrie on a course among the dunes where on some tees you could see neither fairway nor green, and putting became a test of negotiating a path between the droppings of sheep. In the evenings my parents attempted the *Times* crossword: the clues were beyond me, but I became a dab hand at the anagrams. I also wrote some execrable poems including 'The old cock grouse of the moor' and 'Ode to a dead trout'.

Over the years we had our share of adventures. My mother was chased by a bull (no comment!). Ben, the family spaniel, sank his teeth into a visiting Peke whom he found guzzling his dinner, to such effect the Peke had to be put away; it happened so quickly my father didn't have time (or inclination?) to practise what he had preached about shoving a stick or finger up Ben's bum. Another time, when he got hopelessly lost in a fog while fishing in the hills, he did follow his own advice of finding a stream that would lead to the sea (in Islay seldom more than a mile or two away) and was fortunate to strike a road.

It was in Islay when I was fifteen that I had my first tentative love affair, though it was so mild and idealized that it hardly merits the name. Until then my only physical contact with a woman had been with my sisters' nursemaid, a buxom girl of eighteen. At fourteen I used to creep up behind her in the nursery and tickle her under the armpits, less with the object of giving her a start, which it did, as to brush my hands across her burgeoning bosom. Once, to my surprise, she stood quite still and allowed me (still from behind) to give them a good kneading; then abruptly pushing me away, said, 'You mustn't do that. It's wrong.' So, rather than risk a further rebuff, I didn't.

The object of my affections on this occasion was a family friend and neighbour whom I shall call Myra. She was then, I think, thirty-one, a small woman with a charming doll-like face and Clara Bow mouth, quite unsophisticated in the ways of the world, but of a romantic turn of mind. For three weeks one summer at Islay she became the focus of my desperate need for somebody to love. Sometimes in the evenings after supper when the only sounds were the distant, melancholy cries of the sheep, we would go for a walk or a drive, then sit on the grass in some remote spot. 'Gosh!' Myra would begin, 'what a perfectly *heavenly* sunset!' or '*Look* how calm the sea is – not a ripple anywhere.' But it was Myra I had come to admire, not the bloody sea or sunset. I shall never forget the first time we kissed. I knew no other way of doing it than to rain little dry kisses on her cheeks, forehead, lips. After a bit Myra said, 'Can I show you a different way to kiss?' I wondered what it could be. 'Open your mouth a little,' she said.

That first proper kiss, that intimate physical contact was for me like a sort of cloudburst, for not only had I found for the first time a woman to love but – far more important and also for the first time – a woman who was actively loving me; and with the intense surprise and joy of it, I burst into tears. 'Don't, my dear, don't,' said Myra, and cradled my head against her breasts and stroked my hair, and because nobody had ever done that either, I wept even more. And even after the novelty had worn off, the discovery of what it was to love and be loved after a lifetime without it, was so great that the act of kissing would still bring tears to my eyes. Between kisses we talked. I told her of some of my hang-ups, and she told me she had never been to bed with anybody (which was not as unusual in those days as it would seem today): she had once been engaged to a man called Roger, but he had died, I think she said, or maybe had gone and married someone else.

And then an odd thing happened. I had to leave Islay early that year, at about the same time as Myra. So my parents said why didn't we go together in Myra's car, which made sense, and to save the expense of a hotel, *why didn't we take the two tents and sleeping-bags we had, and camp on the way?* I could hardly believe what I was hearing. I supposed that the possibility of their son of fifteen and friend of thirty-one having any kind of physical relationship had simply never occurred to them. For days before our departure I was in a ferment of excitement, and could think of nothing else. I felt I was on the brink of some new and earth-shaking experience, but had no clear idea of how it might end.

We set off together like some honeymoon pair, and at about seven in the evening entered a field. After I had put up one of the tents, I said to Myra, 'Do you want me to put up the other one?' She blushed a little, and said with a disarming directness, 'Oh, Ludovic, you *are* wicked.' So I put the sleeping-bags into the tent, and after we had sat in the car drinking coffee and eating the remains of our sandwiches, Myra went into the tent to undress and get into her sleeping-bag. By the time I had smoked a cigarette and walked round the field, it was almost dark, and I had the hell of a job crashing about in the tent taking off my things and finding my pyjamas – all of which sent an invisible Myra into giggles. Then I said, 'I don't think we need two sleeping-bags any more than two tents, do we?' When she didn't answer, I crept in to her sleeping-bag and put my arms around her. It was a tightish fit. Then it began to rain.

And that, believe it or not, was that. For apart from a deal of kissing, absolutely nothing happened. I was far too nervous to do any exploring, having no clear idea of where to go and what to do if I ever got there; also, since fear of my mother had made me basically fearful of all women, I was frightened on two counts; of being rebuffed, or alternatively of giving Myra a baby. She on her part was equally apprehensive, feeling perhaps that this tent in this field in the pissing rain with someone young enough to be her son was not really the time or place to start. If she had been able to give me some small encouragement, some guidance, I'm sure I would have found the way and the ensuing coupling might have been an initiation to remember. As things were, we lay clasped in each other's arms, myself hard against her, until we fell asleep.

Myra was not the only person I was half in love with that summer. Another, at Eton, was a yellow-haired boy called Butler whom I thought of constantly. To show him how much I cared I did a very rash thing; left my house by the fire escape at 2 a.m. in gym shoes, made my way through the streets of a darkened and deserted Eton, climbed up the fire escape of his house, and, where it passed his bedroom window, clambered in. I intended to do no more than plant a chaste kiss on his forehead and, as it were, plight my troth. But he woke with such a shriek and gave me such a blast of early morning halitosis that I was obliged to beat a hasty retreat and was lucky, I suppose, to arrive back in my own house undetected. Later, at summer camp, Butler and I used to go for evening walks in the woods, and lie down in a hollow. But what I wanted to give Butler was not what he wanted me to give him. 'Oh, do stop kissing me,' he said. 'Do get on with it.'

My mind at this time was a maelstrom of thoughts of love and sex. I loved and I lusted, separately and together, boys and girls. I lusted equally after one of the master's wives, the daughter of a local colonel who came regularly to College Chapel, and a female shop assistant in W. V. Brown; and when the shop assistant was on her way home, I would sometimes put myself in her path and smile, and if she smiled back, I would tremble at the knees; but I never had the guts (as I learned later some boys had) to take things further. Then I found my scheduled bath time (9.42–52) coincided with the time a nubile young maid in the house next door undressed for bed. To see what I wanted meant turning out the light and standing in the bath. One evening I slipped on the soap, lurched forward and crashed my hand through the window. There was blood everywhere. It took some explaining. I have the scar on my wrist to this day.

Were we all at this time as over-sexed as it might seem? I do not think so. Deprive boys at the age of greatest sexual awareness of the company of girls and such diversions will follow. Today with boys and girls mixing freely, libidos that used to boil now simmer.

Eventually Billy Cassels and I decided it was time to be initiated, and sought the advice of Volkoff. Volkoff was a Danish count of our age who knew the address of every brothel and high-class tart in London, Paris and Copenhagen. Volkoff said, 'You couldn't do better than French Marie. Say I sent you.'

So Billy and I went to London and after a good lunch spun a coin as to who would go first, and I won. French Marie had a flat in Shepherd Market which contained, to my surprise, a maid, a dog, a set of Molière and a baby grand. She greeted me in her negligée, a well-built woman of about thirty with raven hair and an olive skin.

'Hallo,' I said, 'Peter sends his love.'

'Oo eez Peetair, dulleeng?'

'Peter Volkoff.'

'Oh, Peetair. You gnaw eem?'

'He sent us. I mean, he sent me.'

'Peetair is a nize boy, yes? And I sink you are a nize boy too?'

'Oh, I don't know.'

'I gnaw you are.' She laughed. 'And 'ave you brought Marie a nize beeg present?'

I handed over an envelope which, on Volkoff's instructions, contained three £1 notes. I had thought she would put this discreetly on one side but she opened it and counted the notes. '*Bon!*' she said, putting the envelope on the mantelpiece. 'And a leetle sumsing for ze maid?'

'The maid?' I said. (Volkoff hadn't mentioned the maid.) 'But I'm not going to –'

'I gnaw, dulleeng,' Marie said, 'but eet ees normal.'

I delved into my trouser pocket and found a half-crown which she put by the envelope. 'And now you are going to be a nochty boy, yes?' She brushed her hand against my crotch and laughed. 'What a beeg boy, eh! Come wiz me and Marie will geeve you a good time.'

And she did. But afterwards I reflected how much better it might have been with old Myra.

4

The Flight to Le Touquet

My last year at Eton was quite enjoyable. In the Easter half I was elected to Pop and also became captain of my house games, which both resulted in certain perks as well as doing much to further self-esteem. In the school play I acted Horatio to Michael Benthall's Hamlet. And to prove what a brave chap I really was and at the same time gain a cup for my house (we were a pretty unathletic lot) I went in for the school heavyweight boxing competition. Although I had never boxed before I managed by some hard slogging to reach the final. I had hoped my father could have come over to see it, and was disappointed when he said he couldn't. In the end I was glad, as my fellow finalist was a boy called Philips who had boxed all his life and, in the second round, knocked me out.

Having left the Officers' Training Corps as a result of being one of a group of boys who had placed a 'No Thoroughfare' notice on the Salisbury–Tidworth road during the previous summer's camp (an action which caused unimaginable chaos among cars bound for the Tidworth tattoo) I joined the newly formed Air Squadron. (There was, alas, no naval unit.) This meant attending lectures by RAF officers on Monday mornings instead of boring old corps parades, and on field days being taken to Northolt aerodrome for practical instruction: this included a flip (and a loop and a roll) in an Avro training plane with a Flight-Lieutenant John Grandy (later Marshal of the Royal Air Force, Sir John Grandy), followed by lunch in the officers' mess. In the holidays I sat the entrance examination for Christ Church, Oxford, and passed. And in the summer half, having had two years of undistinguished cricket and another two of equally undistinguished rowing, I took up rifle shooting at the Butts, became a member of the 2nd VIII, and spent a happy four days pooping off at targets at Bisley.

But by far the most memorable thing I did occurred in my last week. When I was talking one day with my friend Maurice Buxton, the conversation turned to what were known in the school as 'stunts' – illegal expeditions to Ascot or Hurst Park races or nocturnal trips to London or Maidenhead. Neither of us had embarked on any of these, not finding them attractive enough to risk expulsion. Was there not some other ploy, sufficiently bold and imaginative, that would make the risk worthwhile? After a bit we hit on it. We would charter a small plane to fly us to Le Touquet and back between noon Absence (i.e., roll-call) and 6 p.m. Absence on the last whole holiday of the half. (This may not sound much today, but to fly anywhere in 1938 was quite an adventure.) With luck we would have time for a brief flutter at the casino, and with our winnings cover the cost of the trip. If we were caught, we would probably be expelled, which would be a pity; but a week later we were due to leave for good anyway.

Looking back, I am staggered how easily it was all arranged. The hire of a five-seater plane from Croydon to White Waltham aerodrome near Maidenhead, then on to Le Touquet and back presented no problems, and at £3 5s each all-in the cost was well below expectations. Maurice very sportingly said he would master-mind the trip for us and if it succeeded make a second trip with others a few days later. There was a long list of applicants for the remaining four places, among them the notorious Gully Mason, school correspondent of the *Daily Mirror* and owner of a greyhound which he raced locally under the auspices of one Slosh Rimmer. Sadly he had to drop out at the last minute, being in enough trouble already, and the final party besides myself was Philip Denison, who was in sixth form and spoke a species of French, Michael Evans, Alan Tyser, and John Pelham. John Wyndham agreed to be in charge of administration at the Eton end and would arrange for volunteers to relieve us of top hats and coats after the noon Absence and to stand by to answer our names at evening Absence if for some reason we didn't make it. But it was to be a point of honour to return on time. We would break one law (being out of bounds) and one only; otherwise we would feel we had failed.

Although we had tried to keep things secret, there were too many involved; and I was quite alarmed as I strode to noon Absence by the numbers of boys who accosted me with messages of good luck. John and his volunteers were waiting in School Yard and he confirmed that the plane had taken off from Croydon and was due at White Waltham at 12.30. Having answered our names we sprinted out to a lane behind the pavilion where the Eton taxi-driver, a notorious character called Hearn, was waiting in his Armstrong-Siddeley. We piled in and lay on the floor until clear of the school limits; and soon after 12.30 we reached the aerodrome.

Our plane had arrived, but we had a problem finding the pilot who had gone off to the local for lunch. We retrieved him, embarked and took off. Our first port of call was at Lympne for customs, but first we made a slight detour to dive-bomb School Yard. From Lympne we crossed the coast over the Romney Marshes, and first Boulogne and then Le Touquet came up ahead.

76

We noticed some French warships riding at anchor off shore, but in our ignorance did not question the meaning of the bunting that decked each ship from stem to stern. Nor, as we circled the airport to land, did we think it strange that at the height of the holiday period there should be no planes either on or above the ground.

We landed and taxied towards the white-fronted control tower. We were now a little behind schedule and realized that if we were to be back at Eton by six there would be no time to visit the casino. But we were so excited at having successfully achieved the first leg that it no longer mattered. Instead, having not yet lunched, we adjourned to the refreshment bar for ham sandwiches and champagne. The pilot went off with three or four dour-looking officials and promised to join us when he had obtained clearance.

We had downed several glasses when the pilot returned, looking none too happy.

'Don't know how to tell you this,' he said.

'Trouble?'

'We can't get clearance.'

'Why not?'

'Because a screaming little bald-headed Frenchman says so. He'll be here in a minute. I don't speak the lingo myself, but I thought one of you boys might. All I can get out of him is that we can't leave.'

Presently the official came in, shook hands all round and at our invitation, addressed Philip. He spoke for some time. I caught the words 'Le roi' and 'La reine'. Philip listened attentively and increasingly quizzically. At length the Frenchman stopped.

'What did he say?'

'You won't believe this,' said Philip, starting to giggle, 'but the King and Queen have just arrived in Paris on a state visit, and while they're there, no planes are supposed to land or take off from French coastal aerodromes. Some sort of security measure. It seems we shouldn't really have landed, but there was no way of stopping us. So we're here for the next three days.'

'*What?*'

'That's when the King and Queen return.'

'Tell him about Absence.'

'It's no good,' said Philip. 'He says it's nothing to do with him. He got his orders from the local chief of police.'

At this point the official bowed deeply and left.

We didn't quite know how to react. It was a wonderfully comic situation, but it meant the end of our enterprise. Even if we abandoned our pilot and took the ferry from Boulogne, we couldn't be back until well after dark. John Wyndham's volunteers might get away with answering our names at evening Absence, but we would all be missed at house prayers. I had visions of ringing up Brian Whitfield. 'I'm terribly sorry, sir, I won't be back tonight.' 'Oh, why's that?' 'Well, sir, I'm in Le Touquet. Our plane's been grounded.' When we did return, we would be expelled: worse, we would have to acknowledge that our stunt had failed. We ordered another bottle of champagne.

A couple of glasses later, Alan let out a cry.

'I've got it.'

'What?'

'He said it was nothing to do with him, it was the chief of police who had ordered it. Why don't we try him?'

The official was in his office. He considered the point carefully. Yes, he would ask the chief of police, but it would, he assured us, be quite useless. He reached for the telephone and dialled a number.

''Allo?'

Between him and the chief of police there followed a lengthy exchange of compliments. How was his *cher ami*? And his *cher ami*'s wife? And when were they going on their *vacances* this year – assuming Monsieur Hitler would allow them all *vacances*? At last he came to the point.

'*Ecoutez, mon cher ami, cet aprés-midi cinq jeunes hommes du collège anglais d'Eton sont arrivés par avion. Eton. C'est un très grand collège, n'est-ce pas? Eh bien . . .*'

He spoke for a very long time. Afterwards Philip said he couldn't have put our situation better himself, that the importance of our being back for evening Absence had been forcibly stressed. There followed what seemed to us a very long silence. The Frenchman lit a Gauloise and said, ''E is sinking.'

And then, through the earpiece of the telephone, there came a sound that was music to our ears, the sounds of a tinny, throaty laugh that indicated that the chief of police had understood our predicament and responded to it. We knew when we heard that laugh that our detention was over, and a moment later the official confirmed it.

'*Eh bien*,' he said, 'you may depart.'

Depart? The Gadarene swine would have been left standing at the speed we left that room. The clock on the control tower showed five minutes to four. We hardly dared ask ourselves if we were going to make it. At the far end of the airfield we spent a frustrating five minutes while the pilot warmed up the engines, then we trundled down the runway and headed up and over the French warships to the north.

There was no avoiding landing at Lympne for customs, but at least it allowed us to tell John, waiting beside a telephone at Eton, to ask his people to stand by for Absence in case we didn't show up. Six minutes later we were airborne.

Of the journey back I remember and care to remember little. The pilot who on the outward leg had given the impression of being a rather lackadaisical type, now wanted us to succeed as much as we did. To this end he announced he would fly at what he called nought feet: it would be less comfortable, not to mention in breach of the regulations, but quicker. Trees, fields, houses rose up at us and fell away; an electric pylon stayed where it was and we had to swerve sharply to avoid it. The plane dipped and juddered and rolled. Our faces changed from pink to grey to sea green. We swallowed and yawned and opened up our paper bags in anticipation. When it seemed we could hold on no longer, the airport loomed into sight ahead.

Ignoring the protests of some RAF people on whose operational runway we had just landed, and shouting perfunctory thanks to the pilot (I often wondered how he fared in the war), we ran to the gate where the faithful Hearn was waiting in the Armstrong-Siddeley, its engine ticking over.

'You gents don't leave much time,' he said, as we clambered in.

'Eight miles in fifteen minutes,' we said. 'Think you can do it?'

'I'll do it easy,' said Hearn, and banged in the clutch.

If flying at nought feet had had its problems, it turned out to be a picnic compared with tearing down country lanes at over 60 m.p.h., the horn sounding continually, pedestrians flattening themselves against the hedge as they heard us coming, cars drawing in to the side. In the end I found it less worrying to look at the floor. We reached the edge of the school at five to six, and now there could be no question of Hearn dropping us by the pavilion as planned; and we told him to take us to the very centre of the school, between School Yard and the Burning Bush. We also abandoned the indignity of crouching on the floor: we were conquering heroes and as such we would return.

As we drove up Keate's Lane, through crowds of boys on their way to Absence, we heard the tower clock sounding the first notes of the hour. Hearn spurted across the main road and came to a halt.

Philip, being in sixth form, was out first, Alan and I close behind him. As we raced through the School Yard archway, we heard the masters already calling the names. A great throng of people, led by John, came whooping up to us. I hardly saw them. My eyes were on Philip, fighting his way through the crowd.

'Denison!'

No answer.

'Denison for the second time.'

A cap rocketed into the air and Philip's voice rang out clearly, 'Here, sir.'

Honour was satisfied. We were home.[1]

I see I have come to the end of my schooldays without once mentioning religion, and as I had to attend two Sunday services and a short daily service every term or half for ten years – a total, I reckon, of some 1,300 hours – it may seem a strange omission. In fact religion hardly impinged on our lives at all. Some boys, I know, were committed Christians by upbringing or conviction, but most of us regarded the services unthinkingly as a daily chore, like algebra and compulsory exercise, that had to be suffered for the alleged good of our souls. Although from an early age I developed a strong scepticism about the historical (as opposed to the mythical) truth of the Christian story, I had not yet come to disbelieve in the external existence of the Holy Family. As a result, whenever I got in a rage with myself for stubbing my toe

---

[1] A few days later Maurice Buxton, John Wyndham and a boy called Robert Orr-Ewing made the same trip in a three-seater; this time there were no hitches and they were able to spend an hour wind-surfing on the Le Touquet beach.

Of the first expedition, Michael Evans and Philip Denison were killed in the war – Philip accidentally by an Allied plane as he was marching to freedom after five years in captivity. John Pelham later became Earl of Yarborough.

Of the second expedition Robert Orr-Ewing was killed in the war. John Wyndham was made Lord Egremont for his services as Harold Macmillan's Private Secretary, and died in 1972.

or knocking my funny-bone and wanted to compensate for the pain, I would say out loud, '*Fuck the Virgin Mary and bugger the Holy Ghost*' which was the most blasphemous thing I could think of and which gave instant relief. (I thought of the Holy Ghost as an elderly man with a white moustache, looking much like the College Chapel verger whom we called the Holy Ghost.) Each time I said it, I expected to be struck by a thunderbolt.

The only time when religion might have been of practical use was when I was being prepared for confirmation. Confirmation was said to make a new man of you, and I had high hopes it might help to rid my mind of all the wicked, lustful thoughts that seemed to inhabit it day and night, month in, month out. For about a week afterwards it did. For a whole week I felt incredibly virtuous, purified of all sin, clear and unspotted, and looked down with lofty disdain on those with their smutty jokes and carnal longings who were still wallowing in the slime. I walked with head high, thankful to have been liberated at last. Then the old Adam began knocking gently at my door. For a time I ignored him, pretending he wasn't there; but soon the knocking grew so loud and insistent he could not be denied; and early one morning, looking at a photograph of Miss Hedy Lamarr, I opened wide the door and let him in.

That summer holidays my father said he would give me a car if I first learnt about its parts and how they worked. So I spent a week acquiring this knowledge which I then fed back to him; after that it went clean out of my head and has remained out of it ever since. The car was a baby Austin and in it I drove to Islay and then on to Skye where I stayed with friends for the Skye Gathering – Highland Games in the daytime, at night reels and country dances, ending with a thirty-twosome on the quay at dawn. One afternoon at the Games I met, to my surprise, Eton's headmaster, Claud Elliott. I had never seen him out of black gown and white cravats, and in tweed coat and flannel trousers he looked diminished. After exchanging some pleasantries, he asked if I was doing anything particular the next day. I said I didn't think so. 'Would you care to come for a climb?' he said.

I mentioned earlier that when confronted by any unusual invitation in life, I find it virtually impossible to refuse; a blend of the pull of a new experience and not wanting to disappoint. I imagined that I was in for a fairly long trek up and down one or more of Skye's numerous hills and that there might be tea and toast by a cosy fire in the hotel on return. Would I be at his hotel at ten o'clock with a packet of sandwiches? I said I would. Lastly – and I should have taken this as a warning – did I have a pair of shoes with nails in them? I said I had a pair of old golfing brogues, but didn't add that the nails were badly worn. 'They'll do splendidly,' said Claud.

I was therefore unprepared for the sight that greeted me next morning. Claud was dressed in what I can only describe as a pair of mackintosh plus-fours. His boots were like boats with sharply inclined prows, the nails on them the size of small obelisks. Round one of his shoulders were coils of rope. Dangling from his waist was – of all things – *an axe*. 'Where are we going?' I said, hoping my voice was not betraying my panic. 'Up there,' said Claud, pointing way above the roof of the hotel to where some jagged peaks showed between a gap in the clouds. 'Good God!' I said, 'I hadn't expected that.' Claud said, 'It's called Pinnacle Ridge. There are five peaks altogether and the last one is the top.' Later – much later – I learned that even among seasoned mountaineers Pinnacle Ridge is considered quite a tough proposition.

I suppose if I had not been so dismally lacking in courage, not to say plain common sense, I would have told Claud there and then that I had had no previous climbing experience, that the very thought of it filled me with dread, that I would be more of a liability than an asset, and please could I now go home? But this would be even more craven: to bow out now was to invite this headmaster to think as poorly of me as the Bug had done at Highfield for not taking my medicine like a man. Yet in my flannel shirt and shorts and golfing brogues I felt I had wandered on to the wrong set. 'All ready then?' said Claud. 'Shall we go?'

For about an hour we walked steadily across moor and bog, then came to the beginnings of the rock face. Here Claud uncoiled his ropes, fastened one end to me and the other to himself. Then he delivered himself of this:

'On the way up you must go first.'

'Oh, no,' I said laughing, and rather touched by his courtesy in suggesting it, 'I'll be happy enough in the rear.'

But we were not, it seemed, in an after-you-Claud, after-you-Ludo situation.

'You don't quite understand,' he said – and here I noticed for the first time a curious habit he had at certain moments of punctuating his speech with a little squeaky sound in the throat, a sort of 'm'm, m'm' like a dog makes when it wants attention or its dinner – 'The reason you must go first going up is because if you – m'm, m'm – fall, I'll see or hear you coming and be able to – m'm, m'm – do something about it, whereas if I were to go first and fall –'

'I wouldn't have a clue what to do?'

'Exactly. For the same reason I'll go first – m'm, m'm – coming down.'

On this encouraging note I led the way upwards. The first two pinnacles were mild affairs and scaled without much difficulty. The next two proved harder. The higher we climbed the steeper became the rock face: in some places it had the appearance of sloping *outwards* or towards one; and the worn nails in my brogues didn't give much of a hold. However, by concentrating only on what was immediately above me, I found I could just about manage; and from below came encouraging comments on our progress.

At the foot of the fourth pinnacle I met my Waterloo. The face of the fifth pinnacle rose sheer above us, and it was evident even to me that we would not be attempting it. Claud came up and said, 'Now this bit is rather – m'm, m'm – tricky. You must lower yourself over the cliff edge until your feet touch a small ledge. I'll – m'm, m'm – guide you with the rope. Find your way along that for a few feet where you'll find a sort of – m'm, m'm – funnel. Climb up that and – m'm, m'm – wait for me.'

I crept forward and peered over. Having had my face close to lumps of rock for the past two hours I at first found it hard to focus. This was not surprising, for there was nothing between me and the valley a thousand feet below. Small objects at the bottom, the size and colour of golf balls, were, I assumed, sheep. I looked for the ledge that Claud had mentioned but the cliff dropped so sharply that I could see nothing between the lip and the sheep. If old Claud thought he was going to lower me blind over that lot, he had another think coming to him; and I said as much, if not forcibly, at least in tones that brooked no opposition.

'Never mind,' said Claud airily, and as though half expecting it, 'we'll go round by my – m'm, m'm – patent path. It's a way I discovered a year or two ago.'

Claud's patent path was only marginally less harrowing than

the drop over the cliff. It was never more than three feet wide and had sheer rock on one side and a precipice on the other. On such a path Moriarty met Holmes. But we negotiated it successfully and came at last to the top of the mountain. Below and around us was a stunning view: to the north the hills of Harris and Lewis in purple order beyond the Minch; to the east Raasay stretched like Cerberus across the approaches to Portree; to the south Rhum and Eigg and far beyond the twin paps of Jura; and on all sides the sea shimmering and simmering in the summer sun. If it hadn't been for the thought of getting down, I might almost have enjoyed it.

We found a little hollow and sat down and unwrapped our sandwiches.

'Now,' said Claud, 'tell me all about – m'm, m'm – Le Touquet.'

He proved a good listener. When I'd finished, he said, 'We knew about it next day. The word had spread.'

'But you didn't expel us?'

'You all got back in time. You didn't disgrace yourselves or the school in any way. You were leaving anyway. What would have been the point?'

We had finished our sandwiches and I had just lit a cigarette when I saw to my astonishment two men and three women walking towards us. They were dressed as casually as I was, the women in blouses and slacks, the men in sports shirts and trousers. One carried a picnic basket, another a camera. For a moment I thought I must be seeing things.

'How on earth did they get here?' I asked.

'Oh, they came up the tourist route,' said Claud dismissively. 'A lot of hikers and people come that way to see the view.'

I was about to float the idea of our returning by this route when Claud said, 'Well, we'd best be off. I thought we'd go down by the Policeman.'

We set off in a southerly direction and for a time made good progress. Then we descended a long, scrabbly slope and turned into a gully. At the end of the gully Claud said, 'There's the Policeman.'

Consider a piece of paper folded in two and placed on a flat surface, crease upwards like a tent. Consider also a ping-pong ball balanced on top of the crease. The ping-pong ball is the Policeman, the crease the ridge on which it stands.

We advanced gingerly along the ridge, Claud leading; there

was just room to walk in single file. When we reached the Policeman, I saw that it was about 10 feet high and that its sides bulged out either side of the ridge. It seemed to me to be impassable.

'Now this,' said Claud, 'is – m'm, m'm – *very* tricky. If you don't think you can manage it, you must say so. I'll go first and you can see what happens.'

He untied my end of the rope and made up several lengths into a sort of lasso which he flung over the top of the Policeman. Taking in the slack, he secured the loose end round his middle, joining it to the end already there. He was now in a sort of cradle, with the rope biting the base of the Policeman on its other side. Without further word he leant outwards and at an angle of some 45 degrees, with his feet firmly planted on the rock face of the ridge and both hands working the rope, he slowly edged himself forward and sideways. At any moment I expected the rope to break with the strain, for Claud to go tumbling down the ridge to his death below, and for me to be marooned for the night.

He disappeared from sight round the bulge and gained the ridge the other side. A moment later I heard him say, 'Do you think you can – m'm, m'm – manage that? I'll send over the rope.'

The rope landed with a swish at my feet. I had already decided the task was beyond me; even the thought of it gave me goose-flesh. But somehow I *had* to conquer the Policeman; if I didn't Claud would have to return the way he had gone, which would have been humiliating for both of us. Then I had a brainwave: to make use of my golfing shoes and light summer wear in a way that the expert mountaineer, lumbered with ropes and axes and ten-league boots would have found impossible.

'How are you getting on?' said the voice from the other side.

'Fine,' I said, fastening the rope round me.

A pause. 'What are you going to do?'

'I'm coming over the top.'

A longer pause. 'I don't know if you can do that. No one's ever – m'm, m'm – done that before.'

'Stand by,' I said, 'here I come.'

I retired a little way along the ridge, turned, and like Fred Trueman *en route* to the crease, ran in towards the Policeman. There I leapt forwards and upwards and the impetus, aided by some scrabbling with my hands, was enough to carry me to the top. I lay there motionless until Claud, like a farmer with his cow, took in the slack of the rope and gently pulled me to the ground.

'*Well done!*' said Claud in admiration, 'Well done!'[1]

The rest of the passage down the mountain was free of any major hazards, though Claud couldn't resist pointing out places where his fellow mountaineers had met with death or disaster. 'You see that gully on the left. That's where old Bimbo Smith slipped in '29 taking Bill Lazenby with him. It was blowing a blizzard at the time and they didn't find the – m'm, m'm – bodies till a week later.' A couple of hundred feet lower down he indicated a ledge in the cliff face. 'Had a nasty experience there in '33 with Jake Wiseman and his brother Charles. Jake missed his footing and broke his – m'm, m'm – ankle, but the ledge saved him. I stayed with him while Charles went off to get help. I gave him some brandy to ease the pain but he'd had no lunch and was soon pretty – m'm, m'm – tight. I thought he might get violent and have both of us over, but all he wanted was to sing. He sang "Danny Boy" and "Roses of Picardy", that sort of thing, and then dropped off to sleep. We had quite a – m'm, m'm – time getting him down.'

Over tea and toast at the hotel (the only part of the day I had predicted accurately) Claud said he hoped I had enjoyed it. In a weird way I had, though rather more in retrospect than at the time. But driving back to Portree, the black silhouette of Pinnacle Ridge standing out sharply against the western sky, I was puzzled by one thing. Why had Claud asked me – a completely unknown quantity – to accompany him? Was there no one else around? And was he not risking his own life as well as mine in inviting such an absolute beginner? After all, he knew nothing of my aptitudes or dependability.

Or did he? Had he reckoned that a boy who was capable of flying to Le Touquet and back between noon and evening Absence was one you could probably rely on? I liked to think so.

---

[1] In 1988 Mr Hamish M. Brown of Kinghorn, Fife, wrote that he had just read an earlier account of my adventures on Pinnacle Ridge, published in *Blackwood's Magazine* in 1948. 'Having crossed the Policeman many a time,' he said, 'I was shocked at this respectable gent's demise early this year. One day it just was not there! Perhaps your behaviour caused the beginnings of a fatal weakness.'

5

Death of my Father

The Oxford I went to in the autumn of 1938 was, if one had the money and the connections, still very much the Oxford of Brideshead; and the year I spent there was, for me and many of my contemporaries, largely a year of self-indulgence. Club dinners, lunch parties in one's own and other people's rooms, gambling parties, river parties, visits to race meetings and to dances in London seemed to fill the calendar. Two or three times I found myself in debt and on each occasion was baled out by my beloved grandmother. It could be said of our generation that we shared a prescience of the coming war, and were determined to make hay while we could. In fact we were all young men experiencing for the first time an unparalleled freedom, and I think would have behaved as we did – and as our predecessors had done – whatever the state of international relations. My life was further complicated by my having fallen deeply in love with the sister of one of my Le Touquet companions, a strikingly beautiful girl of eighteen; and on many mornings I was to be found at the foot of my staircase waiting for the arrival of the post and a sight of her familiar blue envelope. But, alas, she loved another, and one morning the blue envelope brought the shattering news that she was going to marry him, which in due course she did. Later she became a lifelong friend – but the first falling in love is like no other, and today, half a century later, when I hear a snatch of 'Deep Purple' or 'Love Walked In' or even 'Jeepers Creepers', it all comes flooding back.

When in London for a dance, I would often stay with one or another of my Grant grandfather's sisters, Great Aunt Ju or Great Aunt Susan. Aunt Ju was a tall, thin old lady whom I remember wearing a black choker and a little lace cap on her silver hair. She had as equable a temper as her brother and was always full of anecdotes and sayings of times past. She never married and for sixteen years was on the staff of a famous girls' school, St Leonards at St Andrews – the last eleven as headmistress and, I am told, a very successful one. She was an avid reader and a dab hand at solving difficult crossword puzzles; and when at the age of ninety she died in her wheelchair soon after breakfast, they found the *Times* crossword puzzle for that day, already completed, on her lap. It seemed not a bad way to go.

Aunt Susan was a smaller, rounder woman with a great zest for life and a curious (though not unattractive) habit of speaking through her nose. When I first knew her, she was married to a Hungarian diplomat called Aladar de Bajza who wore pebble glasses so thick you could barely see his eyes. Uncle Aladar had an atrocious accent and would say incomprehensible things like, 'If I vould be a vorrier, vich I am not, I tink I vould vorry very, wery much.' Of his own country he said, 'Ve haff two classes of persons in Hongary – aristocracy and scum.' Asked what happened to the scum, he said, 'Ve vip them.' Once, answering the doorbell, he found two nuns on the step, and before they could state their business, he said, 'I loathe wirgeens', and shut the door. Another day he chastised a newspaper boy whose bicycle on the pavement had nearly mowed him down. 'Dam-ned dog!' he shouted after him, 'Ven I see you again, I vill horsevip you.'

After Aladar's death I used to lunch with Aunt Susan regularly. She was very interested in genealogy and once gave me a table she had compiled showing that I was a direct descendant of King James II of Scotland. When I passed this on to my friend Iain Moncreiffe, the Albany Herald, he told me that while it was quite true, around 30,000 other people could legitimately claim the same. In later life Aunt Susan developed an eccentric habit of collecting dirty stories which she wrote down in a little black book. 'Ludovic dear,' she would say over coffee, 'have you heard the one about the nun and the fish-monger?' And she would pull out the book and read it. Sometimes the stories were so obscene I was at a loss to know where to look.

In June of 1939 I passed the exams I should have passed in December of 1938 had I even half-heartedly applied myself to the syllabus, and soon after left with a Christ Church friend for a month of studying at a villa at Mouans-Sartoux near Grasse. In that beautiful, perfumed and as yet unspoiled part of France, unravelling itself to me for the first time, with the sea and the fleshpots of Cannes and Antibes close at hand, it would have been hard to concentrate anyway; but with Hitler's demands still unsatisfied one had to ask oneself what was all this reading *for*? Would we be back at Oxford in the autumn as planned? For how much longer could a confrontation between the European powers be avoided?

Another indication of the way things were going came to me in Islay a month later. One evening after supper my father and I found ourselves together in the sitting-room. He pulled a long envelope from his pocket and said, 'I didn't show you this before because when I first received it, there didn't seem much likelihood of it happening. It's the best news I've had for some time.' He handed me the letter. 'I am commanded by my Lords Commissioners of the Admiralty', it said in so many words, 'to inquire whether in the event of hostilities, you would be prepared to take command of an armed merchant cruiser.' My father said nothing to suggest that this letter was anything but a bolt from the blue. In fact, as I discovered from records made public long after the war, he had earlier that year travelled to London for an appointment with his old friend and former shipmate, Admiral Sir Charles Little, then Second Sea Lord and in charge of officers' appointments, and asked point blank if, in the event of war, he could have a ship. He did not tell my mother what he had done (presumably for fear of her lodging an objection and then thrashing the whole thing out). It was, I think, something more than a desire to help defend his country in the only way he knew how; it was an opportunity to redeem himself, to expunge once and for all the ignominy of his court-martial and the cutting short of a successful naval career. 'I shall be sixty next week,' he said to me, 'and they still have enough faith in me to offer me a ship. Eighteen years on the beach and they offer me a ship. Gosh, what a chance.' For him the war could hardly come soon enough.

At the end of August I left Islay for Skye to stay in a house party for the Portree Games – the same place I had stayed the year before. Despite our youth and appetite for life we were a sombre little gathering, for Hitler had already begun to mobilize against Poland, and I think we all sensed that this time there could be no turning back. On 1 September our hostess took us to a bay on the east coast of the island where at low tide you could still gather wild oysters. We spent most of the day there, finding that many of the shells we picked up were empty husks, picnicking in a little wood in the shadow of Pinnacle Ridge and my adventure of the year before, gathering oysters. By the end of the day we had gathered some two hundred; and it wasn't until we returned to the lodge that evening that we learned that Germany had marched into Poland at dawn.

After so many days of tension, of pretending to a normality that none of us felt, it was a relief to know the worst. Next morning, in response to telegrams to join their units, some members of the house party packed and left. As yet I had no unit, but that afternoon, feeling that I too should leave the periphery for the centre, I joined the exodus south. It was, I recall, a lovely summer's day, with a light wind stirring the roadside grasses and moving the shadows of the clouds over sunlit heather and bracken. All the way south, across blue water at Lochalsh and over the moors to Invergarry, by Loch Ness and Ballachulish to the great cleft of Glencoe and on to the bare uplands of Rannoch, my eyes and senses absorbed that marvellous country with a heightened awareness, seeing it as it were for the first time because – who knew? – it might also be the last. Passing through Stirling after dark I saw the shape of things to come. Not a light showed anywhere. The war had begun.

I reached my grandmother's flat in Edinburgh around midnight, and there found a telegram from my mother. It said that my father had flown south from Islay to join his ship, the 17,000-ton former P and O liner, now HMS *Rawalpindi*, then refitting in the London docks; and that Bob Boothby had said that he might be able to arrange a commission for me in Henry Dundas's old regiment, the Scots Guards. But I had long ago decided that soldiery was the last thing I wanted. Wherever I went in the war and whatever I did had to be in some outfit where there was the minimum likelihood of personal combat. Ever since Highfield days I had had a recurring nightmare of being pursued by a Uhlan in a spiked helmet intent on skewering me with his bayonet – a situation I would have found no more acceptable had I been asked to skewer him with mine.

On trips to Northolt from Eton I had toyed with the idea of becoming a fighter pilot, but couldn't rid myself of the image of some latter-day von Richthofen screaming down at me with guns blazing; and my mechanical incompetence combined with congenitally sluggish reactions to the unexpected were not characteristics likely to help one to survive. That left the Navy, the service I had always set my heart on entering, which went about its business on an element which had never held any fears for me, and where personal combat was a thing of the past. There was no need to think further.

Next morning the air raid sirens sounded for the first time, and my grandmother and I stole down to the cellar where we sat petrified for half an hour, fully expecting the annihilation of Belgrave Crescent, if not of all Edinburgh. After the All Clear I went upstairs and wrote a letter to the Admiralty, offering my services. Their answer reached me in my destroyer at Scapa Flow several months later, regretting there were no vacancies at present and advising me to apply again in six months' time.

Two weeks later I visited my father on board *Rawalpindi* in the London docks and took tea with him in the large and comfortable captain's cabin behind the bridge. He was in civilian clothes, for the ship was still in dockyard hands. I have seldom seen a man so changed. He had never liked the agent's job, for he often found himself dealing with people who thought they were better than they were, who took offence over trifles and constantly squabbled among themselves. In an instant, it seemed to me, the traumas of those years and the bitter memory of what had happened before that, had evaporated. It was as though some hidden tap had been turned on to release latent energies and enthusiasms. He was back in the element he loved and whose parameters he knew, where business was conducted along well-established and, above all, impersonal lines; for in everything an officer does, he has the cushion of the service behind him.

Over tea he told me how *Rawalpindi* would be employed: as part of the Northern Patrol, a collection of armed merchant cruisers and trawlers whose job was to intercept German merchantmen attempting to run the British blockade between the Faeroe Islands, Iceland and the north of Norway. He would have an ex-RN first lieutenant and a crew of some 300 reservists, many of whom had served in the ship in peacetime. They would be based at Greenock on the Clyde, and in order that my mother could see him during the brief periods between patrols, she and my sisters would move into a friend's cottage in Perthshire.

After tea he took me on a tour of the ship and explained the alterations being made, many of which he had asked for himself. From time to time we were interrupted by an officer wanting a signature or a dockyard official seeking clarification; and it was plain that he loved every minute of it. He led me to the gangway, and as I said goodbye, I hoped in my romantic way that a day might come when I in my naval uniform and my father in his would meet on *Rawalpindi*'s quarterdeck and exchange salutes. At the foot of the gangway I noticed some big guns lying on the dockside preparatory to being fitted. These were the guns about which my father wrote later to a friend: 'They have given me some guns, good guns, and I am going to use them.'

My own entry into the Navy came soon after. Summoned to Oxford by the Joint Universities Recruiting Board, I was asked which service I wanted to join and why. I mentioned Uncle Will and my father and a little later came a letter saying that I had been commissioned as an acting probationary temporary sub-lieutenant in the Royal Naval Volunteer Reserve and been appointed to HMS *King Alfred* for training. I was overjoyed. For me the Navy had always been a world apart, remote and exclusive; and yet now, almost without warning I was about to become part of it; part of a fabric 400 years old, of a family which numbered among its members not only my father and Uncle Will and the young midshipman whom I had hero-worshipped in command of the *Nelson*'s picket-boat, but Nelson himself, Drake, Jellicoe, Beatty. At that moment I was never happier, and the pride and joy of having once served in the Navy has lasted all my life.

HMS *King Alfred* turned out to be the Hove Corporation underground car park, taken over for the duration; and I look back on my time there, as indeed that of all my wartime appointments, with a clarity and intensity not given to any other period of my life, for I was not yet twenty and in the prime of health and well-being. On my first morning at *King Alfred* I was taken before the captain, named Pelly, who turned out to have known my father in the First World War. He asked me how old I was.

'Nineteen, sir,' I said. 'I shall be twenty in two weeks' time.'

'In that case,' he said, 'I shall have to disrate you to midshipman. You were born two weeks too late.'

We were all billeted in Hove's numerous genteel hotels where the residents were mostly retired service people and old ladies: Rattigan's *Separate Tables* could have sprung from any of them. At first I shared a room with a rather dreary man who claimed that he was kept awake by my flow of language during the night (in those days I used to talk and shout in my sleep regularly) and fortunately after a few days he left.

At 7.30 each morning we walked the few hundred yards to the car park, dressed (for our uniforms took time to be made) in an odd assortment of sports jackets, casual trousers, Trilby hats and caps. At the steps leading down to the car park we learnt to say we were coming aboard, and when we left in the evening to declare we were going ashore. In between we did extensive drills, learnt the rules of the road and the meanings of flags, practised boat handling in nearby Shoreham harbour – and one dreadful day were taken to a nearby football field to be instructed in the one form of warfare I had joined the Navy to avoid: bayonet attack.

Our mentor in this was a tubby little chief gunner's mate by the name of Vass. Having suspended a sack full of straw between one of the goalposts and fixed a bayonet to the end of his rifle, Vass would address us as follows:

'There are three parts of the body at which the bayonet may be aimed.' (Pregnant pause to allow us to wonder which they were.) 'The first is the throat.' (Pause) 'The second is the stomach.' (Pause) 'And the third is the privates.' (Pause) '*All mushy areas.*' (A quick look at the class to see how we were taking it.) 'The throat and the stomach is self-explanatory. *Re* the privates, you all know 'ow much it 'urts when a cricket ball 'its you on the privates. Let me tell you (pause) it 'urts a bloody sight 'arder when the point of a bayonet separates the port and starboard privates in one stroke – *thus*.' And with this he lunged at the sack with his bayonet so that the point came out the other side. Then we had a go. Afterwards I wondered if it was not too late to transfer to the RAF.

At *King Alfred* I met old friends from Eton and elsewhere, among them Bill Richmond, brilliant member of a brilliant family. His father, the admiral and naval historian, was Master of Downing College, Cambridge, one of his sisters was to become Lady Plowden, Chairman of the IBA, and he himself had won a scholarship to Eton. But Bill had his problems and after a year or two there he was moved on to a less demanding, more informal establishment in Kent, where the aim was to rid boys of their repressions by having a minimum of rules and regulations. 'I had a fine time with my repressions,' Bill told me. 'I hate washing and I hate exercise, and I didn't do either and nobody cared.' He said he didn't do much work either, but still managed to win an exhibition to Trinity College, Cambridge.

Bill was one of the funniest, least pretentious, most companionable men I ever knew, who from an early age came to recognize the essential absurdity of the human condition, from which he himself seemed oddly detached. There were few people or situations on which he did not hold a refreshingly original, almost surrealistic view. Our friendship deepened as time went by and he was the only man I regularly corresponded with throughout the war. In letters and on the telephone we addressed each other as 'Goat', though I forget now why.

Another oddball at *King Alfred* was Peter Beatty, the younger son of the admiral. Being very rich – his mother was a Marshall Field from Chicago, and he had won the Derby with Bois Roussel a year or two before – he came to Hove with chauffeur and valet and had the chauffeur take him to the car park in the Rolls each morning and wait outside the steps each evening for his return. One morning in a semaphore class I noticed he was paired with a man from Aberdeen in the fish and chip business, and a little older than us. At lunch I asked Peter how he had fared. 'Oh, I fooled my fellow properly,' he said. 'He couldn't make head or tail of what I was semaphoring.' 'What were you semaphoring?' I asked. Peter gave a manic laugh and said, 'Bois Roussel.'

The reader who has progressed so far will recall in the early pages of this book references to Great-uncle Will, my Kennedy grandfather's naval brother. However cavalier he may have been in his treatment of native property and possessions, I had always thought him a man of high moral standards; and a story about his starting family prayers when he became commander-in-chief at the Nore, seemed to bear this out. One morning he found himself reading about Lot's daughters – how they made old Lot drunk and then committed incest with him to continue the line – and he was so appalled that he put the Old Testament aside and, for fear of finding himself reading something similar, or worse, never opened it again.

During my time at *King Alfred*, however, a different side of Uncle Will emerged. One evening a small party of midshipmen and sub-lieutenants which included myself were invited by the Commodore of the Brighton Yacht Club as guests at their annual dinner. After dinner the Commodore made a speech which ended thus: 'And now, gentlemen, I want to give you a toast which was a favourite of an old seafaring friend of mine, the late Admiral Bill Kennedy.' I stopped day-dreaming and sat up. '"Boys," he used to say at the club dinner after he'd got back from a hard day's yachting, "Here's to cunt and gunpowder – the sailor's two best friends."' We raised our glasses. 'Cunt and gunpowder,' we solemnly intoned, as if it had been 'The Queen' or 'The Squadron' or 'Absent friends', and one wag at the back, remembering the toast to wives and mistresses, piped up with 'And may they never meet', and everyone laughed. But from then on I looked on Uncle Will through rather different eyes.

My father meanwhile had taken *Rawalpindi* up north and was in Scapa Flow on the night of 13–14 October when Gunther Prien in *U.47* penetrated the anchorage. 'But,' he wrote, 'he was after bigger fish than us' – referring to Prien's sinking of the battleship *Royal Oak*. Then he went off on patrol; and in a few days captured the German blockade runner *Gonzenheim*, took her crew prisoner, and sank her. Later he wrote to my mother: 'Everything is slowly and surely shaping itself. After my rounds this morning I was able to congratulate various people on the way they had cleaned up their departments. An excellent atmosphere is beginning to prevail.' He introduced the practice of marching the ship's company round the deck after morning prayers. 'I warned them we would do it and I myself led them with the first lieutenant. Some of the mercantile men thought it a bit of a joke till I made them run the last lap of over 300 yards. They were all so pumped (except me) that they became quite subdued and appreciated they were all the better for it.' About himself he wrote, 'I wondered from the start if I had got too rusty. Some things certainly were a bit strange at first, but I feel now as if I was back in the last war and there had been no interlude at all . . . But I feel I must make good and I realize the responsibility of this command more than I ever did in my former commands.'

And then one day I had a letter from him myself:

My dear Boy,

I have several letters of yours to answer. Some I fear are rather old, but that cannot be helped, as I have no time when we are in harbour for perhaps a couple of days, and then we are at sea for several . . .

Yes, I did shake hands with the King when he visited the Fleet, and we had quite a chat. His equerry, Harold Campbell, I know well, and I was glad to meet him and others whom I have not seen for years. It's very amusing meeting some of the bigwigs now who were contemporaries of mine. They are all very jolly and welcoming.

While writing the above, the bridge reported that our pet iceberg was again in sight, a formidable, ghost-like object, so I thought that a good opportunity to do some more gunnery. We had a very spirited attack on it this afternoon at long range, and with considerable motion on the ship, which made it difficult but very instructive . . .

What I want to know is how long you will remain a midshipman, what work and general training you do (this your next letter will probably tell me), when you are likely to get a sea appointment and what form it is likely to take.

Another thing I want to know is the question of your finances. Tell me frankly, have you any debts now or are they all paid off? And if they are, pray do not involve yourself in any that you cannot meet. What pay will you get, what will your messing cost, what do they allow you for uniform? All this I want to know, and then I will see what allowance to give you. Now is the time when we must all live as economically as possible. Income-tax has soared, and I don't know what I shall be doing, if anything, once we have seen this show through.

Another person with whom my father was corresponding was the CO of *King Alfred*, Captain Pelly. Towards the end of my training, he sent for me.

'I think I ought to tell you that your father wrote to me a little while ago to ask if you could be released to join him on his next patrol. I told him I didn't think you were far enough on with basic training. But if an opportunity presents itself later, and the Admiralty agrees, I see no reason why you shouldn't.' He smiled. 'He'll be a lot tougher with you than we've been.'

'Thank you, sir.'

'Meantime, when you leave here next week, you're going on a rather strange course. A batch of you are being sent to RAF Cardington to learn how to fly balloons.'

The Admiralty have dreamed up some rum schemes in their time. One of the rummest was a proposal during the first war to train seagulls to land on the periscopes of enemy submarines.

The idea this time was to attach barrage balloons to the quarter-decks of warships as protection for them and any convoy against air attack. All those with whom we discussed the idea thought it barmy. If the weather was fine and the balloon directly above the ship, it would hinder the ship's anti-aircraft fire; while in bad weather, with the ship making drastic alterations of course and speed, the balloon would be slewing about all over the place, a menace to other ships and itself, and no protection at all. The RAF's fleet of training balloons were housed in the two vast hangars at Cardington which had been built for the airships R.100 and R.101, and here we would be instructed in how to handle them, to send them up and then, after a decent interval, to bring them down.

We were billeted in hotels in nearby Bedford, but I had neither the time nor the inclination to visit old haunts. For it was now the middle of November, cold and often foggy. We left the hotel for the airfield before it was fully light and returned to it as it was growing dark: all one craved then was tea and sleep. One evening I was invited to nearby Ampthill House to have dinner with the son and daughter-in-law of the man who had been the Conservative MP for the constituency at the time my father was his agent. After dinner, we went into the library to hear the BBC nine o'clock news.

I was not listening very carefully to what was being said when one word struck a chord in my sub-conscious and immediately the whole message struck home.

'The Secretary of the Admiralty', said the announcer, 'regrets to announce the loss of the armed merchant cruiser HMS *Rawalpindi*. The *Rawalpindi* was a former P and O liner of 17,000 tons. Next of kin are being informed.'

I went to the telephone and was put through to the Admiralty. A disembodied voice a long way off said, 'The captain? No, I'm afraid he's gone.'

The German surface fleet at the outbreak of war was minuscule compared with that of the Royal Navy, but two months after hostilities had begun its commander-in-chief Admiral Erich Raeder had reason to be pleased with its operations. The two pocket battleships *Admiral Graf Spee* and *Deutschland* had been operating against our shipping in the south and north Atlantic respectively, resulting in powerful British forces being diverted from the Home Fleet at Rosyth and Scapa to search for them. In mid-November the *Deutschland* was due back in Germany, but in order to hide this from the British as long as possible, Raeder ordered his two fast battleships *Scharnhorst* and *Gneisenau* to sail for the Iceland–Faeroes gap (attacking anything worth while on the way), and there to make a feint into the north Atlantic before returning home. This would keep the pressure on the British forces still hunting for the vanished *Deutschland*, and might also ease the pressure on the *Graf Spee*. It was not a risky operation because aircraft reconnaissance had confirmed that there were no British aircraft carriers in northern waters, and the only two ships capable of taking on *Scharnhorst* and *Gneisenau*, the aged *Rodney* and *Nelson*, were incapable of catching them.

Accordingly at noon on 21 November the *Scharnhorst* and *Gneisenau*, wearing the flag of Vice-Admiral Marschall, cleared Wilhelmshaven Roads and steered to the north. By noon the next day the ships were in the Shetlands–Norway gap where Marschall had hoped to intercept a Norwegian convoy; but with his speed down to 12 knots because of the weather, he abandoned this and headed for Iceland. By dawn on the 23rd he was north of the Faeroe Islands and he continued on a northerly course until at a little after 4 p.m. the foretop look-out in the *Scharnhorst*, which was in the lead, reported a steamer on the starboard beam.

Scharnhorst's captain, Kurt Cesar Hoffmann, climbed to the foretop to check for himself and formed the opinion that it was an armed merchant cruiser. However, he had to be careful: it could be a neutral. At first the steamer appeared to be heading in his direction, then abruptly turned away. Having informed Marschall by radio and brought the ship to action stations, he signalled the steamer, at first in German, then in English: 'What ship? Origin and where bound? Stop and do not use wireless.' The only reply to this was the letters FAM, which meant nothing. By now *Scharnhorst* had worked up to speed and the gap between pursuer and pursued was gradually closing. Then Hoffmann saw smoke floats being dropped over the ship's stern to disguise her escape, and knew she must be British. An hour after the first sighting, he gave the order to open fire.

A week earlier *Rawalpindi* had left the Clyde on what was to be her last patrol. The weather was consistently vile, the horizon (when it could be seen) was empty, and to pass the time a ship's concert was arranged for the evening of 22 November. It was a great success. My father was asked to do a turn and to everyone's surprise agreed. He sang 'Tom Bowling', which he had often done at my mother's Conservative Party concerts. It was decided to hold a repeat performance the next day for the benefit of those who had been on watch.

Next morning a Swedish ship was sighted and in case she was carrying contraband the boarding officer, Sub-Lieutenant Anderson, was ordered to sail her to a British port with an armed guard. Anderson was also appearing in the concert party and had no wish to leave the ship, so he spun a coin with Lieutenant Pickersgill, the second boarding officer, to decide who would command the armed guard. Anderson lost and left the ship.

In mid-afternoon as it was beginning to grow dark the look-out in the crow's nest sighted a ship some seven miles distant. This was reported to the captain who, assuming it to be another blockade runner, ordered the second boarding party to muster, and altered course towards. Within a minute or two it became obvious that the ship was not a merchantman but a warship, so my father sheered away, increased to full speed of 17 knots and ordered action stations. He also sent out by wireless two enemy reports. The first said, 'Am being chased by enemy battleship.' Then, on the bridge, looking at the *Scharnhorst* through binoculars, he was heard to say, 'It's the *Deutschland* all right,' and made the second signal, 'Enemy is *Deutschland*'. It was an understandable mistake. *Deutschland* (already back in Germany) was the one enemy ship he had been warned might come his way; and the outlines of the main surface ships of the German Navy were very similar.

I have sometimes wondered what my father's thoughts were during that long hour between the *Scharnhorst* first sighting him and her opening fire. Did he realize that his time had come, that nothing short of a miracle could now save him, his crew and his ship from total destruction? My guess is that the minds of all of them were so occupied with ways of preserving themselves, cramming on every knot of speed and steering for the already darkening eastern horizon, broadcasting enemy reports, seeing the guns were primed and ammunition ready, dropping smoke floats over the side, that they had no time for introspection. Yet at some moment fear must have brushed them in the gut; and it may well have occurred to her largely peacetime crew that had the ship still been flying the Red Ensign rather than the White, they could with honour have scuttled or surrendered. But now *Rawalpindi* was as much a unit of the Royal Navy as *Hood* or *Nelson*, and from the days of Sir Richard Grenville, the tradition of the Navy was to fight, however hopeless the odds. So all they could do was give as good an account of themselves as they were able, even if it meant dying for King and Country in the process.

Scharnhorst's opening shot fell short, perhaps a final warning. It was ignored. The following salvo was also short, and gallantly *Rawalpindi* replied to it with those of her ancient six-inch guns that could be brought to bear. She also hoisted battle ensigns. *Scharnhorst*'s third and fourth salvoes were deadly, a cloudburst of eleven-inch shells tearing into her superstructure and sides, and in an instant reducing this once graceful liner to an inferno of flame and smoke and twisted metal. The bridge was destroyed and everyone on it, the wireless room and everyone in it, also the generating room which resulted in loss of power to the ammunition hoists and the dousing of all lights. Yet those of *Rawalpindi*'s guns not yet knocked out continued to fire, and one registered a hit on *Scharnhorst*'s quarterdeck. Then the *Gneisenau* appeared on *Rawalpindi*'s other side and poured in a withering cross-fire. Within fifteen minutes it was all over. With fires raging amidships and ammunition exploding below, a group of sixty to a hundred men, many wounded and in pain, assembled on the stern; among them was Lieutenant Pickersgill who must have been cursing the luck that had lost him the spin of the coin to Anderson. 'Through our binoculars,' wrote a *Scharnhorst* officer, 'we watched with awe at their attempts to lower boats.' Some forty men managed to get away in three boats, but others remained; and presently one of them picked up a signal lantern and flashed to *Scharnhorst*, 'PLEASE SEND BOATS'.

This was impossible, but seeing the three boats in the light of the blazing *Rawalpindi*, both German ships manoeuvred to go alongside them. *Gneisenau* rescued twenty-one survivors from one boat and *Scharnhorst* six from another. *Scharnhorst* was about to help on board a further ten from the third boat when she received a peremptory signal from *Gneisenau*: 'CEASE PICKING UP SURVIVORS IMMEDIATELY. FOLLOW ME.' *Gneisenau*'s look-outs had spotted a strange ship approaching. It was the cruiser *Newcastle*, hurrying to the scene in response to *Rawalpindi*'s signals. At the same time *Newcastle* had seen the German ships and intended to shadow them until superior strength arrived. But it was a dark, blustery night, and lacking radar, she soon lost them in a rainstorm.

With the whole of the Home Fleet now after him, Marschall took his ships up to the Arctic for two days, then, in minimum visibility, passed through the Shetland Narrows at speed and reached Wilhelmshaven just six days after he had left.

The day after the battle, *Rawalpindi*'s sister-ship *Chitral*, searching the area for more survivors, found the boat with the ten men in it, also another survivor spreadeagled across an upturned lifeboat: he had been like that all night and was still alive. My father and 263 other men had gone down with the ship. I have often thought about his death and hoped it was quick; that before it came about, he was not mangled or maimed.

The Admiralty did not release the news of the battle until after *Scharnhorst* and *Gneisenau* had arrived back at Wilhelmshaven and their triumph had been released to the German press along with pictures of *Rawalpindi* prisoners; so that when, after hearing the BBC announcement, I caught the night train to Scotland to join my mother and sisters, my father had been dead five days. Had such an action taken place later in the war, it would still have attracted attention but been given less widespread coverage. As it was, when I stepped off the train at the Waverley Station in Edinburgh in the morning, I found that every newspaper in the country had given it front-page banner headlines. Nothing excites the British in wartime more than news of a defeat against odds, and this was a classic of its kind: the first surface action of the war in which an old, semi-armed former passenger liner had defied two powerful battleships; in which the bulk of her crew were pensioners and reservists and the captain at the age of sixty had been recalled to sea after seventeen years on the beach; in which the ship had been battered into a burning wreck and most of her company killed. Defeat it may have been; but it set the stamp on how the Navy was going to fight the war. In the House of Commons the Prime Minister, Neville Chamberlain, summed it up: 'They must have known as soon as they sighted the enemy that there was no chance for them, but they had no thought of surrender. They fought their guns till they could be fought no more. They then – many of them – went to their deaths and thereby carried on the great traditions of the Royal Navy. Their example will be an inspiration to those who come after them.'

Nor did it end there; for such was public interest and national pride that it became a running story. Next day there were pictures of the man who appointed my father to the *Rawalpindi*, his old friend Admiral Sir Charles Little the Second Sea Lord, inspecting on Horse Guards Parade the eleven survivors picked up by the *Chitral*. Later there were feature articles on the action, graphically illustrated, and on my father's naval career and life as a Conservative agent, pictures of him as cadet and captain, pictures of my mother, my sisters and myself. Editorials honouring my father ('the war's first hero') as well as some execrable poems appeared in every kind of paper from *The Times* and *Telegraph* to the *Biggleswade Chronicle* and *Horse and Hound*; and other tributes to him from the eminent and less so were expressed both in the press and in hundreds of letters to my mother. 'It was a bitter blow', the Northern Patrol's admiral, Sir Max Horton, wrote to her, 'to lose our crack ship, its captain, officers and so many of its crew . . . how profoundly we admired your husband for what he was, what he did, what he stood for and how he died.' Loving my father as I did, I found the combination of grief for him, pride in him, and an unutterable sense of loss emotionally shattering, and there were many times during the next couple of weeks when I dissolved uncontrollably into tears.

There was an added cause for pride. When I looked back on the whole of my father's career, particularly the affair of the mutiny at Newport, his court-martial and reprimand and axeing from the Navy – and after that the memories of it which he could never entirely expunge – it seemed to me that when he first took *Rawalpindi* to sea, he had in his own mind wiped the slate clean. Indeed in one of the last letters he ever wrote, he told a friend, 'All the bitterness of the last seventeen years has been swallowed up in the mists of the North Sea. I am as content as any man can be.' But he had done something else too. 'I feel I must make good,' he had written to my mother from Scapa Flow, 'and I realize the responsibility of this command more than I ever did in my former commands.' *I feel I must make good.* He had done much more than that; paradoxically he would never know of it.

The only honour awarded to my father was a posthumous mention in dispatches, and in view of the way the action had caught the public's imagination, many people thought this inadequate. It was said openly that he should have been awarded a posthumous VC, a view which gained momentum a year later when Captain Fogarty Fegen, in command of another armed merchant cruiser, the *Jervis Bay*, was awarded a VC for going out to attack the German cruiser *Hipper*, itself about to attack the convoy the *Jervis Bay* was escorting. Questions about this apparent discrimination were raised in Parliament, and from their prison camp in Germany *Rawalpindi* survivors wrote to my mother regretting that my father had not been similarly honoured. In fact the VC is only awarded for actions above and beyond the call of duty, and there *was* a difference between Fegen deliberately sacrificing his ship to save the convoy and my father going full belt in the opposite direction (had he had a convoy to protect, I have no doubt he would have done as Fegen did). In lieu of this the country could not have behaved more handsomely. The Board of Admiralty sent my mother a unique letter of appreciation for my father's services, scripted and embossed on parchment; the First Lord of the Admiralty unveiled a plaque to his memory in High Wycombe Parish Church; and best of all, in 1943 my mother joined the ranks of those widows whose husbands have rendered special service to their country by being granted by the King a Grace and Favour apartment in Hampton Court Palace – a far more tangible and lasting manifestation of esteem than would have been a posthumous VC.

Yet the belief of many that my father did in fact win a VC persisted for many years, indeed still does today. Quite recently (1987) I received a letter which credited him with the award. The writer was on the staff of the National Maritime Museum.

6

HMS Tartar

After Cardington, we were sent to Portsmouth for a week of practical balloon handling. A balloon had been fixed to the stern of a rather elegant yacht in the harbour and every morning we were ferried out there to winch it up and down. It was not arduous work and there were generous intervals for elevenses, lunch, and mid-afternoon coffee in the teak-panelled saloon. Another balloon had been set up on the dockside close to Nelson's flagship at Trafalgar, the *Victory*, and we took it in turns to take charge of it during the night and to sleep in one of the officers' cabins. I was told that my cabin had formerly been occupied by

Lieutenant Pasco, Nelson's flag-lieutenant, the man who had hoisted the famous 'England Expects . . .' signal just before the start of the action. We had a little mild action the night I was there: around midnight a Miss Crump, on her way to the dockyard gate after a wardroom party, tripped over one of the balloon's mooring wires in the dark and cut her leg quite badly. I told one of the crew to take her to the dockyard sickbay. When he returned, I heard him tell his mates, 'Silly effing cow. Didn't effing look where she was effing going.' During the next five years I would become used to this prolix way of putting things.

During a second week we spent afternoons at the Physical Training School, a time of day when some of the more elderly members of the course had been accustomed to lolling in club armchairs sipping port: before the week was out one had broken his ankle and two had fainted. And to acquaint us with the meaning of flag signals at sea, we were drilled on the parade ground as though we were ships. Instead of being ordered, 'About turn!', the flags for 'Turn together 180 degrees to starboard' were called out, and in place of 'Halt!' we got 'Stop engines!' At the end of the week we expected to receive orders to join balloon units in ships of the fleet; but were not altogether surprised, or disappointed, to be told that the Admiralty had now concluded what we had suspected all along, that the scheme was wildly impracticable and had been cancelled. So in the New Year, Bill Richmond and I, having been promoted to sub-lieutenant, were sent to HMS *Osprey* at Portland to learn about Asdics, the echo-sounding device that gave destroyers the whereabouts of enemy submarines; this included a day at sea at the receiving end, in the *Osprey*'s training submarine, two of whose three officers would later win the VC.

At the end of February 1940 my seagoing posting came through at last. 'You are hereby appointed Sub-Lieutenant RNVR of HMS *Tartar* for watch-keeping and other duties and are instructed to join her' – the next bit was written in ink – 'at Greenock on March 9th 1940. A first-class railway warrant is enclosed. You are to acknowledge receipt.' Immediate inquiries revealed that the *Tartar* was one of the famous Tribal class destroyers, completed a year before the war, the fastest, biggest and most modern destroyers in the fleet, formidably armed and superbly appointed and commanded by the cream of the Navy's destroyer captains. There were two flotillas of eight ships apiece and the *Tartar* belonged to the Sixth flotilla, based at Scapa Flow as part of the Home Fleet. Each ship had a complement of around a dozen officers and 250 men. Of the sixteen built, only four would survive the war.

I could not have asked for a better appointment, and as I sat in a comfortable compartment of the Scottish express on the morning of 9 March, my mind was in a turmoil of delight and nervous anticipation. In the guard's van lay my tin trunk, my name and rank painted in white lettering on the top, and in which I had packed everything I thought I would need – spare uniform, Messrs Gieves's inflatable battledress, woolly stockings, sweaters, balaclava and duffel coat, fur-lined seaboots, shirts and under-wear, a carton of Balkan Bairam cigarettes and half a dozen favourite books. But what would it all be *like*? What would I have to do? How would my fellow officers regard me? Would I be seasick? It was a new and quite unknown world I was entering, and I had no pointers to guide me. At Glasgow I changed trains for Greenock, and as we drew into the station I saw a variety of warships, some grey, some in pink and mauve camouflage, riding at anchor off the town. One of them was mine; and within the hour I would be stepping on to her quarterdeck, saluting the officer of the day and saying as I had been told to say, 'Sub-Lieutenant Kennedy. Come aboard to join, sir.'

But imaginings rarely match reality. At the Navy office on the pier where I asked for *Tartar*'s whereabouts, I was taken to see a spindly lieutenant-commander.

''Fraid you've missed her, laddie.'

'Oh dear!'

'She sailed this morning.'

'Oh! Should I now go somewhere else?'

'You might if we knew where she had gone. But we don't. We seldom do. No one tells us anything. We could send you on to Scapa, but then she might come back here. Equally if you stay here, she might go to Scapa. Or Rosyth. Or anywhere. It's a toss-up really.'

'Yes.'

'I had a fellow here yesterday looking for his ship who'd been to four different ports and missed her at each one.'

'Did he find her here?'

'No, she'd just sailed for Southampton. Bad luck, wasn't it? He's on his way to Southampton now, but I wouldn't be surprised if in a few days we saw him back here. It happens all the time.' He looked vacantly out of the window where a light rain was falling. 'I think on the whole, laddie, we'd better keep you here, and see how the situation develops. I'll arrange a billet for you in *Warspite*.'

Warspite was the battleship I had seen lying out in the bay, one of the oldest ships in the Navy, a survivor of the battle of Jutland, a legend in her own time. Late that night I and my tin trunk were dumped on board her, and while I was wondering where to go and what to do, a marine approached and said, 'Will you please follow me, sir.' I followed him up and down half a dozen ladders and along dim passageways until we came to a door marked 'Captain of the Fleet' where he knocked. The title had a fine, romantic, Elizabethan ring to it but what on earth did such a personage want with me at this hour of the night? There was no answer to the knock so the marine opened the door. It was quite dark. When he had found a light-switch I saw we were in a large cabin, empty except for two chests of drawers and three camp-beds, two of which were occupied. 'There you are, sir,' said the marine, 'and I hope you have a comfortable night.' Presently my tin trunk arrived and was put down noisily on the deck. One of the sleeping figures stirred and muttered, '*Bloody hell!*'

They woke me in the morning, sub-lieutenants like myself also waiting for their ships, and told me that if I wanted breakfast before the gunroom table was cleared, I had better shake a leg. The word 'gunroom' struck a brief chill, for I had recently been reading Charles Morgan's early novel of the same name, with its horrific accounts of beatings and bullyings in the pre-First World War fleet gunrooms. I need have had no fears, for when I finally reached it (having lost my way three times) not one of the many boisterous midshipmen and sub-lieutenants seemed the least interested in my presence. Subsequently I did my best to join in, but the conversation was largely unintelligible. Things and events were referred to as fish, guff, gash, a bottle, the rattle, the first dog, the last dog, kettles, bricks, whizzers; people as the O.O.W., the E.A., No.1, the S.O.O., Schoolie, Toothie, the Chief, the P.M.O., the Pusser. Physically and psychologically I was lost in that battleship, and with nothing to occupy my time, waited fretfully for *Tartar*'s return.

On the afternoon of the third day I was told she was back and alongside an oiler. Tin trunk and I embarked once more, and a little way downstream I glimpsed her for the first time – as sleek and elegant and powerful-looking a ship as I had yet seen. From the bow there rose in successively higher tiers A gun, B gun, the convex armoured wheelhouse and – the high point of the ship – the open bridge, some 40 feet above the waterline. At the back of the bridge was the foremast with its aerials, aft of that the raked funnel, and then in the waist of the ship the four torpedo tubes. Up again to the pom-pom and X gun and then down to Y gun, the quarterdeck and the stack of depth charges. The whole effect was one of symmetry and grace, and as we approached I felt a quickening of the senses, the near fulfilment of a long cherished dream. Already I belonged to the Navy; soon, like the midshipman in the *Nelson*'s picket-boat at Invergordon long ago, I would belong to one of its ships.

In the wardroom I met my fellow officers: the captain, Kim Skipwith, small, dapper, almond-eyed, a brilliant ship-handler and of much conscious charm; No.1, Pinky Holland-Martin, country gent and future admiral, ginger-haired and blue-eyed; No.2, Henry Durrell, the cheerful former Reserve officer who would soon relieve him; Spider Wilson, the navigator, a lean, hook-nosed sub-lieutenant RN who smoked cigarettes through a holder and had a habit of saying 'Great Land!' when surprised (his father being a parson, this was the nearest the family ever got to swearing); Tiny Archer-Shee, the ponderous 6 foot 6 inch RNVR lieutenant, a City man in peacetime, whose uncle had been Rattigan's the Winslow boy; the doctor, the chief (engineer) and the gunner. In time others would join us: George Whalley, a Canadian who was transferred to Intelligence because the captain thought him too bright for destroyers, and who later became a Professor; another chief who became known as Windy-pops because he thought each day would be his last (and one day, in another ship, it was); and an RNVR midshipman named Juncker whom we called '88' after the German bomber. My own nickname of Uckers was also inevitable, being the Navy's name for the popular messdeck game of Ludo. Spider and 88 are the only ones of that little company to have survived and today, nearly fifty years later, I am still Uckers to them, as they are still Spider and 88 to me.

I was given a hammock and shown where my servant would sling it (a good thing too, as I had not a notion how to), in a little lobby called the midship flat. The first lieutenant said, 'We're sailing again after oiling. You'll be keeping the morning watch with me, so you'll want to turn in early. The bridge messenger will call you at three forty-five.' That night I had the utmost difficulty climbing into my hammock – for again no one had taught me – failing at five or six separate attempts; and, once in, I wondered how I would ever get out. But it was snug in there, and as I drifted to sleep to the sounds of the creaking of the plates and the gentle throb of the propellers, I wondered where we were going. I had wondered about it all evening, but no one told me and somehow – and I can't think why – I was too shy to ask.

It seemed only a moment later that I woke to find myself looking into the bearded face of the bridge messenger and heard him saying, 'It's a quarter to four, sir, and the officer of the watch says to tell you it's a fine night.' Heavy with sleep, I somehow managed to reach the deck, put on my clothes and new fur-lined seaboots and duffel coat, make my way up to the after lobby, push aside the black-out screen and step into quarterdeck blackness. I stood there a moment, letting my eyes grow accustomed to the texture of the night before turning forward into the wind, towards the high rampart of the bridge superstructure. My boots squeaked a little as I walked. In the waist of the ship, as the phosphorescent bubbles danced along the ship's side and little waves slapped playfully against the thin plates, the loom of a light appeared out of the darkness to starboard, focussed momentarily in my direction, slid into darkness again. An artificer, his middle watch completed, was climbing out of the engine-room hatch as I passed, and a gust of warm air brushed my face. I passed the ship's motor-boat, lying snugly in its davits, and the galley, now secured for the night, entered the bridge superstructure by another black-out screen and climbed the three ladders to the open bridge.

There were some shadowy figures moving about there, but having been in the light again, I at first found it difficult to focus. A voice which I recognized as that of an RN midshipman on board for training, said, 'Ready to take over the watch?' I said I was, although I felt far from it. 'We rounded the Mull of Kintyre an hour ago. Our 0350 position is on the chart. Course 017, speed fifteen knots, ship at cruising stations, captain's in his sea-cabin. Well, night-night.' He disappeared and another took his place.

'Bridge messenger, sir. Here's your cocoa.' He handed me a

mug of steaming, sweet sludge and I sipped it gratefully. Then the head and shoulders of someone emerged from behind the little screen that covered the light on the chart table. It was the first lieutenant.

'Ah,' he said, 'so you got here all right. Any problems?'

'No, sir.'

'Good. When you were at *King Alfred*, did they teach you how to take bearings on a gyro compass repeater?'

'Yes, sir.'

'Well, you can make yourself useful right away. See that lighthouse flashing fine on the port bow and that other one almost abeam to starboard?'

'Yes, sir.'

'You'll find compass repeaters either side of the bridge. You take bearings on them and I'll pencil them in on the chart.'

So I did, and he did. Like Boswell being handed a rope by Coll in a storm in these same waters, I don't believe it was strictly necessary, but (like Coll) he obviously wanted me to feel I had some function to perform, and I was grateful. From the chart table he said, 'Come and have a peep,' and he showed me where the two bearings cut, almost plumb on the course the navigator had pencilled in, and a bit further on from the last plotted position. 'That's where we are now,' he said. I felt enormously proud, as though I had just put the ship there myself.

There were four lookouts in the wings of the bridge, and presently one shouted out, 'Lights bearing green one five.' I looked through the binoculars they had given me and saw several small vessels bobbing up and down. 'Fishing-boats,' said the first lieutenant, and went to a voicepipe and said, 'Captain, sir?'

A sleepy, tinny voice came up from below. 'Yes.'

'Permission to alter course to avoid some fishing-boats?'

'All right. Let me know when you're back on course.'

'Aye, aye, sir.' He moved to another voicepipe. 'Starboard ten.'

Another tinny voice, this time from the wheelhouse.

'Starboard ten.'

'Steer 030.'

'Steer 030, sir.'

And so it went on, with hardly a quiet moment; buzzers sounding and being answered, look-outs reporting their reliefs, bearings being shouted out (with sometimes the first lieutenant and I reversing roles), the Asdic operator reporting an echo, permissions for a dozen different things (including an odd one from the engine-room to make smoke) being asked for and granted. When the night began to ebb, the first lieutenant said, 'Now I'm going to show you where the various voicepipes and telephones are, so when you hear a voice saying "Wireless office – Bridge" you don't answer the voicepipe to the captain's sea-cabin which would make him very annoyed if he was asleep.' He showed them to me one by one, and then he came to some large instrument covered in canvas. I think he was going to pass it by when, keen to show interest, I said:

'What's in there, sir?'

'That,' he said, 'is a thing called the Mountbatten station-keeping gear. It was invented by Lord Louis or his father, I forget which. We keep it covered because the captain finds it quite useless.'

A little later, looking through my binoculars to starboard, I saw a coastline that somehow seemed familiar. A glance at the chart confirmed it. It was the west coast of Islay. There was the Mull of Oa where my father had taken his first shoot; and the cliffs where the dog Ben, having chewed up the Peke, had fallen down a crevasse on to a ledge and had to spend the night there before being rescued. There were the golden sands of Machrie where old Myra had admired the bloody sunset and taught me how to kiss. There was the hill where my father had got lost in the mist, and the Rhinns of Islay where we often used to picnic and where once Ben had rolled on a dead sheep. I remembered leaving the island for the last time, on my way to Skye in the week before the war, and my father shyly pressing a fiver into my hand and saying, 'You may find this'll come in handy.' What a world away it was now.

The sun came up over Jura, and the wardroom steward arrived on the bridge with a plate of hot buttered toast and a jug of tea. I leaned on the bridge counter, looked at the smudge of Harris and Lewis away to the north-west, at the bows slicing cleanly through a calm sea, the ship lifting a little to the swell. I munched my toast and sipped my tea and thought I had never been happier. I was officer of the watch (well, *second* officer of the watch) of a crack fleet destroyer going about (well, *about* to go about) its business in great waters. I could not ask for anything more, and I smiled with the joy of it.

'I think you've quite enjoyed your first watch,' said the first lieutenant.

'I was just thinking,' I said, 'how marvellous it is that we are actually being paid for this.'

He looked at me in astonishment. 'I can think of quite a few other things', he said, 'I'd rather be doing instead.'

I couldn't think of one.

'Forgive me asking,' I said, 'but where are we actually going?'

'Did no one tell you?'

'No.'

'How very remiss. Why, Scapa of course. Where else?'

It was to be my home from home for the next two years, and in that time I came to know it well – a sheet of water some ten miles by eight lying south of the mainland of Orkney, a natural harbour if ever there was one, a long-time refuge for war-weary ships. The Vikings had first discovered it on their terrible raids south, and given to the ring of islands that surrounded it their lovely Norse names – Hoy to the west, Switha and Hoxa and Flotta to the south, Pomona and Ronaldshay to the east. Here in the First World War had been quartered the battleships of the Grand Fleet, and on a May evening in 1916 Admiral Jellicoe had led them out of harbour to join with Beatty and the battlecruisers from Rosyth to meet the German High Seas Fleet off Jutland. And it was here two years later that the High Seas Fleet was brought in chains after the Armistice; to lie and rot until Midsummer's Day 1919 when Admiral von Reuter hoisted the signal to scuttle and all his proud ships sank slowly to the sea bed. (A party of Stromness school children on their summer outing in a pleasure boat thought it had been arranged for their benefit and gave three lusty cheers.) And it was only five months ago that Prien had with much skill and daring brought his U-boat in through a narrow unguarded eastern entrance to sink the *Royal Oak*. In Germany Prien and his crew had been hailed as heroes and fêted by Hitler. Yet on balance it had been a poor reward for an enterprise so brilliantly planned and executed, for had the bulk of the Home Fleet not taken up temporary residence at Loch Ewe, losses in ships and men could have been devastating.

Admiral Beatty called Scapa the most damnable place on earth, and most of the Navy agreed. The islands were treeless, just heather and grass, seabirds and sheep, and across the bare face of the Flow tempests blew, often for days on end. There were no women, shops, restaurants, just a couple of canteens that dispensed warm beer, a hall for film shows and the occasional concert party, and football fields that too often displayed the sign 'All grounds unfit for play'. This was depressing for many, particularly the lower deck, but I preferred a war without distractions. In any event, on the few days we were in harbour each month, we had enough to occupy us on board. We fed well, cigarettes and spirits were duty free; and sometimes in the evenings there would be darts competitions in the wardroom flat, tribal parties where we and flotilla friends dressed up as Tartars, Eskimos, Bedouins, cinema evenings often improved by the last reel appearing first and upside down. We sang songs too:

> Oh, we had to carry Carrie to the ferry,
> And the ferry carried Carrie to the shore,
> And the reason that we had to carry Carrie was,
> Poor Carrie couldn't carry any more.

And in summer when the hills of Hoy were touched with purple and green and the Flow sparkled blue in the morning sun, at night too when the Northern Lights wove pale patterns in the sky, the place had a rare beauty. Then I would take my fishing rod ashore, climb a hill above the anchorage on the other side of which lay a small loch and, away from all Navy sights and sounds, spend a contented afternoon with only skuas and curlews for company. Whether I caught any trout or not didn't matter; I invariably returned on board refreshed.

Scapa was an advance post for the Home Fleet to apprehend German warships trying to break out into the Atlantic. The Home Fleet's task would have been made much easier had it been able to make use of Norwegian harbours too; and plans to forestall German intentions by occupying them were already far advanced when the Germans struck first. On the night of 9 April 1940 a signal arrived to sail immediately after oiling. That morning, in a secret and well-planned operation, the German fleet had taken possession of all the principal Norwegian ports from Narvik in the north to Oslo in the south.

When I came on watch next morning I was met by an impressive sight: all around us the ships of the Home Fleet which we had joined during the night – battleships, battlecruisers, a carrier, cruisers and destroyers – steaming south-eastwards at high speed in search of the German fleet. But the sea remained empty, for most enemy ships not destroyed in the harbours they had captured (at Narvik the German Navy was to lose half its entire destroyer force) were able to slip back home without leaving the shelter of the fjords. Yet the sight of our own ships – and there must have been some forty – manoeuvring at high speed as one unit, many of them shipping green water over their bows, their halyards billowing out a succession of brightly coloured flags, was a heartening spectacle. From the turn of the century, such fleet manoeuvring was commonplace; after 1945, it never happened again on such a scale.

The Norwegian campaign was a brief one, for with German air superiority unchallenged, it was only a matter of time before the troops that we had put ashore had to be evacuated. We were ordered to evacuate any troops that had made their way to Molde, and for me this meant a return journey along the fjord where once my parents and I had sat on the deck of the *Sigurd Jarl*, listening to Norwegian folk songs on the gramophone as we made our leisurely way from Bergen to Trondheim. I remembered Molde as an attractive little fishing-port; but the night we reached it in *Tartar* it was burning from end to end, having been attacked by German dive bombers for the past five days.

After making fast alongside the jetty, word reached us that the commander-in-chief of the Norwegian Army, General Ruge, was in the town, and the captain sent me ashore to find out if he would like to come to England and join the Norwegian forces there. I finally tracked him down in a wood above the town, standing with his staff officers in a clearing in the snow. There were perhaps a dozen of them and I had never seen a more dispirited-looking group, saying nothing and looking down at the burning town with glazed eyes. The light from the fires lit up their blue-grey cloaks and peaked caps, making them look like mummers in some Ruritanian play. I gave the general the captain's message: his response was to smile and shake his head. Weeks later he was captured near Tromso and sent to a concentration camp.

We saw the campaign out in the far north when the sun shone all through the middle watch, and the last British troops were embarked from Harstad. On our final journey to Scapa we met the hospital ship *Atlantis* who told us she had just seen the *Scharnhorst* and *Gneisenau* sink the transport *Orama*, but her own neutrality had been respected. The day after, the Germans sank the aircraft carrier *Glorious*.

At the end of May came the evacuation of the British Army from Dunkirk, and after that, a question-mark arose in the minds of many. What was going to happen next? The German Army now occupied Europe from the North Cape to the Pyrenees. How could we continue to survive alone? Our Army was in disarray and practically weaponless, and even if the Navy could prevent sea-borne landings on any scale, what about the air? Would it not be only a matter of time before German parachutists in their thousands descended on our fields and meadows as they had done in Holland and Belgium? And were there no doubts at all that we would be able to repel them? The question-mark remained.

And then one day we were given an answer. On the wardroom wireless on which, far out in the North Sea or Atlantic, entertainers like Vera Lynn, Tommy Handley, Ted Ray and others enabled us to forget for a while where we were and what we were doing, came a voice that was to become ever more dear and familiar, a voice that without hesitation or equivocation pointed the way ahead: 'We shall not flag nor fail. We shall fight in France, we shall fight on the seas and oceans, we shall fight with growing confidence and growing strength in the air, we shall defend our island whatever the cost may be, we shall fight on the beaches, we shall fight on the landing-grounds, we shall fight in the fields and in the streets, we shall fight in the hills; we shall never surrender.'

With these words and the conviction with which they were uttered, the question-mark was obliterated, never to rise again. I think we all knew then instinctively that, however long it took, we would eventually win the war.

This new Churchillian mood of resolution and defiance was behind the ruthless (and little-known) task we were now ordered to perform: to sail with two others of our flotilla to the Faeroe Islands and seize four Swedish destroyers. The neutral Swedes had just bought them from the Italians and were steaming them home to Goteborg with a transport and an oiler. As the British government had given the Swedes express permission to enter the Faeroes, which we then controlled, it seemed a somewhat churlish thing to do. But Churchill was concerned that the Swedish government, many of whose members were pro-

German, might dispose of the ships to Germany to make good some of the heavy losses in destroyers they had suffered at the two battles of Narvik. The Swedish Commodore would be asked to sail his ships to a British port. If he refused, our orders were to sink them at anchor. (Two weeks later, and for the same reason, Admiral Somerville was ordered to sink the French fleet at Oran when its commander refused to capitulate; and this he partly did.)

In the early hours of the next morning, while it was still dark, we crept into the Faeroes and lay to across the entrance of the fjord where the Swedish squadron was at anchor. The motor-boat was lowered and the flotilla captain (a rather pompous little man who had temporarily relieved Kim while his own ship was refitting) went away to call on the Swedish Commodore. He was told the Commodore was not yet up, but insisted on seeing him all the same. Arrayed in pyjamas, the Commodore said, 'I have orders to fight or scuttle, captain. When does the fight begin?' Our captain said it would begin at 10 o'clock unless he had received a favourable reply before then; and added that his orders were explicit.

It was now full light. We could see the destroyers lying in a little bay at the head of the fjord, with their transport and oiler in their national colours of blue and yellow anchored close by. A Faeroese fishing-boat chugged past us on its way to the fishing-grounds, and on the bridge the chaplain and the engineer officer discussed the prospects of buying cod. This brought a rejoinder from the captain, who was clearly a little on edge, 'We did not come here for cod.'

By 9.15 no message had been received from the Swedish Commodore, so to encourage him we all put on tin hats, went to action stations and steamed up and down to show we meant business. This had the desired effect. A message came from the Commodore that while he was not willing to steam his ships to a British port, he would evacuate their crews to the transport and we could seize them if we wished. This was a cunning move as it put the onus of responsibility on us.

Spider and I and twenty ratings were detailed to steam one of the destroyers to Scapa. It was called *Puke*, and, as things turned out, aptly named. After the Swedish crew had left it, we went over in the motor-boat. In the wardroom I found a Portuguese magazine giving a vivid account of my father's action in

Rawalpindi, together with a photograph I had once taken of him. Elsewhere I found a parrot in a cage and a suitcase left behind by their owner. So I put them in the motor-boat and took them over to the transport. Several hundred Swedish sailors watched the boat come alongside, and I expected hisses and cat-calls. But sailors everywhere appreciate the bizarre, and as the parrot was handed over, there was quite a cheer. That night I slept in a four-poster bed in the *Puke*'s captain's multi-mirrored cabin.

We had a horrid journey back to Scapa. It was blowing a gale as we reached the open sea, and first one engine packed up and then the other. A trawler turned up to take us in tow, but this did not prevent us rolling so violently from side to side that there were several occasions when I thought we were going right over. This went on for two days and nights; we had no sleep apart from catnaps and were soon pretty well out of food and water. On the third day a destroyer arrived to spread oil on the sea ahead of us, and eventually we tottered into Scapa.

During the next few days the British government received cast-iron assurances from Sweden that if returned, the ships would not be sold or otherwise handed over to Germany, and agreed to pay £50,000 to the Swedish government for any damage or inconvenience caused. Before the destroyers were handed back, Admiralty experts came on board to look for secrets (they found none) and an order was given that any 'mementoes' which the steaming-parties had taken were to be returned. As a result enough things were dumped on the *Tartar*'s quarterdeck to stock a pawn-shop. But we refused to give up a gay red and yellow lifebuoy marked in bold lettering PUKE: it found an honoured place in the after lobby, a reminder, an exhortation and a warning.

There was a postscript to the story. As the Swedish ships, once more reunited with their Commodore, were passing through the Skaggerak, they were spotted by a British bomber whose pilot had not, as they say, been put in the picture. And insult, though not injury, was added to insult.

'Have bombed four destroyers proceeding east,' the pilot signalled. 'Estimate no hits.'

One afternoon when we were lying in the Flow alongside the aircraft carrier *Ark Royal*, and separated from her by a kind of floating pontoon, I was informed the captain wished to see me. This was still the flotilla captain, Kim having not yet returned. He was writing at his desk when I entered.

'Ah, Kennedy. You officer of the day?'

'Yes, sir.'

'I was on deck a little while ago and I see the cat's gone adrift.'

I looked at him goggle-eyed.

'The cat, sir?'

'Yes. It's not where it was this morning. It seems to have got shifted. Has it been reported to you?'

'No, sir.'

'Well, you might look into it, will you?'

I stood rooted to the spot, like what's-his-name on the peak in Darien, gazing with wild surmise.

'See what's happened to the cat, sir?'

'That's what I said. Now, get on with it, man.'

'Aye, aye, sir.'

I tottered out of the cabin in a sort of daze, trying to assure myself I had not been hearing things. For what possible reason could the captain want to know the whereabouts of the ship's cat? Was it perhaps an April Fool? No, that had gone by some weeks ago, and anyway, the captain didn't seem to be made in the mould of an April fooler. Alternatively, had the stress of war temporarily unhinged him? And if so, was he safe to be left in command? Should I perhaps arrest him? I had half a mind to ask the first lieutenant for guidance, but since it was mid-afternoon he and all the other officers were asleep, and I didn't think he'd be too pleased to be woken with a cock-and-bull story about the ship's cat.

There was nothing for it but to find the cat myself. This was not too easy as it had always been a cat of no fixed abode. I looked for it in all the most likely places, such as the wireless office where they kept a permanent saucer of milk for it, the captain's sea-cabin where it often favoured his leather bunk, and the wardroom pantry where it sometimes lurked for tit-bits. As I went around the ship I asked in an offhand way the few people I met whether they had seen the cat anywhere, and they looked at me rather strangely and said No. I even shouted across to the quartermaster of the *Ark Royal* to inquire whether it had come his way and he gave the same answer. I eventually ran it to earth asleep on a coil of rope on X gundeck. Now came another dilemma. Did the captain want me to take the cat physically to him – for what purpose I could not tell – or did he just want to be reassured it was okay? Somehow the scenario of my entering the captain's cabin with the cat in my arms was not one that seemed likely to attract a favourable reception. So I left the cat where it was, and went along alone.

'Ah, Kennedy, there you are. You've been a devil of a long time. What have you got to report?'

'I've found it, sir.'

'You've found what?'

'The cat, sir. It's up on X gundeck.'

The captain stared at me in the same sort of uncomprehending way as I at first had stared at him.

'Are you trying to make a fool of me, Kennedy?'

'No, sir. You asked me to find out what had happened to the cat. I thought it an odd request at the time, so I asked you to repeat it, which you did. I've now done what you asked.'

The captain's expression changed. His pupils dilated, his cheeks bulged and took on a purplish tinge. He looked as if he might do me physical damage.

'No, no, you bloody idiot,' he bellowed, 'not the cat, the *catamaran*. Bugger the cat!'

Today the word 'catamaran' has come into general use as a form of sailing craft with two keels. Then it was not a word most people had ever heard of. By devious means I found out that what the captain was referring to was the floating pontoon separating us from the *Ark Royal*, and which had slightly shifted its position. So I called for the bosun's mate.

'Sir?'

'Bosun's mate, the catamaran seems to have got shifted. Call out the duty watch, will you, and have it secured.'

'Aye, aye, sir.'

He disappeared forward at a trot. I went down to my cabin, took out the dictionary and turned to 'catamaran'.

'A raft,' it said, 'used by the natives of Madras to paddle from one village to another.'

But I never told that to the captain.

By now I was making my way in the world. I had exchanged my hammock for a small but snug cabin which had running water, a generous bookcase and a niche for my wireless which the Chief

Petty Officer telegraphist was good enough to link up to the ship's receiving aerial. I was permitted by the officer of the watch to make adjustments to the ship's course and speed to keep station; and I became the ship's correspondence officer. This involved sorting through the documents sent us each week by the Admiralty of which the most interesting by far was called WIR, or Weekly Intelligence Report.

WIR was a booklet which included fascinating information on the suspected whereabouts of the ships of the German Navy. For instance: 'Recent aerial photography of Wilhelmshaven showed *Scharnhorst* and *Gneisenau* both in harbour, the former in dry dock, the latter alongside the inner basin. Agents' reports indicate that neither vessel will be operational for at least two months.' Or, 'The raider G disguised as a merchantman with three masts and two funnels (one of which may be a dummy) was observed going down Channel on August 14th and is believed to be bound for the Indian Ocean, though the white uniforms and solar topees reported as being loaded on board before sailing, could be a blind.'

These reports were read avidly by every officer in the ship, for they gave a tantalizing glimpse of the activities of an enemy with whom we were at war, but whose ships and sailors we never saw. For me they fuelled a question which had first arisen at the time of the sinking of the *Rawalpindi*, and later became a kind of obsession: *what were German sailors like?* Were they all fanatical Nazis, like the jack-booted, goose-stepping soldiers we had seen so often on the newsreels? Or were they more like us, not greatly interested in politics, officers and men of a navy which, when first formed, took the Royal Navy as its model? After all, we shared the same sort of uniforms, spoke the same sort of language, issued the same sort of orders, shared the common disciplines of navigation, seamanship, gunnery, torpedo-firing, wireless telegraphy. So what divided us? Was it no more – though Heaven knows, it was enough – than the policies of our two governments, imbuing each side with a will to win? Aside from that, how might we have regarded each other? These questions stayed with me, demanding answers; but it wasn't until after the war that I began to look for them.

And so that strange and beautiful summer went by, in which for some twenty-five days a month we went into the Atlantic on patrol, sometimes on our own, more often as a screen for the battleships and carriers; while 700 miles to the south the Spitfires and Hurricanes from Tangmere and Biggin Hill took issue with the Luftwaffe in the first exchanges of the Battle of Britain.

It was about this time that the flotilla captain returned to his own ship and Kim came back to us; and he decided that I had become enough of a pro to be given a watch at sea by myself, first during daytime, then at night.

Night watches in rough weather weren't much fun – feeling but not seeing the bows rise steeply and dramatically like a roller-coaster to surmount the crest of some monster wave, then holding on tight while they dropped swiftly and sickeningly into the trough, and the keel plates shuddered with the shock and the spray rained down like confetti. As each new crest was breasted and the wind beat a tattoo on the halyards and the water sloshed around the bridge, it was a question of learning to stand upright, to adjust one's body to the motion of the ship so that spray-spattered binoculars could still be trained on other ships and confirm their presence. As hour succeeded hour of cold, fatigue and discomfort, one began to think the watch would never end.

But there were other nights of sheer joy, when the sea was calm and the moon shone, when the ship hummed and trembled as she sliced through the water at speed, delighting, or so it seemed, in her own power and beauty. From the bridge one could look aft and see the whole graceful length of her, the wake bubbling and frothing astern; and, nearer, the foremast like a giant inverted metronome, swaying to and fro against a backcloth of stars. On those nights one hardly noticed the time go by. One read with keener interest the routine signals coming in from the Admiralty (anything from Wrens clothing to the nightly U-boat Disposition Report), gave with greater grace permission for the bosun's mate to take the wheel, was less crotchety with the look-out who failed to report a ship or light. There was time for reminiscences with one's fellow officer of the watch or, if alone, with the duty signalman, and sometimes during the first watch (8 p.m. to midnight), the doctor, who had little enough to occupy him, or the first lieutenant after his rounds, or even the captain, might turn up for a gossip over a final cigarette or pipe. Later, beneath the stars and with the ship asleep, there were moments when I felt that sky and sea and I were one, concordant and indivisible, and remembered Rupert Brooke's 'a width, a shining peace under the night'. Would a day ever come when I could say the same of myself in terms of time, when I could find continuity and reconciliation between my past and future? For a long time to come, indeed long after much of my future had become my past, I doubted it.

Yet if I was by this time a quite efficient officer, I was also, as my mother never tired of telling me, inclined to fecklessness, and presently I did something so crassly feckless as to bring me within an ace of court-martial and the abrupt ending of my sea-going career.

We were escorting from the Faeroes to Scapa a tug towing a destroyer whose engines had broken down. To avoid U-boats we were zig-zagging either side of the tug's course, five or six minutes on the starboard leg, five or six on the port. It was as boring and routine a task as one could imagine, and a calm, moonlit sea and warm, windless middle watch did nothing to make it less so.

At about 3 a.m., having reached the end of the starboard leg, I gave the order to the wheelhouse, 'Port twenty!' and heard the quartermaster reply 'Port twenty', followed by 'Twenty of port wheel on, sir!' Presently I should have told the quartermaster to steady on the new course, but instead I drifted off into some reverie of my own, having forgotten I had ordered any change of course at all. Fortunately the quartermaster was a man of sensibility and initiative and brought me back to reality with an urgent, 'Twenty of port wheel still on, sir!'

Looking up, I saw that we had travelled way past the course on which we should have steadied and that the bows were now swinging round towards the tug.

'Hard a starboard!' I bellowed down the voicepipe. 'Stop starboard. Half astern starboard. Full ahead port.'

There was a jangle of telegraph repeats in the wheelhouse, and the whole ship shuddered and trembled at the sudden strain put on her. With the tug no more than a couple of hundred yards away and still closing, the bows at last stopped their swing to port, then slowly – agonizingly slowly it seemed to me – began to turn to starboard. The tug crossed our stern not fifty yards away.

Any hope that the captain might have slept through all this was in vain.

'Bridge?'

'Sir?'

'What the hell's going on?'

I told him.

'I'll come up.'

By the time he did I was back to half ahead on both engines and had almost regained the proper course. I waited for the coming blast, for the news that I wasn't fit to keep a watch on my own, that my watch-keeping certificate would be taken away from me. Instead he walked past me to the bridge counter, looked at the tug – now a decent distance away – and without turning said, 'Any cocoa going?'

The bosun's mate brought him a cup and put it on the bridge counter. He stayed sipping at it for perhaps ten minutes, then abruptly turned and without a word went down the ladder to his sea-cabin.

Perhaps he figured that we are all allowed one mistake, and that having made it, I had done everything I should have done to correct it. Whatever his thinking his continuing trust in me endeared him to me more than ever; and imbued me with a determination not to be feckless again.

7

The Pursuit of the Bismarck

We went down to Plymouth for a refit in the autumn and all had two weeks' leave. After six months at sea it was good to lie abed of a morning, drink fresh milk, walk on green grass, go dancing, make love; but all too soon we were heading back for Scapa. It was a gruelling winter, for first the German pocket battleship *Admiral Scheer*, then the heavy cruiser *Admiral Hipper*, and finally in January 1941 the *Scharnhorst* and *Gneisenau* all broke out into the Atlantic undetected and between November and March sank a quarter of a million tons of Allied shipping. For us this meant almost continual sea-time, screening the battleships and carriers on long patrols in what turned out to be a vain attempt to find the enemy. The weather was at its worst; bitterly cold, with leaden skies that gave minimum visibility; seas that tossed us unceasingly to and fro, up and down, and sent food, mess traps, and even furniture shooting from one side of the wardroom to the other. Each day seemed to slide into the next, watch, sleep, food following one another in an unvarying pattern; mind and body became numb with boredom and fatigue.

But towards the end of February 1941, while the *Scharnhorst* and *Gneisenau* were still at sea, it was our turn to take the offensive. *Tartar*, with three other destroyers and two assault ships carrying landing craft and commandos, was to sail across the North Sea to northern Norway, proceed by night up Vest Fjord, the long channel that leads to Narvik, and at dawn attack various ports in the Lofoten Islands, some ninety miles inside enemy-held territory. It was a bold plan and one that assumed that neither enemy warships nor planes would be at hand to offer resistance.

The passage across the North Sea was uneventful. We entered Vest Fjord soon after midnight and steamed parallel with the coast. At around 5 a.m., as the night was about to dissolve, we nosed our way with one of the assault ships into the approaches to Svolvaer, the Lofoten Islands' capital. I could just make out mountains towering above us and, at the foot of one, street lights and the black smudges of houses. It was so still I heard quite clearly the voice of an officer in the assault ship ordering the lowering of the landing craft. Presently, having embarked the commandos, they moved off like ghosts towards the town. The commandos were to cut the telephone wires, blow up storage tanks, capture the German garrison and recruit Norwegian volunteers.

Dawn broke and brought with it as lovely a sight as I have ever seen. Above Svolvaer and stretching out of sight to north and south were range upon range of mountains entirely blanketed in snow; to the east, across the flat, empty waters of Vest Fjord were the distant mountains of the mainland, similarly whitened. Over their tops the sun appeared and shone from a blue cloudless sky.

But so exquisite a backcloth was hardly in keeping with our mission. A small coaster flying the Nazi ensign chugged out of harbour and not imagining for a moment that we could be anything but German, dipped her ensign in salute. Our reply was to send a shot across her bows, then, when her crew had abandoned ship, to sink her. We did the same to the factory ship *Hamburg* of 10,000 tons which refined fish oil for use in explosives; and a third victim was a smaller ship laden with fish and due to sail for Germany that day. Soon after came a huge explosion from the shore where the commandos had blown up two refineries. A thick column of black smoke rose into the air against the white mountain and I took a photograph of it through the barrels of the pom-pom gun with my grandmother's ancient folding Kodak. Later in the war this picture was used as the cover for the government publication *Combined Operations*.

The morning wore on, the sun continued to shine. By noon the time limit of our stay was drawing near. The landing craft, each with its quota of German prisoners and Norwegian volunteers, headed back to the assault ship and were hoisted on board. Together we turned and on a glass-like sea began the long journey down Vest Fjord, the other ships joining us *en route*.

This was the first combined operation of the war, and it had been resoundingly successful. We had remained unmolested in enemy waters for nearly twelve hours, done considerable damage to German shipping and installations, and brought back with us 200 German prisoners and more than 300 Norwegian volunteers – all without a single casualty. The press gave the operation widespread coverage and praise, for it came at a time when Britain was still facing Hitler alone, and we had little enough to celebrate.

And yet I could not bring myself to feel as euphoric as others did and as perhaps I should have done. I thought of many things: of the contrast between the astonishing beauty and tranquillity of the day and the fearful havoc we had caused – three fine ships with their valuable cargoes sent to the bottom, two refineries on which local people depended for a living gone up in smoke. I thought of the reprisals the Germans would take when they found out what had happened.[1] I thought of all the Norwegian mothers that night contemplating the empty places at the table and not knowing when, if ever, they would see their sons again (some never did). And I could even spare a thought for some of the 200 young German seamen and soldiers of the Alpine Corps whom I had seen pass by in the landing craft; some looked little more than boys, plucked without warning from their beds at dawn and borne away across the sea to prisoner-of-war camp in

[1] Many houses in Svolvaer and Stamsund were burned to the ground, and sixty-three of the inhabitants were carted off to a labour camp at Grini in southern Norway.

England. Oh, sure, they had only themselves to blame, they shouldn't have been there in the first place. But they must have felt much as I had felt as we steamed up Vest Fjord the night before. Whatever happens tomorrow, I had prayed, please, please, let me not be captured, be taken from my beloved ship, be deprived of any further part in the war. My prayer had been answered, theirs never had the opportunity to be made.

I had the first watch that May evening, a day out from the Clyde. With *Somali*, *Eskimo* and *Mashona* we were escorting the troopship *Britannic* and the battleship *Rodney* westwards across the Atlantic. It was, as I recall, an uneventful watch, and at about 9 p.m. while checking bearings and distance from *Rodney* for perhaps the sixth time, I heard the buzzer from the wireless office. Signalman Pearson, with whom I was sharing the watch, a barrel-shaped fellow partial to chocolate 'Nutty', thrust his flabby fist into the voicepipe and hauled up the signal box.

'U-boat Disposition Report, I expect,' he said.

He unravelled the signal, scanned it, then handed it to me. It was prefixed MOST IMMEDIATE, came from the cruiser *Norfolk* and went something like this: 1BS 1CR 66.40N 28.22W Co220 Sp 30.

'Pearson,' I said, 'does that mean what I think it means?'

'Yes, sir. One enemy battleship, one enemy cruiser, position sixty-six forty North, twenty-eight twenty-two West, course 220, speed 30 knots.'

'Christ!' I said, and pressed the captain's buzzer.

In such a manner did I learn of the break-out into the Atlantic of the giant *Bismarck* together with the *Prinz Eugen*, an event followed by the most exciting week of my life. A glance at the chart showed that the German ships had been picked up in the Denmark Strait, the stretch of water that lies between Greenland and the north of Iceland. Although of intense interest the news did not then affect us personally, as we were 600 miles away and fully occupied with protecting *Rodney* and *Britannic* against U-boats. But it was the one topic of conversation throughout the ship. In the wardroom that night we discussed the likely eventualities into the early hours, and when my servant called me with tea at 7.30 next morning, I was already awake.

'Heard the news, sir?'

'No.'

'*Hood*'s gone.'

'*No!*'

'Yes, and *Prince of Wales* damaged.'

The *Hood* gone — the most famous, most loved of British warships, the one above all others that epitomized the Navy and the country? It seemed impossible to believe. And the brand new battleship *Prince of Wales* damaged! If this is what the *Bismarck* could do in six minutes flat, what might she not achieve against the convoys from America? The question-mark that had arisen at the time of Dunkirk rose again. Loose in the Atlantic and supported by supply ships and tankers, she could prey on our shipping for months and cut the supply line on which we depended for survival.

After breakfast I went to the charthouse where Spider had put up a large scale chart of the Atlantic, and pencilled on it the position of the first sighting of the German squadron, the location of the sinking of *Hood*, and the squadron's present position as received from the signals of the pursuing *Norfolk*, *Suffolk* and wounded *Prince of Wales*. He had also marked the positions of the British ships closing in on *Bismarck*, and as the day passed and assuming she kept her present course and speed, it looked as though the commander-in-chief, Admiral Tovey, in his flagship *King George V* with the battlecruiser *Repulse* would be the first to engage her in the morning and (if the result was inconclusive) that we would be the second.

Eskimo and *Britannic* went off to the west, while we steamed south-westwards all day, the seas getting higher, the wind rising hourly. Inevitably that evening, as the gap between us gradually narrowed, one's thoughts turned to the action that lay ahead. Inevitably too one had mixed feelings, partly a desire to stop the *Bismarck* at all costs and by so doing perhaps win honour and glory, partly — and I'm not sure if it wasn't the stronger part — a reluctance to get embroiled at all. Our task, if we met, was to close in to some 6000 yards to deliver our four torpedoes. With *Rodney* soon outdistanced by the swifter enemy, we would have to undergo the full weight of his broadsides during the run-in; and we knew, without having to say it, that if we survived that, it would be a miracle.

When I came on watch again at midnight, it was blowing a gale. We had had to reduce speed to 15 knots, while *Rodney* with her long dachsund's snout pushing through the crests had lumbered past at her maximum 22 knots and was now out of sight ahead. I think that was the most uncomfortable watch I ever kept. The motion was like that of a hovercraft in a bumpy sea, greatly magnified, for we lunged at the waves rather than rode them. Throughout the watch the signals from the shadowers kept coming in, and it looked as though the commander-in-chief would make contact with the enemy at around noon. When I reached my cabin via the engine-room and boiler-room (for there was a danger of being washed overboard along the upper deck) I found the place a shambles – books, wireless and broken water carafe strewn about the deck. I left them where they were and clambered into bed.

'Sir?'

Where was I?

'Seven-thirty. Here's your tea. I've cleaned up the mess on the deck. And Jerry's done a bunk.'

I thought sleepily, this man has got his priorities right.

'Lost contact, have we?'

'Not a whisper since you came off watch. Can't say I'm altogether sorry.'

This is not the place to recount the changing events and fortunes of either side during the rest of the operation, for we had little knowledge of them at the time, and I have described them fully elsewhere.[1] Suffice it to say that two days later when we had begun to think that *Bismarck* had disappeared off the face of the waters, she was spotted alone (for she had detached *Prinz Eugen* for independent warfare) some 700 miles north-west of Brest. Her speed was down to 20 knots which suggested damage or a fuel problem (it was both) but which would bring her under German air cover within twenty-four hours. At that time *Rodney, Tartar* and *Mashona* (*Somali* had left us to refuel) were still bucketing around the ocean at high speed, but we were some 150 miles to the north of her, and with only a couple of knots' advantage had virtually no chance of catching up.

There was still however one British group between *Bismarck* and France, Vice-Admiral Somerville's Force H, steaming north from Gibraltar; it included the aircraft-carrier *Ark Royal*, and if one of her torpedo-planes could slow down *Bismarck* a little more, there might still be a faint chance of bringing her to book.

---

[1] *Pursuit* (Collins, 1974) from which one or two passages are included here.

At six that evening Admiral Tovey in *King George V* thundered over the horizon to join us, and took station in the van.

Presently a signal lamp began flashing from the flagship's bridge.

'To *Rodney*,' sang out our signalman, 'from C-in-C. What is your best speed?'

Then it was *Rodney*'s turn.

'To C-in-C. From *Rodney*. Twenty-two knots.'

Gradually the distance between the two ships lengthened and *Rodney*'s lamp began flashing again.

'To C-in-C,' shouted the signalman, 'from *Rodney*. I am afraid that your twenty-two knots is faster than mine.'

The flagship dropped back, and we all steamed on, less with any real hope of *Bismarck* being delivered to us than for the lack of any alternative; if failure had to be admitted, let it not be admitted until the last possible moment. At 6.30 p.m. Tovey signalled the Admiralty that unless *Bismarck*'s speed had been reduced by midnight, *King George V* would have to return to harbour for lack of fuel; *Rodney*, with *Tartar* and *Mashona* also very short of fuel, could continue until eight the next morning. A little later came a report from Admiral Somerville that he had launched a torpedo attack with Swordfish aircraft, but they had registered no hits: if the light held, he aimed to launch another. For two hours we waited in anticipation of this, praying, hoping that it might be successful. Then came a second signal: 'Attack completed. Estimate no hits.'

So that was it. The long week's night was over: we had lost *Hood* and gained nothing in exchange, and *Bismarck* was freed to fight another day. In *Rodney* the captain told the crew over the public address system that their last chance of bringing the enemy to action had gone, and his commander ordered guns' crews to stand down. As for *Tartar*, it is difficult to convey the extent of the gloom in which we sat down to supper in the wardroom; nor, now that the week-long tension had been broken and the banging and buffeting were almost over, the overwhelming sense of exhaustion we all felt.

And then a most extraordinary thing happened. A signal was received from the cruiser *Sheffield*, shadowing *Bismarck* from astern: 'Enemy's course 340°.' Now 340° was almost due north, towards us, almost the opposite of the course of around 120° which she had been steering for Brest. On the bridge the general feeling was that the captain of the *Sheffield* must have made a mistake and thought *Bismarck* was steaming from right to left instead of left to right, understandable enough in the prevailing weather. But a few minutes later came a confirmatory signal, 'Enemy's course North', and when further signals came in saying her speed was no more than a few knots, we all realized that *Bismarck* had been crippled by the last Swordfish attack, (one torpedo had hit and jammed her rudder) and that she was going to be delivered to us after all.

So we made preparations for a battle which – unless *Bismarck* was able to slip away in the night – now looked inevitable; I stowed away all things breakable in my cabin, put on clean underwear and filled the brandy flask, mounted to my action station at the pom-pom, and wondered how it might be when the time came.

And then an odd thing occurred. An army officer, what the Navy calls a pongo, had come aboard when we first sailed as a wardroom guest; he had been given a week's leave, was hoping for a spot of sea breezes, had not thought to get involved in this. After dinner, not knowing the rules and having nothing to do, he had got rather tipsy, and now he appeared on the upper deck singing to the wild night his repertoire of pongo songs. When it was reported to the captain, he was ordered to go to his cabin and stay there. In former times, I suppose, he would have been clapped in irons or shot.

The weather worsened as the night wore on. The same head-wind into which *Bismarck* had involuntarily turned gave us a following sea; one in which the bows yawed sideways like a car in a skid, so that the ship leaned heavily to starboard and stayed there like a determined drunk until the quartermaster gradually eased her back to the given course. All night long we stayed at action stations while the ship slewed first one way and then the other and great rafts of spray, flung up from the bows, slapped at our oilskins and sou'westers. At first I had turned over in my mind what our role might be – perhaps a night torpedo attack – but soon anything beyond the next five or ten minutes seemed remote and irrelevant. After what felt like an eternity dawn came, with curling wave-tops, a leaden sky, wretched visibility. Presently the commander-in-chief sent a signal asking *Tartar* and *Mashona* their fuel situation. When he had been told, he sent another signal: 'On receipt of executive signal, proceed as convenient to refuel at Plymouth or Londonderry.' Were we not going to be allowed to be in at the kill?

During the morning watch, guns crews were allowed to go off in ones and twos for breakfast, and around 8 a.m. I went down to the wardroom for mine. Returning, I saw that *Rodney* and *King George V* had drawn well ahead of us, so popped up to the bridge for the latest news. There I found long faces and silence. I looked at the Yeoman of Signals quizzically and he handed me the signal log. '*Tartar* and *Mashona* from C-in-C,' I read. 'Proceed in execution of previous orders.' So, thanks to our critical fuel situation (for if ordered in to a torpedo attack at speed, we would use up a great deal more), we were to be denied any part in the battle. But Tovey's original signal had said to proceed to refuel *as convenient* – 'and what I'm going to find convenient,' said the captain, 'is to stick around for a bit and watch.' I had reason for disappointment too. I had with me both my grand-mother's Kodak and also a 16-millimetre Bell and Howell movie camera lent me by the father of a girl-friend; and with the pom-pom gun having no role to play, I could, had we been sent in on a torpedo attack, have obtained some unique footage.

A moment later I saw a big puff of cordite smoke above *Rodney*'s main armament and a second later heard the thud of her guns. Through my binoculars I saw in the distance, on the edge of a patch of rainfall, the dull smudge of a ship. There she was at last, the vessel that these past six days had filled our waking thoughts, been the very marrow of our lives. And, as the rain faded, what a ship! Broad in the beam, with long raked bow and formidable superstructure, two twin 15-inch gun turrets forward, two aft, symmetrical, massive, elegant, she was the largest, most handsome warship I, or any of us, had eyer seen, a tribute to the skills of German shipbuilding. Now there came flashes from her guns and those of *King George V*. The final battle had begun.

In all my life I doubt if I will remember another hour as vividly as that one. It was the colour contrasts I recall most, so rare in the eternal greyness of voyaging at sea. The sun appeared for the first time in days, shining from a blue sky between white, racing clouds; and the wind, still strong, was marbling and stippling the green water, creaming the tops of the short, high seas. There was the sombre blackness of *Bismarck* and the grey of the British ships, the orange flashes of the guns, the brown of the cordite smoke, shell splashes tall as houses, white as shrouds.

It was a lovely sight to begin with, wild, majestic as one of our officers called it, almost too clean for the matter in hand. It seemed strange to think that within those three battleships were five thousand men; it seemed almost irrelevant, for this was a contest between ships not men. And who was going to win? None of us had any illusions about the devastating accuracy of *Bismarck*'s gunfire. She had sunk *Hood* with her fifth salvo, badly damaged *Prince of Wales*, straddled *Sheffield* and killed some of her crew the evening before, and hit an attacking destroyer in the course of the previous pitch-black night. But there were factors we had not reckoned with: the sheer exhaustion of her crew who had been at action stations for the past week, the knowledge as they waited through that long, last dreadful night that the British Navy was on its way to exact a terrible revenge, that they were virtually a sitting target.

Rodney was straddled with an early salvo but not hit, then with her fire divided, *Bismarck*'s gunnery sharply fell off. But that of *Rodney* and *King George V* steadily improved. As they moved in ever closer, we observed hit after hit. The hydraulic power that served the foremost turret must have been knocked out early, for the two guns were drooping downwards at maximum depression, like dead flowers. The back of the next turret was blown over the side and one of its guns, like a giant finger, pointed drunkenly at the sky. A gun barrel in one of the two after turrets had burst, leaving it like the stub of a peeled banana. The main director tower had been smashed in and part of the foremost was in shreds. Through holes in the superstructure and hull we could see flames flickering in half a dozen places. But still her flag flew; still, despite that fearful punishment, she continued, though now fitfully, to fire.

It was not a pretty sight. *Bismarck* was a menace that had to be destroyed, a dragon that would have severed the arteries that kept Britain alive. And yet to see her now, this beautiful ship, surrounded by enemies on all sides, hopelessly outgunned and outmanoeuvred, being slowly battered to a wreck, filled one with awe and pity. As Tovey said in his dispatch: 'She put up a most gallant fight against impossible odds, worthy of the old days of the Imperial German Navy.' And George Whalley, our Canadian lieutenant, wrote, 'What that ship was like inside did not bear thinking of; her guns smashed, the ship full of fire, her people hurt; and surely all men are much the same when hurt.' It was a thought shared by many British sailors that day,[1] yet one rarely expressed by airmen who incinerate cities or by soldiers of those they kill in tanks.

By 10 a.m. the last of *Bismarck*'s guns had fallen silent. She was still making headway through the water, though now listing heavily to port. The fires had spread, and now smoke was issuing from a hundred cracks and crevices in the deck. And then, as we looked at this silent, deadweight shambles of a ship, we saw for the first time what had previously existed only in our imagination, the enemy in person, a little trickle of men in ones and twos, running or hobbling towards the quarterdeck to escape from the inferno that was raging forward; and as we watched they began to jump into the sea.

We had seen enough. It was time – way beyond time – to go home.

'Make to *Mashona*,' said the captain, 'course 045°, speed 15 knots.'

We had missed taking part in one battle; but another, unsought and exclusive to us, lay just ahead.

In the end the captain decided to make for Londonderry, for although eighty miles further than Plymouth, it meant less time within the range of enemy bombers. All that day in a moderating sea we and *Mashona* steamed northwards at 15 knots, the most we could manage with so little fuel but greatly to be welcomed after the high-speed junketings of the past five days. In the afternoon everyone not on watch slept: I didn't stir from 1.30 p.m. until six.

At dinner that night there was much talk of the battle, the weakness of *Hood*'s armour, the whereabouts of *Prinz Eugen*, the one in a million chance of a torpedo from one of *Ark Royal*'s aircraft bringing *Bismarck* virtually to a halt; but there was talk too of the celebrations we would have when we reached Londonderry the following night. 'We'se going to give ourselves a party,' said the gunner, a West Country man, 'such as never was.'

[1] And, a few days earlier, by German ones. When the gunnery officer of the *Prinz Eugen* saw *Hood* blow up, he murmured to those around him, 'Poor devils, poor devils!' No sailor of any nation enjoys watching the end of any ship.

Next day I had the forenoon watch and was in the wardroom for breakfast by 7.30. I had hoped to hear an announcement of the sinking of the *Bismarck* on the news, but there was nothing. After the news, and while tucking into eggs and bacon, I listened to a man encouraging me to grasp the back of a chair and kick my legs sideways in time with the music he was going to play. Then I put on duffel coat and seaboots and made my way to the bridge.

It was a fine, fresh summer morning, with a bit of a wind and quite a few passing clouds. Spider was on the compass platform, drawing at a cigarette through his holder.

'What's for breakfast?'

'Bacon and eggs,' I said, 'plural. Anything happening here?'

'Not much.' He gave me the course and speed, pointed out *Mashona* on the beam, said he expected us to be in harbour by 6 p.m. Then, as I was about to take over the ship officially, I saw him looking intently through his glasses.

'Take a look at that, Uckers,' he said. 'I don't think I like the shape of it.'

I put up my own glasses and trained them in the same direction. A big, black, four-engined plane swam into the field of vision. I could see the crosses on its fuselage distinctly.

'It's a Focke-Wulf,' I said.

'I'll tell the captain,' said Spider. 'You press the alarm bells.'

I went to the front of the bridge and pushed the alarm button that would set bells ringing in every compartment of the ship. *Short-long, short-long, short-long*, it went, the signal for anti-aircraft stations.

When the captain reached the bridge, I went down to my action station at the pom-pom. The crew were manning the telephones, checking the feed belts, setting the levers to fire. I took up position between the layer and trainer and stood by to await events.

'Aircraft to starboard,' shouted one of the crew, and the gun swung round on its turntable. A bomber was approaching at around 3000 feet. A moment later all eight guns of the main armament were loosed off at it. That must have scared the pilot, for he turned away before finishing his run.

'Two aircraft to port,' came a voice.

We swung round again, and lined up on them. Just before they reached their bomb-release position, I shouted 'Open fire!' At the same time the captain ordered full speed and hard a port which made things difficult for the layer and trainer as the ship leaned heavily over. To add to the din of the pom-pom, the main armament was fired again, and the oerlikon gun, though it could hardly have been in range.

Two clusters of bombs were released almost simultaneously. At first they looked like blackbird's eggs, then, as one watched, they grew rapidly larger, so that one felt they were aimed at one personally, had one's name on them as the saying went. 'It's all right,' I shouted to reassure myself as much as the crew, 'they're going to miss.' I was right. They landed in the wake and went off with a tremendous blast.

We had hardly regained our course when another pair was sighted. They were no more successful than the first but after a salvo, I noticed two or three pieces from one falling into the sea. It lost height and let off black smoke, staggered on for quite a way, then tipped over and dropped into the sea. We saw a wing-tip sticking out of the water like a giant fin, then that too disappeared. We all gave a great cheer.

And so it went on; the aircraft made their runs, the guns fired, the ship turned this way or that and the bombs fell in the sea, many too close for comfort. It was when the planes first turned to make their approach that one felt a chill in the pit of the stomach. But once action was joined, then, as one of Nelson's sailors said at Trafalgar, 'I bid fear kiss my bottom and set to in good earnest.' Being under fire wonderfully concentrates the mind; as with an orgasm, you become oblivious to anything else.

During a lull one of the crew said, 'Looks as though they've got *Mashona*, sir.' We had been too occupied with our own defence to consider how *Mashona* was faring; but now I saw she had taken a list and that steam was rising from her amidships. She must have been hit in the boiler-room. The captain turned *Tartar* towards her, and as we watched, the list increased and she came to a standstill. When she was leaning right over, she signalled 'Abandoning ship', and men began sliding down her hull and into the sea. History was repeating itself. Two days ago we had seen the destruction of one marvellous ship and her crew taking to the water; now it was happening to another.

The captain manoeuvred the ship to a position where *Mashona*'s rafts and groups of men in the water would drift down on us. By some miracle of fortune there was then a lull in the attacks. Had bombs still been falling, the safety of our own ship would have been paramount and we would have had to leave the *Mashona* people to drown. As it was, we were able to help them up the scrambling nets and over the side, stripped them of their wet clothes and wrapped them in blankets before sending them below to be rubbed down and given hot soup and dry clothes.

There was one officer, the only one, who didn't make it. He was a retired lieutenant-commander in his forties, not on the ship's books but sent on board for further sea experience before taking up his own command. I lowered a rope and told him to hang on to it while two of our people began to hoist him up. But when he was almost level with the deck, his strength failed and he fell back into the sea. He succeeded in grasping the rope again but only just, and it was then, I realized afterwards, that I should have jumped down beside him, fastened the rope under his arms and had him hauled up without further exertion. It wasn't that I thought of doing it and rejected it, rather that it never occurred to me. For he had not the strength to keep hold of the rope and now he went down for the last time. I had a brief glimpse of his hair undulating like seaweed just below the surface. Then he disappeared, for ever. Today I still see and am haunted by the manner of his going; for I believe I could have saved him, and didn't.

Last to reach us was *Mashona*'s captain, pushing two exhausted men on a rubber cushion. Of her ship's company of 250 we picked up all but forty-five, half of the dead killed when the bomb exploded, the other half drowned before we could pick them up. *Mashona* was lying bottom up now and the captain ordered Spider to fire a torpedo to sink her. But it missed, and rather than waste another, he told the destroyer *St Clair* which had just joined us to sink her by gunfire. Then, with an extra 200 men on board, we resumed course for Londonderry.

But if we thought that our troubles were over, we were all too soon disillusioned. I had gone down to the wardroom to lend the doctor a hand when the alarm bells sounded again. On my way to the pom-pom I heard a cry of 'Aircraft approaching from astern', and had barely reached the gun when I saw it. It was flying much lower than any of the others, perhaps hoping to take us by surprise. We couldn't fire the pom-pom because one of the main turrets was in our line of sight. The whine of the turbines took on a higher pitch as the captain increased speed and turned sharply away. *He's too late this time*, I said to myself, as I watched the bombs fall, *he's left it too late*. The bombs came on at us unwaveringly, growing larger and more menacing with every fraction of a second. I heard the whish of them as they sailed past my ear and landed in the sea not thirty feet away. Had they exploded, I doubt if I would be writing this today. But there was no explosion; just five little *phuts* as they disappeared beneath the surface. Truly the good Lord was with us.

Nor was that the end of it; for by now the enemy was back in force, and all afternoon and evening, in relays of two and three, they hammered away at us. Only the captain's brilliant ship-handling saved us from the fate of *Mashona*. Admiral Tovey in *King George V*, 100 miles north-west of us (and for whom these attacks were obviously intended) gave us permission to proceed to Cork or some other Irish port to obtain fuel; but by the time we had received the signal we were slightly nearer Londonderry. Our signal log for that day was a litany of 'Enemy still bombing' and 'When can we expect fighters?' In the early afternoon we were told that three fighter aircraft were being diverted to us, but there was no sign of them until 7.15 when one arrived on its own. It was a wonderful tonic to us all – I had a strong urge to fall on the pilot's neck and weep with gratitude – and he at once celebrated his presence by shooting down one of the planes. After that it was quiet for a bit, but there was one final attack at 10.30 p.m., only an hour from Londonderry. In his report the captain said that there had been over fifty separate attacks and that at least 160 bombs had been dropped near *Tartar*.

Turning to go up the River Foyle, we had so little fuel in our tanks that the ship heeled over sharply to port and stayed there; it took a good few minutes before she decided to come back. In the morning after fuelling we sailed for Greenock at 30 knots to land the *Mashona*'s survivors. Hearing that the singer and actress Evelyn Laye was appearing in some show in Glasgow, the captain dispatched me there that evening to ask if she would give us a concert next day, a Sunday, on the deck of the destroyer depot-ship. She said she would and, wearing the captain of the *Mashona*'s cap, she did. And that was as happy an end to the *Bismarck* story as one could wish.

The next day we sailed for Scapa.

*

By this time *Tartar* had established two records. We were the first destroyer in the Navy to have steamed more than 100,000 miles since the outbreak of war, and in doing so had put in more seatime than any other destroyer; a statistic celebrated by a special feature in the *Illustrated London News* and mentions in other papers. We also became known as 'lucky *Tartar*', as several of our sister ships had been sunk or badly damaged. Perhaps as a reward (though I doubt it) we had several days in harbour during June; and I recall some happy afternoons fishing for trout on Hoy, though every hour or so I had to climb the hill that separated the loch from the anchorage to make sure the ship was not flying the signal for recall.

At the end of the month, in company with a cruiser and our sister ship *Bedouin*, we sailed for the Arctic in search of an enemy weather-reporting trawler called the *Lauenberg*. Radio Direction Finding had placed the ship in the general direction of Jan Mayen Island, inside the Arctic Circle. We steamed north for three days: south of Jan Mayen the force was spread five miles apart to widen the area of search, and in *Tartar* the first lieutenant promised £1 to the first man to sight the enemy. Within a short time a sailor in the crow's nest started shouting and waving, and, hoisting the signal 'Enemy in sight', the captain went on to full speed. He also ordered practice shells to be fired so as to burst above the target and bewilder the crew but not damage the ship. With *Bedouin* following, we came alongside, and a boarding party led by Spider clutching a revolver jumped on board; by this time the *Lauenberg*'s crew had abandoned ship and the boarding party searched cabins and compartments for whatever they could find.

In the next forty minutes they returned with armfuls of papers which were taken to the captain's day-cabin. Meanwhile *Bedouin* had lowered a boat and sent over a RNVR lieutenant called Bacon from naval intelligence, an expert on German naval documents, who had been specially embarked for the operation. After the *Lauenberg*'s crew had been shepherded below and the last of the papers had come on board, we lay off a little and sank her.

During the return to Scapa, Lieutenant Bacon hardly moved from the captain's cabin. We all hoped he was having a happy time there, though we rather doubted whether the pickings from a little weather ship in the Arctic would reveal much that wasn't already known: we were far more interested in the workings of the *Lauenberg*'s powerful Telefunken radio receiver which we had looted for the wardroom and which gave outstanding reception. But Lieutenant Bacon was bringing home the bacon; for what none of us knew were the efforts then being made by the Admiralty to crack the German naval ciphers, and the imperative need to obtain, as opportunity offered, whatever scraps of intelligence they could. It wasn't until long after the war, when the secrets of Ultra were finally revealed, that I learned that codebooks and signals found in *Lauenberg*, plus a set of rotor arms discovered in the trawler *Krebs* during the Lofoten raid, plus material taken three weeks earlier from another Arctic weather ship, *München*, and finally and most important of all the Enigma machine and codebooks captured from the U-boat U.110 all, when pieced together, enabled the Bletchley Park codebreakers to penetrate the principal German naval cipher and continue to penetrate it, with a few breaks, until the end of the war. This penetration, in conjunction with High Frequency Direction Finding and other factors, was what enabled us to win the U-boat campaign – a campaign which, had we lost it, would also have lost us the war.

One of *Lauenberg*'s two officers was accommodated in an unused cabin in the after flat, and on several occasions I was detailed to take a revolver and accompany the sailor who brought him his meals in case he cut up rough. But he was a pleasant enough young man, with blond hair and a moustache, who smiled and bowed and seemed genuinely grateful for his food and the way he was being treated. I deeply regretted my inability to speak German, and when we reached Scapa and he and his crew were led blindfolded ashore (to prevent them seeing what they shouldn't, but I daresay they thought they were going to be shot), I thought once again, what are these people like, what do they think of Hitler and the war, do they want to beat us as much as we want to beat them? One day I would try and find out.

8

Convoy to North Russia

By early September, having been in northern waters ever since our refit at Plymouth just a year before, we were due for another refit, and soon came the joyous news that this was to take place in London's Albert Docks, where I had visited my father on board *Rawalpindi* at the beginning of the war. As we steamed down the east coast into unfamiliar waters, past Flamborough Head and Orfordness and places which had previously been names on the map, there was a feeling of exhilaration that infected the whole crew. And going up the Thames into the heart of the capital, it seemed almost unbelievable, after the barrenness of Scapa Flow, that this place with all it had to offer in the way of theatres, restaurants, nightclubs, cinemas, and the opportunity of seeing old friends, was to take over from Scapa as our home for the next six weeks.

First, though, I went north to where my mother and two sisters were living in my grandmother's Edinburgh flat. She was fully occupied in war work, helping in a sailors' canteen in the Leith Docks in the evenings and running a thing called The Naval Officers Leave Bureau in the day. The object of this was to fix up accommodation for officers on leave with nowhere to go (those whose parents lived abroad, Australians, Canadians, etc.) in country houses whose owners had offered hospitality. Some owners also offered rough shooting, and I spent two happy days pottering round the fields and woods of an estate in Fife in the company of the spaniel Ben, now rather longer in the tooth since Islay holidays. As a retriever Ben was more of a liability than an asset, for if after a long search he found a bird I had dropped in the undergrowth, he became so excited he was apt to start eating it. If, on the other hand, the bird landed where we could both see it, he would stand stock still, ignoring all exhortations to fetch it, knowing (and knowing that I knew) that his services were unnecessary. He was a wayward dog; but I think he enjoyed the outing.

Then it was back to London and to wardroom parties (which, despite the blackout, few friends refused, for a visit to a warship was a rare treat) and to parties in London, most of which arose spontaneously. There was bombing on some nights, I believe, but I do not recall much about it. It was a strange time, one of heightened relationships, making instant friends with strangers, men and women, exchanging confidences, going here or there as the mood dictated, waking up in strange beds, sometimes with a girl beside one. Yet the intensity of each relationship did not disguise its ephemeral nature, for one knew, even as one lived it, that it would be ended abruptly by duty or departure. Yet there was a carefreeness, a lack of commitment to an uncertain future that expressed the mood of the times. Solemn thoughts and long-term planning would come later. There were few evenings when I did not find myself heading for the West End, invariably ending up in Al Burnett's Stork Club singing 'Shoe Shine Susie' ('sitting in the shoe-shine shop') or on the darkened dance floor of the 400 Club, pressed hard and almost stationary against some lissom thigh.

And suddenly it was over, and the sea took us again, and Orfordness and Flamborough Head appeared to port not starboard and we were back at Scapa for what I look back on as the bloodiest (though not literally) winter of the war. For the convoys to North Russia had started, and because of the proximity of the route to German warships lurking in the Norwegian fjords, the Admiralty sent a covering force of battleships, cruisers and destroyers each time a convoy sailed. This meant long patrols in the vilest weather, in an area that covered the Faeroes, Iceland, Jan Mayen and the North Cape: it was always cold, sometimes unbearably so, and often dark. The only happy memory I have of that time is of a beautiful ice cold New Year's Eve at anchor in Seidisfjord on the east coast of Iceland. At two minutes to midnight the *Tartar*'s officers gathered on the quarterdeck in fancy dress: the captain in silk pyjamas and carpet slippers, an open shirt and a fez; the chief as a Cossack; the gunner as a clergyman; I forget what I was wearing. When the quartermaster sang out, 'Midnight, sir!' the youngest member of the wardroom grasped the clapper of the ship's bell and sounded the full sixteen strokes. Then under a dazzling display of Northern Lights which seemed to fill the night sky, we joined hands and sang 'Auld Lang Syne'.

The next day, in company with another destroyer, we were ordered to leave Seidisfjord to reinforce the escort of the first section of a Russian convoy. For two days we steamed steadily north-east, then in the middle of my middle watch entered an ice-field. Presently the moon came out so that one could see the ice stretching away in every direction. There was no wind and the only sound was the crackle of breaking ice as the ship's bows sliced a passage through the field. The stillness was uncanny. Above, the stars shone brightly and the Northern Lights, like serpents' tongues, spat white daggers of light across the sky.

The further we advanced, the darker it became, until by the time we picked up the convoy south of Bear Island and north of the North Cape, it was totally dark from about three in the afternoon to eleven the next morning, after which there was a kind of murky twilight. Depressing though this was, it afforded the best possible protection against sighting by aircraft or U-boats.

Yet worse than the dark was the cold, of an intensity I did not know existed. When the spray came over the bows, as it did when steaming into a head sea, it froze where it landed. After a while the extra weight caused by chunks of ice on gun turrets, guardrails and rigging became so great that we were in danger of becoming top-heavy. So each morning parties with axes and crowbars were detailed to prise away these chunks and throw them overboard. These people wore not only two or three layers of underclothing and sweaters but balaclava helmets that covered everything but the eyes; for the spray froze on the skin too. The two officers of the watch were allowed to alternate an hour each on the bridge with an hour in the charthouse below it. The three bars of the wardroom electric fire were on continuously but you could feel no heat further than a couple of feet away. Bed was the warmest place, but it was hell climbing out of it. There was no moment of the day or night when we did not feel cold.

It was in these conditions that the incident of the messman's menu occurred. Our messing arrangements were taken care of by a petty officer steward called the wardroom messman who provided us with three excellent meals a day for some absurd sum like half a crown. He was a bit of an oddball, this man, and one of the oddest things about him was a speech impediment which caused him to pronounce his W's as V's and his L's as D's when they formed the first letter of a word. We had two officers named Wilson and Whalley whom he called Dootenant Vearlson and Sub-Dootenant Volley and two on his staff whom he called Vearlyamson and Vearlkinson.

It had been his practice in peacetime to provide the wardroom with a menu for dinner and to place it on the table. Just because there was a war, he saw no reason to discontinue the habit. Usually it said simple things like 'Brown Windsor', 'Roast Lamb and Redcurrant Jelly', 'Spotted Dick', etc., but we had noticed a growing tendency on his part to adapt more exotic names like 'Soup de Legumes' (sic) and 'Beef Scapa Flow'. The longer we were away from base and the more the food stocks dwindled, the more extravagant became the names. On this trip, somewhere to the east of Bear Island, he excelled himself. As we sat down to dinner, we saw the last item on the menu advertised as 'Rêve de Debussy'. It gave us the giggles; and for the first lieutenant it was too much.

'Messman!'

'Sir?'

'Rêve de Debussy?'

'It's the savoury, sir.'

'Yes, we assumed that. We don't much like it.'

'Dootenant Vearlson was here earlier and he seemed to like it.'

'I'm sure he did, and I expect we will too. It's the name we don't care for. Try something simpler in future, eh – something that tells us what it is?'

The messman retired, defeated. But when he gave us the same savoury on the return voyage, he got his own back, as I shall presently relate.

After six days, and undetected by the enemy, we reached our destination, the small port of Polyarnyy, at the mouth of the Kola inlet; and here we made fast alongside the jetty while the merchant ships went on to Murmansk.

Polyarnyy, deep in snow and in almost perpetual darkness, was a cluster of dreary-looking wooden buildings about half a mile inland. There was a sort of track leading to it which we had permission to use for exercise, but every hundred yards were sentries in fur hats and with fixed bayonets, ready to prod us back if we dared strike out on our own. The people in Polyarnyy looked Mongolian, with high cheekbones, narrow eyes and almost total lack of expression. The women carried shopping bags but we never found any shops. We had expected the men to be bearded but all were clean-shaven. The people seemed indifferent, though sentries badgered us for cigarettes; in return they gave us the little red stars from the front of their fur hats. There was little to do in Polyarnyy but walk to the village and back, read and drink. (And write a letter to the headmaster of my prep school, declining in no uncertain terms his invitation to the school's fortieth anniversary party.)[1]

[1] See pages 43–45

On our last night before sailing with the homeward-bound convoy, and to dispel Polyarnyy gloom, we decided to dress up as a mid-Victorian cricket team posing for the annual photograph. This fondness for dressing up, which may strike the reader as childish, was in fact therapeutic: it allowed us to slough off our collective identities as officers engaged in a war to become, however briefly, other people. From scarce resources we managed to fashion top hats, caps, bats, whiskers, and stumps; and having consumed a generous quantity of rum punch, to position ourselves, some seated, some recumbent and holding aloft a ball or bail between finger and thumb, in front of the camera.

The doctor volunteered to be the photographer. To represent the camera he placed a megaphone – the small end towards the cricketers – on top of a tripod; then hid himself and the megaphone under the green baize cloth from the wardroom table. What he hadn't divulged was that he had secreted about his person a large syringe filled with water and that when he had the team's attention, he intended to squirt it at us through the megaphone. That moment had arrived. 'Watch the birdie,' said the doctor, and the captain, who was observing proceedings from the side and had had rather more rum punch to drink than was good for him, murmured inconsequentially, 'Attaboy!'

It was then we heard the clatter of feet on the ladder and there, framed in the doorway, were the Russian port admiral, his flag-captain and flag-lieutenant. We stared at one another uncomprehendingly. At this moment the doctor, unaware beneath the green baize cloth that we had visitors, squirted the contents of the syringe.

The captain looked at the stunned faces of the Russian officers, standing immobile in the doorway. But he was equal to the occasion. 'Well, make up your minds,' he cried, swaying gently on his feet, 'either come on inski or else bugger offski.' They came on inski and were proffered rum punch. Happily they had never tasted it before and were soon even merrier than we.

Next morning we embarked what fresh food the local quartermaster could spare: mostly yellow bread the texture of three-ply, and evil-looking sides of yak. We wondered whether we might see 'Yakski Polyarnoe' on the menu, but the messman had learnt his lesson. At sea that night the 'Rêve de Debussy' savoury showed up a second time. Eagerly we read the menu. 'Tinned sardines on fried bread', it said, and it didn't taste half as good.

Five days later we heard that our sister ship *Matabele*, escorting the second section of the same convoy, had been torpedoed off the Kola inlet and had gone down within minutes. There were just two survivors.

The following is written with the benefit of hindsight. In January 1942 the *Bismarck*'s sister ship *Tirpitz*, of more than 52,000 tons, arrived in Trondheim from Germany, her Baltic training completed. Although she was not spotted by British aircraft until a week later, the Admiralty knew of her arrival, as they were to know much else about her future movements by the deciphering at Bletchley Park of German naval signals coded on Enigma machines − one of the first fruits of all the intelligence we had captured. Information from intercepts that bore directly on current operations was immediately sent to senior commanders in the field in signals that bore the prefix Ultra: this denoted the source (and its reliability) as well as ensuring severely restricted distribution.

Tirpitz and others of the German surface fleet were in Norway for two reasons: as defence against an allied invasion of that country which, ever since the raids on Lofoten and Vaagso, Hitler had come to believe increasingly likely ('Every ship that is not in Norway is in the wrong place'); and as an advance post for making lightning attacks on the now regular Russian convoys, as and when Hitler permitted. A month later and as part of the continuing movement north, the heavy cruiser *Prinz Eugen* with the pocket battleship *Admiral Scheer* and three destroyers sailed from Germany to join *Tirpitz* in Trondheim. Operational orders concerning them from Admiral Carls at Naval Group North in Kiel were decrypted at Bletchley in time for four British submarines to take station off the approaches to Trondheim and for one, the *Trident*, to torpedo and severely damage the *Prinz Eugen* as she was about to enter harbour.

Nevertheless, with such a powerful squadron now in Trondheim, Admiral Tovey at Scapa decided that he must cover the passage of the next Russian convoy with the Home Fleet. So when the convoy sailed from Iceland, he had at his disposal two battleships, a battlecruiser, the aircraft carrier *Victorious*, a cruiser, and twelve destroyers including *Tartar*. When he was some 200 miles south of the convoy, it was sighted by a German aircraft; and next day the submarine *Seawolf*, stationed off

Trondheim, reported *Tirpitz*'s departure. Wearing the flag of Vice-Admiral Ciliax and escorted by three destroyers, she was on her way to attack the convoy.

If the weather during the next couple of days had been less thick, there would have been a fair chance of Tovey bringing Ciliax to battle. But with visibility often down to under a mile, both sides were groping in the dark; Ciliax for the convoy, Tovey for Ciliax (who had no idea he was at hand). As it was, the German destroyers, spread on a wide range of search, missed the convoy by only a few miles. Timely receipt of a further Ultra intercept from Admiral Carls giving Ciliax a fresh area of search enabled the convoy to be routed away from danger.

By now Ciliax's destroyers were running short of oil, so he detached them to Tromso to refuel. He continued looking for the convoy all that day, but having seen nothing by evening, decided to abandon the operation and steer for home. Tovey at this time was 150 miles south-west of him; having received no further Ultra intercepts and with some of his own destroyers having to leave because of shortage of fuel, he was making towards Iceland to collect more. A signal from the Admiralty that *Tirpitz* might still be to the north of him led him to reverse course in that direction at the very moment that *Tirpitz* had turned for home. Then from the Admiralty came the break that Tovey had been waiting for – an Ultra intercept from Admiral Carls to *Tirpitz*'s destroyers oiling at Tromso giving them the exact position for rejoining *Tirpitz* in the morning. A glance at the chart showed Tovey that *Tirpitz* must now be some 150 miles to the east of him and within aircraft striking distance. He ordered the fleet to turn south-east and increase speed, and signalled to *Victorious*: 'Expect *Tirpitz* in 68° 15′ N, 10° 38′ E steering to southwards. Report proposals.'

For us this news came as a bombshell. We had been told before leaving Scapa that we would be going to sea to cover the passage of the convoy. Of the break-out of the *Tirpitz* and the reasons for the frequent alterations of course during the last two days we knew nothing. Nor did we think to question it: banging about the ocean, going this way and that, keeping watch, sleeping, eating, was our accepted way of life. So what for Tovey and his chief of staff and secretary must have been a period of the most intense excitement was for us as monotonous, boring and tiring as it always had been. Now came this staggering news that *Tirpitz* was within range of our aircraft, and that an attack on her was imminent. Could it be that history was about to repeat itself, that what *Ark Royal*'s planes had done to *Bismarck*, those of *Victorious* would now do to *Tirpitz*? Was Jack Tovey about to bring off the spring double?

A further consideration entered my mind. Spider had recently left the ship, and I was now torpedo officer. So if *Victorious*'s planes could slow down *Tirpitz* enough for the fleet to catch up, *Tartar* and the three remaining destroyers would be sent in to torpedo her while the battleships attacked with guns. To my surprise I found this prospect wonderfully exhilarating, and prayed that the opportunity for it might come.

Presently *Victorious* replied to Tovey's signal. She would send off a search force of six aircraft in an hour's time, and a strike force of twelve others an hour later. From *Tartar*'s bridge we watched the search force take off and head south-east. Then, as the strike force was ranged on deck, Tovey signalled *Victorious*, 'A wonderful chance which may achieve most valuable results. God be with you.'

But, alas, God was elsewhere that day. The search force had no difficulty finding *Tirpitz* – almost exactly where the Ultra signal had indicated she would be – and with only one destroyer escorting her (the other two were still en route from Tromso). Then the strike force arrived. These were not the old Swordfish biplanes with which *Ark Royal* had attacked *Bismarck* but the new, faster Albacores. However their crews had had very little training, and their newly appointed leader had never flown with the squadron before. Instead of attacking from ahead which the conditions demanded, the planes approached mostly from astern; and when the captain of the *Tirpitz* turned to avoid the tracks, all the torpedoes missed (one by ten yards astern which was the nearest *Tirpitz* came to sharing *Bismarck*'s fate). Two of the planes were shot down. When last seen, *Tirpitz* was running east for the shelter of Vest Fjord and the Lofoten Islands, now beyond our reach; and there was much gloom in the fleet that night as a chastened Tovey took us back to Scapa.

But again thanks to Ultra, there remained one further chance of bringing *Tirpitz* to action. From an intercept of a signal from Carls to Ciliax now at anchor off Narvik, it was clear that the battleship was to return to its old berth at Trondheim as soon as considered safe to do so; and three days later Carls signalled

Ciliax to sail for Trondheim after midnight on Friday 13 March. A superstitious man, *Tirpitz*'s Captain Topp sailed at 11 p.m. on the 12th.

When this intelligence reached Tovey, he ordered a flotilla of eight destroyers including *Tartar* to sail for the Norwegian coast north of Trondheim and to try to intercept *Tirpitz* on her way south. We left at high speed at dusk and at 10 p.m. the following night went to action stations. Presently the coast of Norway, snowy white in the darkness, showed up ahead, and the eight ships took station two miles apart, reduced speed to lessen the bow waves, and turned to the north. Although neither side knew it, we and *Tirpitz* were now approaching each other head on.

For nearly four hours we maintained our course northwards, expecting at any minute the giant silhouette of *Tirpitz* to loom out of the darkness ahead. For nearly four hours I stood close to the torpedo firing levers at the back of the bridge pondering on the role and responsibility allotted to me – to fire torpedoes at the biggest battleship in the world and perhaps, in the process, to sink her. It seemed absurd. Yet there was no denying the reality; and what I remember most was the extraordinary silence on the bridge, a silence broken only by the sound of the bows slicing through the water, by the ticking of the compass in its bowl and, very occasionally, by the captain's almost whispered orders to the wheelhouse. Did we keep silence because we wanted nothing to distract our attention as we peered into the darkness ahead? Was it because, with an enemy coast in sight to starboard, we unconsciously felt our voices might be carried ashore? Or was it simply because we had nothing to say? A little, I think, of all three.

We had been ordered to break off the operation by 3.30 a.m. if nothing had been sighted so as to be clear of the coast by dawn; and on the half-hour we turned. It would be hard to say whether relief or disappointment was uppermost; the relief was instant but the disappointment lasted longer. A little later we fell out from action stations; but many of us were too keyed up to go to bed, and made up for our previous silence by empty chatter over cups of Bovril in the wardroom.

And where had *Tirpitz* been? It was not until long after the war that I learnt that despite having left Narvik an hour earlier than ordered, she had not entered our area of search until we had left it. We had missed her by a couple of hours. In life timing is all; though looking back on it now, I am less surprised at Tovey getting it wrong than by how very nearly he had it right.

Nor in the long term was *Victorious*'s attack on *Tirpitz* without its rewards. The German naval staff had had no idea the British fleet was at sea, and were much mortified. Hitler was particularly concerned; and remembering what had happened to *Bismarck*, ordered that *Tirpitz* was not to operate against future Russian convoys without confirmation that there were no British aircraft carriers in the area. As this was almost impossible to confirm, she never did operate against another convoy (though the possibility that she might led to the scattering of the convoy P.Q.17 and the subsequent destruction of two-thirds of it). Apart from a foray against the weather station in Spitzbergen, she remained for the rest of her career a prisoner in the Norwegian fjords where, often apprised of her movements by Ultra, we attacked her with Fleet Air Arm bombers and fighters, RAF bombers and midget submarines. In the last of these, an RAF high-level attack in 1944 with blockbuster bombs, she capsized and turned turtle at her moorings off Tromso with huge loss of life.

And now my time in *Tartar* was coming to an end, and *Tartar*'s time too, at least for this commission. Soon after the abortive attempts to sink the *Tirpitz*, the captain was informed he had been appointed to another job. To say we were depressed would be an understatement. For the two years I had been in the ship the captain and the ship had been inseparable: to us he was the ship. We had admired him for many things, for his brilliant ship-handling which had served us so well, not least on the day *Mashona* was sunk, as much as for his lightly worn leadership. He was utterly unpompous, a respecter of talent but not of rank, possessed of a natural authority without ever being authoritarian, even-tempered, lively, funny, generous (one rarely entered his cabin without being offered a drink) and, for those of us in the RNVR wonderfully tolerant of early crassness and ineptitude. We loved him dearly and would have followed him anywhere; and when the time came for him to be piped over the side for the last time, the ship's company came spontaneously to the rails to cheer him on his way.

The new captain seemed a nice enough fellow, but we approached him warily, like one pack of dogs accosting another, wagging half-heartedly, keeping our distance. Poor chap, it was not his fault that we regarded him as a usurper; we would have felt the same about whoever succeeded Kim. The grace and precision with which Kim, with the minimum of orders, would bring the ship alongside an oiler, was always a joy to experience; but the first time the new man attempted it, not yet having the measure of the ship, he failed to pull up in time and sailed gaily past. But at least he had shown himself to be human, and after that we gradually came to accept him.

But the new regime was not to last for long. Soon after, we were again up in the Arctic, providing cover for another Russian convoy in case *Tirpitz* came out again. When I handed over the first watch, it was blowing a monstrous gale, and our speed was down to a few knots. At midnight I lost no time in reaching my bunk, but later was woken by a terrific crack followed by a shudder which seemed to run right through the ship. At first I thought we had been torpedoed, but when no alarm bells rang and the occupants of the other cabins in the flat stayed put, I went back to sleep.

It was my servant, harbinger of all night-time events, who woke me the second time.

'Seven-thirty, sir. Here's your tea. Heard the news?' (He knew as he said this, there was no way I could have heard it.)

'No.'

'Bloody great wave bashed in the foc'sle. We're going back to Scapa.'

It was true. A freak sea had landed tons of water on the fore part of the ship, stove in the deck to a depth of two or three inches, buckled the deck plates and the bulkheads below. The general view that repairs to the damage were beyond the resources of Scapa was confirmed when we arrived there; and the next day we sailed for Hull to be paid off into dockyard hands.

The Sw"itha gate opened to us, we edged into the swirling tide race of the Pentland Firth and shaped course to clear Duncansby Head. On the hilltop to starboard lay the Hoxa Head signal station, always the first to welcome us home from sea, bringing news about mail, where to oil, which buoy to secure to. For two years this place and this ship had been my life. Would the war, or the peace, I wondered, ever bring me back to these arcane islands, and indeed did I want to come back, if not in *Tartar*? For I had come to love the ship no less, and when I looked back on all we had shared, from my initiation as a seafarer to the last attempt to engage *Tirpitz*, I thought how bloody good to us she had consistently been, never refusing anything demanded of her, preserving us always, as the saying went, from the perils of the deep. For although I had no yardstick of comparison to go by, I knew instinctively that this had been not only a happy ship and a lucky ship, but a quite exceptional ship and ship's company. A week later I left her lying forlornly in dry dock at Hull, the comforting sea no longer lapping her sides, propped up by timber shores to prevent her tumbling over, an invalid ship almost bereft of life. And I, bereft too, turned my back on her and drove to the Paragon station.

9

Newfoundland

I was given a month's leave and saw it as a wonderful opportunity to take up some much-neglected writing. During the refit in London in the autumn I had picked up a book called *It was Good While it Lasted*, the pre-war memoirs of the golfer and golfing writer, Henry Longhurst. It was a lively, witty, hedonistic account of a cosmopolitan life, in which he had travelled the country and the world to report on golfing events, mixing with celebrities in other fields, always enjoying himself hugely. I found his style beguiling, and when I had finished the book, I thought, why don't I do something like that: write a light-hearted account of my early life and the high points of the last two and a half years in the Navy? And one evening in my cabin in Scapa Flow I made a start. 'Autobiography of a Sub-Lieutenant', I wrote on a piece of paper. 'By Ludovic Kennedy. Chapter 1.' It was ridiculous, really; but I had never felt more mentally alive.

With so much fatiguing seatime during the winter, progress had been slow, though whenever we had a day or two in harbour, I managed to add a few more pages. Now, with empty days stretching ahead, I gave all my attention to it, and by the time my leave was over, I had pretty well finished. But then what to do with it, for I was a complete stranger to the world of publishing? Here I was lucky. My friend Bill Richmond, whom the reader may recall from my time at *King Alfred*, had just returned to England from Madagascar, his ship having taken part in the landings there. But finding progress inland too slow for his liking, he had set out on his own for the capital to capture the island single-handed; and had advanced a considerable distance, I gathered, before being apprehended and returned to his ship. There was some talk of a court-martial, but in the end it was decided he had not been quite himself, and the idea fizzled out. Now he was back on leave with his family in the Master's Lodge at Downing College, and invited me to spend a weekend there. I found him grown enormously fat – some trouble with his glands, he told me – but as witty and companionable as ever. I asked him if he knew any publishers and he said, Yes, he did know one by the name of Charles Fry, a senior editor at the fine art publishers, B. T. Batsford. 'I don't really think it's his sort of book,' said Bill, 'but he might advise you where to go.'

But miraculously it turned out it *was* Charles Fry's sort of book; and so I was spared having to hawk it round from publisher to publisher which has been the lot of the first books of so many established authors. There being little demand for new fine art books in the middle of the war, B. T. Batsford had begun to diversify. The year before they had published with great success a book called *Fighter Pilot*, the memoirs of a Battle of Britain pilot, Paul Richey. Now they were looking for naval and army counterparts. 'I enjoyed your manuscript very much,' Charles Fry wrote to me, 'and would like to publish it with some mutually agreed cuts. Perhaps when you are next in London we could meet.'

Charles Fry was around forty, with shiny, rosy, tautly stretched cheeks in an egg-shaped head and with thinning yellowish hair brushed flat like a 1930s crooner. He had long, rather delicate hands whose two index fingers were almost black from the nicotine of the fifty or sixty cigarettes he smoked a day. In his office he handed me my manuscript, saying, 'I've made a few cuts, as you'll see. But you may not find them acceptable.' The first thing I noticed was that he had shortened the title to the single word 'Sub-Lieutenant'. I then found his 'few cuts' to amount to an emasculation of the first fifty pages, though he had left the naval chapters more or less intact. There was no way I would have found the cuts unacceptable, so thrilled was I at the prospect of being published. The book then went to the Admiralty Press Division for censorship. The only thing they took out was the story of how Chief Petty Officer Vass conducted bayonet drill at *King Alfred*: they said it smacked of blood-lust.

To publish a book today, from the time of delivery to distribution of the finished copies, takes some nine months. In 1942, in the middle of the war, with all the handicaps of bomb damage and shortage of staff and paper, it took just five. In July, when I was billeted in the Royal Naval Barracks at Devonport to attend a gunnery course, the galley proofs arrived, the metamorphosis of my manuscript into 12 point Perpetua. In the evenings I corrected them at one of the tables in the wardroom ante-room, and people passing by would stop and ask (for galleys are a yard long) what I was doing. When I told them, they were a little discomfited, never having met a writer before and not quite sure how to react. 'Whacko!' they'd say, or 'Bit of a scribbler, eh?', or 'So we have an author in our midst!' I was reminded of Robert Louis Stevenson on his way to America.

> The fact that I spent the better part of my day in writing had gone abroad over the ship and tickled them all prodigiously. Whenever they met me they referred to my absurd occupation with familiarity and breadth of humorous intention ... 'Well!' they would say. 'Still writing?' And the smile would widen into a laugh. The purser came one day into the cabin and, touched to the heart by my misguided industry, offered me some other kind of writing, 'for which', he added pointedly, 'you will be paid.' This was nothing less than to copy out the list of passengers.[1]

In August, having been promoted to lieutenant, I was appointed gunnery and watch-keeping officer of HMS *Watchman*, another destroyer; but in every way different from *Tartar*. She was a very ancient ship laid down in the First World War and recently pulled out of mothballs and given an extra fuel tank to help shepherd hard-pressed convoys across the Atlantic. We were to be part of an escort group consisting of another destroyer, ourselves, and six corvettes. Our armament consisted of a single 4-inch gun below the bridge for loosing off at U-boats (and *Tirpitz* too if she happened to pass our way), a couple of anti-aircraft guns and lots of depth charges.

But we had also been supplied with one brand new and quite

---

[1] *The Amateur Emigrant* by Robert Louis Stevenson.

revolutionary piece of equipment, a circular radar scan called the PPI which was set up in the charthouse. Until recently primitive radar antennae had been in fixed positions pointing only in the direction of ahead, and any contacts gained were passed orally by the radar operator. But the antenna that fed the PPI revolved on its own axis and all contacts made were translated into luminous blobs or lines on the screen which were calibrated in yards or miles from the centre. This was the forerunner of what is in common use today in every modern ship, aircraft and aircraft control tower in the world; but ours was the first to be installed operationally. When with a convoy, the scan showed us the exact positions of all the ships in it and their relationship to us and each other; and, in inland waters, the delineation of the coastline with its bays and promontories, a luminous replica of the chart. All this is old hat now; but to us then, it was breath-taking. And it wasn't long before we realized its future implications: that in time the open bridge would be a thing of the past; that you could do everything you wanted by way of navigation and pilotage without ever having to move from the snug of the charthouse.

At the end of August a parcel arrived from Batsford's containing the author's six complimentary advance copies. Never was a parcel opened with a greater sense of anticipation and joy. The dust-jacket was a handsome navy blue with my name and the title in white, and a white crown and anchor in laurel leaves set between the two. I stroked it a couple of times, then turned the pages delicately and lovingly, lingering over 'Publisher's Note', 'Acknowledgements', 'Contents' and 'List of Illustrations' as though they were cast in gold. Next I inspected the photographs, most of which I had taken with my grandmother's old Kodak, and thought they could not have been bettered. Then to Chapter One and the brash opening sentence, 'The first nine years of my life are of no importance', which, as the present reader will know, was quite untrue. But being then twenty-two and not wanting to expose myself, I thought it an arresting opening of which the London School of Journalism might have approved.

I read on without pause, increasingly enamoured of what I had written, and when I reached the end, I went back and started all over again. In the course of the next week or two I must have re-read the book a dozen times and my relish and admiration for it never palled. Then one day I put my own copy aside and never opened it again. I have found the same thing happening, though less obsessively, with subsequent books.

And that was not all I read. I cut out and pasted into a scrapbook not only every review that appeared, even one-liners in the *Runcorn Courier* and *West Highland Gazette*, but every advertisement for it too. And to add to the general euphoria came a stream of fan mail, some from old chums at Eton and Oxford, some from relations, lots from contemporaries of my father, pleased with what I had written about him, some from total strangers. One letter I particularly cherished was from Stanley Baldwin to Lord Dudley who (as the father of a friend at Eton) had sent him a copy of the book. 'The boy has a real talent for writing,' Baldwin had written. 'Beautifully done.' Even better was a letter to Charles Fry from Noël Coward, then making his naval war film, *In Which We Serve*. 'I was tremendously touched and impressed by *Sub-Lieutenant*,' he wrote to Charles Fry. 'It is simply and movingly written with that typically naval genius for understatement. Do please tell the author from me how very, very much I enjoyed it.' This was hugely heartening, as despite having had this one book published, I did not yet know if I had it in me to write another. I also, on advice, joined the Society of Authors and found the Council of Management to consist of such illustrious names as Maugham, Wells, Forster, Shaw, Wodehouse, Coward. From then on I nurtured a secret ambition that one day I might reach the giddy heights of the Council of Management myself: then I would know for certain that I had arrived. (I never did, and in 1980, realizing I never would, I resigned.)

The escort group to which *Watchman* belonged was based at Londonderry, poised between Ulster and the neutral Irish Republic. Once a month or so the group would slip down the River Foyle, watched from the left bank by representatives of the German ambassador in Dublin who lost no time in informing Berlin of our departure. At sea we would join with the next outward bound convoy from the Clyde or Liverpool and take station round it. The Atlantic crossing took eight to ten days depending on the weather and the speed of the slowest ship; and having handed over the convoy to a Canadian group off the south coast of Newfoundland, we entered Argentia Bay (where the year before Churchill and Roosevelt had signed the Atlantic Charter) to rest and repair damage alongside an American depot-ship. After two or three days there, we would sail round to St John's, the capital, for shopping and a night ashore, then back with the next eastbound convoy to Londonderry. This routine never varied.

When we sailed with our first convoy the Battle of the Atlantic was at its height. In June U-boats had sunk 144 ships, in July 96, in August 108. Now, with no less than forty-two U-boats on station between Greenland and the Azores, Admiral Dönitz was about to launch a new offensive. We guessed it would be only a matter of days before we were in action.

Astonishingly we had an uneventful passage, both on the outward and homeward legs. For a total of eighteen days we zigzagged to and fro across the front of the two convoys, lookouts straining their eyes to catch a glimpse of conning-tower or periscope. But none came. Convoys ahead and astern of us were mauled, some savagely, but we remained inviolate. Back in Londonderry we thought, oh well, we'll buy it next time, but amazingly next time was the same as last time, and so were all the future times. For as the months went by and the shipping losses again mounted (94 in October, 119 in November) and we heard on the radio the Admiralty warning convoys that U-boats were gathering to attack them, and later their escorts reporting ships burning and sinking, our convoys remained as untouchable as pariahs. On one occasion, it's true, we did sight a U-boat far away on the surface, and chased it; and when we were a couple of miles off, I pooped off at it with my little gun and one of the shells fell quite near. Then it dived, and that was the last we saw of it or any other U-boat. Luckier even than *Tartar*, we came to assume that every trip would be a peaceful one; and – the weather apart – every trip was.

Yet it was not satisfactory; for I had exchanged a ship whose duties were mainly offensive and whose movements were varied and unpredictable for one whose role was primarily defensive and whose task was always the same. A taste of action would have given our lives an edge, broken the pattern, tested the ship's and our own capabilities. As it was, the monotony and boredom as we crawled to and fro, back and forth, were stupefying. Nor were things helped by the ship's low morale, especially in the wardroom. The captain, a retired lieutenant-commander, was a dear man, large, bald, unflappable, as slow-moving as his ship and unlike in every way the dapper Kim. (He had a nice sense of humour too. 'I see you're wearing your lifebelt round your tummy,' I heard him say to a look-out. 'In the water you'll float bottom up. What makes you think you can breathe through your arse?') But at sea he remained in his tiny cabin below the bridge and, except when on watch, we never saw him. Our *bête noire* was the first lieutenant, disliked equally by wardroom and lower deck. A peacetime RNVR officer, he was as petty-minded and obsessed with detail as his background of a solicitor's office in a small town in Wales might have led one to expect, and we all resented the high-handed, often petulant way he addressed the crew.

By the end of 1942 I was beginning to feel I had had enough of *Watchman*, and was wondering what the chances were of a transfer, when the matter was taken out of my hands. I have mentioned that before leaving Newfoundland with the homeward bound convoy, we always spent a night in St John's. On Christmas Day – the first I had spent ashore for three years – I received an invitation to a lunch party at Government House. I had no idea why I had been asked until I found that the Governor of the island, a charming, stocky, rosy-cheeked, retired vice-admiral with an equally charming wife, had been an old naval friend of my father, and that his wife had known my Grant grandmother in Edinburgh during the first war. We sailed that afternoon, but on the next visit I was invited there again, this time on my own. The Governor lost no time in coming to the point: his ADC and private secretary would be leaving shortly; would I be interested in taking his place? My naval pay would continue for my duties as ADC, and he would give me a personal allowance for my work as private secretary. The appointment would be for a year. I asked time to think it over, and said I would give him a definite answer on the next visit.

It being an offer of the kind I cherished, an opportunity to explore new territory, meet a new challenge, my instinct was to accept; moreover it was the sort of invitation that was unlikely to occur again. Then doubts began creeping in. I would not have been offered the job if I had not been in the Navy, and the reason I had joined the Navy was to take part in the war. Yet after three years at sea a shore job of some kind might be coming up anyway, and being ADC to the Governor of Newfoundland would be a lot more interesting than mouldering in some shore base. The more I thought about it, the more confused I became and, awash in indecision, took my dilemma to the captain. 'What do you *want* to do?' he asked. I told him. 'Then do it,' he said. 'And the war?' He smiled. 'I expect it will manage to get along without you for a bit.' So a signal was sent to the Governor accepting, and when we reached St John's, I stepped ashore from *Watchman* for the last time.

If life in *Watchman* had been a contrast to life in *Tartar*, life in Government House, Newfoundland, was of a different order altogether. It was like staying in a well-appointed English country house, complete with cook and butler, chauffeur and gardener. I lived with the Governor and his wife as part of the family. The Governor was a jolly old soul, laughed a lot and had a curious habit when animated of splaying the palms of his hands across his chest and puffing it out like a pouter pigeon. As the King's representative he took precedence over everyone else on the island, including his wife, who had to follow two steps behind wherever he went, even in his own dining-room. His official title was 'His Excellency the Governor and Commander-in-Chief', but everyone called him 'H.E.'

A couple of Border terriers completed the menage, the aged, grizzled Beano and his yapping son Pepper whom I sometimes used to give a little rootle up the arse when the yapping became intolerable and I thought no one was looking. Once the Governor caught me at it, chuckled merrily, put his hands across his nipples and said, 'Nice work, Ludo. Often wanted to do that myself.'

Like my father he was a simple sort of man, practical and forthright. Once when presenting the prizes at a graduation ceremony, he said to those who'd been studying for three and four years, 'Now you are going out into the world, try and make yourselves useful. Know how to mend the tap and the electric light. There's no place in this world for bookworms.' His favourite game was snooker, at which he punctuated the play with cries of 'Down, dog, down!' and, when his opponent was about to pot a sitter, 'I've seen people miss that shot.' When his side was winning, he'd hum a hymn tune, usually 'Holy, holy, holy'.

My duties as private secretary were to take charge of the Private Office which employed three or four girls, draft the Governor's correspondence and quarterly reports to the Dominions Office in London, decode the confidential ciphers and make arrangements for official visits; and as ADC to accompany the Governor on visits, make sure the car was at hand and the driver sober, and persuade him to rise to his feet when it was time to move on to the next port of call (not always easy when he had a glass in his hand). On weekly visits to Canadian naval headquarters I reported on the latest news from the Atlantic battlefield; and the Governor took up my suggestion of giving dinner parties for captains of the escort groups during their one night in St John's. These parties were much appreciated: candlelight and silver, the company of local girls aiming to please, saddle of lamb and claret all gave a helpful lift to the morale of battle- or weather-weary men between one crossing and the next. Twice, on visiting the operations room, I learned that one captain who had dined with us a few days before and another whom we expected in a few days' time would not be completing the passage: black crosses on the chart told their own story. But *Watchman*'s charmed life continued until eventually she was taken off the Atlantic run.

Until the war St John's had been little more than a shanty town, with all the shops in the one main street running parallel with the waterside; most buildings were of wood, the most noticeable exceptions being Government House and the huge, gaunt Newfoundland Hotel. War-time needs had led to some new construction (a road to Argentia, the development of the port and of Gander Air base) but there was still no highway to connect the island's towns. So for longer visits – to the paper mill towns of Grand Falls, and Corner Brook on the west coast – we embarked in the *Terra Nova*, the vice-regal carriage which was hitched on to the rear of the daily, creaking Newfoundland Express. This ancient contraption consisted of a dining-room and kitchen, washroom and loo, a bedroom each for the Governor and his wife and a drawing-room cum observation car at the rear. Here slept the butler and I in hammocks slung beneath the roof, with Beano and Pepper on the floor. The butler snored, Beano snored, and Pepper in his dreams made muffled yaps as he chased imaginary rabbits. I thought of mentioning this to the butler in the morning, but he got in first. 'Ever been told you talk in your sleep, sir?' I said I used to but thought I had given it up. 'Oh gracious me, sir, no, no, no. Yelling like billy-ho you were. On about man-eating geraniums and shark pudding and heaven knows what.'

The best time of the day was around noon when the Governor declared the sun was over the yardarm and called for pink gin. In comfy armchairs we lazed in the observation car, rattling along at all of 30 m.p.h. and sipping our gin while on either side the wilderness of Newfoundland, barrens and forest, rivers and lakes rolled by. Today, I am told, the railway has gone out of business, its place taken by a trans-island motorway.

Newfoundland was Britain's oldest colony, having been taken for the Crown by Sir Humphrey Gilbert in 1583. It was given restricted self-government in 1832, but during the depression of the 1930s the economy collapsed and Britain had to resume direct rule. When I was there the question everybody was asking was what would happen when the war-time boom was over; for with almost no agriculture and the economy dependent on timber and fish, the economic future looked bleak.

To make recommendations a three-man Parliamentary delegation came out from Britain: Charles (later Lord) Ammon, Labour, with a white Stalinesque moustache and a face so square and dead it might have been lying in state; Sir Derrick Gunston, Bart, Conservative, a bibulous, red-faced ex-Guardee; and the markedly eccentric and vastly entertaining A. P. Herbert, Independent. I was interested in meeting A.P.H. Then one of Britain's leading writers of comedy, he was also author of a remarkable book that I found few people had ever heard of: *The Secret Battle*, based on his own experiences in the trenches, about a man who had been shot for cowardice yet was, in the words of the narrator, 'the bravest man I ever knew'.

This ill-assorted trio were lent the *Terra Nova* and a cook for a week in order to tootle around the island and see what was up. But the atmosphere on board was fraught. Not only did Ammon, a dim man if ever I met one, insist on referring to himself as 'Your Chairman' when addressing the other two, but being a lay preacher and teetotaller, had declared the *Terra Nova* dry. So before lunch and dinner, instead of convivial sessions in the observation car, the other two would slope off to one of the bedrooms where I had secreted a small cache of spirits beneath the bunk. Of the three my favourite was A.P.H. and during his time on the island I came to know him quite well. He invariably turned up in petty officer's uniform (he was a member of a river patrol unit operating near his home on the Thames at Hammersmith) which meant we both called each other 'sir'. Thin and tall, with a slight stoop and markedly hooked nose and an endearing habit of twitching and stuttering whenever he spoke, he resembled a kind of manic flightless bird. We all loved his company (he was wickedly funny about his two colleagues), especially after dinner at the piano when he sang us comic songs. Three times he stayed at Government House and three times left something behind – a sponge, a whale's tooth, a razor strop, a map of Labrador. Once, when calling for him at the Newfoundland Hotel, I was told by Derrick Gunston that he was having a Turkish bath. I said I didn't know the hotel had any. 'He undresses and goes into the bathroom,' said Derrick, 'turns on the hot tap until the room is full of steam, then sits on the loo seat for quarter of an hour.' To get away from the others A.P.H. commandeered a boat to go to Labrador where local people mistook him for the travelling dentist and asked him to pull their teeth. He told H.E. how worried he was that Canada had been given a 99-year-lease of Goose Airport in Labrador. 'Barren piece of land,' said H.E. shortly. 'No use to anybody.'

The report of the Commission was never made public because it seemed that while they all agreed that the link with Britain should be maintained, they had quite different ideas as to how this should be done (A.P.H. wanted a Northern Ireland-type 'solution'). But after the war there was a referendum, and by a narrow majority the islanders voted to become part of Canada, the wisest decision they could have made in geographical and economic terms.

In my leisure time I pursued those activities which had always interested me – public speaking and performing – and which I hoped to take up professionally after the war. I joined the St John's Players and acted the part of David Bliss in Noël Coward's Hay Fever; addressed a variety of Rotary and other clubs; read (very badly, I now realize) some of H. E. Bates's short stories on the Newfoundland radio; and sometimes in the evenings would take a girl to dance at the local country club. I also wrote a play called Wardroom, a sort of naval Journey's End; not knowing what to do with it and remembering his generous remarks about Sub-Lieutenant, I wrote to Noël Coward asking if he would advise. Not only did he agree to do so, but having read it, wrote in his own hand a long and helpful letter recommending improvements; and when I wrote to thank him for these, I received a second letter saying that I was to be sure to let him see a revised version. In the event I never did revise it, finding it on reflection altogether too shallow.

I knew from one of the books of my Great-uncle Will (whose ship had been stationed in Newfoundland for a year) that he had enjoyed the sport there. So did I; walking up ptarmigan on the barrens, shooting a caribou and missing a moose, and fishing for sea-trout in streams close to St John's. But the highlight of the year was the Governor's annual salmon-fishing holiday when I accompanied him, his wife, a friend, and Beano and Pepper on a visit to Big Falls on the Upper Humber. Most of the party went there by train and canoe, but the Governor and I, delayed by the arrival of the Parliamentary Commission, travelled in style, flying from St John's in a Canso seaplane lent by the local air vice-marshal and putting down on a lake among the forest and mountains to the north. Here guides who had spent the last few days portaging across country came alongside in canoes, and having embarked our gear, took us across the lake to where the Humber emptied out of it. There followed a leisurely twenty-mile paddle downstream, forests of fir and birch on either side, and occasionally, peering out of them, an inquiring bear or moose.

In the late afternoon we reached Big Falls, a ten-foot drop into a long, wide pool where the salmon used to gather until the water rose high enough for them to continue upstream. Forty feet above the falls stood three huts owned by one of the paper companies: the Governor, his wife, and the dogs slept in one, the friend and I in the second, and the guides, who also cooked for us, in the third, though the constant hum of mosquitoes and the discomfort of sleeping bags laid on branches of spruce gave few untroubled nights.

Here we stayed for eight days, anchoring in our canoes in line abreast below the falls and casting our flies either side of the stern. Whenever one of us hooked a fish, the guide would lift the anchor so as to drop down clear of the others, then landed one on the bank to bring the fish ashore. Altogether we caught sixty-one salmon, none bigger than twelve pounds, most around seven or eight, which averaged out at between two and three salmon per rod per day. One evening a bear, smelling the fish we had already caught, swam the river to investigate, but was headed off by the guides. I had hoped he might have come for Pepper who spent most days yapping on a rock. Before long I got the measure of Pepper by carrying around a tin of his staple diet, stuff called Pard, and when the yapping seemed it would never end, took him behind a bush and shovelled some into him. This worked wonders, though in time the Governor's wife did comment on his girth.

On the ninth day we embarked in the canoes with our gear and two barrels of salted salmon, and pointed the bows downstream; and after a day's peaceful paddling in sunshine along the Humber and the many lakes through which it ran, we reached the railhead where the *Terra Nova*, the butler, and pink gin were waiting.

For most of my time in Newfoundland my relations with the Governor's wife were particularly gratifying. I think she looked on me as another son (her own son was also in the Navy, the other side of the world) and I found in her qualities of gentleness and affection which had been quite missing in my mother. She asked me about the girls I saw, whom she knew only as dinner-party guests, and I was able to fill her in about them. She on her part was charmingly indiscreet about her own past life (not that she had much to be indiscreet about) and I vividly remember one conversation in which I asked her at roughly what age married couples gave it up. She gave a wickedish smile. 'I can't say yet,' she said. '*Really*?' I said, thinking at twenty-four that by sixty-four one was long past it. 'H.E.,' she said with a giggle, 'likes it every two or three weeks.'

Unfortunately towards the end of my stay, I took up with a girl of whom – for some reason I never discovered – she violently disapproved, and there was a subsequent coolness in our relationship. Things picked up a bit after the girl left for England, but the old cosiness had gone; and when, soon after, my year was up, rewarding and unusual though it had been, I was more than ready to return to the Navy.

It was while I was in Newfoundland that I first discovered a book which was an eye-opener to me and helped greatly to change my thinking. It was *The Age of Reason* by the radical reformer Thomas Paine, author of the more celebrated *The Rights of Man*, and written mostly in prison in Paris in 1794. I have mentioned earlier the difficulties I had, despite ten years of indoctrination at prep school and public school, in accepting the Christian faith. These had persisted. I could not understand how it was that others, bishops and headmasters and so on, wiser and older than myself, could embrace it with such confidence and display, while I was unable to; and I had put it down to some defect in me, a similar defect to the one that prevented me having a satisfactory relationship with my mother. But Paine, with unreserved commitment, and a conviction no less sure than that of the bishops and headmasters, removed in an instant my doubts and hesitations; and in the process, it seemed to me, reduced to rubble the rock on which the Church was founded.

'It is necessary for the happiness of man,' he began, 'that he be mentally faithful to himself. Infidelity does not consist in believing or disbelieving; it consists of professing to believe what he does not believe.'

That was a life-giving start; and it was music from then on:

Every national church or religion has established itself by pretending some special mission from God . . . Each of these churches shows certain books which they call revelation, or the word of God. Each of these churches accuses the other of unbelief, and for my part I disbelieve them all.

When I am told that a woman called the Virgin Mary said, or gave out, that she was with child without any cohabitation with a man and that her betrothed husband Joseph said that an angel told him so, I have a right to believe them or not; such a circumstance requires a much stronger evidence than their bare word for it.

The history of [Jesus Christ] is altogether the work of other people; and as to the account of his resurrection and ascension, it was the necessary counterpart to the story of his birth. His historians having brought him into the world in a supernatural manner were obliged to take him out again in the same manner; or the first part of the story must have fallen to the ground.

The resurrection and ascension, supposing them to have taken place, admitted of public and ocular demonstration, like that of the ascension of a balloon, or the sun at noonday, to all Jerusalem at least. A thing which everybody is required to believe requires that the proof and evidence of it should be equal to all, and universal . . . Instead of this a small number of persons, not more than eight or nine, are introduced as proxies for the whole world, to say they saw it, and all the rest of the world are called upon to believe it.

If we are to suppose a miracle to be something so entirely out of course of what is called nature, that she must go out of that course to accomplish it, and we see an account given of such a miracle by the person who said he saw it, it raises a question in the mind very easily decided; which is, is it more probable that nature should go out of her course, or that a man should tell a lie? We have never seen, in our time, nature go out of her course . . . it is therefore at least millions to one that the reporter of a miracle tells a lie.

These books, beginning with Genesis and ending with Revelation . . . are, we are told, the word of God. It is therefore proper for us to know who told us so, that we may know what credit to give to the report. The answer to this question is, that nobody can tell, except that we tell one another so.

It is a matter altogether of uncertainty to us whether such of the writings as now appear under the name of the Old and New Testament in which the collectors say they found them, or whether they added, altered, abridged or dressed them up; who the people were that did all this, we know nothing of; they called themselves by the general name of the Church, and this is all we know of the matter.

About three hundred and fifty years after the time that Christ is said to have lived, several writings of the kind I am speaking of were scattered in the hands of divers individuals; and as the Church had begun to form itself into a hierarchy or church government with temporal powers, it set itself about collecting them into a code, as we now see them, called *The New Testament*. They decided by vote . . . which of those writings out of the collections they had made, should be the word of God and which should not.

As the object of the Church, as is the case in all national establishments of Churches, was power and revenue, and terror the means it used, it is consistent to suppose that the most miraculous and wonderful writings they had collected stood the best chance of being voted. As to the authenticity of the books, the vote stands in the place of it, for it can be traced no higher.

Now, for the first time, I came to realize that the Christian religion was as much founded on fantasy and myth as every other religion (how could it be otherwise?). But if that was so, why did so many millions of people subscribe to it? And the answer to that surely was not, as its supporters (and the supporters of all religions) claimed, that it was about the discovery of external truths, but rather the fulfilment of internal needs. Yet having reached that point, the question still remained, Did God exist? And it was to be a lifetime before I would begin to find a satisfactory answer to that.

10

The Invasion of Europe

On arrival in London I found that my mother and sisters had recently moved into the Grace and Favour apartment she had been given at Hampton Court Palace. It was in fact a house with four floors and an attic, being part of the Tudor wing on the extreme left-hand corner as you face the entrance to the Palace. One side of the house bordered on Tennis Court Lane, the other on the tiny Lord Chamberlain's Court, while the magnificent forty-foot drawing-room looked out towards the entrance gates and the river. With walls several feet thick and no central heating, it was the coldest house I have ever been in, and as we huddled round a small coal fire on winter evenings, I was reminded of *Tartar*'s wardroom on the journey to Russia. Seemingly impervious to the cold, my mother adored it, and lived here happily for the next thirty-three years. An additional perk was having a key to the gardens, so that when on summer evenings the public had left, my mother had the run of the place for her dinner-party guests. She also cultivated a small garden of her own between the Banqueting House and the Orangery.

Pleased though I was at my mother's pleasure in her new home, I was deeply distressed to find her bullying my sister Morar, six years my junior, in the same way as she had once bullied me. Though Morar was now seventeen and about to join the Wrens, my mother treated her like some recalcitrant child, criticizing her for this, blaming her for that, *ordering* not *asking* her to perform some household chore. It was painful to watch and listen to, because Morar was no more capable of standing up for herself than I had been in my day; and there were times when my mother was thrashing things out with her, bombarding her with rhetorical questions ('Have I or have I not spoken about this before?') to which the poor girl had no answer, that I tried to intercede for her as my father, long ago, had occasionally tried to intercede for me. But I was no more successful than he had been. 'This has nothing to do with you, Ludovic, so will you kindly not interrupt!'

Strangely, my mother's attitude to my other sister Katherine, a year younger than Morar, was the very opposite. 'My wee bead', she used to call her, and while not spoiling her, cuddled and cherished her as any loving mother would. As a result Katherine grew up a normal, healthy, assured young woman, without any of the hang-ups that plagued her sister and myself. Since those days the three of us have sometimes mulled over the different ways we were treated, but without coming to any conclusions.

Two interests of my mother at this time were the Drown Box and spiritualism. She was introduced to the Drown Box (named after its inventor) by a man called Brigadier Firebrace who said it would cure her of arthritis. So far as I can remember, you had to put a few drops of your blood on a piece of blotting-paper and send it to an address in, I think, Herefordshire. There they put the blotting-paper into a special box which in some way or other determined the wavelength of the owner of the blood, and with this knowledge, sent out beams to settle the person's disturbed vibrations. Something like that. My mother became quite excited about this box, and persuaded me to send off blood on blotting-paper to Herefordshire in the hope that the beams might soothe the vibrations in my sometimes troubled stomach; but they were no more successful with that than, in the end, they were with her arthritis. The box and its beams are still in use today, though I am told that tufts of hair have taken over from blood; and that 'the box' has been very successful in diagnosing, though not curing, disorders in horses.

My mother's interest in spiritualism had begun within two months of my father's death, although by this time it was beginning to wane. But for more than four years she attended seances in Edinburgh and London, and in two fat notebooks she left accounts of them. Sometimes she sat alone with a medium, sometimes there were others present; but within a very short time she was claiming to be in touch with my father through one of a number of 'guides' – an officer killed in the First World War, two Red Indians (Red Eagle and White Feather), a French child called Deville and a black child, Poppet, who called my father 'Massa Kennedy'. It was evident from my mother's records that she was much closer to my father in seances than she had ever been in real life; and it was striking how vacuous if cheerful those messages from the other side were. My mother was not to worry about anything: my father, her father and various other dead relations were keeping an eye on her and helping in all sorts of ways. And there were homely bits of advice. My sister Morar was to take plenty of acids to counteract excessive starch. My sister Katherine was to take halibut oil to lubricate her nerves which had become very dry. I myself had a stomach full of gasses (too true!) but no cure was suggested.

There are entries about a trumpet floating round the room, of tables levitating and moving about (once at a seance at Belgrave Crescent a table banged into the dog Ben who was asleep and much surprised) and of ectoplasm 'streaming like butter muslin' out of the nose and mouth of a medium called Mrs Duncan, who was subsequently imprisoned for fraud. On one occasion my father said he had Admiral Beatty with him to gain first-hand experience of a seance, but there was no record of Beatty's reactions. Another time my father said, 'What people do on your side they also do on our side. Take a racing motorist. When he comes to this side, he can still race his car. He would fret if he couldn't. And there are pubs and clubs on this side just as there are on yours.' He told my mother that when she fell asleep in the bath (which she often did) he made knocking noises to wake her up. 'This', wrote my mother, 'I was sure of.' My father seems to have been appreciated by his guides. The guide Poppet told my mother, 'I love your massa man. I may be black but my spirit is white.'

Apart from all this tosh, some things were said which seemed to be beyond rational explaining. At one seance where seven or eight were present, the medium said, 'Does the word "Fareham" mean anything to anyone?' My mother said that Fareham didn't but that Farnham did, for Farnham Common was where we had lived before the war. The medium said she saw a red brick house with a blue roof close to some woods where there were beech trees. This was an accurate description of our house. The medium said, 'It seems that there are also Hubbs or Tubbs and Bubbs living there. This sounds like nonsense to me. Do you understand it?' My mother said she did, as there were three families living there called Tubb, Bubb and Jubb. Then, at a seance in Edinburgh on 12 November 1940 the medium said, 'Your husband says that a big naval battle is being fought now in the Mediterranean. Italy's Navy will be almost obliterated. You will hear nothing for two or three days.' Beneath this entry my mother wrote, 'The above sitting was held at 10.30 a.m. on Tuesday, November 12th. The news of the naval battle at Taranto when half the Italian fleet were destroyed was announced on Wednesday afternoon, November 13th.' On the other hand my father said on several occasions at this time that the war would soon be over, and that the ship which had sunk the *Rawalpindi* had itself been sunk. In fact the war was to last another five years and the *Scharnhorst*, which had sunk the *Rawalpindi*, survived until December 1943. It was quite a puzzle to know what to make of it all.

After two weeks' leave I reported to the Admiralty where I was told (as a result of *Sub-Lieutenant*) that I was to join the Admiralty Press Division. This consisted of a room occupied by four people: Nicholas Monsarrat, who had already written a couple of light, witty books about life in corvettes and presumably even now was laying the foundations of *The Cruel Sea* – he sat at a desk in the corner and rarely spoke; the West Country novelist John Moore, chainsmoker, raconteur and most clubbable of men who was to become a lifelong friend until his early death from cancer; Commander Anthony Kimmins, the playwright and broadcaster, larger than life, bursting with vitality and of the most telling charm with the biggest, broadest smile of anyone I ever met – he stayed away from the office as much as he could but every so often he would appear, beaming, with a suitcase to be briefed on some coming operation, then re-appear a week later to broadcast a vivid account of it; and in general charge of the place a Commander Kenderdine, RN, who I think found us all a little mad. John, Nicholas and I were kept occupied putting together and pasting up official naval publications, but I forget now what they were.

All the talk at this time was of the coming invasion of Europe, and in the middle of May I was appointed Press Liaison Officer to one of the five major naval forces taking part in the attack. My duties were to distribute a score of war correspondents among the ships of the force, and to embark three others and myself in the headquarters' flagship *Largs*. At the briefing in the cinema hall of HMS *Vernon* in Portsmouth I met Henry Durrell, the *Tartar*'s old first lieutenant, now in command of the destroyer *Isis*. Spider was there too, and we agreed to meet for dinner on our return from France. But I would never see Henry again: within a few weeks the *Isis* was sunk and he was not among the survivors.

The force sailed on the night of 5 June. It was an odd feeling to be steaming south again across the Channel, to be about to re-enter a country which for more than four years had been entirely cut off from us. John Moore, who was in the adjoining force, had told me he thought there would be horrendous casualties and had equipped himself with a box of morphine ampoules. My three correspondents, for whom this was just another assignment, were rather more fatalistic and sat up late, as journalists do, drinking whisky out of tooth-mugs, and gossiping.

I took a few hours' sleep but was on the *Largs*'s bridge by dawn. The surrounding sea was a mosaic of ships of every description. Bombers passed overhead in waves and above the French coast, now fifteen miles away, red and white flak curled upwards. Someone shouted, 'Torpedoes approaching from port,' and the captain turned to port to present a smaller target. One passed astern of us but the other hit the Norwegian destroyer *Svenner*. Although she was the ship nearest to us, we didn't hear a sound. Within minutes she had broken in two, bows and stern pointing to the sky just as had happened with *Hood*; as we watched, they slid beneath the surface. The speed and silence of it was uncanny.

We came to anchor a few miles from the shore. The sea was still choppy and as the landing craft moved off, they were tossed around mercilessly. I thought how wretched the soldiers must be feeling, rotten with seasickness and knowing that within an hour they were going to have to land on a heavily defended shore. But many of them burst into song, and in one craft a man stood up with a bugle and turning towards the *Largs*'s bridge, blew the General Salute. It was a strangely moving moment.

In war things seldom happen as anticipated. I had thought that by this time we should be under heavy and continual air attack, and that many of our ships would have been sunk or severely damaged. But not a single German aeroplane had come into view and among the ships the only casualty had been the *Svenner*. Not able to see what was happening on the beaches, I went to the wardroom for breakfast. There was, as usual, a hum of conversation and the clink of cutlery: we might have been alongside the jetty in Portsmouth. I sat down and a white-coated steward appeared and said, 'Porridge or cereal this morning, sir?' It was not what I had expected.

Next day I cadged a lift ashore with the admiral and his staff and with them walked along the beach. Invasion craft of all sorts lay in grotesque positions, some high and dry on the sand, others half in the water, some burnt out, others apparently undamaged but with their bottoms blown out by mines. The engine of one landing craft was still running, with blue smoke streaming from its exhaust.

There had not yet been time to bury all the dead. They lay where they had fallen, looking as if they had never even lived, let alone sung and waved as the assault craft took them inshore. The tide had covered them once and some were half buried in the wet sand. They looked as if they had been dead a hundred years.

All except one. He lay higher on the beach than the others and the sea had not touched him. He rested on a slope, face down, his head towards the enemy. So natural was his attitude that he might have fallen forwards while standing at attention. There was no knowing how he had died, for his uniform was unblemished and he bore no marks. I guessed he was about twenty.

We had just stopped for the admiral to talk to a German officer who had been taken prisoner with fifty of his men when there was a peculiar roaring sound and a cry of 'Lie down!' All of us – British and German alike – hit the sand, by which time four German jet fighters flying at around a hundred feet and firing cannon shell were already a mile down the coast. Luckily no one was hit. I wandered off into the outskirts of Ouistreham and met an ancient apple-grower who told me how happy he was we had come and gave me a glass of milk and cried '*Santé*!'

I had been instructed before leaving London to write daily 'colour' pieces for a pool, in case papers' accredited correspondents were unable to file. So after the battle had moved inland I sat with my typewriter in the sunshine on the *Largs*'s deck, churning out a thousand words a day, not a paragraph of which was ever used. Still, it was good practice. A friendly reporter from one of the dailies, hearing that this was the first time I had ever filed, said, 'Let me give you a tip. With your first sentence you must grab the reader's attention.' Wasn't this what the London School of Journalism had always advised? I asked what the first sentence of his first despatch had been, and he said, 'The Navy's done it again' (i.e. put the army safely ashore). It reads like a tired cliché now, but I remember how impressed I was at the time – a handful of words to encapsulate a huge theme: what the invasion had been all about.

Back in London I received two invitations, one from Commander Kenderdine to write a history of the Home Fleet, another from Tony Kimmins to be his assistant on a tour of the Pacific theatre. Both were quite tempting, but by now I had had enough of observing others take part in the war, and put in for a sea-going appointment. It came through surprisingly quickly, as watch-keeping officer of HMS *Zebra*, a brand new destroyer building at Dumbarton on the Clyde. But first I was sent to the once and future Roedean Girls' School near Brighton ('If you need a mistress in the night, please ring the bell') for a torpedo course in which I came out top, and (as I was to be navigator too) a crash navigation course from my friend Dick David whose ship was also in the Clyde.

And so it came about that just four and a half years after I had first joined *Tartar* at Greenock and sailed in her up the Minches to Scapa Flow, I made the same journey in *Zebra*: then I had been allowed to pencil in our position on the course laid by the navigator, now as navigator I laid the course myself. Returning to Scapa was a spooky experience. Superficially the destroyer anchorage seemed much the same (though a large colony of Wrens was now administering the base), but for me the place was full of ghosts – of Kim and Henry and Spider and Tiny and others in *Tartar* with whom I had shared two years of war, ghosts of fellow tribals – *Punjabi, Mashona, Eskimo, Ashanti, Bedouin* – which had lain at neighbouring buoys and some of whose officers we had come to know almost as well as our own. Twelve of the original sixteen had been sunk, and their replacements were complete strangers. All was changed; and I had a hard job restraining myself from telling my shipmates how different and how much better it had been in the old days.

Our employment was what it had always been, screening the big ships whenever they put to sea; formerly battleships, now mostly aircraft carriers which launched attacks off the Norwegian coast against enemy shipping going up and down the leads. For us it was as monotonous and dull as ever, though no less necessary; for while the German surface fleet in Norway now hardly existed (*Scharnhorst* had been sunk the previous Boxing Day, *Tirpitz* by the RAF on 12 November) the enemy could still field a formidable force of U-boats.

For me there was one compensation: the job of navigator, unique in the general raft of an officer's duties in that like being the author of a book, it involves no one but oneself; and I enjoyed the mystery of taking sun sights and star sights far out at sea, then applying logarithmic tables to the angle of observation to determine in terms of time and space precisely (well, to within a mile or two) where one was on the surface of the sea. I remember one occasion when we were instructed to take two other destroyers under our orders and sail to the assistance of a Russian convoy being harassed by U-boats. For three days it was overcast and I had to navigate by dead reckoning. Then at dawn on the fourth day I managed to snatch the faintest of star sights, the fruits of which led the captain confidently to signal to the others our noon position. Less confidently I waited for them to demur, but neither did; and the day after, guided by the radio chatter of the convoy's escorts, we joined the convoy. I felt quite proud when the senior officer signalled 'Congratulations on finding us'. We must have brought them luck too, for after our arrival there were no more attacks.

By March 1945 it was clear the war was coming to its end, and I looked forward to finishing it where I had begun it, at Scapa Flow; though some said that we might be sent to ports in Norway, Denmark, or even Germany to see to the disposal of German warships. But early in April a signal arrived appointing me first lieutenant of the destroyer *Wheatland*, then refitting at Taranto in Italy for service in the Far East; her captain, oddly, was Tiny Archer-Shee. I went there in a troopship and of the journey out remember two things: an enchantingly pretty girl with (I thought) an enchantingly pretty name – Dorothea Orbell – a member of a concert party troupe with whom I passed many a cosy evening under a rug in the lee of the after funnel (where are you now, Dorothea?); and the night of VE Day when all the scuttles and deadlights in our blacked-out ship were thrown back so that lights from every cabin and compartment blazed out triumphantly across the darkling sea — nothing else could have proclaimed more dramatically and with such certainty that the war was over.

Tiny, as large and ponderous as ever, seemed as glad to see me as I was him; though it required an effort on my part to address him as 'Sir', not 'Tiny'. Soon after I joined, he took himself to Cairo on a fortnight's leave, so I was left in temporary command. There was plenty to do during the daytime, supervising the running of the ship and the alterations being made by the Italian workmen, seeing requestmen and defaulters, receiving officers from the base. But the evenings were apt to hang heavy. The air was warm and sultry, stars crowded the sky, and I was consumed by unfocussed lust. Sadly there were no means of assuaging it. My Italian teacher was happily married, the bars and cafés of Taranto were off-limits and in any case lacked appeal. The only possible candidates were a pair of tremendously brisk, friendly, English girls who ran with great competence a rest-house in the hills where we sometimes went for weekends. They were not unattractive either, but had one made a pass, I think that to avoid embarrassment they would have professed not to have understood what one was suggesting. And for a man there are few things more humiliating than that.

We were due to leave for the Far East in August. But in August the two atom bombs fell on Japan, bringing the war there to an end; and so on leaving Taranto we turned west instead of east, and my sea-going time as first lieutenant lasted no longer than the journey to Plymouth, where the ship paid off. I spent a further six months at the Admiralty awaiting demobilization, sharing a flat in Sidney Street with Bill Richmond who was doing the same, at the end of which time my naval career was over.

11

Oxford, Ashridge and The Red Shoes

What to do now? In fact the question had already been answered.

Since my return home from Newfoundland in the spring of 1944, I had become increasingly aware of my ignorance of so many things, in particular literature and art, seldom the leading topics of any wardroom conversation. My father, as the reader will recall, had rarely read a work of literature in his life while my mother's repertoire did not go far beyond Dickens, Robert Louis Stevenson and parts of Walter Scott. When I was small, she tried reading aloud to me, at first *The Old Curiosity Shop*, later *Kidnapped*. From anyone else I might have enjoyed it, but coming from her I professed to be bored, and yawned and fidgeted to show how much I resented it; and in the end she gave up. Her only other attempt to instil culture into me was to take me to a performance at the Old Vic of what she called *Hamlet-in-its-Entirety* which lasted five hours and put me off Shakespeare for years.

It was not that I was unread, but that my favourite authors – Maupassant and Maugham, Wodehouse and Waugh, Saki, O. Henry, Damon Runyon – were all moderns, and of those of earlier times – apart from a smattering of Stevenson and Dickens – I knew nothing. A door was opened for me in that summer of 1944 when I came to know and love a woman who, among many other admirable qualities, was educated in a way that I was not; and when she spoke knowingly of those who to me were hardly more than names – Hardy and Chekhov, Donne and Keats, Manet and Monet, Wren and Nash, I felt I was at the portals of a new country, one that no one had told me about and whose highways enticingly beckoned.

So I began to read, and the more I read, the more I wanted to read; for in literature too the appetite grows by what it feeds on. And when the war ended and I heard that the government was ready to give grants to undergraduates whose studies had been cut short by the war, there was no question of my not applying. If I was going to be a writer, the first thing I had to do was acquaint myself with the great writers of the past. And so in October 1946 I returned to Christ Church to resume my studies, while Bill Richmond returned to Trinity, Cambridge.

The Oxford I came back to was altogether different from the one I had left. The indolence and hedonism that had characterized the pre-war period, at least for some, had given way to application and austerity. Rationing was still in force and those of us – in 1946 the great majority – who had come back from the war and felt that time was not exactly on our side, wanted to make full use of the opportunity offered. That is not to say that we did not enjoy ourselves (and the authorities sensibly let us come and go as we pleased), but the priorities of a student of twenty-six who has just been released from the services are not those of a boy of nineteen tasting freedom for the first time.

I had a slight setback on arrival to find that the English literature tutor assigned to me, while a dab hand with a golf club (he had been a Blue), was somewhat less expert at guiding one down the fairways of Eng Lit. I put a lot of effort and enthusiasm into the weekly essays I wrote for him, but received little in return. Then I had a stroke of luck; an introduction to David Cecil, an English Literature don at New College who had a brilliant reputation both as teacher and talker. After I had met him two or three times, he agreed to allow me to attend, in addition to my own tutorials, one of his.

The group I joined was a mixed one; a Roosevelt (name of Dirk), George Scott, later editor of *Truth* and later still the representative of the EEC in London, and a little Chinese man who was so short that his legs not only did not reach the floor but stuck out from the sofa horizontally. The routine was for one of them to read out his weekly essay, on Dryden or Dickens or whoever, after which David would lead a general discussion.

In all my years spent acquiring knowledge of the past, I look back on those sessions with David and his pupils (and the crowded lectures he gave in the hall of New College) as the high point: he was an astonishing communicator. Today, forty years on, I see him as vividly as then, standing before the fireplace in his rooms in New College, wearing a pair of corduroy trousers, a nondescript tweed coat and a badly tied bow tie. With his slight build, high domed forehead and slender fingers, he looked always a little poetical, an appearance that belied the robustness of his views. 'Who are we doing today?' he would say as he burst breathless into the room, invariably late; and after the essay had been read he would discourse for perhaps twenty minutes on the author in question. For an academic he could not have been less academic. Where other tutors would treat a text as a corpse and dissect it as in a post-mortem, David's first criterion was whether the author had succeeded in entertaining one and why; then to consider his intentions and how far he had succeeded in realizing them. And so infectious were his enthusiasms and so wise his judgements that inhibitions one had set up against this writer or that were soon broken down. As George Scott wrote later,

'Literature became what it had never been at school, an integral part of life.'

He always listened sympathetically to his pupils' views, however immature or unformed, and never told them where they were wrong, rather where his views differed from theirs. And when someone mentioned that he had been enjoying a writer not of the first rank, he would often say how good he thought him. I think he hated as much as anyone the narrow academic notion that there are only a limited number of writers worthy of serious study. In this way he let us form our own conclusions.

He had many endearing idiosyncrasies. Sometimes to drive home a point he would fling both arms downwards like a piston; or interlock his fingers and set his thumbs criss-crossing against each other in semi-perpetual motion. He talked extremely fast and not always audibly, his tongue outdistanced by his thoughts and struggling to keep up with them. Like my Aunt Moggie he had trouble with his R's, and had an odd habit common to some Cecils and Cavendishes of pronouncing 'th' as 'f' (I once heard him say in a lecture, 'Of all fe Womantic poets, Byron was weally fe most womantic, for as well as being exceedingly beautiful, he was also a lord', which resulted in much laughter when people saw the point).[1] Another mannerism was finishing a sentence an octave or two higher, or lower, than he started it.

He was a chain-smoker of Craven A cork-tipped cigarettes which he fished out of a battered packet deep in his pocket, then lit by poking the end against a bar of the electric fire; this usually left shreds of tobacco on the bar which then began a little conflagration of their own. And he held his cigarette, not like most people between the index and middle fingers, but between the middle and third fingers, close up to the knuckle. While others were talking, he smoked normally; but when he was holding the floor, and so as not to interrupt his flow, he took quick short puffs like a steam engine leaving St Pancras.

I was aware at the time how much I – and so many other undergraduates – owed him, and I have been aware of it ever since. One of David's many delightful books was *Two Quiet*

---

[1] As a younger son of the Marquess of Salisbury, David had the courtesy title of Lord David Cecil.

Lives about Thomas Gray and Dorothy Osborne. Twenty years after I left Oxford, I tried to acknowledge my debt by dedicating to him my book on the *Bismarck* operation, *Pursuit*. 'For my friend and former tutor David Cecil,' I wrote. 'This tale of unquiet lives. With gratitude and affection.'

In addition to English I read some philosophy and history and also joined in various extra-curricular activities. Appearances in my mother's amateur theatricals as a child had given me (and later my sisters) a taste for acting which had led to my joining the Oxford University Dramatic Society briefly before the war and the St John's Players in Newfoundland. But I knew by now that I had very little talent for acting, and that whatever I did in life I would have to achieve as myself and not as imaginary people. One day, perhaps, I might write lines for an actor to speak; but I did not want to be one. I did join the Union and spoke once or twice on fairly frivolous motions; but essentially the Union was for budding politicians and my interest in politics then, as now, was peripheral to my writing.

Instead I joined the undergraduate magazine *Isis*, and soon found myself literary editor. This was enormously satisfying, not only in learning how a magazine was put together but in the pleasure of reviewing or sending out for review books which London publishers were prodigal enough to send. Looking back at the cuttings I am embarrassed at how portentous and opinionated some of my notices were, airily dismissing Terence Rattigan's *Flarepath* at the Oxford Playhouse, picking holes in L. P. Hartley's *Eustace and Hilda*. Reviewing Bob Boothby's memoirs, I wrote, 'The second half of the book is too complex and comprehensive to do justice to here', a sentence which Evelyn Waugh (to whom the editor had sent a copy of the magazine for comment) said in the next issue that I shouldn't have written and the editor shouldn't have published. I also wrote an *Isis Idol* profile of Bill Richmond when as President of the Cambridge Union he came over to take part in the Oxford Union presidential debate. Unlike myself, Bill was in love with politics: he had served in all the offices of the Union before becoming President, he was President of the Cambridge University Conservative Association and had been elected unopposed a Cambridge town councillor. He was travelling a well-worn route to what could be a distinguished Parliamentary career.

I also became founder member of the Oxford University

Writers' Club, whose object was to gather together a score of hopeful scribblers like myself and four times a term invite some literary figure to address us. Fellow members included John Watney, who had written a good war book, *The Enemy Within*; Michael Croft, subsequently director of the National Youth Theatre; Francis King, the novelist and critic; Maurice Cranston, the philosopher; Kenneth Harris of the *Observer*; James Leasor, the writer and journalist; John Synge, who became director of the Redfern Gallery; Michael Meyer, translator of Ibsen and Strindberg; John Herbert, who became a pillar of Christies; and George Scott. David Cecil became our President. The meetings took place in a private room of some college or restaurant, dinner being followed by the talk and questions. Few of those I approached refused. I think they were attracted by the informality of the occasion and also perhaps felt a moral obligation to pass on what they thought of value to their profession's apprentices. Evelyn Waugh came, so did Cyril Connolly, V. S. Pritchett, John Betjeman, Elizabeth Bowen, John Lehmann, Charles Morgan, Godfrey Winn.

Most of the meetings took place in such a haze of claret that it is not surprising that surviving members can recall only fragments. Many remember the first meeting, which took place in freezing weather at the Trout Inn. The guest was Charles Morgan whose talk Michael Meyer recalls as lofty and dull. George Scott noted Morgan's silver hair and polished jackboots, and his telling us that he always wrote the last act of a play first. George says he had to leave the Connolly meeting because of an attack of hiccups, but Francis King, who was present, remembers Michael Croft being irked by Connolly's ivory-tower attitude (he also had a very soft, flabby, girlish way of speaking) and Connolly then being upset by Michael Croft's abrasive questioning. Maurice Cranston remembers Connolly in his cups admitting that for all his critical writings on French literature, he could hardly speak a word of French.

Perhaps we didn't always treat our guests with the reverence they expected or deserved, but at our time of life we were less concerned with which act you wrote first than with the practicalities of living; in particular with how to exist while trying to complete a book or play. 'Be a roadsweeper,' said Evelyn Waugh helpfully, puffing at a Havana cigar. 'Become keeper of a railway crossing,' said John Betjeman with his Boy Scout smile, 'where there's only one train a day.' 'Be a journalist,' said Godfrey Winn. 'It's an interesting life.'[1] Michael asked Godfrey how much he earned, and when Godfrey told him, Michael asked if he wasn't ashamed. Fortunately for the evening he wasn't.

I'm glad to say that the club continued for another ten years after I left, and that among its future members were Godfrey Smith, Alan Brien, Al Alvarez, John McGrath, Derwent May, George Macbeth and Anthony Thwaite. It would seem that in later years the practice of inviting a literary figure to dinner and to give a talk was dropped in favour of informal meetings where members brought their own liquor and read their own works. After that it was hardly surprising that the club failed to survive.

My own writing, meanwhile, was having its ups and downs. *Lieutenant*, a sequel to *Sub-Lieutenant*, had found no takers, nor had *His Excellency*, another play. The *Isis* launched a short story competition which I entered for fun under an assumed name. Mine was not a story aimed to bring about suspension of disbelief – an unlikely little tale about a sailor with a hangover left behind in his ship on the eve of its destruction in the Bikini atoll atom bomb tests – although re-reading it today I recognize its pace and tension. 'There were nine entries,' said Gwil Owen, the editor of *Isis*, when I came into the office, 'and this one' – handing me my entry – 'is the only one with any merit.' I owned up and it was duly published. Fired by this modest success, I wrote more stories and in the course of the next couple of years had them accepted by the *New Statesman*, the *Strand*, *English Story*, Cyril Connolly's *Horizon* and – best of all – the *New Yorker*.

From time to time I visited my mother at Hampton Court Palace. Living with her at this time was our old family nanny whom we called Nanny-Noo. Then well over eighty, she had in her youth been my mother's nanny (and still sometimes referred to her as

---

[1] Evelyn Waugh touched on this in reply to a letter I wrote asking him to expand on his 'be a roadsweeper' remark. 'Under present conditions,' he said, 'daily journalism would be positively harmful to a man seeking to prepare himself for the work of a creative writer.' He went on: 'I may add that I think it important for a writer to keep in practice, as a pianist plays scales. If you have no imaginative theme in your mind demanding expression, write hard and often nonetheless.' After suggesting beginning with a biography, he concluded: 'If you are obliged to earn a living, choose a trade or profession which will bring you in touch with the widest variety of people and places, and will afford physical privacy, and some leisure.'

Miss Rosalind), nanny to various cousins and, on occasions, nanny to my sisters and myself. I had never thought of her as anything other than Nanny and was quite surprised one day when my mother told me her name was Rose Ashdown: it seemed unlikely.

Nanny's appearance from as far back as I could remember was unchanging: brown eyes, grey hair and a stoop. I had the happiest memories of her, for she was one of the kindest, gentlest souls there has ever been. Unlike other nannies, she never nagged or lost her temper. She always called me 'Dear' or 'Dear boy'. If she wanted one to eat something particularly unappetizing, she would say it was good for the blood, and the nearest she ever came to a show of authority was to say 'Make haste, dear' when faced with procrastinations which would have driven any other nanny demented. She had a choice phrase for describing those of my playmates who had made a good impression on her. 'Such a nice boy, madam. He responds and aspires.' When some minor illness had confined me to bed, she would say, 'The boy must lie quiet, madam, and take plenty of fluids,' and she would keep me supplied with muslin-covered jugs of fresh lemonade. Once, when I was in bed for ten days, she helped me build a Spanish ship.

One winter evening around teatime one of the Palace security men came to the door to say that Nanny had fallen over one of the iron wastepaper bins in the Palace gardens, and hurt herself quite badly. Presently two other of the Palace staff carried her into the house and up to her room. She was clearly in a state of shock, and moaning with pain. The doctor was sent for and arrived surprisingly quickly. He said he thought she had broken her hip and must go at once to hospital. He gave her an injection and telephoned for an ambulance.

Sitting on one side of Nanny's bed with my mother on the other, I remember how shocked I was by what had happened. For more than twenty years I had looked on Nanny, not as a person with hopes and desires and emotions of her own, but as a never-changing pillar of strength, a never-failing source of love and gentleness. Now she was made plain, an old, frail, injured woman named Rose Ashdown: there was something about her suffering which I found deeply distressing.

By the time the ambulance had arrived, the injection had taken effect and she had ceased moaning. Two men came in carrying a stretcher. They lifted Nanny on to the stretcher and then strapped her injured leg so that she could not move it. They worked with a cool, matter-of-fact precision. Then my mother put together a little bundle of Nanny's overnight things – a nightdress, bedroom slippers, hairbrush and wash bag. I had never seen these before and in some odd way felt I should not be seeing them now, as if I had stumbled on private love letters.

The men took Nanny downstairs and lifted her into the ambulance. I asked them where they were taking her and they said Kingston Hospital. Although this was no more than a ten-minute drive, I could not bear the thought of Nanny going there alone, and on an instinct asked the driver if I could come too. Hardly looking at me, he said, 'Jump in, mate.'

We set off. There was a full moon shining so brightly that its light penetrated the smoked windowpane and suffused the knees of the second ambulance man and myself with a violet glow. Presently I became aware of Nanny stirring in the shadows. Then I heard her say, 'What's this?' It didn't sound like her speaking at all. The ambulance man leaned forward and said, 'It's all right, lady, you just lie back and rest. We're taking you along to the hospital and everything's going to be all right.' I was aware then of a significant pause, after which Nanny said, 'You want my money, don't you? I've hidden it.' This was followed by a sort of manic laugh and then Nanny said, with all the suddenness of an exploding bomb, 'You buggers!'

The ambulance man leaned forward again and took hold of Nanny's arm to comfort her. It was a well-meant but mistaken gesture. The touch of another's hand gave her mania an external reality. With the quick instinctive movement of one trapped, she rose so that the top of her head was caught in the light from the moon and her grey wisps of hair glowed violet. 'You keep your hands to yourself, you filthy bugger,' she said; and then the ambulance was drenched in a flow of invective and abuse with oath following oath and obscenity on obscenity. It was like a sewer pipe bursting; memories from way back that froze the imagination, things observed and experienced in nearly a century of living. It continued unceasing as the ambulance drew up at the emergency entrance to the hospital and while she was being taken out of it. A nurse standing in the doorway received the full blast. 'Effing cow!' Nanny cried as she sailed past. The nurse took from me the bundle of overnight things. 'We'll let you know how she is in the morning,' she said with a smile, as though being called an effing cow happened to her every day.

I went abroad next day and was away for a month, but heard of Nanny's progress in letters from my mother. There had been fears that she might become bedridden, but the broken hip healed well, and within a few weeks she was back at the Palace. On none of her visits to the hospital had my mother noticed any peculiarity of behaviour.

When I came back myself and was walking from the station across the bridge that leads to the Palace gates, I felt a great uneasiness about meeting Nanny again. Did she know or had some busybody at the hospital told her what I knew? And if she did, was she going to refer to it, and if so, how? I prayed not, because if she did, the cosy trusting relationship we had shared for more than twenty years would be changed for ever.

She was sitting at the kitchen table when I came in, looking much as she had always looked, on her lap some sewing.

'Hallo, Nanny,' I said, and went over and kissed her.

She looked up.

'Hallo, dear. Your mother's gone to Kingston. She said to start tea if she wasn't back when you arrived.'

'How are you, Nanny?'

'Well, I've been poorly, you know. But I'm right as rain now. Never better. You're looking well, I must say. All that foreign sunshine would do you good.'

I looked into her eyes for the thing I hoped I would not see; and saw only what I had known and cherished through the years.

'Come and sit down, dear boy,' she said. 'Here are some crumpets for your tea. You always did like crumpets, didn't you?'

Looking recently through my scrapbook for this period I was astonished to find a letter from the Queen, then Princess Elizabeth, beginning 'Dear Ludo' in her own hand and thanking me for a copy of a book I had sent her as a wedding present. This reminded me of something I had entirely forgotten, a week in Edinburgh that summer when, as the guest of friends, I had met and danced four nights in a row with the two Princesses at the Assembly Rooms, Holyrood Palace and elsewhere and, in that brief period, come to know them a little; the King had also talked to me about my father, whom he had known in the Navy during the First World War, and about meeting him again when he inspected the fleet in Scapa Flow in October 1939. At that time I was a keen and quite competent exponent of Scottish reels and country dances at which the two Princesses, especially Margaret, seventeen then and wonderfully attractive, were also accomplished performers.

I went to France soon after, but on my return to England a few weeks later for the beginning of the Oxford term I was told by my mother that the King's equerry, Group Captain Peter Townsend, had been on the line from Balmoral, and would I please call him? I did, and was told that the King and Queen had invited me to spend a few days there. It was not a party, he stressed, just the two Princesses and a man called Fane: he very much hoped I could come.

On past form the reader might think that this was the sort of new and unusual experience I was always seeking, and that I would have lost no time in accepting. Had I been one of a party, I think I would have done. But nothing that had happened in my life so far had quite prepared me for joining such a gathering. I could tell myself that this was one of the most ordinary of families in that they were easy-going, natural, unassuming. But they were also something else. To me the divinity that hedged a king – and his family – was very real, and in bed that night, imagining life at Balmoral, I was assailed by feelings of inadequacy. What to do or say when I got there, how to comport myself? In waking nightmares I came down to breakfast with shaving soap on my ears and my flies undone, appeared in the wrong clothes, set fire to my sheets with a cigarette, sounded off during a break in conversation at the dinner-table, peppered the King with shot on the grouse-moor – scenarios that all added up to the same thing, *fear of making a bad impression*. But why so obsessed about impressions? Because, I reflected ruefully, that is how it had always been, the childhood straw to stop myself from drowning. If I took myself rather too seriously, I suppose it was because I feared that no one else would.

Nothing ventured, nothing lost; and in the morning I called Townsend to say I hoped I might be excused but the invitation clashed with the beginning of the Oxford term. It was a genuine excuse because it was true; and although I had few doubts that the Dean of Christ Church would have given me leave of absence had I asked, I had no wish to do so. However unenterprising my decision, that is how things were at the time.

At the beginning of my last term, when considering what to do after going down, I received a note from the historian A. L. Rowse at All Souls. Would I care to call on him to discuss a proposal that might be of interest? Intrigued, I accepted. He said he had been asked by Odhams, who normally published text-books but were now going into general publishing, to commission a number of books on historical subjects. He had read *Sub-Lieutenant* and some of my reviews in *Isis* and wondered if I would be interested in writing a book on Nelson's captains. I was flattered and pleased, both at having been asked at all, and because Nelson had long been my principal historical hero. At Eton I had chosen Southey's *Life of Nelson* for one of my English literature prizes.

Next came the problem which had been aired at so many Writers' Club meetings: how to support oneself while writing? — for although there was to be an advance against royalties on exchange of contracts, and I had a very small private income, together they would not be enough to live on. Then another piece of luck came my way. Bill Richmond, who was leaving Cambridge at the same time, had heard of a vacancy for a librarian at Ashridge Adult Educational College: the librarian would be fully occupied at weekends when the courses took place, looking after lecturers and guests, but Mondays to Thursdays would be more or less his own. I lost no time in applying, and having been interviewed by the Principal, General Sir Bernard Paget, and the Chairman of the Educational Council, Dr Arthur Bryant, I was offered and accepted the job.

And because both the job and the book on Nelson's captains had reflected so precisely what Evelyn Waugh had advised, I wrote to tell him so. 'Delighted to hear of your well-planned start,' he replied on a postcard. 'The architecture of Ashridge is all that can be desired and from what I hear of the goings-on there at weekends it should make an ideal setting for a novel.' And he added generously, 'I greatly enjoyed your stories in *Horizon* and the *New Statesman*'.

Ashridge stands in its own extensive grounds on a wooded crest of the Hertfordshire countryside, a few miles from Berkhamsted and hard by the golf course made famous by Henry Cotton. It is a huge grey pile in nineteenth-century Gothic, built for the Earl of Bridgewater in 1808 by James Wyatt, who performed much the same service for Mr Beckford at Fonthill. In mediaeval times Ashridge was a monastery whose occupants, according to the records, spent much of their time drinking, fighting with jugs, playing practical jokes on visitors and having women from St Albans to stay the night. On the dissolution of the monasteries, Henry VIII had Ashridge converted into a palace, and the future Queen Elizabeth spent some of her childhood there.

After the First World War the place was bought by a Mr Urban Broughton who endowed it as a college for adult education in memory of his friend Bonar Law. Although it was supposed to be non-political, the chairman (Stanley Baldwin) and members of the governing body were all Conservatives, so that while organizations connected with the Conservative Party held courses there (I remember my father going over for an agents' course), those connected with the Labour Party did not. However after the Second World War (when it was used as a hospital), the new charter said the education was to be 'uninfluenced by bias or loyalty towards any political party'; and on those conditions General Paget and Dr Bryant agreed to serve.

The courses lasted from Friday night to Monday morning (though sometimes there were weekly courses too) and were catholic in subject – Music, the Sea, Agriculture, the Law, Britain's economy, the Commonwealth and Europe, the Theatre, etc. Each course consisted of four lectures, two on Saturday and two on Sunday, followed by discussion groups and questions. The guests – some sixty or seventy at a time – were a mixed lot. There was the usual sprinkling of lonely-hearts, mostly widows and spinsters, less in search of education than company, one or two servicemen and civil servants from Whitehall, several retired people, workers from both sides of industry, the odd sixth-former, and always a few foreigners. One morning I arrived at breakfast to find a Turk heaping butter and mustard on his porridge.

I was given a study of my own on the first floor and a bedroom nearby; all the beds were on wheels, however, a legacy from the hospital days, so that if at all restless in the night one was apt to wake up the other side of the room. There were only three of us on the teaching staff, so at weekends one was on the go almost continually, taking turns to chair the lectures, organize the discussion groups and look after the guests. My only duties in the week were to run the library, which I did in a fairly *ad hoc* fashion, having had no previous training or experience, and to edit the *Ashridge Quarterly*, a magazine which contained transcripts of the best of the lectures and to which I contributed brief, windy editorials. Both the General (a darling man but short of views on adult education) and the director of studies (a delightful, bald, chain-smoking ex-Army Education Corps colonel) were happy to let me run the library and edit the magazine as I wanted. As a result I had plenty of time to push on with my book on Nelson's captains – though initially this meant visiting museums in London and elsewhere in search of archive material.

Glancing recently through the four *Ashridge Quarterly*s I edited, I was interested to see how many of the contributors, then well-known names, are almost unknown today. Who under the age of forty now is familiar with the works of Nigel Balchin, Ronald Knox, C. E. M. Joad, Roger Fulford, G. M. Young, Hannen Swaffer, James Laver, William Haley? But many of their talks read well, even now; and when I could not reprint a talk in full, I'd include some of its more informative aphorisms: 'A third of the causes of all illnesses in this country are psychiatric in origin. This is not an opinion but a statement of fact', 'Every other person who goes to prison has been there before' – and one that I knew to be true from painful experience, 'A human being's strongest motivating power is not the sex urge and not the power urge, but the desire to give and receive affection, admiration and praise'.

One of the wittiest talks was called 'The Needs of Youth' and given by a wonderful old girl called Dr Macalister Brew, educational adviser to the National Association of Youth Clubs. 'I do not propose in this talk,' she said, 'to touch on the best way of explaining to youth the facts of life. But I only hope that you do not do it in the way my father did it to me, which was to take me into his study and explain all the facts at great length and in some detail. Then he said, "Now I want you to understand that everybody does that – *except the Queen and your mother*."'

With the guests I can recall only two awkward moments. The first was when giving a concert on gramophone records. In those days symphonies were recorded on both sides of four twelve-inch records, and I somehow managed to put on the records of a Beethoven symphony in entirely the wrong order. Several times

I braced myself to apologize until I realized that none of the audience was aware of anything amiss.

A more embarrassing moment occurred with my predecessor as librarian, Leslie Paul. Leslie had lectured on Modern English Poets on Sunday afternoon, and we gave a joint reading of them in the evening. This included extracts from Eliot's *Four Quartets*, and at the end I thought our audience might enjoy Henry Reed's parody of Eliot, *Chard Whitlow*. It was not until afterwards that I realized they did not know what parody meant, so that when I began, 'As we get older, we do not get any younger', and paused for the collective chuckle, none came. That line, the silence seemed to say, was a profound truth, one that they often proclaimed themselves and much more understandable than the Eliot that had been read to them earlier. Manfully I pushed on,

> 'Seasons return and today I am fifty-five,
> And this time last year I was fifty-four,
> And this time next year I shall be sixty-two'

Silence again. I looked up and saw baffled faces that seemed to say, There must be some reason why this man says that next year he will be seven years older than he is this year, though we do not know what it is; but he is a poet, and poets write in riddles, so we must give him the benefit of the doubt. It was like that right to the end; and afterwards I began to think we had been too clever by half. Would I, eight years ago in the *Tartar*, have been able to distinguish between *Burnt Norton* and *Chard Whitlow* on hearing them for the first time? Probably not.

Sometimes in mid-week I drove over to Hampton Court Palace to lunch or dine with my mother. She was involved in many pursuits: children's amateur theatricals; King George's Fund for Sailors; the Bach Choir and, when it came round, Poppy Day. The children's theatricals consisted of an annual production of Thackeray's *The Rose and the Ring* in the Palace Oak Room, an activity that allowed her to order little people about without the slightest fear of mutiny: a clapping of hands followed by the cry of 'Silence, everyone!' were sounds I often used to hear coming from rehearsals in the drawing-room. She also entertained fairly frequently, and among her regular guests were Dr Jaques, the conductor of the Bach Choir, and Bob Boothby, whose obscene anecdotes embarrassed and political reminiscences delighted his fellow guests. Guests who came by public transport and hadn't been before were invariably asked by my mother what route they had taken, and were apt to be told, 'Oh, that's *miles* out of the way. When you go back, you want to . . .' and there followed instructions of bus and tube connections far too long and detailed (as they sometimes confided to me afterwards) for any well-lunched guest to memorize. But it provided my mother with another opportunity to impose her will on others.

In addition to the dog Ben, now nearing the end of his days, which he passed mostly in an old suitcase marked No.1 underneath the kitchen dresser, she also had a cat called Wolsey. When the *son et lumière* performances of the history of the Palace began, Wolsey, as befitted his name, became a devotee. With an uncanny sense of timing, he left by the cat-window a few minutes before the show was due to begin, settled himself comfortably near the front row, and returned as soon as it was over. I often wondered what he saw in it.

It was about this time that my sisters and I noted the curious vocabulary of personal clichés that my mother was now increasingly adopting, and we started collecting them:

'We *foregathered* at *crack*' (met early in the morning), *tapped* (joined) the A1 at Hatfield, and made a *tryst* (rendezvous) for breakfast.'

'Shall we *lush up to* (splash out on) champagne?'

'My dear, I'm *radiant*' (happy). Once to Ben, eating his dinner, 'He's *yagging* (wagging) because he's *radiant* with his sheep's head.'

'Would you like some *grit on the tongue?*' (sugar).

'This is like *weasel's pee*' (a weak drink).

'Are you *wilting/champing/yearning?*' (for food).

'For supper, *Kalter auschnitz* (cold cuts) or *hoosh-magoo-magrundy?*' (left-overs warmed up).

'If you *delve/rummage/routle* in the drawer, you may find it *lurking*. Or it could be *perched* on the shelf.'

'Is he *quite?*' (a gentleman).

'Have they *tucked up?*' (made love).

'He was *mast-high*' (in a state of euphoria).

'Is she a *spin?*' (spinster).

And if very surprised by some news, she would exclaim either 'God's Teeth!' or 'Yesu Chreest!'

One evening when a cousin was staying, the suggestion was made that we go into Kingston after dinner to see the ballet film,

The Red Shoes. I wasn't too keen myself, but as my mother and the cousin wanted to go and the alternative was spending the evening with Ben and Wolsey, I agreed to accompany them. I had never seen a ballet, but had a gut feeling that I would not enjoy it. In the event the ballet was incidental; for what I had not bargained for was the impact the star of the film, the dancer Moira Shearer, would make on me. In the same way as Lord Bootle had a thing about butlers, I had always had a thing about red hair. At my prep school, as the reader may recall, I had first hero-worshipped an older boy with red hair and later had a crush on a younger boy with the same. Now here was this apparition with the reddest of red hair, a figure like an hour glass, blue-green eyes the size of saucers, the prettiest of noses and a most pleasing voice. And, if that weren't enough, she danced with a grace and lightness that were breathtaking; and her death under the wheels of a train in Monte Carlo station was almost more than one could bear. On the way home, my mother said, 'Well, I enjoyed that mast-high. How about you two?' The cousin was also mast-high, but I said nothing for I was already in love. During the next few weeks I brooded constantly and was not helped by meeting others who had also seen the film and felt (or so they said) as I did. I wanted to meet this girl more than anyone in the world, but the chances of doing so were infinitesimal. Only a miracle could bring it about.

And, then, amazingly, the miracle happened. On visits to naval archives in London at this time, I was seeing something of Pauline Pitt-Rivers whose husband Julian, an Oxford friend, was on an archaeological dig in Spain. One day she told me that her mother, the actress Hermione Baddeley, had been asked to judge the fancy dress at the coming Sadler's Wells–Old Vic ball, and had been given two complimentary tickets: would Pauline like them? Would we like them? asked Pauline. I said I was easy and so did she. We decided to give it a whirl and leave when we had had enough.

On such seemingly trivial decisions do our destinies sometimes depend, for when we reached the Lyceum ballroom and had been shown up to the box where Hermione Baddeley and other principal guests were assembled, who should also be there but the red-haired beauty from *The Red Shoes*: she and Ralph Richardson were going to present the prizes. I felt a tremor run through me when I caught sight of her. She looked even lovelier than in the film, her hair dazzling in its richness, and was holding herself as upright as ballet dancers do: it was an aesthetic pleasure just to look at her.

I longed to introduce myself (in that press of people there was no question of anyone else doing it) but at first was too shy. What would this beautiful, successful, sophisticated creature have in common with me? So I stood on one foot and then on the other, and once or twice started out in her direction before thinking better of it, then cleared my throat and lit a cigarette and went to the edge to observe the dancers below; eventually, realizing that if I did not make a move soon the opportunity would vanish for ever, I walked boldly up, gabbled my name, and said in a rush, 'Would you like to dance?'

I had half hoped she might refuse, opening the way to conversation, however awkward it might turn out. But it was not to be. 'I'd love to,' she said.

As I followed her down the stair to the dance floor, I thought, This is madness. Here am I who can just about manage quick-quick-slow so long as I am not also expected to chat, having the effrontery to beg a dance from a woman whose fame as a dancer is already well-known. We reached the edge of the floor, and I wished I was almost anywhere else. I put one hand in hers and the other round her waist (Oh, boy!). Then she said, 'Before we start, I must tell you something.' What could it be? 'I don't dance very well,' she said.

How to react? It was a joke, of course, but surely a rum sort of joke? Where exactly was the humour in saying you didn't dance very well when dancing well was what you were known for? Still, because *I* couldn't see the joke didn't mean that there *wasn't* a joke. So I put my head back and gave a kind of silent manic laugh.

We set off, and within a step or two it was clear she couldn't dance for toffee; she was as rigid as a telegraph pole and quite unwilling to be led; she trod on my feet, pushed me, and came within an ace of tripping us up. Several times we had to stop and re-start, and the end of the number came as a divine relief: there could be no question of hanging around to wait for the next. As we made for the stairs leading to the box and she prettily gathered up her skirt, she said, 'Well, I did warn you, didn't I?' I nodded. 'You see,' she said, 'I've only done that sort of dancing once or twice. Does that surprise you?' I said it did.

But at least the ice had been broken, and though I did not have the nerve to ask for her telephone number before the evening was out, I knew that the Opera House would always find her. But I took my time in following things up. Was this girl not really out of my class? Did she not live in a world more cosmopolitan than any I had known? If I started dating her, would she not expect to be taken to places that, on a regular basis, would be more than I could afford? Then I remembered (how could I forget?) our dance: could her ignorance of ballroom dancing belong to someone as sophisticated as I believed? After a fortnight of dithering I decided that whatever the difficulties, I had to see her again – though I did wonder if she would remember me. So I sent a postcard to Covent Garden suggesting a date for dinner; and she sent one back saying she was dancing that night, so it would have to be after the performance. I booked a table at the Savoy Grill: she could hardly baulk at that.

And so began our courtship, and before long I discovered that far from being the worldly creature I had imagined, she was in fact quite unworldly, had led a very sheltered life and even now, at the age of twenty-three, was still living at home (the only child) with Mum and Dad. Dad was a civil engineer working at the Admiralty, a tall, mild, handsome man whom I remember as being full of laughter, though often I couldn't figure out just what he was laughing at. Mum was small and very Scottish, with a will of iron within her family, though somewhat mouse-like without; it was she, recognizing Moira's talents as a child, who had pushed her into the ballet and who in true Scots fashion had kept her to the sort of disciplined regime that commitment to ballet demands. So that the film star image that I (or rather *The Red Shoes*) had created of a Moira lunching daily at the Mirabelle or Caprice, flying to Paris for weekends, always surrounded by admirers, soon gave way to something quite different; an immensely hard-working girl who spent every morning limbering up at the barre, most afternoons at rehearsal and half the evenings of each week performing; after which it was back by tube to the flat for a meal prepared by Mum, often followed by the washing or darning of tights. No time for ballroom dancing. This was hardly glamorous, but to me a great relief.

For the next two months we met every week or ten days, either in London for dinner (she rarely ate lunch) or sometimes, when she was not dancing, at Ashridge for the weekend: the General adored her and called her 'My fairy'. All this time I never ceased to marvel at her beauty and the way people looked at her when she came into a room. Oddly, though, instead of this giving her the self-assurance one would have expected, she saw it as something that marked her out from others, and became acutely self-conscious. Nor could she cope with compliments on her looks or dancing: they made her – to the *chagrin* of those who gave them – uncomfortable and embarrassed. Congratulated on a particular performance, she would invariably find some fault with it.

The day before she and the company were due to leave on a tour to Florence and Turkey, I picked her up at Covent Garden to take her to lunch with my mother at Hampton Court. What happened that day was what happened to the suitor of John Betjeman's Joan Hunter-Dunn. After reaching home the night before, we had stayed in the car park until a quarter to one. Now, as we drove down Bow Street, I asked if her mother had commented on her lateness. 'Yes,' she said, 'she was waiting up,' and then, 'I don't think she was altogether happy.' I have since told Moira that that remark of hers was her way of bringing me to the post – the unconscious speaking to the unconscious. Whether unconscious or deliberate, it had its effect. I couldn't bear the thought of Moira's mother being unhappy; so, on the spur of the moment, I turned the car into Tavistock Street and stopped outside a greengrocer called V. Coffey (as I discovered later) and behind a van unloading Brussels sprouts. Moira says that I then leaned over and said (though I have no recollection of it), 'Are you ready?', to which she replied, 'How do you mean?' To this I said (which I do remember), 'Will you marry me?' and she said, 'Well, yes.' We then drove in total silence the seventeen miles to Hampton Court.

In July Moira and I in one car and my sister Katherine and her husband Ion Calvocoressi in another, motored to a villa we had taken at Opio near Grasse in the south of France. We encountered Gallic understatement in Rouen where the Guide Michelin described the almost devastated cathedral as '*très touchée*', and overstatement in a field near Roanne where a perfectly ordinary dog-show was described as '*Exposition Canine Internationale de Sud-Est*'. And at a café in Tournon where we had lunch I heard a man decline the offer of a further dish with the words, '*Merci, je suis* full-up.'

My father as Commander, 1916.

Aged two with my mother.

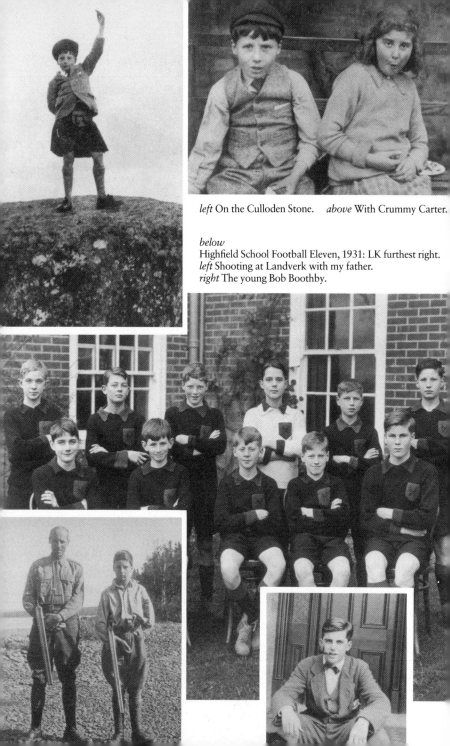

left On the Culloden Stone.   *above* With Crummy Carter.

below
Highfield School Football Eleven, 1931: LK furthest right.
left Shooting at Landverk with my father.
right The young Bob Boothby.

The Fourth of June at Eton, with my mother and sisters Morar and Katherine.

The flight to Le Touquet. From the left: Alan Tyser, Michael Evans, LK, Philip Denison, John Pelham.

Eton leaving photograph.

above right My father at Belgrave Crescent before sailing on his last voyage.
above HMS *Rawalpindi* in action with the German battleships *Scharnhorst* and *Gneisenau*. From the painting by Norman Wilkinson.

With Spider Wilson on *Tartar's* bridge.

HMS *Tartar*.

The raid on the Lofoten Islands, 1941. Taken with my grandmother's postcard-size folding Kodak camera through the barrels of the pom-pom gun.

Admiral Gunther Lütjens (left) and his staff officers before embarking in *Bismarck*, 1941.

Bismarck at anchor near Bergen on the eve of her break-out into the Atlantic. Taken from *Prinz Eugen*

The end of HMS *Mashona*

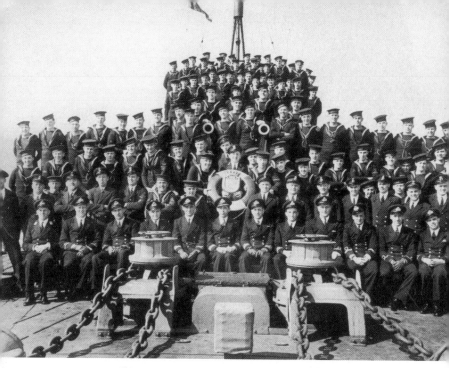

Ship's company, HMS *Tartar*. LK front row, third from left.

As ADC to the Governor of Newfoundland.

The villa was charming, an old building on the side of a hill a little way down a lane, and a tiny garden with fig and orange trees and a swimming-pool which took all of three strokes from end to end. Here lived the resident couple Charles and Josette with Gerard, aged two, a couple of friendly flea-bitten dogs called Bobby and Folette, and a cat, very thin. We asked Charles why there were so few oranges on the orange trees and he said they had been mostly picked by the previous tenant whom he called 'Sir Olivier'. Was it true, he asked, that Sir Olivier was a great English painter? No, we said, he was a great English actor: why a painter? Because he had spent much of his time here painting, said Charles, and he had heard it said that Sir Olivier was *un très grand artiste*.

We spent a lazy two weeks, swimming in the sea and in the little pool, reading, exploring restaurants in Mougins and St Paul de Vence, and one memorable day, as a result of an introduction from Cyril Connolly, lunching with the writer Willie Maugham at the Villa Mauresque at Cap Ferrat. At this time Maugham was one of my literary heroes: his beguiling style, lofty yet confiding, was one I much envied and had tried to use as a model for my own; and it was an odd sensation to see on the entrance gate the evil eye sign so familiar from the title-pages of his books. It was a sophisticated gathering of perhaps eight or ten people, and although Moira was looking stunning, neither of us felt wholly at ease. After lunch the old boy, now wizened as a walnut, was good enough to take me aside and engage in literary conversation. A writer must write from his own experiences, he said, and the more of human activities and relationships he experienced, the richer his writing; and he had this advantage over his fellows in being able to purge himself of painful or shameful memories by putting them into fiction. The greatest novelists in the world were Tolstoy, Dostoyevsky, Dickens and Balzac, because their range and depth of characterization were greater than those of other novelists. Writing a play was a knack: many successful novelists like Henry James had failed as playwrights simply because they didn't have the knack. If I had read most of this before, in the pages of *The Summing-Up* and elsewhere, it in no way diminished the pleasure of hearing it from his own lips. I doubt if he had read a word I had written, so he had no need to single me out in this way.

We motored home by the Route Napoleon, the way the

Emperor had gone after his arrival at Frèjus from Elba in 1815. Past Grasse and Digne and Serres and Grenoble the road leads over bare, pink quartz-like mountains and through broad empty valleys under a huge expanse of sky; on no other artery in France is there such a sense of space and freedom. At Laragne, where we breakfasted, the patron of the Restaurant des Terrasses advised us to make a detour beyond Serres along the road to Gap, then at Veynes to take a little secondary road across the hills to join the Gap-Grenoble road at Corps. He said it would be a detour worth making, and it was. For the first part we climbed steeply upwards, running beside a fast mountain stream, turning and twisting and skirting huge ledges of overhanging rock. Then a broad valley opened up leading to a high, flat plateau of cultivated land. Here were crops and cattle grazing and lush fields bright with alpine flowers, and beyond them jagged mountains, their tops still white with snow, their sides a rich ochre reminiscent of the Red Hills of Skye. The wildness of the mountains and the soft hues of the fields made a pleasing contrast. Beyond the plateau the road fell sharply into another gorge, even steeper than on the ascent, a country of rocks and thick pinewoods and tumbling water. We came down at last into Corps and the great dam over the Drac: in the hour we had taken to cover twenty miles we had not met a single car.

We joined the main road at Pont de Claix, south of Grenoble, and at once met other British cars hurrying south whose owners in those far-off, unsophisticated days hooted and waved to show they were British, we were British, and how splendid it all was. Next evening we arrived in Paris, where outside the Madeleine cinema Moira saw, to her dismay, a full size effigy of herself wearing a real tutu. *The Red Shoes* marched on.

I was back at Ashridge in August, but not for long. The college had been steadily losing money, and now the General and Dr Bryant had been told by Lord Davidson, Baldwin's old crony and chairman of the governing body, that they were bringing in as residents the members of a girls' finishing school called The House of Citizenship. This was not to the liking of Dr Bryant and the Educational Council who had always insisted that no one class of people should predominate, and they resigned en masse. The General fought a rearguard action for some time but was eventually told to hand over his duties to the bursar; and in

September the three of us on the teaching staff were given a month's notice.

In many ways this suited well, for Moira and I were to be married in the New Year, and I would have been leaving before Christmas anyway. So I moved in to the top floor of my mother's apartment at Hampton Court Palace, and when Moira had time off we went house-hunting in London. We met some rum people. A very old man who owned a flat in Campden Hill showed us round twice but on both occasions avoided a particular door. When I asked where it led, he leaned towards me conspiratorially and whispered so that Moira couldn't hear, 'It's the gentleman's WC.' A woman who said she had been to dancing classes in Edinburgh with my mother volunteered the information that she had a house in the country called 'Gracious Pond'. And there was the *memsahib* of a flat in Pont Street, full of Victorian furniture and bric-à-brac, whose husband had recently died after a lifetime in the service of the Raj. As we walked through the rooms she spoke of him and their life together almost continually, and on entering a room overlooking the back, she turned dramatically and said, 'And there is my husband.' We half expected to see him come through the door but found ourselves looking instead at an oil portrait of an immensely old and jaded-looking lion. Further inspection revealed a tiny bust of her husband perched on a shelf beneath.

In the end we found what we were looking for in a charming small house in Clabon Mews, just off Cadogan Square. It consisted of a drawing-room cum dining-room and garage on the ground floor and three small bedrooms above. On the day we exchanged contracts I heard that a 1950 Rockefeller Foundation Atlantic Award in Literature, for which I had applied on leaving Ashridge, had been granted me: it was not a fortune but would help to cover household expenses while I was completing my book on Nelson's captains.

We were married on 25 February 1950 in the Chapel Royal of Hampton Court Palace, where I had already given away my two sisters. Bill Richmond, who had been narrowly defeated in the general election two days before, standing for Churchill's old seat in Oldham, was best man; Bob Boothby proposed our health and mercifully kept it clean. Moira was given away by her father: their car arrived so early they had to make several circuits of the pond in Bushey Park before arriving at the chapel. Moira's dress had been made by the woman who had also made her dresses for *The Red Shoes*. She carried a bouquet of jasmine, orange blossom and lilies of the valley, but had no bridesmaids. The service was conducted by Canon Collins of St Paul's, a friend of Moira's father and later an activist in CND. The photographer Baron took the photographs (including a private one of me doing an *entrechat* on the Vecchio staircase); and we had a reception for 250 in the Palace Oak Room. The press were there in force and in next day's papers under such headlines as 'Red Shoes Star Weds Naval Hero's Son', they estimated that some two thousand people had crowded into the Palace courtyard to see Moira arrive and the two of us drive away. It was a wonderful, memorable, happy family day.

In the evening we flew to Paris for a night at the St Regis Hotel, and next evening caught the Barcelona Express to Perpignan where, in the morning, we changed into a local train for Vernet-les-Bains in the foothills of the Pyrenees. Why we chose Vernet, I can't remember, but we spent a blissful seven days in a hotel where yellow mimosa bloomed outside our bedroom window, and the maids, being so near to Spain, pronounced *chambre* as *shumburra*, and in the dining-room our fellow guests shouted Gallic witticisms over our heads; and we went for walks up Mont Canigou and drank Cinzano in the town's cafés and began to know each other a little better (though today, looking back, we are agreed we hardly knew each other at all). And then suddenly it was over, and it was home to Clabon Mews and *Sleeping Beauty* and *Nelson's Band of Brothers*, and whatever else the slumbering future might bring.

PART TWO

12

To America with the Ballet

So far this has been a book about a private person, known only to family and friends: it has been about the closed worlds of school and college and the Navy, about innocence and the loss of innocence and the puzzlement of personal relationships. I half ceased to be a private person when I married Moira because she was known to the public. Yet in time, as journalist, broadcaster and author, I too would be known to the public; and how that came about and what resulted from it forms the second half of this book.

At first, in a back room of Clabon Mews, I ploughed on with *Nelson's Captains* while Moira continued to dance: this included performances at Covent Garden and in the film *The Tales of Hoffman*, as well as a three-week visit to Paris to play the part of Carmen in Roland Petit's Ballet de Paris. I attended two of her performances at the Marigny Theatre and at one of them heard the man next to me pay Moira a charming and untranslatable compliment. '*Elle est très fragile*,' he said to his companion, '*avec la force de tonnerre.*'

Later that summer I was telephoned by a director of the *Sunday Times* by the name of William Mabane. Would I go and see him to discuss an article they wanted to commission? Would I not? In his office in Gray's Inn Road he elaborated. International tension was high: the Korean war had begun, the Iron Curtain had split Europe in two, while in Asia and elsewhere communism seemed to be slowly spreading out and expanding its empire. In Britain there was a feeling of despondency, even helplessness: people looked for a sign and found none. What did I and my generation think?

I had no idea what I or my generation thought, but by looking earnestly at the floor I tried to give Mr Mabane the impression that the matter was uppermost in my mind. Could I let him have a thousand words by Thursday? It was then Monday. 'Oh, I'm sure I could,' I said breezily, though I was never less sure of anything. On the way home I wondered how and why Mr Mabane had picked on me.

I have never been a speedy writer, and in those days my progress down a page was tortoise-like. In a haze of Turkish cigarette smoke I worked at the piece the rest of that day and all Tuesday and Wednesday, chiselling out draft after draft, agonizing over the shape of a paragraph or choice of a word. By Thursday morning I knew I could improve it no further, and being alternately astounded by its brilliance and ashamed of its inadequacy, I sent it to Mr Mabane in a taxi.

I called it 'A Time for Decision' and the general message was that while it was better to resist than submit to communist aggression (if that was the choice), the resistance would only be effective if we made up our minds beforehand to do so. I realized, I said, that this was unpalatable advice to those whose armour still hung upon the wall; 'but', I added, 'to reach a decision is to take positive action. It is in fact the only positive action we can take.' All in all it was pretty gung-ho stuff, ponderous and a little pompous, as much of my early writing was.

Astonishingly, though, it struck a chord, for in the middle of the week after publication Mr Mabane telephoned to say that the article had resulted in hundreds of letters of which they would be printing a large selection the following Sunday. They did this in a special four-column feature, accompanied by a supportive leading article and a separately printed letter from Desmond MacCarthy, David Cecil's father-in-law and the paper's chief literary critic. 'In times of trouble and suspense,' he wrote, 'I have seldom read an article more psychologically profound.' This was heady stuff; others were in the same vein. They ran a further batch of letters the next two Sundays followed by two more articles by a soldier and an industrialist respectively (both advocating a return to Christianity) all of which, together with my original article, were published in a special booklet. Quite unexpectedly my journalistic career had begun.

Nor could it have come at a better time, for when the *Sunday Times*'s editor, Harry Hodson, heard that I intended to accompany Moira on that autumn's Sadler's Wells Ballet tour of America, he at once commissioned a series of articles.

This was the second visit of the Sadler's Wells company to America, the first having taken place between our engagement and marriage the year before, and both sponsored by the Russian-born impresario, Sol Hurok. For Moira that first visit had not been altogether comfortable. Her natural shyness (often mistaken for aloofness), combined with Scottish reserve and even puritanism (once, when we were engaged, she scolded me for watching two dogs rogering on the pavement), had never made her relationship with other members of the company easy. This was compounded by her newly won fame as star of *The Red Shoes* which meant that when the company reached New York, hers was the only name the American public had heard of – indeed some referred to the company as the Moira Shearer ballet. None of this was calculated to gain her popularity with the corps de ballet; equally, although she now alternated with Margot Fonteyn in the leading classical parts, she could never be – and indeed never wanted to be – part of the tightly knit old guard (Ninette de Valois, Freddie Ashton, Bobby Helpmann and Margot herself) who had been the backbone of the company in the years before the war. It was with other leading dancers like Beryl Grey and Violetta Elvin that she felt most comfortable.

Things were better for her on the 1950 tour, both because I was around and also because Margot Fonteyn, with whom Moira shared a dressing-room as well as sleeping quarters on the company train, had now established herself in America, as in England, as the company's principal ballerina. After New York (where I finally finished off *Nelson's Band of Brothers*) the 120-strong company of dancers, administrators, orchestra and stage hands, together with the scenery for nine ballets, embarked in a special train for a series of one-night stands in huge 'Shrine' auditoriums, each seating more than five thousand people, returning after each performance to the train, with longer stops in hotels in the main cities. Altogether the company travelled some fifteen thousand miles, gave 153 performances in thirty-two states in a period of five months and was sold out almost everywhere beforehand. *The Times* called it one of the most exacting theatrical tours in history. The most popular ballets were the three fairy-tale classics, *Sleeping Beauty*, *Swan Lake* and *Giselle*, which some Americans had never seen; and there were ecstatic reviews in both national and local papers.

I followed as best I could in the small Austin car the Austin Motor Company had lent me, driving by way of Philadelphia and Birmingham, Alabama, to New Orleans, then west across Texas to Los Angeles. Near a place called Eutaw in Alabama I took a wrong turning which eventually led into a dirt road. Being very short of gas I stopped a Chevrolet coming in the opposite direction. By now it was almost dark, and to show the driver he had nothing to fear, I walked in front of his headlamps holding a map. It was a mistake. When I came abreast of the driver's door I observed an ugly, white, half-shaven, middle-aged face. Its owner took one look at me, put his foot on the accelerator and shot down the road. It was twenty minutes before another vehicle came, an ancient jeep driven by an old black man. He said that if I trailed him, he would lead me to the nearest gas station, seventeen miles away. I said I doubted if I had the gas to reach it. He said if I followed him to his home, he would give me a couple of gallons from a tin. After three or four miles we reached a shack by the roadside where he was as good as his word. I told him about the man in the Chevrolet and how I guessed he thought he was going to be robbed. He laughed. 'I ain't got nothing to be robbed,' he said. 'I just a poor farmer and reckon it's ma duty to help anyone got stuck on the road.' He refused any payment and responded to my profuse thanks with 'You're welcome, welcome, welcome.' I remembered a Southerner called Mrs Valentine whom I had met on the boat coming over and her saying how offended she had been at being addressed by a black man in her Paris hotel. When I asked why, she said, 'We think niggers are inferior.'

One thing I learnt on my journey across the country was that had I offered my *Sunday Times* article 'A Time for Decision' here, it would have found no readers. For here the people had already decided. The Korean War with its mounting casualties and the slow spread of communism across the globe with the threat it posed to American values had induced in the people a mood of fierce belligerence. 'You just can't do business with those guys,' was a phrase I often heard. 'They lie and they cheat. If they want a war, let's give 'em a war, and I say the sooner the better.' Internally the temper was the same, with the infamous McCarthy hearings in Washington rooting out communists and crypto-communists and past communists with a savagery reminiscent of the Salem witch-hunts. Not even the Sadler's Wells Ballet was immune, for on reaching Los Angeles I was told that in order that the delightful Russian-born ballerina Violetta Elvin might continue with the tour, she was obliged to fly back to London, have her passport validated by the Russian consul, then go to the American Embassy to swear she had never been a member of the Communist Party. Only then would she be allowed to return to the United States, no longer a menace to American society.

Elections for the Senate were in progress in Los Angeles, and I went to a big meeting in Union Square held for the local Democratic candidate, Mrs Helen Douglas. She was a handsome woman in a smart, black tailored coat and skirt and had a fine voice and commanding presence. 'My friends,' she said, 'we hear much talk these days of the threat of communism to the American way of life. But I want to tell you this. It's not enough just to hate communism. You all have to show both in word and deed that you love democracy.' Everyone clapped, myself included. Then she turned on her Republican opponent. 'This young boy,' she said scathingly, 'who thinks he knows so much about communism and doesn't know a thing. This *tricky, Dicky Nixon.*' The phrase would one day pass into political folklore, but this was the first time that I, or I guess most others present, had heard it. But for all Mrs Douglas's eloquence, tricky Dicky was about to outsmart her, beginning his climb to power on the backs of those like her whom he charged, often falsely, with being soft on communism.

The ballet played in Los Angeles for two weeks and was sold out for every performance. Charlie Chaplin and Greta Garbo came (though not together) to Moira's first *Sleeping Beauty* and I found myself sitting next to Artur Rubinstein the pianist. We were placed in the twelfth row which meant we could not see the dancers' feet. Mr Rubinstein said it was as important to see the dancers' feet in a ballet as it was unimportant to see a pianist's hands at a concert. After a recent concert of his, two ladies had told him how disappointed they had been not to see his hands but said they had consoled themselves by looking at his feet. I asked if he liked Tchaikovsky's music, and he said Yes, he was a genius and because of it you could accept lapses of taste which in other composers like Rachmaninov were unforgivable; but you had to take Tchaikovsky in small doses, whereas you could listen to Mozart all night. At a party afterwards Mr Rubinstein told Sol Hurok that the Union Jack and Stars and Stripes flanking the stage were irrelevant and vulgar. Hurok said he would remove them and next time I went they had gone.

One evening Moira and I were invited to dinner with Sam Goldwyn and his wife Frances to hear his plans for the making of *Hans Christian Andersen* in which he wanted Moira to dance and act, to music by Frank Loesser and choreography by George Balanchine. (We had been told about the project when Frances was in Europe earlier in the year, and when Moira asked about the character of the role she might play, Frances said, 'Why, you're just an abused and lovely thing.') Ninette de Valois had been invited too – I supposed so that Goldwyn could sweeten her up to obtain Moira's release. As soon as we arrived, Goldwyn took Moira and me aside and outlined the story. After all the aphorisms attributed to him ('a verbal contract isn't worth the paper it's printed on', etc.) I was impressed by his straightforward, intelligent, lively manner, and how he managed to tell the story without making it seem corny. He had a fund of anecdotes and in relating them, his face puckered up like Popeye's. He said he'd tried to buy the film rights of all George Bernard Shaw's plays, but Shaw had sold them to Pascal: when he'd taxed Shaw on this, Shaw had said, 'Well, I heard the movie business was run by crooks so I thought I'd sell them to the biggest.' After dinner he showed us *Wuthering Heights* with Laurence Olivier as Heathcliff and Merle Oberon as Cathy. We were all very moved by the death of Cathy. Goldwyn said it was the finest picture he'd ever made. 'But we had to shoot Heathcliff's return fourteen times. Thirteen times Olivier ranted. There was no occasion for ranting. The last time he got it right.'

On one of Moira's days off we were given lunch by an MGM executive called Arthur Hornblow who took us round the MGM lot. I was astonished by the size and number of sets: a French village street, a house in Kent, a town in the wild west, a street in Tudor England, a park in New York, a quayside in the Mediterranean, a Chicago slum. Hornblow said that in the dry Californian climate it was possible to keep the sets up indefinitely. On an artificial lawn we met Spencer Tracy making a film called *Father's Little Dividend*. The dividend in question was a baby called Dinah. 'It's the darnedest thing,' said Tracy, 'but we're not allowed to shoot the kid for more than thirty seconds at a time. The mother stands by the director with a stop-watch and when she says "Stop", everything has to stop. That's state law.' On another set we met Red Skelton who was making a film called *Excuse my Dust*. He told Moira he'd seen *The Red Shoes* every evening for two weeks except Fridays and Sundays when he had his radio show, and when he heard Moira had married, he was so upset he went outside and cut down a rosebush.

Another time Freddie Ashton, Alexis Rassine, Moira and myself were invited to spend a day with Christopher Isherwood, and as an admirer of his Berlin stories I greatly looked forward to it. Isherwood lived in a bungalow close to others near the Santa Monica beach. We arrived at noon, as suggested, swam in the sea which was dirty and crowded, then returned *chez* Isherwood for what we assumed would be lunch. Nothing was said, however, and we sat around with glasses of wine waiting for something to happen. At intervals the telephone rang and Christopher conducted quiet conversations. Young men in flowered shirts wandered in and out. Conversation fell away and we picked up books and magazines in a desultory fashion — among them, I recall, a book of Cocteau drawings and a notebook of Truman Capote's jottings. At moments Freddie, Alexis, Moira and I would catch one another's eye, raise our eyebrows woefully, then return to what we were reading. Around 2.30 someone (though not Christopher) said how about some chow, and like Pavlov's dogs we rose together.

Omelettes in Ted's Shack next door worked wonders and gave us the zest to enjoy a drive that a friend of Christopher took us on into the hills above Malibu. It was cool and silent up there, and as far as the eye could see were ridge upon ridge of mountaintops, brown and bare, with layers of blue mist between, like an illustration from a child's fairy book. After that it was back to the bungalow, and more drinks and telephoning and waiting for things to happen. Erika, the daughter of Thomas Mann, came in, and someone called Jay, around fifty, wearing a red and green silk shirt and red and green sandals and a big gold earring in one ear. Jay told me he was leaving for Tangier next week because you could get four servants there for twenty bucks a week, and do whatever you wanted (Arab boys?) and not have to pay income tax. Then a young actor told me about butterflies in Cuba while a woman called Miss Pringle bored Moira to tears reminiscing about her early life on the stage.

I never spent a more empty day. The biggest disappointment was Isherwood. He might not have been there, so little impression did he make. Had he invited us, I wondered, because he wanted to see English people again, and now that we were there, did he perhaps feel a little ashamed at having taken American citizenship? Once he said lamely, 'You've got to live over here to become pro-British,' and was embarrassed when, unable to respond, we left the remark hanging in the air. He seemed to be in a muddle about where he belonged. In a very English voice he would utter Americanisms like 'Oh, sure' and 'Yeah', and then, as if for our benefit, 'Yes, of course. Oh, yes.' And he ended his sentences on an up note, like Katharine Hepburn. Looking at him, I asked myself, was this really Herr Issyvoo, the brilliant snapshot-taker of pre-war Berlin, the friend and confidant of the volatile Sally Bowles? And the short answer was, Yes, it was. (Later Mrs Goldwyn told me that Isherwood collaborated with young boys to send in scripts, all of which were rubbish, and that he was very hard up and reduced to writing captions to photographs to make money.)

In America, as everyone knows, the sublime and the ridiculous are seldom far apart, as with Gutzon Borglum's vast rock sculptures of American leaders and the Forest Lawns Cemetery and Memorial Park. A smaller example came my way when an American cartoonist called Franklin, whom I had met at dinner, invited me to see the collection of Impressionist paintings of Edward G. Robinson, the Hollywood actor who specialized in gangster roles. Although I was aware of its existence, nothing had prepared me for a display which must have been unique outside art institutions, and which hung unostentatiously on the walls of various rooms in his elegantly furnished house.

There were two Renoirs, one, *Après le Bain*, of a nude peasant girl whose skin seemed so tinglingly alive you felt you could reach out and touch it, the other of a young girl's head with a red hat and black plume; Van Gogh's *Landscape at Arles*; a Gauguin of natives riding horses on a pink beach; two little Boudin seascapes; and a wonderful Chagall of a Russian peasant with a black beard, against a background of snow. There were two Rouaults, the huge, infinitely sad *Old Clown*, whose bold lines, harsh colours and stained-glass structure I would have found difficult to live with, and a lovely, much smaller picture of the head of a Chinese girl. There was a Toulouse-Lautrec, two Utrillos (one of the front of Notre Dame), several Degas dancing girls, a Bonnard, a Sickert, a Monet, a Modigliani, one or two Pissarros and a big, brilliant Matisse of a woman laying a dinner-table with the light sparkling on glasses and silver. It was a staggering collection and I came away from it dizzy with such a concentration of beauty.

Then Mr Franklin took me to where he said we would find Mrs Edward G. Robinson herself painting. She was not there but her model was, a large, Spanish-looking woman of the kind William Russell Flint might have painted, dressed in a scarlet brocade evening dress with a generous display of bosom. 'Why, hullo, Mrs Peabody,' said Mr Franklin, 'how are you?' 'It's not Mrs Peabody any more,' said the model, 'it's Mrs Knapp.' 'You were Mrs Peabody last time we met,' said Mr Franklin, 'and that was only five months ago.' 'Well,' said Mrs Knapp tersely, 'I'm Mrs Knapp now.' Mrs Robinson came back from telephoning and uncovered her painting of the model, almost complete. 'What do you think of it?' she said. 'I think it's just great,' said Mr Franklin without hesitation, 'I think it's perfectly beautiful.' Fortunately I was not asked my opinion. Yet on our tour of the Impressionists Mr Franklin had offered no praise of them at all. Maybe for him they were beyond praise, or he felt praise to be superfluous; whereas Mrs Robinson's painting, however trite, was something he felt he could relate to.

In November the ballet moved to San Francisco. But the *Hans Andersen* deal was not yet finalized, and a week later Sam Goldwyn invited me to fly down and stay with him so as to represent Moira's wishes during the final negotiations between his people and Moira's agents.

I arrived in time for a lunch party, and found myself sitting next to the lovely raven-haired Hedy Lamarr, whose picture, torn from a movie magazine, had once adorned the wall of my room at Eton; but I thought it wiser not to tell her so. She had a fuller face than I expected and melting eyes and an entrancing Austrian accent. We talked about the meanness of some rich men. She told me that her first husband who was an armaments baron would buy her anything she wanted, but wouldn't allow her a bank account. She said that to make the lift work in the building where they lived, you had to put a penny in a slot, which enraged him.

Sam was, as always, dapper, cheerful, friendly. After dinner in the evening, although I hadn't asked for it, he said he wanted to tell me the story of his early life.

'I was born in Poland,' he said. 'My father was an antique dealer but lazy. When I was eleven, he died of pneumonia. I didn't get on with my stepmother so I decided to run away. I swam a river which separated Poland from Germany and when I reached the other side a lady in a cottage dried and fed me. I made my way to Hamburg where friends of my family managed to raise enough money to send me to England where I had relations. I got a job in Birmingham as a blacksmith's apprentice, but they gave me the sack because I wasn't strong enough.'

Having emigrated to America he found a job in a glove factory. 'After a while I decided I'd like to go out and sell gloves myself, but when I told the boss, he said, "What do you know about selling gloves?" I said, "Nothing, but I want to try." So he sent me off to some little town in Massachusetts – he wouldn't let me go to any of the big cities – and I went to see the manager of the main store. I was told he was out. I came back later and was told the same thing. I knew he wasn't out and I was determined to see him. I stayed there four days and on the fourth day he agreed to see me. I told him why I had come. "Listen," I said, pulling two of the best gloves from my pocket, "you've got to buy these gloves, my whole life depends on it, if you don't I'm finished." Then I burst into tears. I guess he must have felt sorry for me, for he gave me an offer for the gloves. That was the greatest moment of my life.'

Flush from selling thousands of gloves, Sam went to New York. 'One day I saw some slides in a five cent joint, and I decided I wanted to make moving pictures. I told my brother-in-law Jesse Laski, I'll put in $7500 if you'll come in for the same amount. But Jesse didn't want to make moving pictures. He'd been in San Francisco where they eat a lot of *tamales*. He said, "Why don't we bring *tamales* to New York and make a pile of money that way?" But I was determined to make moving pictures. They'd been going ten years or so then, but only in five- and ten-minute shorts. I wanted to make full-lengths. And then I came out here and got started.'

'Listen,' he said, 'I've never worried about making money. I've never gone out looking for money, but I've found money's always come to me.' I asked if anyone had wanted to write his life, and he said, 'Oh, lots of people, including Hesketh Pearson. But I've refused them all. A lot of my experiences have been bitter, bitter, bitter. All the lying and double-crossing and dirty dealing I've met with. When someone writes my life, I want them to tell the truth and that can't be done until I'm dead. My wife has all the notes.'

A contract for *Hans Andersen* was agreed next day, and I flew back to San Francisco. Two of Moira's guests for *Sleeping Beauty* that night were the jazz trumpeter Muggsy Spanier and his wife

Ruth whom we had met and made friends with in Greenwich Village during our time in New York. After the performance Muggsy had to leave for the Hangover Club where he was playing with Meade Lux Lewis, but Ruth came to the stage door. 'How did Muggsy like it?' I asked, as I walked her along to Moira's dressing-room, uncertain whether it had been jazz trumpeter's fare. She stopped in her tracks. '*Like it?*' she said. 'Why, that girl' – and she searched for the *mot juste* – '*made Muggsy sweat!*' Moira said she could not have wished for a nicer compliment.

After San Francisco, Moira and the company went off in the train for one-night stands in the mid-West, while I took the car through New Mexico and Colorado to Denver, where I sold it. We met in Chicago for Christmas. On Boxing Day a Russian admirer of Moira called Dr Gabrielianz invited me to lunch at the Adventurers' Club, and showed me a collection of the club's exhibits. The first was about nine feet high and looked like an elephant's trunk. I asked what it was. 'Is copulative organ of whale,' said Dr Gabrielianz. 'Whale takes twenty-four hours to copulate. Is long time, yes?' Next to it was a stubbier object, like a sixteen-inch shell. Dr Gabrielianz said, 'Is copulative organ of elephant. You see, compared to whale, is very small.' And next to it was what looked like a walking-stick. 'Don't tell me,' I said. 'Is copulative organ of giraffe?' Dr Gabrielianz smiled. 'No,' he said, 'of walrus. Is funny, yes?' 'Yes,' I said, and we both laughed.

In the New Year the company went on to Canada and I took the *Queen Mary* home. In the ship's cinema they showed a newsreel of the main events of 1950. The two 'weddings of the year' were ours and Elizabeth Taylor's first. The commentator didn't add that Elizabeth Taylor's had also just ended.

I have written before in these pages of my friendship with Bill Richmond, a friendship which grew as time went on. He was the only man I ever felt totally at ease with and to whom I could say whatever came into my head without fear of misunderstanding. He also made me laugh more than anyone I knew. I remember one or two occasions in the old St James's Club when he would beckon me to follow him into a room where some aged member lay sunk in a deep armchair, newspaper spreadeagled across his flies, head on chest, wheezing loudly. Alone one would not have found such a situation funny, but Bill had an odd quirk of making it seem so, and I would find myself joining him in silent, convulsive laughter.

But he was a restless, moody man, and one of the saddest things for me was to observe, in the scores of letters we exchanged throughout the war and after, how difficult he was finding it to cope with life. Paradoxically he had, so far, been anything but a failure. He had won a scholarship to Eton and an Exhibition to Trinity, he had done his bit in the war and after it been President of the Cambridge Union and a member of the Union's successful debating tour in the United States; since then he had landed a steady job as a leader writer on the *Daily Mail* and been accepted as the Conservative Party's prospective Parliamentary candidate for Oldham. But there was some fatal flaw in his makeup, and as time went on and he lapsed into long silences or became offensively off-hand, people found him increasingly difficult to get along with. When he wrote congratulating me on my appointment to Ashridge in late 1948, I asked in reply if he realized how much he had changed. He said he had:

> But the trouble is, I don't really know what to do about it. It's only people I'm fondest of who really catch it, but I didn't realize it was getting as bad as you say. Maybe it has something to do with my fatness, but it isn't as if I haven't tried other things other than that fool box [the Drown box my mother had put him on to]. I spent months under a doctor having injections and pills and so on, and it did bugger all good . . . The trouble may be partly physical but it is also mental or spiritual or whatever you like to call it. I can't spend a quiet evening at home: the prospect appals me . . .
>
> The trouble with me, Goat, is that I'm now 29, and I haven't got a single personal interest in the world. Apart from a few staunch friends – a diminishing few – I know nobody, and it's appallingly lonely. I also suspect that I'm becoming a bore, which I don't think I used to be, and [is] something unforgivable in anybody, but especially in a journalist and would-be politician . . .
>
> You say, 'Perhaps you don't care what people think.' I passionately care what people think, even if I don't appear to. Perhaps it's [because of] the feeling of the strength of friendship with those few people that I bother less about

others. The failure to know either of my parents has been my own *great* failure.

This is a rambling letter, rather typical of me at present. A lot of things have happened since I started off in the cold, wide world a year ago. But one thing hasn't — I haven't grown up yet.

And yet when he had committed himself to something worthwhile, he could swiftly regain all his old sense of enjoyment and enthusiasm. Campaigning at Oldham ten days before our marriage, he wrote: 'I do really wish you could come up here for the last two or three days . . . because it is such enormous fun.' At a meeting the night before, he said, a bench had collapsed under the weight of one of his female supporters, bringing down five or six others, and 'a loopy Catholic cousin' had written to all the local Catholic priests that Bill had risked his life doing secret naval work in the war and was a great Christian who helped the poor in the service of God. 'I understand this is to be read out in the pulpits on Sunday!' He enclosed his election address 'to give you and Moira a good laugh' and ended, 'the confetti situation is well in hand.'

Had he been elected instead of losing by a few hundred votes, life as an MP might have helped him to grow out of himself. As it was, his sense of aimlessness increased and when I came back from America in 1951, he seemed more lost than ever. He had no flat of his own, spent most nights at the St James's Club and would sometimes pop down to stay with my mother, who kept his sheets on permanent stand-by in the linen cupboard. Another cause of low spirits was that a girl whom he had hoped to marry (and who also might have saved him) had in the end turned him down. His black dog moods were increasingly frequent, those of gaiety and high spirits correspondingly fewer; the classic symptoms, though I did not know it then, of progressive manic depression.

One afternoon my mother telephoned me at Clabon Mews with the news that Bill was dead. He had stayed the night before at the St James's Club. The valet had called him with tea at eight when he seemed in normal spirits, but at 9.45, concerned that he had not appeared, knocked at the door before entering and found it locked. Through the door he asked Bill if he was going down to breakfast, and Bill replied that he wouldn't bother as he had letters to write. At lunchtime the valet returned and finding the door still locked and no answer from within, used his pass-key to enter. 'I found Mr Richmond,' he later told the coroner, 'lying on his back with a shotgun between his legs. The barrel was in his mouth.' On the table were letters saying what he intended to do.

As soon as I heard this I went round to his mother's house in Wilton Crescent to give what comfort I could. But I had expected too much of myself. As she came towards me with arms out-stretched, her pale angular face immensely calm and dignified, emotion took hold of me, and instead of my comforting her, I found her comforting me. (I remembered then a letter in which Bill had referred to 'her serenity, the inner peace, the absolute tolerance that enables her to accept things'.) Yet I could gain some solace in that it had shown her how much Bill had meant to me. I went to the funeral at a church near Lady Richmond's family home in Yorkshire and once again, as the coffin was lowered into the grave, found it impossible to contain my grief. I have met no other man whose company I valued more, whose ready wit was also married to a kind of childlike innocence, whom I loved more than a brother.

For a long time afterwards I could not rid my mind of what he had done and how he had come to do it, because however low-spirited friends may be, suicide is rarely a scenario one considers. I was haunted by the careful and deliberate prep-arations he had made: taking a fellow member's guncase from the hall to his bedroom the night before; not killing himself that night, when he would have been quite undisturbed but, as they say, sleeping on it; not doing it on waking either, but taking his tea from the valet and then at some juncture after that finally deciding on it and writing the farewell letters; and then the final horror of removing the gun from the case and putting it together, inserting a cartridge in the breech, manoeuvring the weapon so that the butt was between his feet and the end of the barrel in his mouth, pulling the bedclothes up to his chin (as a shroud? for modesty's sake?), then awkwardly stretching down arm and hand to reach the trigger. For so life-enhancing a man, for so rumbustious a figure, it was a pitifully inept sort of death.

In a milder way I had my own psychological problems. They first showed themselves in physical form soon after I took up my job at Government House, Newfoundland: the manifestations were insomnia, stomach pains, sweating in hands and feet, and general lassitude. The Canadian naval doctor who examined me called my ailment 'soldier's heart', a stress condition brought about by three years of the war at sea. It plagued me on and off while I was in Newfoundland but paradoxically when I returned to sea in the autumn of 1944 it vanished. After the war, however, at Oxford and Ashridge and before and after my marriage, it returned and became something I had to learn to live with; and I sought no cure for it because there did not seem to be one.

One evening in London, having run out of sleeping pills, I approached a local doctor for a prescription. First, though, he questioned me; and when he handed me the prescription, gave me the name of a psychiatrist whom he thought I ought to see. At that time my knowledge of psychiatry was hazy. However I went along as suggested and was told by the psychiatrist that it was not 'soldier's heart' I was suffering from but an anxiety neurosis. In that case, I asked, how was it that when I went back to sea where I might be blown up at any moment, the symptoms disappeared? Because, he said, it was not anxiety about death that was unconsciously troubling me but doubts about my ability to cope with my personal life. At sea in the war the Navy provided me with bed, board, uniform, transport and a daily routine; a personal life hardly existed.

This was the first of hundreds of visits I made to psychiatrists in the course of the next twenty-five years, and which altogether cost a small fortune. During that time I always endeavoured to hide what I was experiencing from the outside world; and it was only when people said, as they occasionally did, 'Cheer up! It may never happen!' that I knew I had not been entirely successful. Some of the initial psychiatric interviews were quite painful because, in answer to questions about my childhood, I had to relate what I had not even confided in detail to Moira – the nightmare of my early relationship with my mother. Although then in my thirties I still felt a residue of guilt and shame about it; and it was my reluctance to accept and articulate what had happened, allowing it to stay locked in the unconscious, I was told, that was a principal cause of the neurosis. Disappointingly, though, when I did come to accept the situation and could talk about my mother without embarrassment, the symptoms continued – indeed it is only in the last fifteen years or so that I have been free of them. This has led me to wonder if all I ever gained from the hours spent and the fees paid was a degree of self-discovery; and that had I never bared my mind to any psychiatrist I might have gained the self-discovery and outlived the neurosis anyway. It is a question I have heard others pose. I kept on going back because I always hoped I would eventually feel physically better; but in twenty-five years I rarely did. So are analysts and psychiatrists anything more than father confessors, sounding-boards, whose reputations for healing are largely illusory?

Two incidents stand out from those twenty-five years. The first occurred at a time when the pains and lassitude had become so acute that on many days I was reduced to sitting slumped in a chair, staring into space for hours on end, unable to concentrate on anything. To counter this I was prescribed a course of electric shock therapy. After the third treatment, when I had come round from the anaesthetic, I experienced what psychiatrists call an abreaction; that is to say, I burst into floods of tears, clung to a nurse who was standing by and told her she was the only woman who had meant anything to me in my life. It was a rum thing to do; but she didn't bat an eyelid. For about a week or ten days afterwards I felt a new man, refreshed and invigorated, and thought my neurosis had gone for ever. Then the symptoms returned.

The other incident took place during one of my twice-weekly interviews with a distinguished Jungian analyst whom I had been seeing for several years. My father always told me never to recount my dreams to anyone as while they might be fascinating to me, they were dead boring to anyone else. But this man could never have enough of my dreams. I had to write them down each morning as I woke (it's amazing what one remembers doing that) and then he interpreted them (trains were wombs, etc.) in his consulting-room.

Usually I sat in a chair opposite him, but one afternoon, having for once no dreams to offer, I was told to lie on the couch and indulge in 'free association', i.e. shut my eyes and tell him whatever came into my mind. I did as he asked, but nothing came. After a few minutes I said, 'I'm sorry, but my mind is a blank,' to which he replied, 'Don't worry. Just relax and wait for something to come. It will.' In another few minutes I saw a white cloud. 'I see a white cloud,' I said. He made no comment but I hardly expected it. Presently I saw a lamp-post. It was black. 'I see a black lamp-post,' I said, and then, 'The black lamp-post is underneath the white cloud.' I was aware this sounded like something from a foreign language phrase-book, but felt that precision was important. More time went by, the cloud and the lamp-post vanished and their place was taken by a herd of trotting pigs. 'I see pigs,' I said, 'a whole lot of pigs, and they're trotting.' I said this quite excitedly because there were so many and I wasn't expecting them. Again no comment, and now something made me turn and open my eyes.

What I saw would have delighted Bill Richmond: a figure with head back and mouth open, deep in slumber. Although surprising, I did not have it in my heart to blame him; what I had been saying was enough to make anyone nod off. I rose and so as not to disturb him, tiptoed to the door. The click of the handle woke him. 'Good heavens!' he said. 'I *am* sorry.' He was obviously terribly embarrassed. 'You may not believe this,' he said, 'but this is the first time this has ever happened.' I was sure he was telling the truth and yet I did find it hard to believe. When you consider the sort of sludge in the way of dreams and fantasies and happenings that patients dredge up from the unconscious every day and which, hour upon hour, week in week out, psychiatrists have to force themselves to listen to, it is a wonder to me that any of them manage to stay awake at all.

13

Hollywood

In the spring of 1951 Moira and I had the idea of making a ballet of Max Beerbohm's enchanting fairy tale, *The Happy Hypocrite*, with her as choreographer and dancing the part of Jenny Mere and the two of us adapting the story for the stage. When we told our friend Roland Pym, the artist, about it, he was equally enthusiastic and offered to rough out some designs for the sets. A letter to the author to ask his permission brought a charming reply from the Villina Chiaro in Rapallo saying he found the idea very attractive, and inviting us to visit him if ever we found ourselves nearby. I replied that we would be motoring through Italy in August and would like to take up his invitation then.

The omens seemed favourable, for when the Sadler's Wells company was in Liverpool, the Covent Garden general administrator, David Webster, invited us to dine with him at the Adelphi Hotel. Over dinner, and as though prompted by some kind fairy, he said that the company was always looking for ideas for new ballets and did Moira have any? When she said she had, he seemed genuinely interested, and when told what it was, asked us to let him have something in writing as soon as convenient. 'Would you like to do the choreography?' he asked, and Moira looked at me and smiled and said she would.

That summer we visited the Cannes film festival for the first showing of *The Tales of Hoffman* and stayed with Alex Korda (for whom I was now working as part-time reader) on board his boat *Elsewhere* in Antibes harbour. Another guest was the playwright Frederick Lonsdale, white-haired, red-nosed, mottle-cheeked, wearing the oldest of old clothes and a hat that might have been picked from a rubbish-tip. Despite urinary problems (I guess a prostate, though nobody referred to such things then) he was in sparkling form. At a local restaurant a French waiter gave him a lengthy run-down on the evening's menu, at the end of which Freddie shouted at him, 'I don't understand a single thing you say.' This was a useful corrective to some of us in the party who liked to think we spoke better French than we did.

He had some good anecdotes too. During the First World War, he said, bombs from a passing Zeppelin exploded quite close to the theatre where Gerald du Maurier was acting. When the scene ended, du Maurier came to the front of the stage and declared to the audience, 'My friends! We are not afraid!' '*Speak for yourself*!' came a voice from the back. Once, said Freddie, when he was being sued for plagiarism, the actor-manager Sir Seymour Hicks gave evidence on his behalf in the witness-box. 'Counsel asked him, "Did you see any resemblance between Mr Lonsdale's play and this other one?" When Hicks said "Yes", I inwardly groaned. Then counsel asked, "What was the resemblance?" and Hicks said, "They were two of the most dreadful plays I've ever seen."' Before he left us Freddie said to me, 'Shall I tell you what the worst thing in life is? It's an unhappy marriage. And if one has to choose between two evils, loneliness is not quite as bad as incompatibility.' I said, 'Do you speak from observation or experience?' and he replied, 'Both.'

The *Elsewhere* took us to Elba and Rome, and from there

Moira and I motored to Rapallo in the Railton motorcar I had recently bought. We found the Villina Chiaro, in the words of David Cecil, Max Beerbohm's biographer, 'a pokey little white cube of a building' overhanging the main road from Rome to Genoa with its roar of traffic and perpetual dust. But when Max had bought it in 1910 it had been a quiet country road; and there was a stunning view of the sea. We were warmly welcomed by Max, looking much as I had imagined he would, small, dapper, the drooping eyes familiar from his own cartoons of himself and wearing a light summer coat and black tie and a soft-brimmed hat which he wore at a rakish angle. With him was Elizabeth Jungmann, his constant companion since the death of his adored wife. Soon I began to notice the mannerisms, the word 'Edwardian' which he pronounced 'Edvardian', the old masher's phrase at the end of a sentence, 'Don't you know?', itself so Edvardian, and reminiscences that began not with 'I remember when I . . .' but 'I remember when my wife and I . . .' We showed him the synopsis we had done and Roland's sketches and he seemed delighted.

Elizabeth Jungmann gave us tea and then Max took us to the little study he had built for himself on the flat roof. It was quite austere, a simple desk and chair in the centre and a single shelf of books running at waist height along two walls. I commented on the bright blue colour of the walls, and Max said his wife had had problems explaining to the Italian workmen the exact shade of blue she wanted. After a bit one of the workmen cottoned on. 'Oh, you mean *Reckitts* blue,' he said.

Most of the books on the shelf were by Max's contemporaries – Belloc, Chesterton, Lytton Strachey, the Sitwells, Arnold Bennett. 'Show them your *special* books, Max', said Elizabeth Jungmann, and Max pulled out *Queen Victoria's Tour of the Highlands*. On the title page he had written in the Queen's hand a spoof dedication from her to him; the whole book was shot through with similar delights, including a balloon over one of the Queen's dogs in which he had written, 'and his loss was *most* heart-breaking and annoying'. Over a picture of Yeats in his *Collected Poems* he had stuck a photograph of the head of a wild-looking Irish labourer wearing a grotesque hat. 'I discovered this pleasant little art some twenty years ago,' said Max. Further along the shelf was a thin book on whose spine was written *The Complete Works of Arnold Bennett*. 'That's a very interesting book,' said

Max. When I took it out, I saw that it was nothing more than one side of a support for a little tray that rested above: the other side said *Herbert Spencer's Poems*; and between 'Spencer's' and 'Poems' Max had drawn a little red heart.

Later he showed us his cartoon murals, one above the inside of the front door, the other along the passage. Zuleika Dobson, the heroine of his enchanting surreal novel about Oxford university life, featured prominently, as did Edward VII, Winston Churchill, George Bernard Shaw. 'Shaw was very ugly as a young man,' said Max, 'and only achieved distinction as he grew older.' And he added, inconsequentially, 'And Ivor Novello was not nearly as beautiful in life as he was in his photographs.' Max's powers of observation, combined with his sense of fun and gift for caricature, had made him, both in pictures and in his parodies of writers collected in *A Christmas Garland*, a unique artist; and although a smaller talent than many of his contemporaries, he has (I have found) outlived many of them.

There was something else about Max that was unique – the disclosure of a chronological fact that has stayed in my mind ever since. I cannot remember now how it arose, but at some juncture during the delightful afternoon he told us that his grandparents had been married – not born but married – *in* 1785. He was seventy-nine then, which meant that he was born in 1872. His father was sixty-two at the time of his birth which meant that *he* was born in 1810. It was therefore perfectly possible for his father's parents to have been married twenty-five years earlier. All the same I found it a staggering thought – to be conversing with a man in 1951 whose grandparents were already grown-up before the French Revolution, before Trafalgar and Waterloo, before Mozart had written *The Marriage of Figaro*, Keats his Odes and Boswell his *Life of Johnson*.

Back in London I made a fair copy of our ballet synopsis of *The Happy Hypocrite* and sent it, along with Roland Pym's sketches, to David Webster, as he had asked. With some anticipation Moira and I waited for a reply. None came. After a month I rang Webster's secretary to inquire whether my letter had arrived, and was told it had. Two weeks later I wrote to Webster again, hoping he might let us have his or Ninette de Valois's reactions soon. But we never had them then or subsequently, and all further inquiries remained unanswered. Finally, in despair, I wrote to Kenneth (later Lord) Clark, whom we knew and who was on the board of Covent Garden; and in January 1952 he replied that the Ballet Sub-Committee had considered the project and turned it down. In a further letter he spelled out the reason: 'Ninette naturally feels that any new ideas for a ballet should at an early stage have been submitted to *her*.' Yet Webster had specifically asked that it should be submitted to *him*. So much for the liaison that existed between them.

Recently I re-read the synopsis and looked again at Roland's drawings, and I am still convinced it would have made, and still would make, a marvellous ballet.

Poor Max was as disappointed as we were. 'I had greatly looked forward to the prospect of Jenny Mere being impersonated – and sublimated – by Moira Shearer.' But out of it all came one lasting compensation. At an exhibition of Max's pictures at the Leicester Galleries, I bought two of his caricatures, one of Lord Savile, bald and bull-necked and gazing vacantly at the sky, the other of King Edward VII on a horse. At the top of the latter Max had written 'THE KING! GOD BLESS HIM!' and then in the bottom left-hand corner added in pencil, 'Done by Max in about 1911 and now belonging to Ludovic and Moira Kennedy, 1952'. It hangs near me as I write.

On our way home we stopped for a week in the villa at Grasse where we had stayed during our engagement, and again were guests of Somerset Maugham at another smart luncheon party at the Villa Mauresque. Afterwards, during a stroll in the garden, Maugham said to Moira that just as he was remembered by most people mainly as the author of *Of Human Bondage*, so he guessed that whatever else she did in her life, she would probably be remembered by most people mainly as the star of *The Red Shoes*. 'It will be a m-m-millstone round your neck', he told her, 'until the d-d-day you die.'

Maugham came to London that autumn as he usually did, and we met again when the three of us were invited to lunch at their house in Hampstead by Kenneth and Jane Clark. As we drove in sunshine through the park in the car that the Clarks had kindly sent for us, Maugham asked me if I had read Graham Greene's latest novel, *The End of the Affair*. I said I hadn't. He said, 'I'm s-s-sorry you haven't, as I s-s-should like to have had your opinion of it. I think it s-s-shows what a really n-n-nasty man he is. I've known him for years and n-n-never thought that before.'

The other guests at the luncheon party were the French

ambassador Rene Massigli and his wife, the sculptor Henry Moore and the poet T. S. Eliot. During introductions Maugham called Massigli *'Excellence'* and said if he'd known he was to be there, he would have worn his *'petit bouton'* (of the Legion d'Honneur). As we were about to enter the dining-room, Maugham stood back to let the ambassador and Eliot go first. Turning to me he said, 'You and I are wr-wr-writers. We have no s-s-social s-s-status. We go last.' I wondered how he classified Eliot, the most famous of contemporary poets – perhaps on this occasion as a publisher, which he also was.

All this buttering me up, seeking my views on *The End of the Affair*, putting me as a writer on an equal footing with him was, of course, immensely flattering. But a week later I saw, as I knew others had sometimes seen, a less attractive side to him. Having twice received his hospitality at the Villa Mauresque, we invited him to drinks one evening at Clabon Mews. Debating who else to ask, we played safe and chose mostly mutual friends, the Clarks, Moira's old friend Sachie Sitwell, Mark Longman the publisher and his wife, half a dozen others. It had occurred to me to ask fellow writers of my generation, but I had lost touch with those in the Oxford Writers' Club, and hardly knew any others. But it was clear that that was what he had been expecting, an opportunity to play the Grand Old Man of English Letters. He stayed ten minutes, looking glum, then abruptly rose and made for the door. 'I have to g-g-go now,' he said. I said I was sorry. He reached for his stiletto. 'I'm s-s-sure your little p-p-party', he stammered, 'will g-g-get more and more upr-r-roarious'; and he turned and left. I could not envisage Graham Greene saying anything like that in a hundred years; but perhaps Maugham meant that Greene was nasty in some quite different way.

Later that month the book on Nelson's captains was published as *Nelson's Band of Brothers*, and was well reviewed: Duff Cooper (whom I hardly knew) wrote saying it ought to be made into a textbook at Dartmouth, and a second impression was ordered. In November Moira and I sailed in the *Ile de France* for America where she was to star with Danny Kaye in *Hans Christian Andersen*. In New York we took the *20th Century Limited* to Chicago and there changed for Denver, Colorado where the Goldwyn Studios had thoughtfully left a swish convertible to drive ourselves to Los Angeles.

We spent a few days at Sante Fe, New Mexico, and at nearby Taos met some of the Pueblo Indians and of the little group that had cultivated them, among them Millicent Rogers, D. H. Lawrence's widow Frieda and her husband Angelo, and the American poet Witter Bynner; my sharpest memory of that visit is of arriving at Millicent Rogers's house for a Thanksgiving Day lunch to find two Indians throwing up in the downstairs loo. Frieda Lawrence told me that the gamekeeper's cottage in *Lady Chatterley's Lover* was based on one at Renishaw, and that the Sitwells, who owned Renishaw, had never forgiven Lawrence for it.

In Los Angeles we had taken Brian Aherne's house at Santa Monica for the estimated six months of Moira's filming. It was a curious sort of house, one of several (including that of Marion Davies) on Ocean Front and built, literally, on the beach. There was a comfortable double bedroom overlooking the sea with a wealth of biscuit-coloured dado work and outside, surrounded by a fence, a small swimming-pool; next to this was the inevitable bar and next to that a gloomy little dining-room with banquette seats as in a restaurant; and across from that an even gloomier small drawing-room with furniture in the French style. With the house came a Filipino servant named Jack, who did the shopping and cooking.

For a week or two all was summer and singing. We went to parties to meet Danny Kaye and Charles Vidor and Rita Hayworth and many others. The composer Frank Loesser from Brooklyn, an addicted wisecracker, took us to a restaurant where he claimed the waiters were named after the apostles ('Hey, Peter, ask Paul to bring us the wine list, will ya?') and afterwards at his home played us 'Wonderful, wonderful Copenhagen' and other songs from *Hans Andersen*. And in his suite at the studio, after a dismal lunch of hamburgers and baked apple, Sam Goldwyn introduced Moira to the press. 'This picture,' he told them, 'will be the greatest picture I've ever made. It'll be the climax of the careers of everyone engaged in it.' To Moira, 'Everyone in America is more excited about your coming over here than any other actress ever.' Moira looked at the floor. 'And this,' said Sam, taking the arm of a handsome young man, 'is Mr Farley Granger who is going to be Miss Shearer's lover on screen.' He spotted the British Consul. 'And this is Mr Hadow, the British Consul, who –' Here Sam forgot whatever he was going to say about Mr Hadow, and in the long pause that followed Moira piped up – 'who perhaps is going to be my lover *off* screen.' Laughs all round, especially from Mr Hadow. 'Jolly well put, if I may say so,' he told Moira. 'Ha, ha, ha! And how was the old country when you left, eh? I want you to come along on Friday and meet some chaps from a Canadian cruiser. I've got a lot of pretty girls coming, but you'll be the prettiest, by Jove. Ha, ha, ha!' Later, when Moira returned to Goldwyn's suite to collect her coat, there was a maid clearing away the lunch. 'Hullo,' said the maid, 'what's your name?' Moira told her. 'Are you in this film?' asked the maid. 'Yes,' said Moira. 'Oh,' said the maid, 'that's nice.'

But a sea-change was imminent. Neither on the boat coming over, nor during the drive from Denver had Moira been feeling her best, which for her was unusual. A visit to a GP, followed by another to a specialist, told her what she had not even suspected: that she had started her first child. It was the best and worst of news, for it meant her pulling out of *Hans Andersen*, with its punishing schedule of dancing stretching far into the New Year. Goldwyn could hardly have taken it worse, insisting that Moira's condition be confirmed by a second gynaecologist and telling her agent, 'If Miss Shearer has a miscarriage, I shall expect her on the set the next day.' But Moira blossomed and wolfed Matsos bread and looked more beautiful with every day that passed; and Goldwyn telegraphed for Zizi Jeanmaire (whose Carmen Moira had danced in Paris the year before) to take over the role.

But what to do now, for we were committed to the rent of Brian Aherne's house for the next six months? Fortunately MGM were able to find a place for her in one of the three short films that made up *Story of Three Loves*. James Mason would play opposite her, she would dance to the music of Rachmaninov's *Variations on a Theme of Paganini*, and Fred Ashton agreed to come over in the New Year to arrange the choreography; Agnes Moorehead would also take part and Gottfried Reinhardt would direct.

So life took on a regular pattern. Moira would leave for the studios early in the morning and return late in the evening, usually very tired. Most evenings we dined in, occasionally accepted invitations out, even more occasionally gave dinner-parties of our own. Once Frieda Lawrence and Angelo brought Igor Stravinsky and his wife Vera, and Aldous Huxley, then almost blind. Vera, Frieda and Angelo bubbled away merrily, Stravinsky rarely spoke, while Aldous Huxley, whose early novels I had once admired, was a walking encyclopaedia. When I remarked (as Robert Louis Stevenson had remarked before me) on how striking I had found the fir trees above the snow line in the Sierras after the heat of the Nevada desert, he gave a rundown on what plants would grow at what heights above so many hundred feet above sea-level.

For me this was not a satisfactory period, for though I had time on my hands, I found I had no theme for a book or a short story that I wanted to write. However, remembering Evelyn Waugh's advice about the importance of scales, I wrote up (for possible publication) a diary I had kept from the time of my arrival at Ashridge to our sailing for America the year before: there were entries on what I had been reading, extracts from Ashridge lectures, descriptions of people and places, opinions on this or that. I wrote each morning, swam in the little pool before a sandwich lunch and wrote again for a couple of hours before Moira's return in the evening. In the afternoons I used to walk along the beach, listening to the sounds of the sea and sea-birds, watching the metal detectors of the beachcombers hovering like helicopters above the sand as they probed for coins or jewellery left by the crowds at weekends. I was surprised by how much they found, though little of it was of value.

I had two or three assignments from the *Sunday Times*. One was to describe an atomic bomb test explosion in the Nevada desert. I stayed the night before in Las Vegas, and in the morning was taken to an observation post nine thousand feet up in the mountains where there were pine trees and snow. The bomb exploded forty miles away, a stab of red light low down in the desert, then the familiar mushroom cloud, beginning just above ground level: this led us to question whether the explosion had taken place underground, which the official in charge would neither confirm nor deny. To me the oddest thing about the explosion was that there was no noise. The official explained this by saying that some sound waves travelled direct into the ozonosphere and by reflection hit the earth many miles from their course. He said that after previous tests, windows in Las Vegas had been broken but those in Indian Springs which was much nearer to the explosion had stayed intact. The same phenomenon, he said, had occurred at Queen Victoria's funeral when the minute-guns at Windsor were heard one hundred miles away.

I also visited the studio where Charlie Chaplin was making *Limelight*, the film based on his early experiences as a music hall comedian (the part of the ballet-dancer which at one time Chaplin had thought might be right for Moira went to the English actress Claire Bloom). The set where he was rehearsing was an old London theatre, complete with stage, auditorium, foyer. Outside, near the entrance, a billboard read: 'GALA BENEFIT FOR CALVERO APPEARING PERSONALLY WITH A GALAXY OF OTHER STARS'.

I knew that Chaplin had written the script and music including a ballet and several popular songs, and that he was both directing and starring in the film; even so I was not prepared for such astonishing energy in a man of sixty-two. Dressed in open shirt and trousers, his white hair shining under the lights, he was for ever on the move, nothing was too unimportant to escape his attention. At one moment he was telling the cameraman, 'No, no, you must have the camera down, low down, to get the sense of the theatre – the camera must see what the audience is seeing', at another prompting the orchestra in their reactions to a disturbance in the gallery or attending to some detail of lighting or dress. And he did it all with a gay, almost boyish enthusiasm.

In the afternoon he appeared as Calvero. The white hair had become ginger and he wore a small toothbrush moustache. He was dressed in a tatty Edwardian tail-coat, high stiff collar, brown trousers cut away at the knees, striped socks and black boots. At once my mind went back to my prep school days and the weekly film show, for this was the Chaplin I remembered: not the actor playing a downtrodden worker, as in *Modern Times*, not the French bourgeois gentilhomme as in *Monsieur Verdoux*, not the Hitler look-alike as in *The Great Dictator*; but simply Chaplin as Chaplin.

For nearly two hours he with a violin and Buster Keaton at a piano gave as part of their stage 'act', a burlesque of a concert. The scene must have been shot a dozen times, and the ease with which Chaplin moved in and out of his roles as actor and director was uncanny, shifting effortlessly from convulsions with his violin to directing the camera and back again. I never saw an artist less conscious of himself or his abilities.

No two versions of the scene were quite the same, as both

Chaplin and Keaton seemed to improvise as they went along, yet each had its own spontaneity and freshness. People around me were laughing (or trying to restrain themselves from laughing) as much at the last version as at the first. When it was over, we all burst out clapping; and Chaplin, dabbing his face with a towel, smiled happily and almost shouted at us, 'You know, all this is nostalgia for me. Sheer nostalgia!'

By mid-April Moira's film was nearing completion, and although she had been required to dance into the fifth month of her pregnancy, it seemed to have done her no harm. I had deliberately kept away from the studio until now, but suggested a day when I might come and see some of the shooting; Moira agreed, though she did not know what was to be shot. When I arrived, I noticed a staircase on one side of the set: quite a few people were milling about, but nothing was happening and there was no sign of Moira. I thought of asking, but knew nobody and didn't want to seem ignorant. Then a voice called out, 'Quiet, everybody, please!' and a little later I heard but didn't see a clapperboard closing and the number of the scene called out. The next thing I saw was Moira at the top of the staircase. Another voice called out 'Action!' Moira took a couple of steps down the stairs, appeared to miss her footing, fell over and tumbled slowly all the way to the bottom. I could hardly believe what I was seeing, but was restrained from rushing over and helping by the apparent lack of concern of those around me. It wasn't until Moira had picked herself up, and called out, 'How was that?' that I realized that this had been rehearsed many times. 'Very nice,' said Gottfried Reinhardt from the top of the stairs, 'we'll print it.'

In May, the film completed, we headed north into Canada, first for a weekend with the Governor of British Columbia and his wife (who referred to her daughters as 'my gulls'), then for a fishing holiday on Lake Cowichan where the juke-box in the local café worked overtime playing Johnnie Ray singing 'Cry'. Then it was two days across the wilderness of Canada in the *Canadian Pacific*, eating, sleeping, playing canasta and on one stretch (such was Moira's fame) riding with the driver in his cab, so high above the track that the rails looked like toy rails, altogether too flimsy to support the weight put on them.

In New York we embarked in the Dutch liner *Nieuw Amsterdam* with a baby's collapsible bath, a present from Agnes

Moorehead. One evening at sea the captain invited us to drinks. He spoke English with a most atrocious accent. In the course of conversation we let fall that we were Scots. Did we know the works of the famous Scots poet, Robert Burns, he asked? Yes, we did. He was a great admirer of Burns too, in fact he admired him so much that he would like to read us one of his poems. He took a book from a glass cabinet and opened it. Moira and I exchanged woeful looks, looked steadily out of the porthole, waited.

> Wee, sleekit, timorous, cowering beastie,
> Oh, what a panic's in thy breastie . . .

He continued to the end. It was, astonishingly, a voice of very passable Scots. I had seldom heard Burns read better. He closed the book and smiled.

'You like?'

'Very much.'

'You vos surpriced?'

'Frankly, yes.'

'That is vy I do it, to surprice. You see, ven I vos at College, I vos studying Middle Dutch. And Middle Dutch and Scots have much in common. The 'och' sound for instance and vords like kirk and so on. Now we fill our glasses and drink a toast. To Robert Burns.'

We raised our glasses.

'To Robert Burns,' we said. And then we went and dressed for dinner.

That summer we sold Clabon Mews and bought one of those elegant, tall Georgian houses in Church Row, Hampstead with barely-sugar banisters and original panelling; previous owners had included Oscar Wilde's friend Lord Alfred Douglas, and the painter Sir William Rothenstein. Rothenstein's son John, then Director of the Tate Gallery, told us that when he was a boy four maids slept in the tiny attic room at the top, one of whom was almost solely employed in taking hot water cans, slops, coal and ashes up or down the stairs.

In August Moira gave birth to our first child, a girl, in the Lindo wing of St Mary's Hospital, Paddington. We called her by the Kennedy name of Ailsa, and Margot Fonteyn and Sachie Sitwell were among her godparents. A rum thing happened on the evening after her birth. Moira was lying in bed reading with Ailsa in the cot beside her when the door opened and a strange-looking man came in and stood at the foot of the bed. At first Moira was quite alarmed, but presently realized the man was weeping. She gave some indication of concern and the man came round to her bedside, knelt down, buried his face in her lap and continued to weep uncontrollably. Moira held his hand and stroked his hair and waited for the weeping to finish. At last the man said, 'Please forgive me, but my wife is having a terrible time next door.' Then Moira realized it was Ian Fleming whose wife Anne, on the verge of giving birth, had developed complications. Eventually Fleming recovered his composure, thanked Moira for her sympathy and left. Later that night his son Caspar was delivered by Caesarean section.

In October Moira was back at Covent Garden, and I was busy reading novels for Korda: I read on average four a week and was astonished by how third-rate most were. My journalistic work was also increasing, with reviews of books, television programmes and plays. On the anniversary of Trafalgar I wrote an article for the *Sunday Times* demolishing the myth that on his death-bed Nelson said 'Kismet, Hardy' rather than 'Kiss me, Hardy' (a myth perpetuated by those who could not accept that our greatest war hero had asked another man for a kiss). Although the 'Kiss me, Hardy' version was attested by Nelson's secretary and chaplain, I was delighted to receive further confirmation from a Mr Corbett, writing from Hardy's home town of Portesham. He said that Nelson's grandson by his daughter Horatia had recently paid him a visit, at the age of over ninety. 'He told me he had asked his mother what exactly had happened when Nelson was dying. She said she herself had asked Hardy, who replied, 'Nelson said, "Kiss me, Hardy" and I knelt down and kissed him.'

In the spring of 1953 the diary I had been writing up in Santa Monica was published under the title of *One Man's Meat*. It had mixed reviews. The *Spectator* called it honest and revealing, the *Star* witty and entertaining, the *Tablet* fascinating. On the other hand my friend George Scott in *Truth* described much of it as ponderous dogmatism, while what struck Maurice Richardson in the *New Statesman* was 'the leaden banality which you might expect to find in the memoirs of a septuagenarian postmaster'. The general consensus was that it was immature and facetious but held a promise of better things to come. Forcing myself to read it again recently, I have to say I think that George, Maurice and the general consensus were right and the others wrong.

Yet although I was now achieving some recognition as a writer, I had not abandoned my other ambition of becoming a broadcaster. Twice I had answered notices in the press advertising vacancies for radio news reader and television commentator; twice I had been to auditions but had heard nothing more. As a result I was having increasing reservations about the quality of my voice, whether it was not a bit too lah-di-dah (my mother said sawft, lawst, awf and gawn till the day she died) and – because I always spoke rather quietly – whether I had enough voice projection. To improve on these I engaged a voice training teacher who came to Church Row once a week for several months; and from her I learnt about breath control and the glottal stop, the use of the solar plexus and resonant lips.

Thus equipped, I again entered for the annual English Festival of Spoken Poetry competition, held every July at Bedford College, Regent's Park. It was a three-day event, and among the judges were such well-known poets as Cecil Day Lewis, Richard Church, Christopher Fry, Louis MacNeice, James Kirkup. In previous years I had won some of the individual events, such as Dramatic Verse, Narrative Prose, Nineteenth-Century Poetry, but had never progressed further. Then in 1952 I came second to Gabriel Woolf in the open finals and in 1953 (Woolf having started his career as a professional reader at Broadcasting House) I won it outright.

I had hoped that this might lead to regular engagements as a poetry reader with the BBC, as had happened to Gabriel, but apart from one or two invitations later in life, they didn't materialize. On the other hand it did lead, through the recommendations of one of the judges who had connections with the BBC, to my being invited that autumn to take over from John Wain as the presenter of the BBC's radio programme *First Reading*, a presentation of newly published verse and prose by budding (and established) writers. Although I wasn't really the right man for the job, being neither a poet nor a critic of poetry, I greatly enjoyed choosing what I thought the best in current literature from the many entries sent in. With the help of my eccentric and boozy producer John Davenport, and a team of first-class readers, I was able to broadcast first readings of the works of Burns Singer, Vernon Watkins, George Macbeth, Terence Tiller, Vernon Scannell and many others. Again opinion was divided.

The Professor of English Literature at Leeds University, the much respected Bonamy Dobree, welcomed some of my strictures but a man in the *New Statesman* said I gave the impression of being in ardent pursuit of the innocuous. 'His linking passages are no more infuriating than those of John Wain. They merely infuriate in a different way.' So I was pleased, when the first series ended, to be asked to present another.

Of the scores of contributions that we broadcast, one has remained in my mind. It was a ballad called 'A Transport Song' by someone called D. Leggett, and without intending to, I came to know it by heart:

> Softly, softly, softly,
> My love's in Austraily,
> He's been bobbing up and down
> Across the mighty sea.
>
> Murder him, I'll murder him,
> He left me in child to him,
> Now he's gone and I am wronged,
> My pocket skinned has he.
>
> Yet if I should murder him,
> I should murder him and him,
> Him alive and him to come,
> And that means the death of me.
>
> So softly, softly, softly,
> My love's in Austraily,
> Come my child, be born my child,
> And take his place for me.

English poetry, which I first discovered in depth in post-war Oxford, has been a source of delight and comfort to me ever since. It has consistently given me that spiritual refreshment that Christians are always asserting is lacking in non-Christians, yet which to me is far more acceptable than a belief in the historicity of a virgin birth, a bodily resurrection, or water turning into wine. Often, and especially in times of stress, I have gained solace not only from the reading of certain poems – Shakespeare's sonnets, Keats's Odes, Donne and Blake and Herbert come immediately to mind – but (and even when alone) reading them aloud. Some lines are etched in my mind for ever:

daffodils,
That come before the swallow dares and take
The winds of March with beauty.[1]

O, but everyone
Was a bird; and the song was wordless; the singing
Will never be done.[2]

Charm'd magic casements, opening on the foam
Of perilous seas, in faery lands forlorn.[3]

The woods are lovely, dark, and deep,
But I have promises to keep,
And miles to go before I sleep,
And miles to go before I sleep.[4]

There was a woman, beautiful as morning.[5]

With the first dream that comes with the first sleep,
I run, I run, I am gathered to thy heart.[6]

[1] Shakespeare [2] Siegfried Sassoon [3] Keats [4] Robert Frost [5] Shelley
[6] Alice Meynell.

14

The Rochdale By-Election

On 2 November 1952 an event occurred in the Croydon area of
London which, though I could have little guessed it at the time,
was to influence to some degree the future course of my life. This
was what became known as the Croydon rooftop murder. Two
young men, both illiterate, Christopher Craig aged sixteen and
Derek Bentley, eighteen approaching nineteen, were observed
breaking into Messrs Barlow and Parker's confectionery warehouse. The police were called and a posse of men sent to apprehend them. Seeing them coming, Craig and Bentley retreated
to the roof. The police followed. Bentley was arrested almost
immediately. When Craig was approached, he pulled out a gun
and fired, wounding one policeman in the shoulder and shooting
another, PC Miles, stone dead.

Such a cold-blooded murder shocked the country, and when
the case came to trial both youths were found guilty of murder;

for, as the Lord Chief Justice, Lord Goddard, told the jury, when two or more men act together in a criminal enterprise which ends in murder, it is immaterial who actually fired the shot.

Craig, being of an age considered too young to hang, was sentenced to be detained during the Queen's pleasure; and Bentley was sentenced to death. There were many who thought that as a matter of egality Bentley should have been given life imprisonment, especially as he was under arrest at the time that Craig fired the fatal shot and because the jury had recommended him to mercy; but the judge did not have that discretion. The appeal was unsuccessful, but it was generally believed that when the time came for the Home Secretary to consider the case, he would commute the death sentence to life imprisonment.

The Home Secretary of the time was an evil-looking cove called Maxwell Fyfe ('the nearest thing to death in life', ran a jingle at the Bar, 'is David Patrick Maxwell Fyfe') and he thought differently. He believed that to prevent this sort of thing happening again, an example had to be set; and two days before the time set for Bentley's execution, he announced there would be no reprieve.

Many people, including myself, found this decision deeply shocking; and there were questions in Parliament, petitions to the Queen and the Prime Minister, and marches in the streets. To all of us it seemed to go against the grain of natural justice that the youth who had not killed the policeman and was under arrest at the time he was shot should be considered beyond human redemption, while the one who had done the killing would, in time, be allowed to rejoin society (and ten years later did so). It was said that Bentley, being the elder of the two, should have exercised a restraining influence. But there was no doubt that Craig was the more dominant of the two. Unable to read or write, he spent most of his time watching gangster films and having the works of Miss Enid Blyton read to him by friends. He collected firearms as other boys collect conkers, and after his arrest the police found in his bedroom an arsenal of ammunition. He admitted he was full of hatred for the police for having helped to put away his elder brother Niven for twelve years for armed robbery, and far from showing any remorse for killing PC Miles, his only regret was that he had not 'done the fucking lot'. Aware of Craig's evil influence, Bentley's parents had forbidden him to continue the association; but it had later been renewed. Bentley was a little better though not much: after a conviction for shopbreaking at fourteen, he was sent to an approved school where he showed signs of epilepsy; as a child in the Blitz he had been bombed out twice and once, after being extracted from the wreckage, was found to have suffered head injuries.

If killing people is wrong, as I believe, then it is wrong absolutely (though cases can be made for killing in self-defence and for euthanasia); and to truss someone up and kill him in cold blood seems to me no better and possibly a great deal worse (because the prisoner is helpless and at one's mercy) than to kill on the spur of the moment. God knows one's heart bled for the widow of poor PC Miles, but killing Bentley could not restore him to her, and at least he had no intimation of his death. Yet Bentley had to live with the contemplation of his death for two months and with the certainty of it for two days; indeed it was the contemplation of it rather than the act of it that was his real punishment. On the eve of his execution I found myself thinking of him sitting in his cell, nineteen years old and on the threshold of life, and wondered how he was filling in the time; and Moira and I were so disturbed by what was to be done in our name that we sent a telegram (as, I found later, thousands of others had done) to Maxwell Fyfe asking for a last-minute reprieve. But there was none; and at nine the next morning Bentley was pinioned, hooded and hanged.

I knew that my response to these events had been instinctive and emotional. Now I wanted to know whether reason could be brought in as slave (as David Hume put it) of the passions. And the more I studied the whole question of capital punishment, the less justification for it there seemed. The great majority of the 140 or so murders that then occurred in Britain each year were the consequence of domestic tiffs (husbands and wives, lovers and mistresses, drunken brawls) where the crime was unpremeditated and the parties known to one another. Clearly capital punishment was no deterrent to them, but how about the remainder? When one had set aside those found guilty but insane and those arraigned for murder but found guilty of manslaughter, one was left with a hard core of some half dozen offenders, mostly those who had committed murder in the course of robbery or rape. It was claimed – and this was the crux of the matter – that were it not for the prospect of hanging, the numbers of these transgressors would dramatically increase.

But how true was this? From my inquiries three counter-arguments emerged. The first was that almost no murders in any category could be said to be foreseen, i.e. almost no murderer intended to murder before the day was out (terrorism was a thing of the future). This seemed to be a poor argument as far as armed robbers were concerned: why take a loaded gun with you if in the last resort you were not prepared to use it? A second argument, gleaned from the criminal fraternity, was that no one who set out on a criminal enterprise ever thought he would be caught; therefore the penalty was irrelevant. This also seemed to be arguable. But the third argument struck me as wholly convincing; that numbers of other countries in Europe and elsewhere had abolished the death penalty without seeing an increase in this or any other category of murder. Were we British so very different? I doubted it.

Having cleared the ground, I set about writing a play based on the Craig–Bentley case, whose object was to show that a youth similar to Bentley, immature and illiterate, was capable of redemption (a Christian concept, though not one subscribed to by all Christians). During his time in the condemned cell, with the help of the prison chaplain and the warders who keep watch over him, he begins to learn to read and write and discover his potential as a human being; and at that moment of self-discovery and self-awareness, his life is ended. For my research into conditions in the condemned cell, I was fortunate in having the guidance of Charles Cape, one of the prison commissioners; as a prison governor, Cape had seen several men hanged and was now a fervent abolitionist. What I had not expected in my inquiries was the revulsion of all prison staff against executions and the effect they said it had on morale throughout the prison for days before and after. Many of those who had to attend executions – doctors, chaplains, and especially prison officers who had sat with the condemned man during his last days and had come to know and like him – said how uneasy they always felt afterwards, as though they had done something discreditable and unclean. 'A horrible business,' Brigadier General Dudgeon, DSO, MC, governor of Saughton Prison, Edinburgh, called it; while a chaplain who had been in the prison service for twenty-eight years spoke of 'horror, humiliation, and shame'.

I called the play *Murder Story* and it was first put on by Peter Haddon (brother of Cicely Courtneidge) at his Aldershot

Repertory Company Theatre. The cast, entirely unknown, were entirely convincing. *The Times* sent down a man on opening night who wrote that while I had loaded the dice heavily, I had scored mostly sixes. After Aldershot the play went on a brief tour of the provinces before Tom Arnold brought it in to the Cambridge Theatre, London with the original cast. The first night was quite an occasion. Bentley's father came with his daughter Iris. Moira and I sat in a stage box, and as the play progressed the stalls below us became awash with weeping. 'The audience,' said the critic J. C. Trewin, 'was in shreds.' After the final curtain came the fulfilment of a Walter Mitty dream – prolonged clapping and cries of 'Author, author!', and I rose to my feet and made a little stilted bow.

We had supper afterwards and waited for the papers. The reviews were surprisingly good. Although some said that I had chosen too easy a target – the Craig rather than the Bentley character, they suggested, might have been more rewarding – and that some of the working-class dialogue was unconvincing, there were some unexpected bouquets. Richard Findlater called it 'the most exciting theatrical experience in town', other reviewers said they had rarely been so moved, comparisons were made with *Journey's End* and *The Times*'s principal drama critic described me as 'a dramatist of thrilling promise'. My old friend Michael Benthall (at Eton, Hamlet to my Horatio), now director of the Old Vic, came round afterwards with Bobby Helpmann and said, 'I think you have a hit on your hands.' So did I, and some said if we had been playing in a more intimate theatre than the Cambridge, we might have done; but West End audiences do not patronize the theatre to have their consciences disturbed, and after a couple of months the play folded. Its life continued for some time outside London with another short tour, several amateur performances, an excellent television production and publication of the text, both in an acting edition and in a Gollancz hardback, accompanied by an essay I was asked to write on capital punishment.

For me *Murder Story* was less a milestone in my writing career than a signpost to a path down which a part of my future lay. For in the following year one of the books sent to *Truth* magazine for review was called *The Man on Your Conscience* by a retired London solicitor, Michael Eddowes: its subject was an alleged miscarriage of justice. Editors always try and commission as reviewers of books those with some knowledge of or empathy with the subject. Casting around for someone suitable for this one, George Scott thought of me and *Murder Story*, and sent along the book for review.

The man Eddowes claimed was on our conscience was Timothy Evans, an illiterate 24-year-old van driver, hanged in 1949 for the murder of his baby daughter Geraldine whose body, with that of his wife Beryl, had been found in the wash-house of 10 Rillington Place, West London, where they lived. At his trial (which was barely noticed in the press) Evans had asserted his innocence of both murders which, he claimed, had been committed by his fellow lodger John Christie, a 51-year-old former policeman who lived with his wife on the ground floor. Evans's story was that his wife was unintentionally pregnant, that Christie had told him he knew about abortions, and that when he came home from work one day, he was greeted by Christie with the news that the abortion had failed and Beryl was dead. Christie, he said, warned him that if it was ever discovered how Beryl had died, they would both be in serious trouble as abortions were illegal; and he advised Evans to sell up his flat and move away to the country until things had blown over: he would get rid of Beryl's body down one of the drains, and arrange for Geraldine to be adopted by people he knew in East Acton.

This advice, said Evans, coming from a former policeman old enough to be his father, greatly impressed him; and he traded in his furniture, vacated the flat and went to stay with an uncle at Merthyr Tydfil in Wales. Then, claiming to be worried about Geraldine, he turned up at the local police station and in order to protect himself and Christie from a charge of abortion, related a cock-and-bull story about how Beryl had died from swallowing a pill that a man in a café had given him, and that he had put her body down one of the drains. The drains were searched but no body was found.

Then Evans told what he said was the truth, his story of the failed abortion carried out by Christie. The house was again searched, and this time the police found the bodies of Beryl and Geraldine wrapped in blankets behind the door of the ground floor wash-house. Evans was brought to London and at the local police station confronted with the clothing of his wife and daughter: he was told that both had been strangled, and that there were no marks of an attempted abortion on his wife's body.

Later that night he signed what he afterwards said was a false confession to both murders.

This was Evans's story, and not surprisingly it failed to convince. Why run away from the flat if innocent? Why lie to the police if innocent? Why confess to murder if innocent? And, above all, what possible motive could Christie have had for strangling his wife and daughter? Christie himself was an impressive prosecution witness and gave evidence of the many rows that Evans and Beryl had had. The jury had no doubts as to which of the two to believe. They were out of court for only forty minutes, and came back with a verdict of guilty; and the law took its course.

The case was soon forgotten by those few who had any cause to remember it. Three years went by. Then Christie sub-let his flat to a black tenant, and walked out. After a few days the tenant began to notice an unpleasant smell and ripped back the covering to the kitchen alcove: there were the bodies of three prostitutes. The police were called and found the body of Mrs Christie beneath the front room floorboards and those of two other women buried in the patch of soil they called the garden: these last had been there at the time of the murders of Beryl and Geraldine. Christie admitted to having murdered all the women including Beryl Evans. He was a compulsive necrophiliac strangler who first rendered his victims unconscious with a home-made inhalation device and then made love to them: the abortion story he told Evans was merely a front to persuade Beryl to undress and then do to her what he had done to the others. At first Christie denied having murdered the baby, but later said that if it could be proved that he had, he would accept it (his reluctance no doubt induced by his knowledge that on that count Evans had been hanged).

While the possibility of there being two murderers living at 10 Rillington Place seemed unlikely, the general view of the public – who knew nothing of the details of the Evans case and anyway had a touching faith in the administration of justice – was that stranger things had been known to happen. They were reassured by a statement by the police that the two cases were not connected, and by another from the Home Secretary, the same Sir David Maxwell Fyfe. 'There is no practical possibility of an innocent man being hanged in this country,' he said with all the arrogance of the truly ignorant, 'and anyone who thinks there is, is moving

in the realms of fantasy.' Still, there was enough general unease
for him to set up a judicial inquiry into the two cases. It was to
be chaired by a Mr John Scott-Henderson, QC who was told
(for reasons never explained) to present his report before the date
set for Christie's execution – then only ten days away. Most
people would have said that to sort out the relevant issues from
two very complex cases, conduct interviews relating to them,
reach a conclusion and write a report on it in that time would
have been beyond anyone's powers. Mr Scott-Henderson did not
think it beyond his. With two days to spare he presented a
report whose conclusions were that 'for reasons of overwhelming
cogency' no miscarriage of justice had taken place. Maxwell
Fyfe concurred and most people greeted the news with relief.

But not everybody, and certainly not Mr Eddowes. He believed
that there were not two killers living in 10 Rillington Place, but
one. It seemed to him really beyond belief that the only two male
occupants of this very small house in West London should both
be strangling women in just the same way without either knowing
what the other was doing; and that it had been entirely chance
that led Evans to accuse of the strangulation of his wife and child
a man who, entirely unknown to him or anyone else, had already
strangled two women and buried them at the bottom of the
garden.

Eddowes's book was very short and – because he was not a
professional writer – poorly assembled. I had to read it three
times to be quite sure I understood what he was saying, and why.
But by the time I had finished, I was in no doubt as to his
conclusions. 'I believe –', I concluded my review, 'and unless
fresh evidence is produced to the contrary will continue to believe
until I die – that on March 9th 1950 we hanged an innocent
man.' Later a pamphlet on the case was published by Ian Gilmour,
MP and Lord Altrincham (now John Grigg) who also could not
agree with Scott-Henderson's findings.

Persuasive as I found both these publications, they made little
impression on the general public who, in any case, had other
things to occupy them. But I found myself thinking about the
illiterate Evans as I had done about the illiterate Bentley. If we
really had hanged an innocent man, then surely the country
should know of it, government should acknowledge it and proper
restitution be made. I was angry too with Scott-Henderson and
Maxwell Fyfe for having destroyed the image I had formed long

ago on the step-ladder of my grandfather's library in Edinburgh of the integrity of British justice, angry that two such charlatans should play this confidence trick on the public and think they could get away with it.

It was then I decided that one day I would write a comprehensive book on the two cases myself. But first I had to attend to other business. My career in broadcasting was about to begin.

When the Independent Television network was set up in 1955, and the companies started to plan programmes, they were faced with a lack of ready-made presenters and commentators. Some came over from the BBC but there was still a gap and approaches were made to actors and journalists. Hence, soon after arriving back from a British Council lecture tour of Sweden, Finland and Denmark (unpaid, but useful practice in learning how to address and hold an audience), I was telephoned by an Associated Television producer by the name of John Irwin. He was planning a magazine programme called *Sunday Afternoon* scheduled to come on the air when the network opened in the autumn. One of its ingredients was to be an item called *Profile* in which a presenter asked three people to describe in turn a third party; at the end of which the third party would be revealed and react to what the others had said about him. Would I like to be that presenter?

It was not the most intellectually stimulating of proposals, but it offered what I had long been seeking, an entry into television; and I accepted without hesitation. The *Sunday Afternoon* team and guests met for lunch at a pub near the old Wood Green Empire theatre, and afterwards broadcast the programme live from the stage (in those pre-videotape days there were no facilities for recording). The only other contributor I remember was a character named Leslie Walsh who styled himself the Memory Man, and in answer to unrehearsed questions would reel off incredibly boring statistics, such as who won the FA cup in 1882. My subjects in *Profile* included the film actor Boris Karloff, the painter Annigoni, the writer Rebecca West, the actress Margaret Leighton, the runner Chris Chataway, the cricketer Peter May, and Moira; and after a sticky start the formula seemed to work well. John Irwin also directed the political chat-show *Free Speech*, ITV's version of the BBC television programme *In the News*, with its original cast of the two MPs Bob Boothby and Bill Brown who, together with Michael Foot and the historian A. J. P. Taylor, discussed the issues of the day (though at the time, strange to relate, views about an issue to be debated in Parliament within the next fourteen days were banned): this was broadcast from the stage immediately before us. The *Free Speech* team also lunched in the pub but were given a four-course sit-down meal with decent wine in a private room, while we had to make do with help-yourself cold cuts in a rather tatty function room nearby. One Sunday Randolph Churchill (Winston's rumbustious son), who had sometimes appeared as a substitute on *Free Speech*, was the principal guest in *Profile*. When Bob heard this, he breezed in during the middle of lunch, a white napkin tucked beneath his ample chin and holding a glass of Château Latour. 'We've been having baby lamb today,' he boomed, 'and redcurrant jelly and new potatoes. What are you tucking into, Randolph?' Randolph was sitting uncomfortably on an upright cane chair, balancing a plate on his knee and picking at a thin, wet, pink, circular object. Bob peered at it. 'Well, well!' he said, 'I haven't seen Spam since the war!' and laughed hugely. Randolph, who liked good food and was a bully by nature, was not amused.

Sunday Afternoon ran through the winter before being taken off. By then I had developed a strong taste, almost an addiction, for broadcasting, and in the process gained some useful experience. Where else, if anywhere, could I offer my services? The BBC Television News Department was a closed institution, its newsreaders being staff men like Frank Philips and Alvar Liddell who had been dishing out the news on radio in a fairly po-faced fashion for years and now, without any effort at adaptation, were doing the same on television. The newly formed Independent Television News, however, seemed to be breaking new ground in allowing its two newscasters Robin Day and Chris Chataway a more informal approach; indeed they were called newscasters rather than newsreaders because they were permitted to dot the i's and cross the t's of their copy to suit their own styles.

Having heard that ITN was looking for a third newscaster, I wrote to the then editor-in-chief, Aidan Crawley, asking for an audition. On arrival at the studios with several others, I was given a copy of a previous bulletin which it so happened I had heard and, having learned how to speak to camera in *Sunday Afternoon*, did not find the reading of it as intimidating as some of my fellow applicants. I was thanked for coming and left. That was on a Wednesday, and having heard nothing by the following Monday morning I assumed I had been unsuccessful. Then ITN telephoned. Chris Chataway was in Edinburgh, Robin Day had the 'flu. Could I come in at once and prepare to read the two evening bulletins? The fee would be seven guineas for the early bulletin of five minutes and ten guineas for the late one of fifteen minutes. I could and did; not only then but for the next two years.

People tell me today that I am one of the most relaxed of television presenters; but it was not always so. Before I read my first bulletin on ITN and for many months afterwards I was as nervous and self-conscious as anyone could be; and as I heard the floor manager counting down the seconds to the start of the title music and saw the lighting up of the signal 'ON AIR', my heart began thumping like a metronome. Apart from my own inexperience, one had some cause for nervousness, for the station's teething troubles were not yet over: reports on film which had been laced in at the last moment sometimes broke during transmission, as did the hand-cranked teleprompter which, unlike modern machines which mirror the words across the lens of the camera, was perched unsteadily on top of it; and when it did seize up, one hoped desperately to find one's place in the script.

Unlike the BBC newsreaders, we also did interviews. The record shows that during my time at ITN I interviewed, among many others, Tennessee Williams, Errol Flynn, Flanders and Swann, Derek Ibbotson, Barbara Kelly; but I have no more recollection of having done so than I have of scores of other interviews I have conducted since. The only person I do remember coming to the studio was my friend John Altrincham, who was in the news for having written critically about the Queen's style of speaking and of the narrow coterie from which her courtiers were drawn. Many people were shocked by what they considered an act of *lèse-majesté*, among them a lunatic body called The League of Empire Loyalists. One of their number was waiting on the pavement when, after his interview, John and I came into the street. Behind him stood several photographers who had evidently been tipped off. Uncertain which of us was which, the man said, 'Lord Altrincham?' John owned up, whereupon the man slapped his face and the cameras clicked. As we walked away, I said to John, 'If only we'd known, I could have

dile in *Swan Lake*.

With Leonide Massine
in *The Red Shoes*.

e Aristocrat in
'zelle Angot.

Moira

With Frederick Ashton in *Façade*.

With my best man, Bill Richmond.

Hampton Court Palace,
25 February 1950.

Margot Fonteyn, a godmother, with Moira at Ailsa's christening.

Piers Place, Amersham. From the left: Rachel 7, Ailsa 12, Fiona 2, Alastair 1.

Fiona as a bridesmaid, 1986.

Rachel just before her wedding, 1988.

Alastair in the Falkland Islands, 198

Ailsa as Miss Yardley, 1971.

As a newscaster with ITN, 1956.

With Richard Dimbleby in the *Panorama* studio.

With Lord Mountbatten.

With Admiral Karl Dönitz.

Sitting on a fortune: filming in the gold bullion vault of the Bank of England.

'LUDO' VIC
(THE ONE JUMP AHEAD
TRAINER)

FLOATING JO
By MARGINAL GAINS out of DON'T NOSE
GREAT TRIER. STAYING POWER SUSPECT. COULD
CATCH POPULAR FANCY IF HE SHOWS RESPONSE
TO HIS TRAINER'S MOD METHODS. SHOWS GOOD
FORM ON TELLY OUTINGS.

Emwood cartoon with
Jo Grimond, the Liberal leader.

left and top The Rochdale by-election

The Timothy Evans Committee outside 10 Rillington Place. From left to right:
Dr J. A. Hobson, Harold Evans, LK, John Grigg, Michael Eddowes, Herbert Wolfe.

With Bryan Magee before delivering
Wicked Beyond Belief to the Home Secretary.

With Anna Hauptmann in Philadelphia.

pretended to be you, and then he'd have slapped my face.'

Robin Day meanwhile was pioneering the style of political interviewing which he was to make his own and which, by its meticulous preparatory work and pointed questioning, was to be a model for others. These were still the days of the paternalistic society, when interviewers were unctuous and their subjects condescending ('So good of you to come along, sir, and may I put to you a few questions about foreign policy?' 'By all means, and let me first say how delighted I am to be here'). Robin would have none of that. He recognized early on that a television interview was unlike a newspaper interview in that in the few minutes allotted to you, there was no time for niceties: you had to go straight to the point. Nor was he intimidated by office. In the course of an ITN interview with the Japanese Foreign Minister, he pulled some Japanese ball bearings from his pocket and taxed the Minister with allowing them to flood the British market. The next day's papers expressed outrage: this was no way to treat a visiting statesman. But Robin (and, I am glad to say, his superiors) were unrepentant. As he said years later at a BBC Current Affairs meeting, 'When I interview a king, I am on a level with the king. When I interview a dustman, I am on a level with the dustman.' (There was laughter when a voice from the back called out 'Hear, hear!', but I did not let on it was mine.) If economic growth and higher living standards are one reason why we are a more egalitarian society today, undoubtedly another has been the advent of television, and the arrival in the market-place of those from Olympus meeting on level terms with the likes of Robin Day.

ITN in those early pioneering days was a happy place to work. This was largely due to the benign leadership of Geoffrey Cox, the distinguished New Zealand journalist who took over from Aidan Crawley soon after I arrived, and stayed twelve years; in format, length and style the half-hour evening bulletin that is with us today was largely his creation. I never once saw him angry or even ruffled, though there were times – soothing the ruffled feathers of the mercurial news editor Arthur Clifford, or engaging in prolonged combat with Robin Day about his contract – when he had every reason to be. He always seemed glad to see one, standing in the middle of his office, leaning slightly to one side like a ship under sail, clinking the coins in his trouser pocket, smiling quizzically and then in his clipped New Zealand accent resolving amiably whatever problem one had put before him. Between bulletins Arthur and Robin would mimic him to perfection. I was grateful to Geoffrey for many things, particularly his ruling at the time of Suez when a memo from the Foreign Office was sent to all news media editors asking that our landings on the coast of Egypt be described as an 'intervention' and not an 'invasion'. I thought this request dishonest, for we were not so much 'coming between' as 'going in'; and when I told Geoffrey I would not comply, he supported me, as I knew he would.

During my early days at ITN I was surprised at the ineptness of some of the copy put before me: this was because most of the sub-editors had been recruited from Fleet Street and were still thinking in terms of writing for the popular press. Clichés of the kind now satirized by *Private Eye* ('Bearded 52-year-old ex-barman husband of blonde model Hilda Spriggs . . .') turned up all too frequently and became known collectively as *100,000 women broke down and wept*. Less objectionable but no less time-wasting was correcting words used more for writing than speaking (*selected* rather than *chose*, *assisted* rather than *helped*, *declared* rather than *said*). Some sub-editors proved unable to imagine, as they were writing the words of their copy, the newscaster in the studio actually speaking them.

At first, until I had come to know and be accepted by the staff in the newsroom, I was reluctant to alter copy too drastically. But in time I began to tailor each item to my own needs, choosing the structure and words with which I would be most comfortable. Then, gaining confidence, I began to consider what I had been too nervous to worry about before: delivery – the one attribute in public speaking that the great Greek orator Demosthenes valued above all others. It is a paradox of public speaking that when you talk to an audience of millions on television, you are addressing one person, and that when you speak to a dozen people in a village hall, you address them collectively. It was on the individual viewers who made up the two million of our audience that I now concentrated; and so as to bridge the gap between us I often personalized a piece of information, as I would had I been in their presence. 'You'll remember my saying on Tuesday . . .' or 'If you play chess you may be interested to know . . .', I would say to buttonhole (or more truthfully pretend to buttonhole) the viewer, and involve him or her in the information-giving process. It seemed to have worked. Peter

Black, for long the *Daily Mail*'s television critic, wrote that I conveyed the news 'as though reading a letter to a faraway relative whom I wished to interest', while another critic said that I showed by my expression that 'the film we had just seen had affected him as deeply as it had affected us'. He concluded, 'Here is the real difference between ITN and the BBC. The ITN newscaster shares the news with the viewers.' Today, I guess, there is not much to choose between them.

I have often been asked if during my time in television I have made any major gaffes. Apart from nodding off briefly a few years ago while interviewing a very boring man after a very heavy lunch (luckily the camera was not on me) I can recall only one, and it happened at ITN. Gaffes were in the air that week because Huw Thomas, the Welsh newscaster who succeeded Chris Chataway, had come to grief telling us of the death of Mr Smith of Smith's Crisps. 'Mr Smimf of Crimps Smimp's' was his first of several attempts at it, each being followed by a giggle and 'I'll start again'. Mine was much worse. Referring to the Liverpool Chamber of Shipping, I inadvertently put two t's where the two p's should have been. But it was late and I was tired.

Moira and I had never much cared for living in London with all its social pressures. I knew what Maugham meant when he wrote of not being able to walk down one side of Piccadilly without wondering what he was missing on the other; and when Moira knew she was going to have another baby, we decided to move to the country. After a long search we found what we were looking for at the end of the High Street in Old Amersham, Buckinghamshire, a classic Queen Anne house of mellow red brick with a white portico, wide staircase with oriel window overlooking a walled garden, and much of the original panelling.

At the time our second daughter Rachel was born in November 1956 we were living with my mother at Hampton Court Palace while waiting to move to Amersham. We considered having Rachel christened in the Chapel Royal where we had been married, but when my mother insisted on us also inviting Aunt This and Cousin That, we shifted the venue to the London RNVR headquarters ship, HMS *President*, moored on the Thames Embankment. Here Rachel was baptized in the ship's bell by a bearded naval chaplain. She gave a loud squawk when the water was poured on her which led my father-in-law, who was by then growing deaf, to inquire whether there was a parrot on board.

Until I joined ITN and despite my father having been a Conservative agent and my cousin a well-known Conservative MP, I had not been much interested in party politics. Towards the end of 1956 two events occurred to change that. The first was the election of Jo Grimond to the leadership of the Liberal Party in succession to the worthy but uncharismatic Clement Davies. There was a quality about Jo which I found instantly appealing, for not only did he reflect and forcefully articulate the views and values which I realized I held, but he did so with a lightness of touch that was lacking in any other party leader. His was a mast I knew I could nail my colours to, and I was so excited by the prospect of what his leadership might achieve that I wrote at once to congratulate him, adding that I was now minded to change from being a 'liberal' to a 'Liberal'. This resulted in an invitation to lunch and for me the beginning of a lifelong commitment to Liberalism.

A month later came the fiasco of Suez, Anthony Eden's pathetic attempt to get his own back on the fledgling Egyptian President, Colonel Nasser, for having nationalized the Suez canal. It seemed to me one of the most crassly stupid political acts of modern times, an example of the kind of gunboat mentality which we should have long since outgrown; and which of the two angered me more, the act itself or the sight of Eden on television with his plummy, condescending voice trying to justify it, deluding himself into thinking that Nasser was another Hitler, it was hard to tell. The whole grisly adventure moreover had clearly not been thought out. How far down the Suez canal were our troops to go? How long was it intended they should stay there? Just what did they hope to achieve? As Edmund Burke said in 1775, when the American colonists were showing the same spirit of independence as Nasser: 'The use of force alone is temporary. It may subdue for a moment, but it does not remove the necessity of subduing again.' No doubt it was partly this anti-colonial folk memory that led the Americans to deny us their backing, so that within days of the landing we had to agree to a humiliating cease-fire and withdrawal. More surprising was the backing the British cabinet gave to Eden's madness, and more surprising still the reluctance of any of them subsequently to resign

(Mountbatten, then First Sea Lord, who disapproved of the whole thing, might have resigned, but that would have meant leaving centre stage, which was more than he could have borne). But I, and others I knew, were immeasurably heartened by the resignations of two courageous Conservative junior ministers, Edward Boyle and the Foreign Office Minister of State, Anthony Nutting. Courageous because Tories do not tolerate dissenters in their ranks, and it meant, as they must have known it would, the end of their political careers.

Just over a year later a certain Colonel Schofield, Conservative MP for Rochdale, died, which meant the holding of a by-election. At the previous general election Schofield had polled 26,500 votes to the Labour total of just under 25,000. No Liberal candidate had stood but the town had a strong Liberal tradition. The great free-trader Richard Cobden had been a former member, and the Co-operative movement had started there in the mid-nineteenth century. In 1906, 1910 and again in 1923 the town had returned a Liberal member, and in 1950 the historian Roger Fulford had polled 10,000 Liberal votes. In the post-Suez climate I felt it was a seat the Liberals could win.

I realized too that this was a moment I had been unconsciously waiting for, that I nurtured an imperative to fight Rochdale for the Liberals. As I wrote later in the *Sunday Dispatch*, 'There comes a time in a person's life when he feels himself being pushed in a certain direction; when he knows he must go in that direction, however upsetting the move, however uncertain the consequences.' I told Jo Grimond of my willingness to stand and after his office had been in touch with the Rochdale Reform Association (as the local Liberal Party was called), I was summoned to appear before their selection committee at Manchester's Reform Club. By this time I had boned up on detailed points of Liberal policy, which was more than the selection committee had done, and had little difficulty in coping with the questions put to me. A week later I received an official invitation to stand.

The fact that after nearly two years at ITN my face was now well known to the public, combined with the news that Moira, then at the height of her fame and beauty, would be helping me in the campaign resulted, from the moment the announcement was made, in massive and continuing publicity. Nor was it initially favourable: the right-wing press labelled me a 'gimmick' candidate, and suggested that a talent for reading the news was no substitute for political knowledge; and there was a clutch of cartoons of us both. But I had scores of supportive letters both public and private. My psychiatrist (the one who fell asleep on me) wrote that my decision to stand showed the emergence of the heroic principle, while my friend Ian Gilmour, editing the *Spectator*, wrote, while wishing me luck, that he could imagine nothing worse than being in the House of Commons. He himself was elected to it a few years later and has been there as backbencher and minister ever since.

So began six weeks of intensive campaigning; canvassing and visiting factories and old people's homes by day, two or three meetings a night. Sometimes during canvassing we would run into our opponents: the Labour man, Jack McCann, who had been defeated at the general election and was being shepherded around by the then President of the Rochdale Trades and Labour Council, the ample Cyril Smith, later Rochdale's Liberal MP; and for the Conservatives a congenial flogger and hanger ('Yes, I would do the job myself') named John Parkinson. Although when canvassing we tried not to get too bogged down at any one house, I was unable to resist the blandishments of one old dear who begged me to step inside and 'tell me all about it'. So I imparted with enthusiasm what I knew about the abolition of Schedule A and the importance of site value taxation and other *recherché* subjects and finally ground to a halt. She looked at me steadily and said, 'You are new vicar, aren't you?'

I found my speeches for the evening meetings a bit of a nightmare, for my knowledge and understanding of detailed policies, especially those of my opponents, were inevitably somewhat restricted. 'Quiet and serious' was how the *Guardian* described my reluctance to bang a drum, but it was too quiet and serious for my chairman, a dentist called Charlie Fearn. 'You want to get some fire in your belly, lad,' he exhorted me, but it was easier said than done. The worst part was question-time, for I have never been able to think quickly on my feet, and some of the questions, especially those on inflation, floored me. Heckling too I found unnerving, though happily there was not much of it. But I gained confidence as the campaign went on, so that towards the end the *Daily Telegraph* was saying that I had 'emerged from being a hesitant and unsure candidate into a fluent debater, fired with enthusiasm for his cause'.

In the middle of the campaign came an interesting development.

Until now television had fought shy of covering by-elections, believing that if they did so they could be contravening the Television Act and the Representation of the People Act. For the timid and conventional BBC it was 'too much of a risk'. But the local independent company, Granada, was braver. Having taken legal advice on the two Acts they saw no barrier to covering the by-election, providing there was balance; and they proposed to the candidates and their agents a series of six programmes covering various aspects of the campaign.

There resulted a lot of hard bargaining, both among the candidates in Rochdale and with Party Headquarters and the Independent Television Authority in London. Morgan Philips for the Labour Party and Jo Grimond for the Liberals welcomed the idea, but for the Conservatives Quintin Hailsham was, true to form, deeply conservative, saying the matter was 'one of great importance' and warning of 'the dangers' of such an innovative step, though without specifying what they might be. The *Daily Mirror* thought such caution ridiculous: 'The government has been thrown into a state of ludicrous dither. TV programmes in this country began more than twenty years ago. Is it going to take the government another twenty to make up its mind?'

By the time the Conservatives had given clearance, the first two programmes had been cancelled, which left four to go. But now I put a spanner in the works. Those who claimed that I might have an advantage over the other two candidates in being a professional television man did not realize that the opposite was true; that while I would be expected to do better as a telly-man, I would in all probability do worse, being the least politically experienced. I therefore called a meeting of the candidates and told them (and later the press) that I thought television was in some ways extraneous to the election, and that the time given to it could more profitably be spent on the doorsteps and hustings of Rochdale, speaking to the people direct. I suggested two programmes instead of four, which McCann and Parkinson agreed to (they had no choice) and was applauded locally (as I knew I would be) when the reasons for my decision became known. The two programmes took place in the main chamber of the Rochdale Town Hall, the first consisting of four-minute statements to camera by all three candidates, the second, on the eve of poll, of a press conference with three journalists. Neither was exactly a show-stopper, but the press agreed we had all acquitted ourselves satisfactorily, and welcomed the initiative that Granada had taken.

The campaign drew to its close. The candidates finished their tour of the old people's homes where Parkinson recited 'Albert and the Lion' and McCann tootled a tune on the piano; my turn was to produce Moira whom they all seemed happy to meet and just look at. On the last Saturday Lancashire and Cheshire Young Liberals organized a motorcade of sixty cars covered in posters which went honking and blaring its way through the town, ending at the Town Hall square where we held a marathon meeting until dusk. The heavy brigade came up from London to spike my guns, among them Attlee and Callaghan. Hailsham had a swimsuit thrown at him in the Town Hall, picked it up with his stick, cried, 'Who will give me a quid for these bumbags?' and rang a bell. We also had a Town Hall meeting with Jo Grimond as the star and a capacity audience that overflowed into an adjoining room; there was a feeling of expectancy and euphoria in the air which my chairman Charlie Fearn did his best to kill by asking us all to stand for one minute's silence in memory of the footballers killed in the Manchester United air crash.

I spent polling day, as did the other candidates, visiting the polling stations and thanking our tellers and others for their support. They were optimistic we would win, but no one else was: all the press commentators put me bottom of the poll, and none predicted that I would get more than 15,000 votes. Granada's cameras came to the poll (another first) and watched the candidates watching the clerks counting the votes. After a time a pattern emerged: McCann in the lead, myself not far behind, Parkinson way in the rear. And that was how it stayed. At 1 a.m. the Mayor went on to the balcony to announce the result to a crowd of several hundred: McCann 22,153, Kennedy 17,603, Parkinson 9827; Labour majority 4550. If it was not as good as we had hoped, it was good enough; the biggest Liberal vote at any election since 1935. When I went on to the balcony after McCann I got a huge cheer, and an even bigger one when I said I would be back for the general election in a year's time and would win. When it was Parkinson's turn he accused the cotton industry of stabbing him in the back and was booed as well as cheered.

Next day the result made banner headlines in all the papers: 'LIBERAL SENSATION', 'LUDOVIC CRUSHES TORIES', 'ROCHDALE SHOCK TO GOVERNMENT', 'P.M. BACK TO LUDO

WEEKEND'. It was all very cheering. The only sour note came from Bumbags Hailsham who proved a rotten loser by claiming in a speech at Glasgow that the Liberals were 'usurpers; a party without a policy, an aim, an outlook or a philosophy'. Yet 17,603 people in Rochdale hadn't thought so.

Since writing the above I have had access to secret correspondence on the Rochdale result between Hailsham and Harold Macmillan, the Prime Minister. Writing as chairman of the Conservative Party on the day after the poll, Hailsham said it had been 'a great personal blow and I should not in the least complain if you told me that it had so shaken your confidence in me that you would wish to relieve me of the chairmanship'. One reason for the poor Conservative showing, he believed, was my being known on television. After seeing the first Granada programme, 'I have no doubt that the Liberal was the worst candidate: this was also the opinion of everyone to whom I spoke . . . The familiarity of his face more than offset the inferiority of his performance.'

In a typically unflappable reply Macmillan turned down Hailsham's offer of resignation ('We all have great confidence in you and your office . . .') but also gave him a mild wigging for his Glasgow speech ('my present inclination is to try to woo away those who have supported the Liberal candidate rather than to attack them'). In a further exchange Hailsham said he agreed about the wooing, when he plainly didn't, adding that 'our own people will demand an occasional riposte to the intolerable drizzle of insult to which they are being subjected by the Liberal organization and leaders.' Two months later Mark Bonham Carter, whose face was not known on television, won Torrington for the Liberals. History does not record what excuses Hailsham put forward then.

With my political allegiance now public knowledge, there could be no question of returning to ITN; in any case I had never looked on my employment as a newscaster as being anything other than a stepping-stone to more adventurous and satisfying work elsewhere. I was then fortunate enough to be offered the chairmanship of Associated-Rediffusion's (now Thames Television's) weekly current affairs programme, *This Week*. Yet although it offered more scope than ITN, it was in those days a scrappy affair, known as the poor man's *Panorama*, in which two, three, four and sometimes even five items were crammed into the programme's running time of twenty-six minutes and fifty seconds. Brief interviews with politicians were juxtaposed with items of quite astonishing triviality.

There was also a lack of foresight in the preparation of the programme which reached its apogee in a trip to Bonn to interview Chancellor Konrad Adenauer. We took with us a 35mm camera and a crew of seventeen. At the request of Adenauer's office, I had sent them a list of the questions I proposed to ask, and after I had put them to him in English and the translator had repeated them in German, Adenauer read out his replies in German from a prepared script, after which the translator repeated them in English. The whole thing took about an hour and a half, lacked any kind of spontaneity, and when viewed by the producers in London was found (as anyone might have guessed) to be totally unusable. On another occasion I flew to Geneva to interview the then Foreign Secretary, Selwyn Lloyd (the monkey, as Aneurin Bevan called him, to Anthony Eden's organ-grinder). The interview was to take place in the studios of Swiss Television, and because he was pressed for time, the Foreign Secretary asked if I would let him know what areas I was proposing to discuss while he was being made up. In the middle of our conversation the make-up girl said, '*S'il vous plaît, m'sieur, levez-vous les yeux.*' Lloyd looked flummoxed, turned to me and said, 'What is she saying?' I said, 'She wants you to raise your eyes, Foreign Secretary,' and then, because he was still uncomprehending, I added light-heartedly, 'so she can have a go at the bags beneath.' This was standard make-up procedure but it was new to our Selwyn. He did as he was asked, but it turned out to be a frosty interview.

On 1 April 1959 Peter Sellers came into the studio and was given a red wig and beard. I introduced him to the viewers as Professor Duncan Grant-Hetherington of the University of Camelford and he said he was just back from the Himalayas where he had been the first European to sight the Yeti or Abominable Snowman. I asked him to describe what had happened. 'Professor Patch and I were about half-way up a crevasse in one of the Himalayas –' (*cutaway shot of Alps with two figures in the distance*) 'that's me leading and Professor Patch, who is quite a nervy type, some way behind – and we suddenly saw those huge footprints in the snow, from which we later made a cast' (*cutaway of cast of elephant's foot*) '– and on turning a corner of the rock face, we found ourselves looking at the Yeti. He was about seven feet high and covered in hair. I was quite alarmed, I don't mind telling you, and Professor Patch even more so.' 'What did you do?' I asked, and Sellers said, 'Well, I had the presence of mind to whip out my wee Box Brownie and take a quick snap – that's it there –' (*cutaway of a still of an ape at London Zoo taken out of focus*) 'and then because he didn't move – tell the truth I think he was as surprised to see us as we were to see him – I made a wee snowball and threw it at him.' I said, 'And what did he do?' Sellers said, 'Well, this was the funny thing. He picked it up and threw it back, just like an MCC man. And then he gave a kind of roar and rushed past us and disappeared. I succeeded in grabbing a piece of his fur as he went by, and here it is' (*close-up of Sellers's hand holding a tuft of coconut hair*). He rambled on about the significance of what had happened ('there are many learned societies wanting me to write papers') and that was that. If it was not as imaginative a hoax as Richard Dimbleby's spaghetti harvest item on *Panorama* the year before, it did manage to fool many people. My secretary at the time was agog with excitement when she came to the house next morning. '*What* an interesting man! And fancy to think that creature really exists! Did he say more afterwards?'

While my work for *This Week* as well as researching my book on the Timothy Evans case, *10 Rillington Place*, and writing a weekly column for the *Star* took up most of my time, I did manage to visit Rochdale every third or fourth weekend to hold a meeting or speak at a dinner. I also found a new and delightful way of going there: direct from Aylesbury to Manchester on the old and now defunct Great Central Line which meandered through the Derbyshire vales and offered a first-class restaurant service where often I was the only diner.

One Friday, when I knew I would be arriving at Rochdale with little time to spare before a public meeting, Charlie Fearn asked me to meet him at his dentist's surgery. The train from Manchester had no loo, so by the time I reached the surgery, I was in some need. 'There's no toilet here,' said Charlie, 'but you're welcome to use the spittoon.' It was one of the rummest invitations I have ever had; and impractical too, as I discovered when I stood against the spittoon and found it was about three inches too high, even if I stood on tiptoe. What to do now? While Charlie was fiddling with his instruments at the other side of the room, I fetched a chair, placed it alongside the spittoon and stood on it. But now I was about two feet too high, and doubted at that height the accuracy of my aim. So all that was left was to kneel on the chair, rest myself on the rim of the spittoon and let fly from there, hoping that someone would give the bowl a good swill-round before the first patient arrived in the morning. Afterwards I wondered, was this how Charlie relieved himself during a long day's drilling?

In the late summer of 1959 the political parties began girding themselves for an autumn general election. So far on television there had been very little to show the human face of those who either were or were aspiring to be our political leaders, so I proposed to the Controller of Programmes at Associated-Rediffusion that we set up interviews with R. A. Butler, then Home Secretary, Hailsham, then Conservative Party chairman, and for the Labour Party its leader Hugh Gaitskell, and Aneurin Bevan. The proposal was approved but only for a fifteen-minute slot at 10.45 p.m. (which allowing for the ads meant thirteen and a half minutes) instead of the half hour I had asked for. Despite these limitations the interviews were a modest success and reported widely in the press. Hailsham, whom I interviewed at his home in Sussex, turned out – as I thought he might – to be as sweet a man in private as too often a clown in public; but only rarely during the interview did he allow the private face to come through. I interviewed Nye Bevan in the swish *Les Ambassadeurs* club in Park Lane where, I was surprised to hear, he was a member. 'Do you want to know what I am going to ask you?' I said, to which he replied in his endearing Welsh lilt, 'No, thank you, boy. Either I know my job, in which case I shall know the answer to your questions. Or else I don't know my job, in which case, I bloody well shouldn't be here.' He talked movingly of life in the Welsh valleys before the First War, and said how bitterly disappointed he was that he hadn't achieved more. Gaitskell, whom I knew as a neighbour in Hampstead, was the most straightforward: as with Jo Grimond there seemed to be no dichotomy between the public and private face. Butler's interview, at his house in Smith Square, was interminably prolonged by a bluebottle which kept alighting on the microphone and then, when approached, retreating to the ceiling. Public or private, Butler was equally discreet: no, there was nothing personal in the Home Secretary having to decide whether a condemned man should live or die; yes, he was disappointed not to have succeeded Eden as Prime Minister, but he had gained much wisdom and experience. Afterwards he gave us drinks and showed his Impressionist paintings.

It was agreed by all the political parties that television should play a limited role in the elections; but so sensitive were the television companies in ensuring that no candidate was given an undue advantage that my final *This Week* interview with the French politician Jacques Soustelle, shot just before the announcement of polling day, had my image and voice removed before transmission and another voice dubbed on. This was reported in several papers, which gave me more publicity than if my presence in an unexciting interview had been allowed to remain.

My campaign in Rochdale was a shadow of what the by-election had been, such interest as there was being exclusively local. During the first week the evening meetings were so poorly attended – most people by now knew what I had to say – that I cancelled the others to concentrate on places of work and the doorstep. However, we kept our one big Town Hall rally to which Robin Day (himself a candidate at Hereford) and Jo Grimond came, and which again was filled to capacity. At the by-election the Tories had plugged their favourite theme that in consolidating anti-Labour forces a Liberal vote was a wasted vote and might let Labour in. Now, with the Liberal by-election vote almost twice that of the Conservatives, I was able to turn this argument on its head: the only way to get McCann out, I reiterated at meetings and in leaflets, was to vote Liberal: a vote for Normanton (Parkinson's successor) was a wasted vote. And it nearly worked, too, for at one moment during the Town Hall count my pile of votes was marginally ahead of McCann's. Then he caught up and the final count was McCann 21,689; Kennedy 18,949; Normanton 11,665; majority 2740.

After so much effort from so many loyal supporters over two years, I was deeply disappointed at failing to win. It had been such a narrow margin too, depending on a swing of no more than 1400 votes; under proportional representation I would have had a comfortable majority. Sometimes I have looked back to that time and with Rochdale a Liberal town under Cyril Smith since 1972, reflected that had I won in 1959, I might have been in Parliament for years (might even have become leader of the Liberal Party!)

Yet with all the disappointment there was relief. There were some aspects of politics like the money supply and interest rates and the public borrowing sector that I felt I could never master; and to pursue a political career without having that knowledge seemed to me to be basically dishonest. And having taken time off from writing and broadcasting to stand for Parliament did not mean that my appetite for a writer's life was any the less; at home and crying out to be completed was work suspended on 10 *Rillington Place*. I would be a liberal and hopefully a Liberal always; but apart from accepting the Presidency of the National League of Young Liberals, and despite many offers over many years to be adopted as prospective Liberal candidate in constituencies ranging from Cornwall to the north of Scotland, I gradually came to realize that for me party politics was a peripheral and not a central activity.

Robin Day failed to make it at Hereford too, and after the election came with Moira and me to Tangier for a week's holiday. We called on David Herbert (who styled himself Lord Herbert in the local telephone book), who showed us his aviary of tropical birds some of which he said he had picked up at Harrods, and in the casbah I bought two Hebrew synagogue lamps and for Moira a pair of gold filigree earrings. One day the three of us hired a pea-green boat and rowed out to sea where Robin taught us the words of The Good Ship Venus:

> The cabin-boy's name was Ripper,
> He was an ugly nipper,
> He stuffed his arse
> With broken glass
> And circumcised the skipper.
>
> Frigging in the rigging,
> Frigging in the rigging.

Our voices rang across the bay, and Rochdale and Hereford and television and *Swan Lake* were as if they had never been.

By now I realized I had outgrown *This Week* (at least the 1959 version) much as I had outgrown ITN two years earlier; and after lunch with Leonard Miall, then Head of BBC Television Talks, I signed a contract to join *Panorama*. In the *Daily Mail* Peter Black quoted my saying that the reason for the switch was that *Panorama* would give me more scope for the sort of work I wanted to do. 'And he won't be the last to switch,' he added, 'so long as ITV stuffs its peak hours with thrills and giggles.'

But before I crossed over, I had one ITV assignment to complete; a series of three interviews with the then Archbishop of York, later Archbishop of Canterbury, Michael Ramsay, who looked as old as Moses but was, people kept saying, younger than Cary Grant. Rubicund, bald and with little bits of white hair sticking out at the sides, he had a disconcerting though not unattractive habit of repeating questions addressed to him before they had been completed, and of emphasizing certain words which didn't need it. 'Archbishop,' I asked, 'what is the Church's view, and indeed your own, about the stockpiling of nuclear weapons?' By the time I had reached 'indeed your own', he was saying '*Church's* – Church's *view*', and when I came to 'nuclear weapons' he was muttering, 'my-my-my *own*'. He also repeated things he originated himself.

One evening after the broadcast, we shared a taxi from the studio. When I asked where he wanted to be dropped, he said, 'I'm staying at the – at the *King's* Cross hotel, and then I'm going – I'm going – *back* to – to York in the morning.' I said if he wasn't doing anything for dinner, would he care to join me at the St James's Club? 'Care to – to – *join*, oh that would be – would be – de*light*ful.'

Seated in a comfortable armchair by the fire, he accepted my offer of a glass of sherry. (They gave you doubles there unless you asked for singles.) Then we had another. At the dinner-table I suggested splitting a bottle of claret over the lamb cutlets. He said, 'Bottle of-of-*cut*lets – would be-be-*most* agreeable.' After dinner we returned to the armchairs and I said, how about a glass of port with the coffee? He didn't demur. The port arrived first and the coffee a little later. When I had poured out the coffee and fixed the milk and sugar, I saw that he had not only downed his own glass of port but was half-way through mine. I waited until he had emptied that too (he didn't seem to notice I had none) and then I said, 'Archbishop, I wonder if I could tempt you to a little more port?' He gave the sweetest of smiles and said, '*Tempt* me, *tempt* me—' paused as if to consider it, then said, 'No, no, dear boy, that would be – would be – *overdoing* it.' And he chuckled briefly and leaned back happily in his chair.

15

Panorama

In the New Year Robin Day and I joined *Panorama*. *Panorama* in those days was, as now, the flagship of BBC Television's current affairs but, as was then the fashion, was a programme of several items rather than one. Its previous reporters had included John Freeman, Woodrow Wyatt and Malcolm Muggeridge, and now at the beginning of 1960 its regular team of Robin Day, Robert Kee, James Mossman and myself was described by one critic as 'the strongest group of contributors to any single programme'. And the still centre around which we revolved was Richard Dimbleby, father of David and Jonathan, a brilliant wartime radio reporter, a no less brilliant commentator on royal occasions (though in a style which today would be considered rather too hushed) and, as *Panorama*'s chairman, avuncular and weighty, though in the presence of those of high office or birth rather too respectful to be a successful interviewer.

Panorama then had a steady audience of some eight million viewers and though this may be hard to believe today, it was a programme which like *Maigret* and *The Forsyte Saga* and later dramas such as *Brideshead Revisited* and *The Jewel in the Crown* was for many people compulsive viewing. Apart from being the only serious current affairs programme on either channel, and thanks to the jet aeroplane, it heralded the arrival of almost instant reporting. Today with satellites we think nothing of turning a knob to watch something happening on the other side of the world. But then it was a novelty for viewers to see one of us addressing them from the fringe of some desert or jungle, knowing he had been there only days before; and sometimes we would appear in the studio on transmission night to give the story an update.

Often our orders to jet off to some other continent came at only a few hours' notice ('Your tickets, foreign money and research material will be handed to you at the airport') and by way of compensation we were sent first-class to obtain elbow-room for homework along the way. In those heady days we thought nothing of covering a country the size of Mexico or Syria or the

Philippines in four or five days' shooting, resulting in filmed reports of no more than fifteen or twenty minutes. The usual ingredients were an interview with the prime minister or president, another with a member of the opposition (assuming there was one), a rundown on the country's economy, a brief look at some singular aspect of it (say, the French Foreign Legion in Morocco, white settlers in Kenya, clocks in Switzerland) and, in Third World countries, a day spent in the country shooting the local crops (rice, sugar-cane, cotton, etc.) plus a man ploughing with a pair of oxen, for which there was a standard commentary: 'For hundreds of years now the country's peasants have been tilling a frugal living from the always inhospitable soil.'

Looking back over the list of items in which I took part, I am surprised how few I can remember. The names of interviewees roll by like bottles on a conveyor belt – Frank Cousins, General Norstad, Peter Thorneycroft, Adlai Stevenson, the Earl of Home, Ingmar Bergman, Sam Wanamaker, Ed Murrow, Dom Mintoff – what on earth did I talk to them all about?

A few things have stuck: the historian Arnold Toynbee telling me that only a religious revival could now save western civilization (not a view, I would have thought, supported by history), and Mrs Pandit, former Indian Ambassador both to Washington and Moscow, saying it was not the differences between Americans and Russians that had struck her but the affinities. Then in Jordan and on the same tack, asking the admirable Antoinette Gardner (later Princess Muna) on her engagement to King Hussein the main difference she found between the Christianity she had recently abandoned and Islam, which she had just embraced, and her replying after whispered exchanges with the king, 'Well, none really'; in Helsinki sharing a Finnish sauna with my sound recordist and our embarrassment at being instructed by the crone in charge on how to whip each other with birch twigs, followed by giggles when the crone applied a well-soaped loofah to the soles of our feet; in the Rif mountains in Morocco coming across a line of spikes stretched across the road, piling out of the car in the belief we had been ambushed, only to find behind a rock three laughing Arab boys who had fashioned the spikes from camel turds; off Leicester Square visiting a charm school for men run by a man with the unlikely name of Eden-Wheen; and on a beach in the Hebridean island of South Uist, while conducting a walking interview with a local teacher, falling flat on my face when the microphone lead wrapped round a stone and broke.

But the major set pieces I do remember. In the summer of 1960 Robin Day and I went to Los Angeles to cover the Democratic Convention at which John F. Kennedy was nominated as presidential candidate. His brother-in-law Stas Radziwill, with whom I used to play backgammon in the St James's Club, was there too, and before leaving London had suggested I contact him in Los Angeles with a view to meeting Jack. But I didn't know Stas all that well and felt the link to be too slender to push myself briefly into the life of a man then fully occupied with his own political advancement and about whom at the time I knew little. Later I wished I had done so, for I had not been long in Los Angeles before I fell under the spell of the Kennedy magic. The extraordinarily compelling voice with its unexpected cadences, the ease and assurance that goes with education and wealth, the sense of history and grasp of international politics so that nothing he spoke about existed in a vacuum, the comparative youth and ready wit, all added up to a *persona* and style that I found beguiling. Here, I felt, was a contender for high office who was in thrall to nobody and who could give politics a new dimension, whose voice would be listened to not only in America but across the world and who, for young as much as old, offered a promise for the future. At the press conference Kennedy gave after his nomination I felt it (as I never felt with any other interviewee) a privilege to be present. One of the two questions I tossed at him mentioned a Lloyd George quote he had brought into his acceptance speech the night before, that a Tory nation (a reference to the Republican administration) was a tired nation. As Britain had been a Tory nation for the past nine years, I asked, did he consider Britain tired? He skirted round it as any self-respecting politician would: it wasn't for him to comment on Britain, but he knew and admired our Prime Minister, Harold Macmillan, and he didn't think him tired at all.

It was a convention with its share of surprises: one of the nominees, the urbane and witty Governor Adlai Stevenson of Illinois, coming down to speak in the convention hall before the nomination ceremony (an unprecedented act) and receiving a twenty-minute standing ovation – as much a vote of thanks for being the Democratic Party's standard-bearer in the past as any real belief that he could continue so in the future; and

Kennedy choosing as his running-mate and against the wishes of most of his supporters, his arch-rival for the nomination and his party's leader in the senate, that old war horse of a politician Lyndon B. Johnson of Texas (with the unforeseen consequence that three years later Johnson would succeed him).

Robin did most of the political interviews while I spoke with Rose Kennedy and various members of the Kennedy entourage. But one afternoon Michael Peacock asked me to go into the convention hall and pull out a coloured delegate from Illinois whom he wanted me to interview about the black vote. Now the BBC had been allocated only three tickets for the body of the hall, and I found they were all out. When I told Michael he said, 'Well, see if you can get in some other way.' This was difficult as the doors were closely guarded; but at one entrance I found a band forming up, and behind them a group of people clutching banners which said 'MISSOURI'S FAVORITE SON'. The Missouri delegation was about to march round the hall, ostensibly as a way of persuading the other delegates to nominate their Governor as presidential candidate, in reality to show everyone that Missouri was alive and well and impress the folks back home. Seeing a spare banner, I seized it; a moment later the doors opened, the band struck up a southern ditty, we raised our banners and spilled into the hall. After some to-ing and fro-ing I spotted where the Illinois delegation was sitting, lowered my banner to the floor, grabbed my man and took him outside.

Just as I was about to begin the interview, Michael Peacock said, 'Good God, Ludo, what's happened to you?' and, looking down, I saw blood streaming from my thumb. I remembered then that in lowering my banner I had felt a slight jab, which must have been a nail in the pole of the banner, but in the excitement of the moment had thought no more about it. Michael said, 'After the interview, you'd better let them see it in the sick-bay. We don't want you to die on us.'

At the sick-bay I was greeted by a tiny nurse called Miss Finkelstein who looked at my thumb and passed me on to swarthy, Hispanic-looking Dr Galumbo who wore a white coat buttoned up to his neck, and had fur all down his arms like that on a chimpanzee. Dr Galumbo looked at my thumb and said, 'Are you allergic to anti-tetanus injections?' I said I didn't know, I'd never had any. Dr Galumbo considered the matter. 'Here's what we'll do,' he said. 'Miss Finkelstein will put a dressing on your thumb and scrape a little of the anti-tetanus solution on your arm. Come back here in a half hour, and if your arm hasn't swelled up, we'll give you a full shot.'

Back in the sick-bay half an hour later I rolled up my sleeve and tiny Miss Finkelstein inspected my arm. 'Looks okay to me,' she said, 'I guess you must be immune.' She rubbed some antiseptic on the arm, fetched a syringe and plunged it in. After she had finished and I was about to roll down my sleeve, I noticed a thing like a small balloon on the place where she had done the scraping.

'Miss Finkelstein,' I said, 'lookee here.'

She did, and said, 'Oh, my!'

'What do we do now?' I asked.

'We'll go right in and see Dr Galumbo.'

Dr Galumbo looked at it and said, 'Oh, my!'

'What do we do now, Dr Galumbo?'

This time Dr Galumbo was more decisive.

'I'll tell you what *you* do,' he said, 'you go right back in there with Miss Finkelstein, and she will give you an *anti*-anti-tetanus shot.'

'Will it prevent whatever it's meant to prevent?' I asked.

'It should,' said Dr Galumbo. 'But it may not.'

It didn't. A week later, having flown to New York and embarked in the *Queen Mary*, I went down with a temperature of 103°, felt as though my body had caught fire, developed pains in my joints, and lost my voice for six weeks. But they weren't too sympathetic at *Panorama*. That's what comes of showing initiative, they said, that's what happens to silly buggers who snatch banners that don't belong to them.

A year later Stas Radziwill was to give me a second bite at the cherry. Kennedy was now President, and on his return to America from meeting Nikita Khrushchev in Vienna and de Gaulle in Paris, he stopped off in London for twenty-four hours to talk to the Prime Minister, Harold Macmillan, attend as godfather the christening of the Radziwills' baby, and dine with the Queen at Buckingham Palace before flying home.

By then Paul Fox had succeeded Michael Peacock as editor of *Panorama*, and all that Monday he hammered away at Kennedy's press officer, Pierre Salinger, in the hope that the President would give us an interview. But Salinger was resolute, not only to him but to other correspondents both British and foreign who were after the same thing. There would be no interviews, period; apart from other considerations the President's schedule was so tight there would be no time for any.

Paul collared me and said, 'The President and Jackie are due to leave the Radziwills' house in Buckingham Street at 8.15 to drive round the corner to the Palace. We're on the air then. Get down there early, try and make a few contacts and see if you can't grab him for a couple of questions as he gets into the car. We'll feed you straight into the programme.'

I can't say I looked forward to the assignment, but I joined an outside broadcast crew in Buckingham Street around 5.30 and waited. Presently I saw Salinger who said, 'I'm sorry, the answer's still no.' An hour or so later the guests from the post-christening party began leaving the Radziwills' house, among them one or two people I knew. Then Stas came out, looked up and down the street, now empty except for a score of policemen, and spotted me standing forlornly on the pavement, a piece of sea-wrack left behind by the tide.

'Hello, Ludo,' he said in his terrible accent, 'what you are doing?'

I told him.

'Why don't you come in,' he said, 'and say hullo to Jack and Jackie?'

They were sitting on two upright chairs either side of the fireplace, wide-eyed Jackie as beautiful as I had imagined, the President seemingly engrossed in the cricket scores in the *Evening Standard*.

'Jack,' said Stas, 'I want you to meet a friend of mine, Ludo Kennedy.'

The President rose and put out his hand. 'I'm sorry,' he said, 'I didn't catch your name.'

'It's the same as yours. The first name is Ludovic.'

He looked hard at me for a moment and said: 'Didn't you write a book recently about a series of murders at Notting Hill here in London, and wasn't there a piece about it by Mollie Panter-Downes in the *New Yorker*?'[1]

I thought, this isn't bad: he's had a tiring time these last few days with Khrushchev, de Gaulle and Macmillan, he couldn't have been briefed because he didn't know I was coming, and yet

---

[1] *10 Rillington Place* had been published two months earlier.

he can remember that: also, as I heard later, he was in some pain with his back.

'I remembered the piece,' he said, 'because of the name. Are you Irish?'

'No,' I said, 'Scots.' I thought of the saw about the Kennedys who couldn't make it in Scotland going to Ireland, and those who couldn't make it there going to Massachusetts, and decided to keep it to myself.

Stas brought me a whisky and soda, and I told the President why I was there.

'Oh sure,' he said, 'what do you want to ask?'

I said, 'Oh, something about Britain's position in the light of these talks with Mr Khrushchev?'

'Certainly,' he said, 'I'd be glad to.'

And so it came about that as the President and Jackie stepped on to the pavement to enter their car, and I came forward, Richard Dimbleby in the *Panorama* studio was able to say to the viewers: 'There is the President, and there also is his namesake, Ludovic Kennedy, about to have a word with him.' And we did have a word, indeed hardly more. It wasn't an interview to go down in history, but it was the only one Kennedy gave in England while President of the United States.

The next year Robin Day and I, with our producer Jeremy Murray-Brown and a camera team, went to Moscow. Under *glasnost* television coverage of Russia is now commonplace, but then it was quite an event. Sponsored by Moscow State Television, we were the first television team to be allowed there, because part of the programme was to be devoted to Richard Dimbleby commentating on the Mayday parade. We flew to Moscow in an old-fashioned Aeroflot plane with brass and mahogany fittings like a Pullman carriage, and bumped around a lot; and the drive into Moscow from the airport, past ranks of shabby, dun-coloured wooden buildings, some seemingly derelict, did little to lift the spirits. They put us up in the huge barrack-like Ukraine Hotel where the basins had no plugs and on each floor (except the thirteenth, which didn't exist) a woman concièrge sat at a desk and kept a beady eye on comings and goings. In the dining-room you had to wait thirty or forty minutes between courses. But the food, when it came, was good: caviare twice a day which led to ebony motions, delicious small fat cucumbers and Georgian champagne.

Work was a different matter. We were supplied with two or three attractive but limpet-like Intourist guides who spoke fluent English; they wanted us to film things we didn't want to, like the insides of factories and the Hall of Science. When I found there were half a dozen churches still functioning in Moscow, and said I would like to attend one of them, my guide was displeased. 'Why do you want to do that?' she said. 'Hardly anyone here goes to church.' I said, 'But in Britain many people still do, and that's what makes it interesting.' She said, 'Mr Khrushchev doesn't believe in God.' I said, 'And you?' and she said, 'I believe what Mr Khrushchev believes.' We were lucky to find a church where a service of baptism was in progress: fourteen tiny babies undergoing mass immersion at the hands of a bevy of white-bearded, robed and hatted patriarchs, and in the background some haunting Gregorian chanting. I also visited one of Moscow's marriage parlours, glorified registry offices which, since the closing of so many churches, have provided young couples with a gloss of ceremony — organ music, flowers, a reception room for the guests.

But the Intourist girls continued to suffocate us, and one day Robin and I decided to give them the slip. He went off to the university where he obtained some revealing interviews with English-speaking students, and I took the crew off to a big open-air vegetable market where there were many queues. Before the day was out the authorities had come to hear of it, and waiting at the Intourist desk that evening was a frosty message for Jeremy that the director of Moscow State Television wished to see him at 9.30 next morning; meantime our filming of the Bolshoi Ballet School, scheduled for the day after, had been cancelled.

That evening we went to a party at the British Embassy. There Jeremy met an English girl who was looking after the children of one of the Embassy staff and his wife who were away on leave. As the evening wore on Jeremy told the girl that he wanted to take her home. She told him not to be silly, she lived miles away in one of the northern suburbs and he would never find his way back. With the obstinacy and single-mindedness of the mildly sloshed Jeremy persisted, and eventually they went off in a snowstorm. I met him at breakfast, his eyes half-closed, but looking quite pleased.

'How did you get on?' I asked.

'Well, everything was fine until it was time to go. When I came

out into the street it was still snowing. It must have been about
2 a.m. I set off in the general direction she said, and I hadn't
gone more than a hundred yards when I heard a rumbling noise.
Guess what it was?'

'Your tummy.'

'A Red Army tank. It seems a lot of them are rehearsing for
Mayday.'

'What did you do?'

'Well, what could I do but stand in the middle of the road and
thumb a lift?'

'And the tank stopped.'

'Yes, and took me on board. I just muttered Ukraine Hotel
over and over again, and they dumped me in the street near the
entrance. Not bad!'

One of the guides came up.

'You will be ready to come with me to Moscow State Television
in twenty minutes.'

'Oh, God, I suppose so,' said Jeremy. 'Will you come too?'

'All right,' I said, 'what about Robin?'

'I think not. He'll start cross-examining everybody, and then
we'll be in deeper trouble. But we'd better tell him we're going.'

We gave several loud raps on Robin's bedroom door, stamped
our feet and said the few Russian words we knew: 'Kaygheebee
Ochi-Chernye Zhazderovya Bolshoi Lubyanka Kaygheebee.'
Presently we heard feet shuffling across the floor, the door was
opened a crack and a bleary figure in pyjamas peered out.

'Oh, it's you,' he said.

We told him where we were going and he seemed relieved
rather than miffed that he wasn't being roped in too.

At Moscow State Television they put on quite a show. We
were taken to the seventh floor, shown into a large room whose
main feature was a long T-shaped table, and given two seats
at the bottom of the stem. Five sober-suited middle-aged men
marched in and took up post at the head of the T, the director
in the centre. They seemed a long way away. The director put
on his spectacles, drew a piece of paper from his pocket and
spoke in Russian. When he stopped, the Intourist guide said to
Jeremy, 'The director says the group of which you are leader has
chosen the wrong path here.' This was too much for Jeremy to
whom the idea of his being a leader was such a novel thought
that, despite his hangover, he burst out laughing. 'Ridiculous

creature,' he muttered: fortunately the guide did not translate. The director chuntered on. Had it not been understood that the Intourist guides would accompany us whenever we were filming? If so, why had we left them behind? Did we think we were showing good manners to our hosts who had made our trip possible? Was this how we behaved in England? He reminded me of my mother in the old days, thrashing things out. Finally he ground to a halt. As regards the filming of the Bolshoi Ballet School, we would have to re-apply, and the decision would be left to the school's director.

The upshot was that we had to cancel seats already booked on the weekly flight to London and stay in Moscow an extra two days. We never did manage to film the Bolshoi Ballet School, though I did secure an interview with a London girl who was training with them. By now, despite an evening of *Swan Lake* at the Bolshoi and a memorable afternoon in the Kremlin Museum admiring the coach that Queen Elizabeth I gave to Boris Godunov and a wealth of jewelled crowns and bibles, Moscow was getting on top of us. Not only were the guides, like the poor, always with us, but we are so conditioned in the West to the colour and liveliness of billboard and other advertisements that to find oneself staying in a city where there are none and which has little architectural merit of its own, had a depressing effect. When I went to the Intourist desk to change my tickets and the girl asked where I wanted to go, I was unaware of saying, as Jeremy said I did, '*Anywhere*!', so desperate was my wish to leave. When she said there was a flight to Helsinki next morning, I jumped at it.

But the feeling of oppression remained with me until the very end. Going through customs where they gave my bag a thorough search, at passport control, at the top of the steps leading to the plane where caricatures of two security men stood in nondescript coats and Trilby hats, even inside the plane itself when the two men came slowly down the aisle giving us all the once-over, I expected at any moment a tap on the shoulder and car ride to, at best, Moscow State Television and at worst the Lubyanka.

Eventually we took off, and when the pilot announced an hour later that we had just left Russian air space, everyone gave a great cheer. That was how it was in those days. That night in Helsinki I dined in a restaurant where there was a floor show and a band, and treated myself to a bottle of Krug.

My last major assignment for *Panorama* took me to Aden

and India. My producer was the programme's assistant editor, Norman Swallow, a cheerful and entertaining companion whose first consideration in judging a filmed report was to ensure that it got past what he called 'the S.H. One. T. point'. Aden was then still a British colony but on the way to gaining independence. I interviewed and dined with the Governor, Sir Charles Johnston, and the next day interviewed one or two Arab nationalist leaders. When Sir Charles heard of this, he sent a frantic message to the Colonial Office in London asking for the Arab interviews to be dropped. Pressure was put on the BBC, as a result of which they complied. Unfortunately Paul Fox, who would never have agreed, was away at the time, and the Director-General Hugh Greene, who would have taken the same view, was never consulted.

Norman and I were in India for eight weeks. The warm air at Bombay airport brought a smell of dung and spices, the Indian smell, ever-present; when I recall India now, that is what first comes to mind. The country also has a bureaucracy more stifling and tenacious than anything the Raj ever handed down: it took us three hours to clear cameras and ourselves through customs, and any request to a government department required several forms in triplicate. Remonstrating was useless: officials wagged their heads and giggled – this was how things were and had to be. In addition cold water taps gushed hot, things ordered never arrived, taxis lost their way. And there were the beggars in rags, some of them children, some on stumps: to toss a coin to one was to open the floodgates to others, a swarm of brown locusts who pursued you down the street. Against this was the exoticism and eroticism of the visual and sensual: exquisite temples and carvings, Shiva's lingam, Vishnu the preserver, a frieze of people making love; the soft, rich looks and classical carriage of raven-haired beauties in saris (a dress which European women should strive to avoid); curries of a fiercer blend than at home, hibiscus and bougainvillea, paw-paws and crimson water-melons, *nimbu pani* and coconut milk fresh from the tree.

A general election was in progress and our first assignment was to cover the sprawling 250-square-mile constituency of Bombay North where lived three-quarters of a million people, the well-to-do minority in houses overlooking the Indian Ocean around Juhu Beach, the majority in the labyrinth of inland slums where five or six often slept in a single hut with leaking corrugated tin roof and, whatever their age or sex, squatted unashamedly on adjoining wasteland to perform their daily jobs. The majority of the electorate were illiterate, so the voting papers carried symbols as well as names, a pair of bullocks for the Congress Party, a pair of scales for the Socialists. The Congress Party candidate was its *éminence grise*, the 64-year-old non-Hindi-speaking Defence Minister, Krishna Menon, once a Labour councillor in St Pancras, later Indian High Commissioner in London but now thought to be tainted with communism and on the defensive because of the Chinese infiltration of Assam. His opponent was a gnarled nut of a man, 74-year-old Acharya Kripalani, a friend of Gandhi and former President of the Congress Party who had broken away to form his own People's Socialist Party. I interviewed both: Menon denied that he was a communist, Kripalani said he was; the mystery to me, having seen the beggars and the slums, was how India had avoided communism so long.

The taxi taking us to the Taj Mahal Hotel from Kripalani's headquarters near the airport was flagged down in the driveway by a short young man in a sky-blue suit wearing steel-rimmed spectacles and with teeth red from betel-juice.

'You are going to the centre of Bombay?' he inquired in that well-known lilt.

'Yes.'

'I am coming with you.' And before I could dispute the point, he had opened the door and climbed in.

'How are you?' he said, putting out a hand. 'I am a helper of Mr Kripalani. I am coming from Kerala which is quite distant from here. I am a student. It is very important that Mr Kripalani beats Mr Menon who is a communist. His victory will be good for India. Are you English?'

'Yes.'

'What do you do?'

I told him.

'For me this is very interesting,' he said, 'for you are just the person to whom I am wanting to ask some questions. Tell me, please, your candid opinions of Mr Charles Dickens, Mr Harold Macmillan, and Mr Kingsley Amis.'

It was a tallish order, but I did the best I could.

'You know *The Caine Mutiny*?'

'Yes.'

'And *A Midsummer Night's Dream*?'

'Yes.'

'And what is your frank opinion of these works?'

We battled on like this for several miles with him firing yet another salvo whenever I thought he had finished. Then, mercifully, it seemed he had dried up. I was just closing my eyes when I heard him say,

'You are probably noticing that I am not asking further questions?'

'Yes.'

'It is not because I am not *having* further questions, you understand. Oh, no! I will tell you why. I have just come from making a poem about you.'

'Oh?'

'Happy in love/And dauntless in work/Is Mr L. Kennedy/Of the BBC.'

At a loss to know how to react, I said the first stupid thing that came into my head. 'But it doesn't rhyme.'

He looked crestfallen. 'That is true,' he said. 'Not rhyming is noticeable omission.'

After a further silence he said, 'Now I am making a poem that rhymes.'

'Yes?'

He turned and gave me a big red betel-juice smile. 'I seal with a kiss,' he said, 'our heavenly bliss.'

I didn't believe he really intended to make a stab at this, but it was an awkward moment and I was glad that just then we reached the hotel and all climbed out.

Completing filmed reports from abroad in those days was something of a hit-and-miss affair. The producer gave the presenter a shot list of everything filmed, the presenter wrote a commentary which he hoped would fit and which he then recorded in some quiet room with the sound man, after which both film and tapes were taken to the nearest airport and shipped to London: there the *Panorama* film editors would chop, change and piece them together for transmission. Back in the hotel one always had a sinking feeling that the film had been wrongly exposed, that the commentary wouldn't match the pictures, that the shipment wouldn't reach its destination or, if it did, that it would miss the deadline. It was therefore always a relief as well as extremely heartening to receive, as we did on this occasion, a cable from London, 'Congratulations splendid coverage Indian elections. Using 17 minutes Monday. Regards Paul.' Of all the editors I ever worked for, Paul Fox was the most meticulous in acknowledging and expressing thanks for reports received from abroad, realizing what it did for the morale of birds in the wilderness.

We were supposed to go to Delhi after that to interview Mr Nehru, but a message arrived that it would be more convenient if we went the following week. So we filled in the time with a visit to Poona, once a famous British Indian Army garrison town, and source of the catch-phrase 'When I was in Poona' that had originated to deflate reminiscences of thousands of old Indian Army officer bores. Ghosts of the Raj still abounded: the Poona Club at the racecourse, baroque silver on display, the click of billiard balls from an adjoining room; the old officers' quarters with its primitive 'suites' of bedroom, dressing-room, bathroom, sitting-room and attendant cockroaches, now part of a hotel; Poona University outside the town, a handsome country house that had been the summer residence of the Governors of Bombay who arrived there each year escorted by a squadron of lancers on horseback with pennants flying and dressed in red and black (in the former ballroom hung two life-size portraits of King Edward VII and Queen Alexandra, and when I asked the Vice-Chancellor why they were still there, he said, 'They're nice pictures and we've nothing to put in their place'); and then the living legacy of the past, scores of handsome Anglo-Indian men and women, fruits of brief unions under the stars, who, as they grew up, found they belonged neither to one race nor the other.

In Poona too was the Indian Defence Academy where, unlike in Britain, officers of all three services train together. The commandant who looked like a tanned David Niven and, like him, was Sandhurst-trained, took us to dine in the staff officers' mess where people said lovely things like, 'Oh that fellow's a bally nuisance. He's always one over the eight and simply won't knuckle down and learn the ropes', and 'We had a ripping match against the President's Eleven. Knocked those bloody geezers into a cocked hat', and (in answer to a question about Defence Minister Krishna Menon, who had just been re-elected) 'It's a free country and people can say what they like, but in my book he's not at all a bad chap.' When I was relating this to a retired British army officer who had once been stationed at Poona, he told me of an evening when the Indian civilian staff at the garrison had put on a play written by themselves, which all the officers and their wives and families were invited to watch. The opening scene was an English orchard and the first words of the squire as he entered from the wings were, 'Oh, my! Oh, my! Someone has stolen my fucking pineapples.'

But there was another side to Poona in the vast and neglected British cemetery on the edge of the town, a wilderness of crumbling gravestones and parched, brown grasses where goats munched and browsed and long ago time had stopped. Here in microcosm was a history of the British Empire; and walking among the derelict plots, abandoned by all except their occupants, one was made aware of the harshness of life in foreign parts in Victorian and Edwardian times, of the self-sacrifice of those in the army, the police, the telegraph service and other branches of the civil administration who had come here with their families to live and die in the service of king and country. 'In loving memory of Trooper David Brown, aged 19. Died of the Cholera.' 'In dearest memory of June Dunn aged 4 and Emily Dunn aged 2, beloved only children of John and Laura Dunn. Died of the Cholera. Ever in our thoughts.' 'To the sacred memory of my dear husband Robert Akester of the Postal Service. Died of the Fever, aged 31.' The graves and headstones with similar inscriptions stretched almost out of sight, monuments to doomed youth. 'Gone but not forgotten', they cried, but it was no longer true. Here at Poona and in England too they had been forgotten as though they had never been.

We also found time to motor down to Goa, the Portuguese colony south of Bombay which four months earlier had been taken over by Indian troops. Because of the heat we broke our journey at a small country hotel whose *patron* said before we went to bed, 'You like good English breakfast? Tea, porridge, bacon and eggs?' and seemed disappointed when we settled for orange juice and coffee.

When we reached Goa next day, I understood how the Portuguese mariner Alfonso Albuquerque must have felt when in 1510 he sailed into one of the loveliest natural harbours in the world: a meandering estuary of green vegetation, red soil, blue water, and long biscuity beaches fringed with grass and overhung with palms that might have come out of a travel agent's brochure. First in Old Goa, several miles inland and then at Pangim on the banks of the slow-moving Mandavi river the capital was established, a complex of warehouses, storerooms, government offices and the Viceroy's palace, low-lying and well-proportioned as might be expected from a people with a long tradition of building in a hot climate and in sharp contrast to the ugly Edwardian architecture which has disfigured so much of Bombay. When we arrived at the palace Indian workmen were dismantling portraits of some of the 150 Viceroys who had governed Goa for nearly five centuries; but the warehouses were still full of duty-free goods, and we stocked up with what we could afford of cigars, cigarettes, watches and scent. But almost the most startling thing about Goa are the four great Catholic churches built in Old Goa and now surrounded by jungle: two had been abandoned to nature but two were still in use, the seventeenth-century Cathedral and the great Church of Bom Jesus; here in a glass case they keep the big toe of St Francis Xavier and take it out for inspection every twelve years.

Nehru had been much criticized by the free world for his invasion of Goa, especially for saying before he launched the attack that his patience was exhausted, a painful Hitlerian echo. In fact he had been more than patient, hoping that the Portuguese would withdraw as the French had withdrawn from their enclaves after independence, then taking part in fruitless negotiations, finally imposing a blockade which the Portuguese had managed to resist by the unexpected growth of the iron ore trade. In addition I met several people who, advocating integration with India, had been imprisoned for years by the Portuguese, some beaten and tortured, others deported to Angola. Now the boot was on the other foot, for outside the town we found several hundred Portuguese troops, Goa's former garrison, locked up in a prisoners-of-war cage. Fred, our handsome, black-haired cameraman, was unhappy filming this. But then Fred had South African connections and had recently been deeply offended at coming across a sign in Poona saying 'SOUTH AFRICANS NOT WANTED'. That evening after filming he said to me, 'Will you help me write a letter to *The Times*?'

'What about, Fred?'

'About these dark-skinned Indian johnnies locking up the Portuguese.'

'But Fred, the Portuguese here are almost as dark-skinned themselves.'

'Yes, but don't you see, it's not right. After all, the Portuguese are Europeans.'

'Well, you draft the letter, Fred, and I'll look at it.'

But, I'm glad to say, he never did.

In Delhi I taxed Mr Nehru with betraying his principles of non-violence by invading Goa, more as a journalistic ploy than with any show of conviction, a charge which he had little difficulty in rebutting. Then we did a story on American tourists at the Taj Mahal (like Venice, more stunning than you could ever imagine) and – which many tourists miss – the nearby fortress of Fatehpur Sikri, abandoned for lack of water in the eighteenth century, but marvellously preserved; then a long drive through the Punjab to Pathankot, trying to dissuade our driver from deliberately running down pye-dogs, and a hazardous 200-mile journey through the mountains to the Indian Moslem state of Kashmir. In Srinagar I talked to the Governor, Bakshi Ghulam Mohammed, and later we threw flour at each other to celebrate the feast of Holi, and I rowed on the lovely Dal Lake and in a mountain stream caught trout whose ancestors had been put there by the British Army a hundred years before. To complete the Kashmir story I needed to visit Azad (Free) Kashmir in Pakistan, but the border, guarded by United Nations troops, was sealed, and so we had to make a 500-mile detour to Amritsar and Lahore and so back up to Azad Kashmir where I interviewed the President, Mr Kurschid. He told me that the day was not far off when his people, fully armed, would stream across the border and reclaim for ever the land that was rightfully theirs – a forecast, like so many given to journalists, that has long been gathering dust in history's roomy attic.

And lastly to Dharmsala, 6000 feet up among the pine trees and rhododendrons of the lower Himalayas to meet the 26-year-old Dalai Lama, a refugee from the Chinese invasion of Tibet. Formerly a British hill station, Dharmsala lacked a hotel, and we were promised accommodation in the tourist guest-house. But several young pilgrims who had been expected to depart had decided to stay on, and so that Norman Swallow and I might have a room, one of them shifted to the attic. I met him at breakfast the next day, and noticing that his black hair was unusually long and curled round the nape of his neck, took him to be a Sikh in western dress. But when I thanked him for vacating his room, he answered in American. I asked him what he did. He said he was a poet. We chatted for a little about poetry, with which he showed more than a nodding acquaintance. When the marmalade came, I asked him his name and he said it was Allen Ginsberg.

Six miles beyond Dharmsala the road ended, and a further half-mile on foot took us to a nursery school where prayer-wheels rattled and squeaked and green prayer flags flew from the tops of the pine trees, and 500 little Tibetan children were being cared for by the Dalai Lama's sister. A secretary took us into the house where the Dalai Lama lived, a modest bungalow with a red corrugated tin roof and derelict tennis court, and, waiting in an ante-room for him to appear, I recalled what I had read about him. First the portents that had led to his discovery at the age of four in a remote Tibetan village – the previous Dalai Lama's face changing direction after death, fungus growing on a pillar, lettering appearing on the surface of a lake (no dottier when you come to think of it than a star in the east, three wise men and a virgin birth); then his intensive education in history, philosophy, metaphysics and religion, and the growth of his interest in things mechanical so he would take a watch or the palace generator to pieces and put them together again; and finally, after all his attempts to appease the Chinese overlords had failed, after he had seen his people massacred and learned that his palace was about to be shelled, the dramatic flight over the mountains to India.

He came smiling into the room, a tall young man with close-cropped hair, dressed in freshly laundered brown and saffron robes and wearing a pair of sturdy, black boots of the kind favoured by Lord Hailsham. His cheeks glowed as though recently scrubbed with Lifebuoy soap, and the skin on his well-manicured hands seemed almost translucent. His arms were bare from the shoulders which gave him an almost girlish appearance, an impression which was strengthened, after the interpreter arrived and we had begun to exchange pleasantries, by his propensity to giggle. This was the most surprising thing about him. Yet they did not seem to be the giggles of a man of nervous disposition or shallow mind, but rather of one who had come to terms with life and could, as it were, afford to giggle.

I asked him if, looking back, he thought there was anything his government could have done to prevent the Chinese invasion, and he said Yes, it might have been prevented if Tibet had not remained so aloof from the rest of the world, had become a member of the United Nations. And how was he spending his time now? Raising money for the Tibetan refugees, he said, and in regular meetings with his cabinet. 'Yesterday we discussed the new constitution we will have when we return to Lhasa.' And when did he think that would be? His answer was to grow as dusty as Mr Kurschid's. 'Soon,' he said. 'In a year or two.' That was twenty-six years ago, and today he is still roaming the world, a middle-aged refugee excluded from his native land for ever, a leader without a government, prince without a principality, monk without a cell.

He had given the interview in Tibetan, but now in near-fluent English he said something like, 'Was that all right? Was that what you wanted?'

'That was just fine,' I said. But then we always said that.

16

10 Rillington Place

When starting researches into the book on 10 Rillington Place, I had not thought that a request to the Director of Public Prosecutions for a sight of the papers on the case would meet with anything but a polite refusal; but to my surprise (and because, I think, it was a case that troubled them) I was given a transcript of the trial, copies of briefs to counsel and all witness statements. Among the last were two batches of statements by three builders' workmen who were in the house at the time, yet who were not called to give evidence. In their first statements the workmen had said that the bodies of Mrs Evans and her daughter could not possibly have been in the downstairs wash-house when Evans in his 'confession' said he put them there, as they were keeping their tools in the wash-house then and going in and out of it all the time. But in the second batch of statements, made two days later, they agreed that they could have been mistaken in their first statements and there might have been a couple of bodies in the wash-house which they hadn't noticed. Having inspected the wash-house and found it to be about the same size as an ordinary lavatory, I knew this was nonsense. What had happened to make the workmen change their minds?

I managed to track down one of them, a Mr Willis, and he told me, 'When we got back to the house after our dinner, there was a black police car waiting outside. The driver said he'd come to fetch us to the police station for more questioning. We said we'd told them everything we knew already, and he said, "What you said before doesn't quite fit in with the chief inspector's calculations."

'They kept us waiting at the station about three hours, and then they started shouting at us that we were wrong to say there were no bodies in the wash-house, they had thirty or forty witnesses to prove there were. Well, we all stuck out for a time saying it was they who were wrong, not us, but in the end – it must have been about five hours after we'd been there – we were all so browned off and exhausted, we were ready to sign anything. I remember our foreman saying, "Well, if the police say there were bodies there, they must be right." Personally, I didn't see it mattered much either way. But knowing what they found out later about Christie, I wish I'd stuck to my guns.'

As the second batch of statements cancelled out the first, the prosecution saw no need to call the workmen as witnesses, and the police had no need to show the statements to the defence; and Evans's legal aid solicitors, having no more reason than anyone else to believe in the innocence of their client, didn't track down the workmen themselves. However, among the papers they still held on the case, I found this, part of their brief to counsel about forensic evidence on the body of Mrs Evans: 'The evidence given [at the magistrate's court] by Dr Teare appears to be open to the comment that his expert opinion travelled beyond justifiable inference . . . in so far as he purports to suggest that there might have been an attempt at sexual penetration after death . . . There is no evidence of that nature during the prisoner's life history.'

Here was the missing link between Evans's claims that Christie had murdered his wife and the reason why he had murdered her; here were Christie's fingerprints; and had what was later known about Christie been known then, this in itself would have been enough for Evans to have been released from prison and for Christie to have taken his place. But since this was not known, it was useless for the defence. 'I had no option but to ignore it,' said Evans's counsel, Malcolm Morris. 'If Evans was guilty, it only made things worse.'

From the time of his trial to the hour of his execution Evans never wavered in asserting his innocence, not only to his family and solicitor but to anyone else who would listen; and I was fortunate in that the former secretary of F. Tennyson Jesse, who had edited *Trials of Evans and Christie* in the Notable British Trials series (but was herself now dead), still possessed the evidence tendered to the Statutory Inquiry (as to whether Evans was fit to hang) from the prison officers who had sat with him. To all these officers and to the prison chaplain he had expressed his innocence, and some had given unsolicited opinions that they believed him. It was therefore vital that I somehow demolish the solid rock of his 'confession', the only evidence of substance against him. The more I examined it, the more it crumbled. For a start it smacked of police phraseology instead of that of an illiterate man ('she was incurring one debt after another . . . no fixed abode . . . I accused her of squandering the money . . . under false pretences', etc.). Secondly the times between which it was said to have been taken were insufficient for the number of words recorded; and from contemporary press accounts it was clear that questioning said to have ended at 11.15 p.m. was still going on in the early hours of the morning. And lastly some of the assertions in it were simply not true, like Evans saying he had put the bodies in the wash-house when the workmen were there and that he had locked the wash-house door when it didn't have a lock.

What I believed happened that night at Notting Hill Police Station was that Evans, having just been told that his wife, whom he thought had died from an abortion, had been strangled, and that his daughter, whom he thought was alive and being looked after by friends of Christie, had been strangled too, was in a state of shock. With an IQ of 68 and unable to write more than his own name, he was confronted by two hostile policemen who were as certain as any two men can be that he was guilty of murder, were determined to go on interrogating him until he 'confessed', and at some time long after midnight (Evans himself said 5 a.m.) succeeded. This – and what they had evidently done to the workmen – was my first experience of the lengths to which CID officers could go in order to secure a conviction, and I was deeply shocked. I was to find the same sort of malpractice repeating itself in case after case in the years ahead.

10 Rillington Place was published in April 1961 and caused something of a stir, most newspapers reviewing it in special feature articles; for although Evans was perhaps not the first apparently innocent man to be hanged in this country, mine was the first book to give a detailed and comprehensive account of how such a thing had come about. In a foreword addressed to the Home Secretary, R. A. Butler, I listed the growing number of people who now believed in Evans's innocence (they included the Home Secretary who had authorized his execution, James Chuter Ede, which for him must have been a painful though courageous admission); and I concluded by asking Mr Butler to set up a new inquiry to look into all those aspects of the case which time had prevented Mr Scott-Henderson from investigating, and which would settle the matter once and for all.

Hopes for a new inquiry rose when, two months after publication, the government announced that the case would be debated in the House of Commons. I attended the debate with the distinguished jurist Lord Birkett, a neighbour of ours at Amersham who had reviewed the book very favourably ('holds one under a kind of spell') in the Observer. From the Labour opposition benches, particularly from Chuter Ede and Frank Soskice, came powerful calls for a new inquiry, even for a free pardon, and the removal of Evans's body from Pentonville to his family for reburial in consecrated ground. They argued that if at the time of Evans's trial it had emerged that two of Christie's victims were lying buried in the garden, it was inconceivable that (a) Evans would have been charged, (b) that he would have been convicted, and (c) that if sentenced to life imprisonment rather than death that he would not have been immediately released at the time of Christie's arrest. 'My appeal to the Home Secretary,' said Sir Frank Soskice, 'is most earnest. I believe that if ever there was a debt due to justice and the reputation both of our own judicial system and to the public conscience, that debt is one the Home Secretary should now pay.'

But R. A. Butler, whom I had always thought of as a decent, if somewhat flabby individual, would have none of it. He said that my book (which he claimed to have carefully read) contained no new facts (as he went along it became clear that he had not read it and was speaking to a Home Office brief). He continued in the same negative fashion. He could not authorize the removal of Evans's body from Pentonville because an 1868 Act of Parliament prevented it; he could not recommend a free pardon because there was no certainty of Evans's innocence; and he could not order a new inquiry because memories had become dimmed and no fresh evidence was likely to appear. For a government minister it was an astonishing display of cowardice and mendacity. In an article I wrote in the *Spectator* I concluded by saying that even if we had lost a battle, the battle to clear Evans's name would, if necessary, go on for another five, ten, fifteen years.

Three years passed; and when in 1964 Labour came into power and Frank Soskice was appointed Home Secretary, a new inquiry was regarded as a certainty. But when in February 1965 Ian Gilmour in the House of Commons asked for such an inquiry, Soskice had had a change of heart. Earnest though he may have been in proposing one in 1961, he was no less earnest in refusing one now. 'I really do not think that an inquiry would serve any useful purpose ... even if the innocence of Evans were established, I have no power to make an official declaration of it.' It was an even more contemptible performance than Butler's. But if Soskice thought he could ride roughshod over public opinion, he was in for a surprise. By now many people had had as much whitewash as they could stand, and among them was an industrialist living in the north of England by the name of Herbert Wolfe, a German Jew who came to this country as a refugee in 1933. Having started life as a ten-shillings-a-week office boy, he was now part owner of a small chemical factory. He had read my book, believed passionately in Evans's innocence, and wanted to do something about it. Like Evans he was a man who had been tossed about by fate; and the integrity of English justice, which the natives seemed to take for granted, was for him, a fugitive from German injustice, infinitely precious. He regarded Soskice's refusal to convene an inquiry as the last straw.

So he telephoned his friend Harold Evans, editor of the *Northern Echo*, and suggested writing an article on the case. He could not have chosen anyone better, for both in the *Northern Echo* and later at the *Sunday Times* Harold Evans became one of the great campaigning editors of his day. Having read my book and other material which left him with a sense of outrage as acute as that of Herbert Wolfe, Harold decided to mount a campaign. He and Herbert published articles on the case every week, reprinted them as broadsheets, sent them to every MP in the Commons and most in the Lords, lobbied ministers, broadcasters and editors. That summer we joined forces and together with Ian Gilmour, John Grigg, Chuter Ede, Michael Eddowes and others who had long championed the cause of

Evans's innocence, formed the Timothy Evans Committee.

From now on events moved reasonably quickly. After 113 MPs had been persuaded to sign a motion for a new inquiry, an all-Party delegation had called on the Home Secretary, and several senior ministers had lobbied the Prime Minister, Soskice caved in: there would be a new inquiry after all, presided over by Sir Daniel Brabin, a High Court judge.

In November Evans's remains were handed back to his family thanks to a new law resulting from the ending of capital punishment (a reform which the Evans case had done much to hasten). Three weeks later the Brabin Inquiry opened in the Law Courts. It sat for nearly two months, examined 79 witnesses including myself, and ran to a million words. In January 1966 Brabin took his million words home and in October delivered his report. As I wrote at the time, if the Scott-Henderson report had astonished by its effrontery, the Brabin report stunned by its absurdity. For whereas all those who had previously studied the case – the prosecution, the trial judge, the Court of Criminal Appeal, Scott-Henderson and myself – were all agreed that whoever had done one murder had done both, Brabin came up with the novel theory that while Evans had probably *not* murdered the baby, for which he had been hanged, he probably *had* murdered his wife, for which he hadn't even been tried. This certainly was an arresting theory, there being virtually no evidence to support it. It was the first case I had investigated which showed not once but twice the deep reluctance of the legal profession to admit that a miscarriage of justice can occur. Like Scott-Henderson, Brabin must have seen where the evidence was leading him and shied away. Yes, he seemed to say, we had done Evans wrong but only on a technicality: the law could breathe again.

There were many diehards who hoped that such a finding would obviate the need for anything further, and that the case could now be quietly forgotten. On television Sir Frank Soskice, reincarnated as Lord Stow Hill, and Lord Dilhorne, a former Lord Chancellor (whom the eminent judge Lord Devlin said had not a grain of judicial sense), pooh-poohed the idea of anything else. Fortunately the new Home Secretary was made of grittier stuff. What Butler and Soskice said they couldn't do for lack of precedents, Roy Jenkins did in an afternoon – recommended a posthumous free pardon which the Queen immediately granted.

So, thirteen years late, this sorry tale at last ended – a tale not only about a grievous injustice but about the pusillanimity of those for whom a belief in the infallibility of the law is more important than a belief in its integrity, who think that when a mistake is made, it is better to pretend it never happened than concede that the law must be human too. Despite *10 Rillington Place* having remained in print from that time to this, the subsequent reluctance of the Home Office and Court of Appeal ever to admit that criminal justice can miscarry continues to this day.

In the summer of 1962 the *Panorama* producer Jeremy Murray-Brown (my director in Moscow) approached several of the programme's reporters with a view to setting up an independent production company to make documentary films. The idea attracted us. We would have a say in choice of subject; we would be freed from boring studio discussions; and as shareholders in the company we would stand to make money if in the long run the company prospered. A further advantage was that we would be our own directors: this would not only cut costs but give us control over every stage of the film from shooting to the final cut. During my last year at *Panorama* Paul Fox had sent me and the brilliant freelance cameraman Eric Durschmied as a two-man team to cover the Chinese invasion of northern India, and I had found the experience exhilarating.

Thus, and long before its time, came into being an independent television company with the grandiloquent name of Television Reporters International. Backers were found and one of them, Michael Astor, became the company's chairman. Robert Kee, James Mossman, Francis Williams, Malcolm Muggeridge and I signed contracts. Approaches were made to Lew Grade and a deal was struck to supply his Associated Television company with four hour-long and nineteen half-hour documentary films during the coming year. We rented a set of offices in Wardour Street, established a billet there for Jeremy and a business manager to look after the shop, hired three top-class technicians, a beaming film editor who had worked with Moira on *The Red Shoes*, a glum cameraman who wore cowpat-coloured shirts and a randy sound recordist who lost little time in bedding our switchboard operator. The setting up of the company attracted several articles in the national press, who on the whole welcomed it. 'The small, independent company', wrote Peter Black in the *Daily Mail* twenty-five years too early, 'may well be the unit of the future', though for the present he wondered whether we would really find the freedom we sought.

In fact we did, and I look back on my time with TRI as the most professionally satisfying in a long television career. The then rumblings in the Middle East led to the making of our first three films, which we called 'The Arab Ferment'. One was a joint effort by Robert Kee and myself on, respectively, Jordan and Israel, our common starting-point being the closed frontier at Jerusalem's Mandelbaum Gate; and when Robert went to the village of Beit Safafa where the border fence, by some quirk of planning, ran slap down the middle of the street, he was able to film a funeral in progress with some mourners on one side of the fence, and others, wailing and frustrated, on the other.

Staying at the King David Hotel in Jerusalem I received the sweetest telegram of my life. The year before Moira had given birth to our third child. I had driven her to the hospital and held her hand as the labour pains increased; and it was a mystical moment when the strange little wet, mauve creature whom we named Fiona emerged from her womb. Although she had always longed for a son, we decided after our three adored girls to call it a day. But accidents do happen and three months later she found she was pregnant again. The telegram said, 'Alastair arrived ten minutes ago 8 pounds 10 ounces very beautiful.' When I reached home, she said that when she saw it was a boy at last, she had wept for joy. I shed a tiny tear too, and made the crew drink Alastair's health in questionable Israeli champagne.

The other two Middle East films were reports by Robert on Egypt and myself on Saudi Arabia. Receiving permission to film in Saudi Arabia was quite a coup, as no professional camera crew had yet been allowed there. It came about by chance: I mentioned to a man at a party what I was after and he told me that a previous Saudi ambassador to Britain and staunch Anglophile called Sheikh Al-Wahhabi was staying at the Dorchester Hotel. 'Why don't you go and see him?' said the man, 'and say I suggested it.' Within a couple of weeks, the Sheikh had fixed entry visas for Eric Durschmied and myself.

Saudi Arabia then was still fairly primitive, and not only because the penalty for thieving was amputation of a hand and for adultery stoning to death. From the carpeted aisle of the jumbo jet that took us from Jeddah to Riyadh a thin sheep with long balls surveyed me with a baleful eye; and the whole journey was punctuated by the cluckings of invisible fowls. Riyadh itself was in a state of transition from windowless constructions of dried mud, the grander ones with crenellated turrets, to steel, glass and concrete. The one hotel was reasonably comfortable but it was a bore not being able to call up wine to wash down our daily mutton (the Americans in the oil community at Dhahran circumvented the law by having home-made stills which enabled them to consume what they called brown and soda or white and tonic). We filmed the Saudi Army on manoeuvres and a great rally of Bedouin tribesmen at the football stadium in honour of the King, but the high spot of our trip was an invitation from a young Saudi prince who spoke excellent English to join him and his retinue on a turkey hunt in the desert.

In the old days this used to be done with falcons and a baggage train of camels, but these had now given way to Fordson trucks. One afternoon the Prince, Eric and myself, some retainers and four sheep (one for each day we expected to be away) embarked in half a dozen trucks and headed out into the desert. The retainers were a fairly ragged lot, and most had a three or four days' growth of beard. At dusk we pitched camp in the middle of nowhere. There was a big kind of drawing-room tent for the Prince, furnished with rugs and cushions, another smaller one for his sleeping quarters and one for Eric and myself: this had been thoughtfully equipped with a bottle of Johnnie Walker and a thermos of iced water. The retainers slept on the sand. When on return to Riyadh I inquired where the whisky had been acquired, I was told that a large truck drove each week to a remote spot on the Jordanian border and there loaded up from a similar truck which had come out from Amman. One of the sheep was soon dispatched and later made its appearance in the Prince's tent where he and Eric and I picked at it with our fingers (the eyes, I was glad to see, had been removed). After dinner some of the retainers joined us and played 'I've thought of something'. One of the retainers thought of the Prince's gold ring and there were many giggles when he told a questioner that his object contained a hole which you could put your finger into.

For the next two days we cruised around the desert looking for turkeys but seeing none. So the Prince decided to organize a sports competition to try out two new toys he had bought, a Polaroid camera and a starting pistol. He marked out a course in the sand of some 200 yards, put the youngest retainers on the starting-line and the older ones (and some were *very* old) at various distances ahead of them. When he had set them on their marks he took a picture with the Polaroid camera, then fired the starting pistol. Away they went, and the Prince leapt into a truck and was ready with his Polaroid when the first of the retainers crossed the finishing-line. Then he made them do it again, and this time I thought the oldest were going to peg out. They perked up when the Prince showed them the developed pictures of themselves and even more when he started dishing out cash prizes. With a few trees around, I thought, this could be the Forest of Arden.

TRI's next project was another three-part series called 'The Jew in the World', with Malcolm Muggeridge considering the Jew in America, Robert Kee examining the history of Zionism, and myself seeking out what Jews remained in Holland and Germany – no easy task, for a pre-war population in Germany of some 500,000 Jews was now reduced to 30,000. Both there and in Holland, I found, Jews who before the war had been proud to be both Jewish and German (or Dutch), now wanted either to emigrate to Israel where their Jewish identities would be fully recognized, or to forget their Jewishness by abandoning Jewish dress and customs, and thinking of themselves exclusively as German or Dutch.

Making the film allowed us to record in Amsterdam a sequence in Anne Frank's house as well as a service in the city's beautiful synagogue. But the most memorable sequence was an interview with a Belsen survivor at Belsen. Her name was Anita Lasker (later Wallfisch), and she now plays the cello in the English Chamber Orchestra. Although to return to the nightmare camp from which she had been rescued emaciated and almost dead at the age of sixteen must have required an extraordinary degree of courage, a part of her wanted to go back to see what her reactions would be. She flew to Germany with us, and although a German born and bred, such was her loathing of her former fellow countrymen and their tongue that at a Hanover hotel she could not bring herself to speak a word of the language, not even to translate our orders to the waiter.

At the camp next day she seemed calm, largely I think because the bland, well-tended memorial park which Belsen had then become had no relationship with what it had once been. I asked her if she would allow me to interview her there, and she readily agreed. We sat on the ground, her back against the trunk of a pine tree, myself a few feet away. I began by asking of her early life in Germany, and she had been speaking less than a minute when a strange thing happened. I had heard it said, before coming to Belsen, that because it was a place of the dead, no birds sang there, and so far had found it to be true. But at this moment a thrush alighted on a branch of the pine tree a few feet above Anita's head, and began to sing his heart out: the trills were so loud as to compete with our conversation. For a moment I wondered whether I should stop the interview, but as the sound recordist (like all his breed a perfectionist) made no attempt to intervene and the bird continued to warble, I decided to push on. It was, I think, as satisfying an interview as any I have done, both for itself and also because Anita, in telling me coolly and factually the story of her life at Belsen and her liberation from it, seemed to have partially exorcized a ghost. Yet when the finished film was shown, there were several who said to me: 'A great interview. But why did you feel the need to add on a studio thrush?'

Another rewarding assignment arose from an approach by Pat Dolin, the dancer. In London in the early 1920s he had partnered the famous Russian ballerina Olga Spessivtzeva in a Marie Rambert production of *Giselle*. Spessivtzeva had been one of the leading dancers of the Maryinsky Theatre in St Petersburg and in 1921, after joining the Diaghilev company, had been the first to dance *Sleeping Beauty* (then called *Sleeping Princess*) in London. Diaghilev had great admiration for her, saying that she and Pavlova were two halves of the same apple, but that Spessivtzeva's half had been warmed by the sun.

Dolin said that Marie Rambert had some interesting scraps of amateur film, none more than twenty seconds long and most rather less, of his partnering Spessivtzeva at the Savoy Theatre in 1924 in the first act of *Giselle*. He also brought news of Olga's later history. Dancing in America shortly before the war she had without warning lost her mind. Her lover, an American businessman called Brown, arranged for her to enter a private nursing home; but he made no provision for her in his will, and when he died, she became a charge on the State of New York and was taken to the state mental institution up the Hudson at Poughkeepsie. When she arrived, and for some time afterwards, they did not know who she was, and when she referred to past roles by saying, 'I was the queen of the swans', and 'I was Pharaoh's daughter', they thought these further indications of her disturbed mind. She stayed at Poughkeepsie twenty years, but in the early 1960s with the help of newly discovered pills she recovered sufficiently to take up residence at the rest home for elderly Russian emigrés run by Alexandra Tolstoy, the novelist's youngest daughter, at Nyack, New Jersey. Did we think, asked Dolin, that her story would make an interesting documentary?

I said I believed it would make a most unusual documentary, the twin stories of the mad Giselle and the Sleeping Princess being so poignantly reflected in her own life; and having been given the go-ahead by the TRI board, began to assemble material. First, and because the *Giselle* scraps had been shot at a different speed, we had to 'stretch' them by reprinting every third frame. Then we hired one of the Royal Ballet's rehearsal pianists to play the *Giselle* music to synchronize with Dolin's and Spessivtzeva's steps; and over a recording of this we laid a commentary by Marie Rambert on Spessivtzeva's dancing. In America I interviewed the director of the hospital at Poughkeepsie and the striking Alexandra Tolstoy, and took pictures of Olga writing in her room, going for walks, attending the onion-domed Russian Orthodox Church. Finally Moira and I found in the archives of the Paris Opera some remarkable still photographs of Olga in all her principal roles. I called the finished product – what else? – *The Sleeping Ballerina*. With the use I was able to make of the haunting, apposite music of Adam and Tchaikovsky, I think it was the best documentary I ever made. Michael Peacock bought it for the opening week of BBC2 – the only TRI product the BBC ever bought – and it received much praise from the critics. Sadly both the BBC copy and my own have disappeared and, so far as I know, there are now no others in existence.

I don't suppose that any of us at TRI had given much thought to the time beyond the expiry of our contract with Associated Television except to assume it would be renewed. But when I returned to London from Cambodia after filming for Columbia Pictures the making of *Lord Jim* with Peter O'Toole at the temples of Angkor Wat (built by the ancient Khmers eight hundred years ago, discovered by a French butterfly-hunter in the nineteenth century, and as astonishing a work of man as Venice or the Taj Mahal), I was told it was not to be renewed. For ATV's Lew

Grade we had been a novelty, and now the novelty had worn off. Looking back, I think we would have been sensible to have fixed up a few contracts for boring industrial films so as not to be wholly dependent on the whim of one contractor. But then we were not sensible people. Renewed approaches to the BBC fell on equally stony ground: they were still too sore at our leaving to want to welcome us back. Today, I think, BBC and ITV would have competed for our services.

In the *Sunday Telegraph*, Philip Purser, one of the best of the television critics, penned our obsequies. Of the films we had made, 'they were better documentaries than any the ITV companies have lately produced themselves, and they deserved an effective network showing: it will be to ITV's eternal disgrace that they were denied this, and the whole principle of freelance production dealt a body blow.'

For me at this time TRI was not the only idea before its time. I have referred to my friendship with John Grigg, and of my preference, which was my father's preference, for spending summer holidays shooting and fishing rather than idling on a beach. For several years during the 1960s my brother-in-law Ion Calvocoressi and I and our families used to take for two weeks a house and grouse moor owned by John and his brother in the central Scottish Highlands. Called Guisachan, it was situated some twenty miles north of Loch Ness and as far up the Rivers Beauly and Glass as you can go, on the watershed between east and west. The original house, built in the park by Lord Tweedmouth, was a ruin (though in my mother's photograph album are pictures of it when she stayed as a guest there before the First World War); but John's parents had converted and enlarged a stalker's cottage into a comfortable and roomy shooting lodge. An attractive feature of the estate was an eighty-foot waterfall, one of the highest in Scotland. The researches of my nephew Richard Calvocoressi, then a schoolboy but later a distinguished art historian, found that it had been painted by the artist Kokoschka. When we first went there, the house had no telephone or electric light. It was an ideal place to relax.

On the hill behind the house and approached by a rough road through dark Forestry Commission woods was the 4000-acre moor with a hill in the centre of it from which on a clear day you could see the mountains of Sutherland. Twice a week a party of three or four adults with guns, three or four children with sticks, and several assorted and often wayward dogs formed up in line abreast and set off across the heather. On most days we had the assistance of two pointers brought by the owner of a neighbouring estate. I have always loved working with pointers. Trained to lope up and down the line, never more than gunshot range ahead, they sniff continually about them. When the sniff is positive, they freeze as if turned to stone, their noses towards where the grouse are sitting, often with a front paw dramatically raised. Then the nearest of those with guns take up position close by and with the pointer's handler encouraging him to move on, advance gingerly step by step. It is as exciting a moment in shooting as any, knowing that the grouse are squatting in the heather only yards away, tensed for the sudden explosion of sound and feathers. You have to be quick on the draw then, for within five seconds at most the birds are out of range. Some pointers like to fool one by pointing at little birds or, on occasions, at nothing at all.

It was not a grand shoot. If at the end of a long day's walking we had killed a dozen grouse, we felt we had done well. On return to the lodge there would be hot baths and whisky, and it was then that I discovered a curious thing: that the local tap water added to the whisky gave the drink a flavour that English – and particularly London – tap water did not give; and a most pleasurable after-taste lingered on the roof of the mouth. And it did not take me long to conclude that this was because the water one added to the whisky was basically the water that the whisky was made from; the one was a brother, not a remote cousin, of the other.

Could not others share what I was finding so enjoyable? Might there perhaps be a market in bottled Invernesshire water? Most of those to whom I put forward the idea pooh-poohed it mercilessly; no one was going to pay for water out of a bottle when you could obtain it free from a tap. (When I mentioned Perrier they said that was French and therefore different.) But I found two friends as enthusiastic as I was. One was a frequent guest at Guisachan shoots, lived near Inverness and knew where to look for supplies of pure water; the other, an old Etonian friend in the City, had contacts in the bottling business. We took expert advice about the arts of bottling, had a tankful of water shipped down from Scotland, added some ingredient to stop the growth of algae, designed and had printed 5000 labels that carried pictures of a thistle, a stag's head and the words HIGHLAND BURN WATER and slapped them on to 5000 bottles. And everyone to whom we offered a blind tasting of whisky with London tap water and whisky with Highland Burn Water knew at once which was which, and said confidently we were on to a winner.

I wish we had been; and had I ever had an ounce of business sense, we might have been. We approached a number of people: a Mr Charrington of Charrington's Brewery who was a friend of my friend in the City, but he wasn't interested; and Sir Frederic Hooper, the chairman of Schweppes whom I had interviewed on television, but he wasn't interested either (no wonder with boring old Malvern Water to protect); they and others were all agreed that whisky with Highland Burn Water beat whisky with tap water hollow, but were equally agreed that marketing it on any scale was not and never could be an economic proposition. What I realize we should have done then was take time off from the City and Scotland and television to go traipsing round every likely bar in London with sample bottles and promise to come back with a follow-up a few days later; that, I knew, was how successful businesses were built up. But to do this would have meant breaking existing contracts and, with wives and children dependent on us, none of us was prepared to take the risk. And so some 4000 bottles of untasted Highland Burn Water languished (and for all I know still languish) in some London warehouse and a venture which had seemed so bright with promise fizzled out. In the long run, I guess, we were right to stick to our lasts; yet there are times today, when seeing on the shelves of Waitrose and Marks and Spencer and Sainsbury what a thriving business the bottled water industry has become, I feel a pang of regret for the millionaire I might have become.

Unlike P. G. Wodehouse's famous character Ukridge, who had so many imaginative but always unfulfilled ideas for making money, I had only one other, so much more complex and capital-intensive than Highland Burn Water that it never progressed beyond an idea; but it has stayed in my mind ever since, and I only mention it here in case the Japanese or some larky home-grown entrepreneur feels inclined to take it up.

The idea sprang from the very first item I presented for *Panorama*, a comparative study of the merits of burial and cremation. While country churchyards have much to commend them, urban cemeteries, it seemed to me, were blots on the landscape, dank, ugly and with tombstones, like the dead they existed to commemorate, far gone in decay. Cremation did not appear to have much going for it either, many finding the transformation from sentient being to a handful of dust too sudden and violent. In the bunkers of the Golders Green Crematorium I had interviewed a stoker dressed like a monk in a girdled brown habit. He lit a cigarette while I was there, and when he was through with it, opened a furnace door to dispose of the stub; and the fierce glare from what looked like a thousand flaming jets lit up a blazing coffin. The stoker said that when the furnace had cooled, they separated the wood ash from the human ash, which they put in urns for relatives who wanted them (it seemed that few did). I asked how long it took for a corpse to become ashes and he said, 'Young people take the shortest time, old people the longest. I've known some old people take nearly two hours. They can be quite leathery.'

It was then, having asked myself if there were not a more agreeable, less violent and primitive way of disposing of human remains, that I conceived the idea of an organization called Burials at Sea, Inc. The British were, and always would be, a people surrounded by the sea; and the sea in the dark beginnings of time was the watery womb from which we had all emerged. What more natural, at the end of our spell on earth, than to return there? What more apposite than to fit out and establish in all our principal ports a fleet of small boats to take loved ones out beyond the three-mile limit where the booze is duty-free and the flying fishes play, and commit them to the deep? Each coffin would have to contain specially drilled holes and be weighted with lead: a single loved one bobbing up to the surface would spell ruination of the venture.

Each boat would require a skipper to navigate, an engineer to prevent breakdowns (unthinkable to have to tow a loved one home) and a steward to fix the gâteau and duty-free fizz. An optional service would be a chaplain to give uplift to the proceedings and mutter comforting things as the coffin was shipped over the side, while in the forward locker would be kept an ever ready supply of plastic wreaths, bought at wholesale prices, for casting on the water. At today's prices one could charge £250 a trip and unless it was *very* rough, fit in four trips a day (more in summer); for six days a week that worked out at £25,000 a month or

£300,000 a year. Multiplying by ten for the boats at other seaports would generate a gross income of £3 million a year – and this in a business where one knew for sure the supply of raw materials would never dry up. If calculations were correct, Burials at Sea, Inc. could go public within months of registration. At times my fantasies about the project knew no bounds. Why use boats that could take only one loved one? Why not have larger boats that could take several, with different times of launchings, and the mourners and their wakes allotted to separate cabins? Why not, for God's sake, charter the *Queen Mary* for a week, equip her with special chutes and dispose of a couple of hundred loved ones a day?

> But that's all over. Here's the world again.
> Bring me the blotter, fill the fountain pen,

as a fellow author once wrote. Still, if my executors think they can afford it, that's the way I plan to go.

Around this time, more or less, I noticed that some hereditary peers I knew were disclaiming their peerages and reverting to their family names, mostly for the purposes of standing for election to the House of Commons. Finding that the names they were abandoning were more mellifluous than the monosyllables they were adopting, I wrote this verse which appeared in *Punch*:

> Hailsham, Altrincham, Stansgate, Kennet,
> English names to flatter the tongue,
> Flattery much less fetching when it's
> Hogg and Grigg and Benn and Young.

17

The Trial of Stephen Ward

Since the publication of *10 Rillington Place* in 1961, I had received a number of letters from prisoners and/or their relatives claiming they had been wrongly convicted. Many had the ring of truth, but I was too committed at this time in making my way in television, both at the BBC and later in TRI, and did not take any of them up. In the summer of 1963 however it seemed to me that a miscarriage of justice of a quite different kind might be about to take place. This was the arrest and indictment of the society osteopath and amateur artist Stephen Ward, for living on the immoral earnings of prostitution.

The story of what has become known as the Profumo affair, of which Stephen Ward was both the beginning and the end, has been told too often to warrant detailed repetition. Briefly, it was that Ward, as a result of his skills as a masseur and manipulator, had come to know several rich people; they included Lord Astor, a wettish individual who gave Ward the lease of a cottage on his Cliveden estate. But Ward was equally a lover of low life and one weekend had invited as guests there Christine Keeler, a night club hostess at Murray's Cabaret Club, as well as the Russian naval attaché, a Captain Ivanov. After dinner one night Lord Astor brought his guests to the swimming pool where Christine Keeler and others were already bathing; they included Jack Profumo, Conservative MP and Minister for War. On return to London Profumo and Keeler had a brief affair. Soon the press came to hear of it, and, knowing that Keeler was also believed to have been to bed with Ivanov, saw the makings of a first-class scandal involving politics, sex and espionage. To save his career Profumo lied to Parliament that he had not slept with Keeler and sued two newspapers successfully for saying so. But he could not keep it up; and two months later, under increasing pressure, resigned as minister and MP.

To say that a scapegoat was needed for this humiliation to the government would be to claim too much; such orchestration is always rare. Truer to say that many felt that had it not been for Ward and his dissolute life-style no scandal would have occurred; for it was Ward who had introduced Ivanov to Christine and Christine to Profumo. Five days after Profumo's resignation the Home Secretary asked the Commissioner of the Metropolitan Police whether there was a police interest in Ward. In fact there was none, but when police receive such a message, they interpret it to mean rather more than it says; not whether there *was* a police interest in Ward, but could they, if they nosed around long enough, find failings in Ward's life and activities with which, as guardians of the law, they ought to acquaint themselves?

It came as a shock to me, and I know to others, to learn that after weeks of police inquiries, Ward had been arrested and charged on five counts: living on the immoral earnings of

Christine Keeler; of another Murray's Club hostess, Mandy Rice-Davies; and of a prostitute called Vickie Barrett; one count of procuring a girl under twenty-one to have sex with a third person and another of *attempting* to procure a girl under twenty-one for the same purpose. I had never met Ward myself, but from those who knew him (including some who didn't like him) I was told that the role of professional pimp and procurer would have been quite out of character; that with osteopathy (from which he earned a comfortable living), drawing and bridge-playing, his life was a full one; and that it was for fun not profit that he brought his friends from high life and low life together. When the date of the trial was announced, I thought I'd like to see it for myself; and with the backing of my publisher Victor Gollancz, I applied for and was given a ticket.

It was as odd a drama as I have ever witnessed, with as rich a *dramatis personae* as you could imagine. First, the judge, Sir Archibald Marshall, a little moley man with an elfin workaday mind that sprouted a rag-bag of clichés ('the heart of this great metropolis', 'one crowded hour of glorious life', 'a great power known as the fourth estate'). Second, the appalling old Etonian prosecuting counsel, Mervyn Griffith-Jones, who had asked the *Lady Chatterley's Lover* jury whether it was a book they would wish their wives or servants to read, who seemed determined to obtain a conviction against Ward at all costs and who set out to prejudice the jury in his opening speech by listing a number of things against Ward which he promised he would prove and half of which he never proved or even attempted to prove. And third, Ward's own counsel, the jolly, sunshiney, Pickwickian James Burge whose defence at the magistrate's court had so pleased Ward that he decided to retain him for the trial, but who proved in the end to be too much of a lightweight for his bludgeoning, moralizing opponent.

And then *les girls*: Christine Keeler, still only twenty-one, a little doll who walked superbly on long, slender legs, but a long-time receptacle for lovers white and black and whose face, painted an inch thick, already bore the ravages of time; Mandy Rice-Davies, mistress of a slum landlord at sixteen, now only eighteen, in her little debutante's petalled hat both saucy and demure, splitting a joke with the judge and originating the immortal line when told that Lord Astor had denied sleeping with her, 'Well, he would, wouldn't he?'; Ronna Ricardo, a homely red-haired tart in a pink jumper who had given evidence at the magistrate's court that she had slept with men in Ward's flat for money, but now declared she had been pressurized by the police into saying this, and so was treated by Mr Griffith-Jones as a 'hostile witness'; and little whey-faced Vickie Barrett, another tart, who looked like an advertisement for famine relief, and who said in a long period of sustained court-room silence that she had caned and whipped men in Ward's flat on many occasions for money, all of which she had handed over to Ward, and not a penny of which had he handed back.

And in the dock the accused himself, the roué of fifty who looked thirty-five, dressed in a sober heather-mixture suit, spending some of his time drawing judge and counsel, maintaining an admirable composure and dignity throughout. I think at the outset he thought he would be acquitted but as the days passed and the false evidence mounted, he realized he was doomed; and on the evening after the judge's summing-up, he went home and took a massive overdose of sleeping tablets. And next day, as he lay dying in St Stephen's Hospital, the jury threw out the two procurement charges and the one concerning Vickie Barrett, which even they could see were lies; but found him guilty of living on the immoral earnings of Christine and Mandy. Why they did this must remain a mystery, for on the evidence given, both girls made it clear he was not pimping for them, that on the only two occasions that they had been given money for sleeping with men while staying in his flat they had not given the money to him, and that neither had ever given back to Ward as much money as he had given to them; in short that they were always in debt to him. Further, it was revealed after the trial that at the time of the alleged offences Mandy was still receiving £100 a week from her slum landlord lover; and had the jury known of this it is difficult to see how they could have convicted Ward on the charge relating to her. 'The English system', wrote Louis Blom-Cooper in his book on the Hanratty case, 'leans heavily on the arrival of a verdict by way of general impressions rather than scrupulous examination of the testimony.' No doubt that was what Mr Griffith-Jones intended; and it is probably as near an explanation of the two guilty verdicts as one is ever likely to have.

I said earlier that what had shocked me most about the Timothy Evans case were the actions of the police who, determined to see him convicted at all costs, first browbeat out of him a false confession, then, when they found that part of the confession did not tally with statements taken from some workmen, browbeat the workmen into making second, contradictory statements, and then shelved both of them. These actions had led directly to Evans's conviction and death. Similarly the actions of the police in the Ward case led, though indirectly, to Ward's death. And with far less excuse, for at least in the Evans case a crime had been committed which needed solving. But in the Ward case no crime had been committed, and the initial efforts of the police were directed exclusively to finding out not whether Ward had done it, but what Ward had done.

It was only when the trial was over that one could look back and see the lengths to which the police had gone and the depths to which they had sunk. They had admitted at the trial that over a period of months they had interviewed an astonishing 140 potential witnesses, interrogating Christine Keeler *no less than twenty-four times.* They had reason to believe that some of the evidence she was to give would be perjured, which it was, and that if this perjury was ever proved (which it was), she would be convicted and serve a sentence for the perjury, which she did. When Mandy Rice-Davies refused to make a statement implicating Ward they arrested her on a trumped-up charge concerning a television set and saw to it she was sent on remand to Holloway. 'After a day or two there, I was ready to do anything to get out,' she wrote. 'They came to see me, and asked if I would like to reconsider my refusal to make a statement about Dr Ward. The prospect of perhaps having to spend a further spell in Holloway was enough to convince me I had better keep on the right side of the police. I told them all they wanted . . .'

It was the same with Ronna Ricardo who said at the Old Bailey that she had testified at the magistrates' court that she had slept with men for money at Ward's flat because the police had threatened to send her daughter into care and put her thirteen-year-old sister Dorothy in a remand home if she didn't. She confirmed this to me when I went to see her after the trial. 'Says police interviewed her nine times and two officers in police car kept watch constantly outside her flat. She thinks they were there to frighten her and they did. Says she finally agreed to say what police wanted because she was thoroughly fed up and was told she would not have to appear in court. Told she *would* have to appear in court only twenty-four hours beforehand. Says that when she reminded officer of his promise, he said if she didn't come, he'd take Dorothy instead.'

Ronna Ricardo had the courage (and it must have needed some courage) to retract her lies at the trial, but Vickie Barrett didn't admit to hers until it was over. Before Ward took the overdose, he left a note for Vickie Barrett reproaching her for what she had done. A journalist from the *Daily Telegraph*, R. Barry O'Brien, took a copy of this note to Vickie Barrett, at the same time informing her of Ward's death. Sobbing, she told O'Brien, 'I did go to the flat but it was only to do business with Stephen Ward. It was not true I went with other men.' Asked why she said she had whipped other men there, she said a police officer had told her that if she didn't, she would never be able to show her face in Notting Hill again. 'He said that girls could get very heavy sentences for soliciting . . . nine months or more.'

Thus, and shamefully, by threats and perjured evidence Ward became a sacrificial goat on the altar of an offended establishment. His junior defence counsel, David Tudor-Price, later a High Court judge, said the trial and conviction had left him with a burning sense of injustice, and the distinguished solicitor Lord Goodman echoed him: 'An historic case of an historic injustice.'

There were few in England who disagreed, but one of them was the judge who had been asked by the Prime Minister, Harold Macmillan, to inquire into the security aspects of the Profumo affair. As a judge Lord Denning was an odd mixture; often an upholder of an individual's liberties against bureaucratic tyranny, but on occasions rigidly authoritarian. Years later he published an autobiography that included some passages so uncompromisingly racist and reactionary that after I had interviewed him about them, the book was withdrawn for the offending passages to be deleted. The *persona* he liked to present of himself was that of homespun Hampshire philosopher, the repository of sturdy common sense; but in sexual matters he was a simpleton, only too ready to condemn practices which were beyond his ken, and yet, as witnesses to his inquiry affirmed, showing a prurient interest in them. Ignorance and salaciousness met when he declared that most people who saw a press photograph of Christine Keeler posing in a swimsuit 'would readily infer her avocation', a sly way of suggesting, and without the slightest justification, that girls who pose in swimsuits can readily be assumed to be whores.

His report was a disgrace, much of it tittle-tattle and gossip in which he whitewashed Profumo (whom he called *Mr* Profumo) and blackened Ward (whom he called Ward). 'Ward', he wrote, 'procured girls of 16 and 17 to be mistresses for his influential friends . . . Ward also catered for those of his friends who had perverted tastes . . . ready to arrange whipping parties and other sadistic performances . . . known to be involved in a call-girl racket.' It was Griffith-Jones all over again.

When preparing my book on the trial, I telephoned Denning's office and asked an official who said his name was Critchley whether Denning was aware that at his trial Ward had been found not guilty on the procurement charges and no evidence had been offered that he arranged whipping parties or other sadistic performances or was involved in a call-girl racket. 'Ah, well,' said Critchley, 'I daresay we were a bit unfair there. We were under a lot of pressure to complete the report, and we didn't really have time to read all the details of the trial.' So much for Denning's airy phrases in his introduction about the overriding interest of justice to the individual and not condemning on suspicion. He also failed to mention a matter favourable to Ward and which has only recently been revealed, that Ward had agreed to help MI5 to try to compromise Captain Ivanov in the hope of persuading him to defect. But to have included that (as MI5 had expected) would have been to blunt the picture that Lord Denning wanted to convey of a monster of sexual depravity.

Any writer who deals with past events needs to be as accurate as possible, and in the course of preparing my book, I applied for a copy of the transcript of the trial for confirmation of what I had heard in open court. To my astonishment this was turned down. There then ensued a long correspondence between myself and a Mr Thompson, Assistant Registrar of the Royal Courts of Justice, as to why it had been turned down, since applications by other authors for transcripts of other trials had been complied with. All that emerged from this correspondence (which I subsequently published in the *Spectator*) was that no reason could be given, but that the decision had been taken personally by the Lord Chief Justice, Lord Parker. What Lord Parker was frightened of I do not know, but I suspect that his awareness of what a disgrace the Ward trial had been, and a wish to pre-empt any further publicity about it, may have had some part in his decision. If so, it failed, for I had the less comprehensive but (so far as it went) equally reliable Press Association transcript to fall back on. Questions asked in the House of Commons as to why I had been denied the official transcript met with a similarly unhelpful response. Had Ward lived, of course, his solicitor would have been supplied with a transcript for the purposes of an appeal, and I should have been able to make use of that.

The Trial of Stephen Ward was published in London and New York the following spring and was widely and on the whole favourably reviewed (Graham Greene called it 'admirable'). It remains one of my favourite books, and I was delighted when Gollancz re-issued it in paperback in 1987. But the trial, the first I had attended in its entirety, had greatly shocked me; not only the deplorable methods used by the police to secure a conviction, but the absurdities of our adversarial system of justice, a system which allowed for Griffith-Jones to vilify the accused as he did (in Scotland they wisely have no opening speeches) and for the accused to be convicted against the weight of evidence. I ended the original edition of the book with this conclusion:

Let no one pretend that our system of justice is a search for truth. It is nothing of the kind. It is a contest between two sides played according to certain rules, and if the truth happens to emerge as the result of the contest, then that is pure windfall. But it is unlikely to. It is not something with which the contestants are concerned. They are concerned that the game should be played according to the rules. There are many rules, and one of them is that some questions which might provide a short-cut to the truth are not allowed to be asked, and those that are asked are not allowed to be answered. The result is that verdicts are often reached haphazardly, for the wrong reasons, in spite of the evidence, and may or may not coincide with the literal truth.

The tragedy of our courts is that means have come to count more than ends, form more than content, appearance more than reality. The antique ritual is positively harmful, for it drives a wedge between the citizen and the law, outlawing him as a stranger in his own land, making him hostage to customs which he has had no share in framing. A small reform like the shedding of horsehair would be a step in the right direction, for it would enhance rather than diminish the dignity of the law. Judge and counsel would be seen to be human too, and would no longer feel the need to go on acting parts which they mistakenly believe tradition demands of them. Wigless they might think twice before saying to a jury *albeit* when they mean although and *avocation* when they mean job. There is need for flexibility instead of fossilization, for all the diverse elements in a courtroom to be brought nearer together, not driven further apart, a need for communication and, above all, understanding.

It is time not only for the rules of the game to be revised, but also, if people like Stephen Ward are to have a just trial in future, to ask ourselves whether the game we have chosen is the one that we wish to go on playing.

Years later a prisoner named Michael Luvaglio, serving a life sentence for murder but whose guilt I felt to be in doubt, spent months and months writing those conclusions out as an illuminated manuscript. Framed, it hangs in my study today. Twenty-four years after Ward's trial, I see no reason to alter them; but it was to be a further two cases and another twenty years before I came to realize that our system of criminal justice was not the best we could do; that there was another that was very much better.

During the first six months of 1965 I travelled the world, gathering material for a book on Americans abroad, those who had eschewed splendid isolationism to spread themselves, as the British had done in the days of the Raj, across the globe. As I had seen on my own travels, there were now few corners of a foreign field without some American presence, where a GI, Peace Corps volunteer, salesman or missionary had not established a billet, where shiny supermarkets, T-shirts and jeans, hamburgers and Coca-cola, which had arrived as novelties, had not come to stay. Some expatriates had gone abroad for commercial reasons, others out of curiosity, others still inspired by Kennedy's promise that America would pay any price, bear any burden, meet any hardship, support any friend, oppose any foe, to assure the survival and the success of liberty. How were they all making out? And how did those among whom they had come to live think they were making out?

With an advance from Simon and Schuster in New York and Hamish Hamilton in London and discounts from Pan-Am and Intercontinental Hotels, I was able to cast a wide net and talk to many; in Paraguay a family of missionaries living with Guarani Indians on an island in the Parana river; in Nigeria a black American diplomat who said he felt no affinity with his black Nigerian cousins, and in the Himalayas a distinguished black American professor whom his Indian pupils regarded, as they did all blacks, as racially inferior; in darkest, telephone-less (though not televisionless) Liberia the admirable Edna McKinnon bringing the gospel of coil and condom; in a des-troyer going up the Dardanelles the officers saying they had never heard of Gallipoli; in Jerusalem tourists shouting 'Say, did you get a shot of the Blessed Virgin's tomb? It's *fabulous*!'; in Vietnam Emlyn Williams reading Dickens at the French Institute; in Bangkok dinner at his house on the klong with the brilliant silk designer Jim Thompson, white cockatoo on shoulder, shortly before he disappeared; in Kyoto the 73-year-old Zen priestess Ruth Sasaki ('The only sin is ignorance'); and in every hotel bedroom from Stuttgart to Teheran to Saigon to Tokyo the voice of AFN, the American Armed Forces network, dispensing moral uplift:

'The words a man uses are the maysure of his mind, the may-sure of his character, his soul, what he is inside . . .'

'This is Walt Sheldon in Fuji, Japan. With me today is His Grace Bishop Hilary Hacker, the Bishop of Bismarck, North Dakota . . . Your Grace? . . .'

'You know when it comes to judging people, the Good Book gives some mighty true advice . . .'

'Steve Allaymo, wrapping up the programme for this week. May I leave you with this thought for the weekend:

> Life itself can't give you joy,
> Unless you really will it,
> Life just gives you time and space,
> It's up to you to fill it.'

A good example of how public attitudes change occurred later that year when my friend Alasdair Milne as producer and myself as reporter were invited to make two films for *This Week* on the workings of the criminal law. In the first, on the police, I advanced the view which I knew from my investigations to be true, that in their efforts to secure convictions against those whom they believe to be guilty, they are apt to bend the rules. But I concluded, I believe fairly:

> If some policemen today are more corrupt than they used to be, the fault is perhaps less theirs than ours. If we want the police to catch criminals, prosecute the guilty but not the innocent, then we must surely establish a new set of rules to let them do so.
>
> This means a greater curb on the liberties of the individual than at present we are prepared to allow. Yet until we do allow it, the guilty will continue to escape and the innocent to suffer . . .

Today with miscarriages of justice falling over one another, it is no longer in dispute that the police are at times inclined to bend the rules. But to suggest such a thing then was to reap a whirlwind, and it came, in letters of inordinate length, in the correspondence columns of *The Times*. 'Bending the rules', boomed Lord Dilhorne, 'seldom occurs.' 'Arrant nonsense,' thundered the Commissioner of the Metropolitan Police. And Lord Shawcross, a contributor to the programme, said of my assertion that bending the rules led to many innocent people landing in prison, 'There is no foundation whatever for such opinions.' All these views were of course articles of faith, not statements of fact, as not only had none of them ever studied the matter, but they assumed that no one else had either.

What seemed to have worried them most though was the way the programme had been edited. 'Faked' was how Sir Lionel Heald, a former Attorney-General, described it. They took particular objection to the intercutting of contributor's views, a standard practice, but which they seemed quite unaware of. Such intercutting, said Shawcross naively, 'might suggest that all appearing in the broadcast were taking part in a joint discussion . . . lending support to other participants with whom they would not wish to be associated.' Just who among television watchers would have thought anything so potty, he didn't say. The correspondence, pro and anti, rumbled on for some time, Dilhorne and Shawcross agreeing that if ever invited to take part in a recorded programme again, they would jolly well insist on seeing a final transcript, so they could withdraw at the last minute if they didn't care for the company they were being asked to keep or the programme's conclusions – terms which no television producer, working to a deadline, could possibly accept, or indeed ever has accepted.

Whatever our present problems in television, and there are some, at least that sort of correspondence could not take place today.

A month later came the general election when I was invited to take charge of the Liberal Party's three party political television broadcasts. It had always seemed to me that the best way of using this prime time slot (then broadcast simultaneously on all channels) was to try and persuade the viewer to one's own point of view, not bore him with lists of past achievements and future promises. I had had some success with this in a Liberal party political in the 1964 general election, a time when Liberal morale was high because of a poll that promised us a 9.5 per cent share of the result or three million votes! My object then was simply to cajole Liberals into voting Liberal, not be frightened into voting Conservative for fear of letting Labour in. 'If you say you are a Liberal at heart,' I said, looking (as it were) the viewer in the eye, 'and don't vote with the courage of your convictions, then you don't have much courage at all, do you?' It seemed to have worked. 'An object lesson in how to use television as a means of persuasion,' wrote Anthony Howard in the *New Statesman*, while a writer in *Tribune* called it 'one of the most compelling appeals for votes which has been seen on television'. And we won a little more than our three million votes!

I used the same technique in 1966. In the second of the three broadcasts I introduced Jeremy Thorpe and David Steel, and in the last Jo Grimond, but for the first they let me go solo. I felt strongly that most party politicals confused the viewer by trying to cover too much ground, and it would be better to concentrate on a single theme. I chose one the Tories might have chosen but had in fact neglected – the threats that the Labour leader Harold Wilson had made in the past to nationalize certain industries and would presumably carry out if he and his party came to power. After referring to this 'bland, benign, reassuring even rather conservative father figure', I listed the industries he had previously said he wanted to see nationalized – among them cement, sugar, machine tools, banks, building land, defence industries, and added, 'Can you believe that Mr Wilson has held these deeply felt beliefs all this time without the intention of fulfilling them? If he has, he is either a hypocrite or a coward, and I have too much respect for him [a bit of a whopper, that] to believe he is either.' After warning the viewers against being misled into thinking the leopard had lost its spots or the tiger its claws, I said: 'If only another twenty or thirty Liberals can be elected to join the ten who are there, Mr Wilson will not have the majority of which he dreams and the country will be spared the nationalization it does not deserve.'

Statistically and critically the broadcast was a success. Television Audience Measurements gave it nearly twelve million viewers or 80 per cent of possible total audience: this was a record, beating the viewing figures for the party politicals of Edward Heath for the Conservatives and Ray Gunter for Labour in the same week: of the three it also had the highest TAM Appreciation Index. 'Tore Mr Wilson's election promises of 1964 to ribbons,' wrote Randolph Churchill in the *Standard*. 'Best of the party broadcasts so far,' said the *Mail*. The *Mirror* called it 'The Night of the Big Hatchet' and the *Spectator*, 'a professional demolition job by a professional communicator'. But the praise I cherished most came from the Guild of Television Producers: 'An example of what a party political broadcast should be'.

Not that it did the slightest good, the Liberal poll being down by more than half a million votes on 1964! So much for the influence of television. After the election, and so as to show there had been nothing personal in my attack on Wilson, I sent a line to Downing Street to congratulate him on his victory and received a charming reply, written in his own hand.

18

Scotland and the Meehan Case

I had composed that party political broadcast in a small bedroom at the back of the Buccleuch Arms Hotel at St Boswells, Roxburghshire, the reason being that after ten years at Piers Place, Old Amersham, we had decided to move. Although Piers Place was the most beautiful house I had owned or ever would own, it always seemed to be in need of structural repairs, there was a large attic floor which we didn't need ourselves and yet were disinclined to furnish for renting out, and the traffic on the main road outside seemed to increase with every year. For some time I had wanted to move further from London with its many social distractions, and now with the half million words of notes I had brought back with me from my world tour waiting to be distilled into a book, I felt the need more than ever.

In the fifteen years since making *A Story of Three Loves* in Hollywood Moira had accomplished much: in films *The Man Who Loved Redheads, Black Tights,* and *Peeping Tom*; on the stage *A Midsummer Night's Dream, I am a Camera, Man of Distinction,* as well as a season with the Bristol Old Vic. Offers continued to roll in, some so tempting that I did not see how she could refuse them, but with four children now of whom none was over twelve, she was adamant that she wished to be with them, and this meant that we could move further afield. When she retired, she was still internationally famous. With her films *The Red Shoes* and *Tales of Hoffman* in addition to ten years at Covent Garden, she had, I think, done as much as anyone to help put British post-war ballet on the map. Over the years there had been many tributes to her beauty and her dancing, but the one I particularly treasure appeared only recently. It comes from *I, of All People*, the autobiography of the poet James Kirkup: 'No other leading dancer – not even Fonteyn or Markova – demonstrated such intelligence in her dancing and such profound musicality as did Moira Shearer, at least among British dancers . . . something intensely warm and human in her dancing . . . a great performer in the style of the classic *ballerina assoluta*.' And he adds, 'I cut a picture of her marriage from a newspaper and carried it with me all my life, through all my moves and all my travels.' He even reproduces among the illustrations to his book this ancient newspaper cutting of the two of us.

At first we considered moving to Devon, which we had come to know during speaking engagements for Mark Bonham-Carter at Torrington and Jeremy Thorpe at Barnstaple, but not seeing anything to our liking, turned our thoughts to our native Scotland. But as the venture was something of an experiment, and we might have to move south again before long, we decided to rent a house rather than buy one. Although this seemed a wise decision at the time, it was anything but wise in the long run, as we had not reckoned on the dramatic rise in house prices. We visited a number of unsuitable lettings as far afield as Dumfries-shire and Loch Rannoch, and eventually settled on a charming Georgian manse in the hamlet of Makerstoun, half-way between Kelso and St Boswells in the Border country, half a mile from the Tweed with, at the bottom of an orchard of Victoria plums, a village school suitable for Alastair and Fiona. Another attraction was knowing from Eton and Oxford days several of the neighbouring landowners, Johnnie Dalkeith at Eildon, Dawyck Haig at Bemersyde, Robin McEwen at Marchmont. Our congenial landlord, Roger Baird, also lived in the village where his wife Margaret was a tenant farmer; he had bought the manse as a long-term family investment.

Here we lived for the next fifteen years, with the eighteenth-century kirk across the road, and from my study window at the front a clear thirty-mile view across the Tweed valley to the distant Cheviots. There was fishing for trout (and sometimes salmon) in the river, grouse-shooting in the autumn and pheasant-shooting in the winter, golf at St Boswells and Goswick and Muirfield. Of our neighbours I saw most of Robin McEwen, a man with a brilliant, mercurial mind, the most generous of hosts and companionable of men yet always hopelessly impractical: sometimes he would blow in unexpectedly to say hello, Kind Dog hat on head, green scarf billowing in the breeze, knees encased in worn plus-fours, always eager to engage in debate while taking a nip of Laphroaig against the cold. Often staying at Marchmont was his dear wife Brigid's father, James Laver, writer on the history of fashion, one time Keeper of Prints and Drawings at the Victoria and Albert Museum, and a marvellous raconteur. South of Naples he had once lunched at a restaurant where they had endeavoured to translate the menu into English. At the bottom he found the three letters CIS and asked what it was. 'Is what he says,' replied the waiter. 'Is "chees"'.' He also spoke of Madame Brillat-Savarin, a great gourmande who, taken queer at a banquet, cried out, '*Vite, vite! Je vais mourir. Passez le dessert!*'

Robin McEwen was also behind my making some money on the horses. I have always found race-meetings very boring, and when we were invited to a box at the Kelso races, I had it in mind to decline. But, having heard I had been invited, Robin persuaded me to accept, saying he was going to meet a trainer friend there who would know all the winners.

For the first race the trainer friend advised us to back a horse called, I think, Super Duper. Super Duper fell at the first fence. For the next race he suggested a nag called My Delight. My Delight completed the course but came in ten lengths behind the rest of the field. Robin was for consulting the trainer friend about the third race, but I felt this was tempting Providence too far. Glancing down the list of runners, I saw to my astonishment that one of the horses entered was called Soixante-Neuf (sired by Coronation Year out of Bewildered Anne!). I said to Robin, 'If its owner has the nerve to call it that, the least we can do is back it.' Robin laughed and said he'd go along with me. So we each put a fiver on Soixante-Neuf, the beast romped home at 10 to 1, and we both collected fifty quid.

Dawyck Haig's son Alexander was much the same age as Alastair and when the two were old enough we used to have fathers' and sons' tennis and golf matches. One afternoon after tennis I was sitting on a drawing-room sofa at Bemersyde when Dawyck's dog, a long black cocker spaniel called Wasp, came and nuzzled up against me in the most friendly manner. When he jumped down some twenty minutes later, I found he had chewed away a large portion of my cashmere sweater. Dawyck said he was sure I could claim on my insurance. A form arrived with the instruction 'State exactly how loss occurred', and I wrote 'Lord Haig's dog Wasp and I were sitting together on a sofa when I discovered he was eating my sweater' with the gravest doubts that I would be believed. But the insurance company promptly sent a cheque for £25 replacement value, no doubt reckoning that such a tale was beyond human invention.

Our Borders MP was David Steel (who had beaten Robin McEwen at the by-election which won him the seat) and as a member of his local Liberal party, I was invited to join the Scottish Liberal Party's Council. Their quarterly meetings were anodyne affairs, chaired by a genial buffer named George Mackie (later Lord Mackie of Benshie), whose deliberations were too often bogged down in the drearier aspects of Liberal Party policy. Although Home Rule for Scotland in a federated Britain was part of that policy, it rarely got seriously discussed. And yet, it seemed to me, this was the most important single issue facing Scotland at that time. All over the world, as I had observed on my travels for *Panorama* and TRI, countries which had long been administered by others were hoisting their own colours; everywhere the idea of new-born nationhood was in the air.

Was Scotland so very different? Ever since my mother had explained to me at Culloden Moor long ago that the English and the Scots were different peoples, I had been intensely proud of my Scottish origins and of Scotland's history as an independent nation. Returning after thirty years I saw the country with a fresh eye. It *was* different from England: it had its own systems of law and education, its own church, currency, literature, music. Like the Jews the Scots were a talented and creative people who had exported themselves all over the world; there was hardly a country anywhere where a quorum of doctors, dentists, teachers, sailors, engineers, could not be assembled for a Burns Night supper or St Andrew's Day dinner. It was Scots who had invented the steam engine, tarmacadam, the telephone, the Dunlop tyre, chloroform, Listerine, penicillin, television; Scots who had risen to command foreign armies and navies and whose courage as kilted soldiers in the First World War had led the Germans to dub them 'the ladies from hell'; Scots, of whom one had helped to found the Bank of England, who had made Edinburgh into one of the great financial centres of Europe; Scots who had provided Westminster with more than her share of British Prime Ministers; Scots who with only a tenth of the population of Britain, had yet supplied England with one fifth of her professional classes. With all this and North Sea (some would say Scottish) oil in the offing, who was to say we were unfit to govern ourselves?

I was told this was a retrograde step: what I was advocating was narrow nationalism in an age of increasing internationalism. Nationalism, yes, but not narrow: what Burke meant by 'the little platoon', and a modern writer in small being beautiful, for the greater the overall unit (and the Common Market was then looming), the greater the necessity for autonomy within that unit, if those being governed were still to feel in touch with those governing. Scotland's affairs had once been dealt with in her own Parliament in Edinburgh; now much of them were dealt with in London; soon more would be dealt with in Brussels. A country that had once been central to itself was on the periphery: it needed to become central again.

At the next Scottish Liberal Party Council meeting I put forward a motion that Home Rule should be the principal aim and object of our policy and that in Scottish domestic matters all other issues should be considered in relation to it. To my utter astonishment the motion was passed unanimously and thereafter, and to my lesser astonishment, completely ignored; at a by-election at Pollok the Liberal candidate devoted just ten out of the 150 lines of his election address to it and came bottom of the poll. Now at that time the Scottish National Party was the only other party in Scotland advocating what we were advocating (though obviously going much further) and it seemed to me crazy to be competing with them for devolutionary votes. So at the SLP's next annual conference I put forward a resolution that talks be opened with them with a view to supporting each other in seats where one or the other of us stood a chance of winning; and to this end arranged a meeting between Jo Grimond and the SNP leader, Billy Wolfe. To no avail: my resolution was never called for debate and another, that if the SNP were to approach us with a view to talks (an unlikely event after the Pollok by-election) we would not close the door, was passed by a narrow majority.

I realized then that my days with the Scottish Liberal Party were numbered and with much sadness wrote out a letter of resignation. For four weeks I let it lie on my desk, unwilling to take the final step. But by now Winnie Ewing was in the throes of her by-election campaign to win Hamilton for the SNP, and aware of how fervently I agreed with everything she was saying (and wished a Liberal had been saying) I felt it would be dishonest to hold back any longer. To my surprise – for I was a very minor political fish – the news of my resignation was given widespread coverage, *The Times* calling it 'startling' and other papers 'sensational'. From Hamilton came a call from Winnie Ewing to join her on the platform at her eve of poll meeting, which (as there was no Liberal standing) I gladly accepted. Next day she was elected by a handsome majority, and I believed the Scottish Home Rule movement to be on its way.

Because of my long commitment to Liberalism, I never in fact joined the Scottish National Party, but I occasionally appeared on their platforms and continued independently to promote the idea of Scottish autonomy. In a television programme networked from BBC Scotland called *The Disunited Kingdom*, I addressed the viewer direct as I had done in my Liberal Party general election broadcast. 'Friends, enemies, Englishmen,' I began, 'hear now the claims of Scotland!', and for four minutes I spelled out what I thought they were. It caused something of a stir north of the border and was reprinted as a pamphlet by the ultranationalist 1320 Club (1320 being the date of the signing of Robert I's Declaration of Arbroath).

I also began a campaign in the press and elsewhere against the lily-livered Scottish Rugby Union. It was the custom before an international match at Murrayfield for the band to play tunes appropriate to the nationality of the visiting team; for the French *The Marseillaise*, for the English 'God Save the Queen', for the Welsh 'Land of My Fathers', for the Irish 'The Soldier's Song'. But for their own Scottish team, instead of 'Scotland the Brave' or some other suitable Scottish air to give a lift to players and spectators alike, they fell back on 'God Save the Queen'. There were two objections to this: firstly it was a *British* tune and secondly (though less important) it was well known that its full version included a line about crushing rebellious Scots; and while the English national anthem may have pleased aggressively Anglophile spectators, it gave immense offence to thousands of ordinary Scots who quite understandably punctuated it with boos and whistles. This in itself was unedifying, and after I left Scotland the SRU at last summoned up courage to change over to 'Scotland the Brave'. But for away matches they still cravenly cling on to 'God Save the Queen'.

I maintained the theme of Scottish self-awareness in my presidential address to the Edinburgh Sir Walter Scott Club. Membership of this club entails attending an annual dinner at which some 400 of Edinburgh's most prominent citizens assemble to celebrate Scott's memory, at which an admiral or general and a judge respond to toasts to the Armed Forces and the Law, and the president speaks on some aspect of the author of the Waverley novels. (The reader may recall that my grandfather, Sir Ludovic Grant, had been president some sixty years before.) Although I would have been surprised if London's Charles Dickens Society required its members to put on a white tie for its annual dinner, the invitation card demanded it for the Scott dinner. After the war I vowed I would never wear a white tie again, and never have, I dislike it so much; so, having been informed that most of those below the salt would be wearing black ties anyway, I put on my Kennedy tartan smoking jacket with green velvet facings which I had recently had made and of which I was sure that Sir Walter, who often wore a plaid, would have approved.

In my talk I mentioned a number of specific things that Scott had brought about for Scotland as the result of his friendship with

George IV. These included the restoration of Scottish peerages forfeited after the rebellion of '45, the continuation of the Scottish currency, and – to me most dramatic and romantic of all – his discovering in a locked box in Edinburgh Castle the ancient regalia of Scotland; the crown and sceptre and sword of state with which the kings of Scotland had always been crowned, and which had last been used at the coronation of Charles II at Scone. I went on:

> Today the Sovereign of the United Kingdom is crowned in Westminster Abbey by the Archbishop of Canterbury in an English Coronation Service ordered by the English Earl Marshal whose authority, like that of the Archbishop, stops at the Scottish border.
>
> Am I alone in this room, I wonder, in hoping that at the next accession there may also be a coronation in Scotland, that the regalia of Scotland be bestowed on the Sovereign by the ministers of the Church of Scotland, according to the usage of the Scottish coronation service, long ratified by Scottish law?

The speech received much applause, and my remarks about the regalia were given prominence in the next day's papers. But there was a small band of Morningsiders, those ever so genteel Edinburghians who say 'Bay-bay' when they mean 'Bye-bye' and ape the English in all things who, I was told, were offended by my rejection of white tie. Their hurt found expression in the person of the secretary's wife, sitting opposite. Fixing me with a beady eye as soon as I had sat down, she leaned over to damn me with faint praise. '*I enjoyed your peroration as much as I deplore your jacket!*' Did I but know it, it was the writing on the wall.

For although the Home Rule movement did for a time grow apace, with an ever increasing number of SNP candidates being elected to Parliament and, under the Callaghan administration, the old High School building on Calton Hill being refurbished to accommodate a Scottish debating-chamber (the old one had become incorporated in the Law Courts), the idea of Home Rule made many of my countrymen uneasy; less, I think, about financial disadvantages (for oil revenue would have compensated for that) than at the prospect of feuding between east and west, north and south, and, for some, the prospect of a semi-permanent Labour administration; and when in 1979 a referendum of the whole Scottish nation was held, the votes in favour of Home Rule did not attain the clear 40 per cent majority on which the House of Commons had insisted. This result was never thereafter challenged: there were no protests or riots in the streets or general mayhem as there would have been, and God knows has been, in that other Celtic country across the water whose struggle for independence has never ceased. A sigh of relief could be heard all over Scotland. The whole Home Rule movement, with roots going far back into the past, melted quietly away as if it had never been.

For many of us it was a huge disappointment; a paradox, too, that a people who had proved themselves historically and geographically over and over again, who had shown a rare talent for managing the affairs of other people, should choose to chicken out when it came to managing their own. But the Scots have always had a deep-rooted sense of inferiority about the English: it was born out of the defeat of the '45 and the surrender of 1707 and, as Boswell and others had observed with chagrin and sometimes rage, the condescension and contempt of the English towards the Scots and their impossible tongue. I thought of Compton Mackenzie's brave words at a Nomads' Club dinner where I was his guest about the mystical experience of people loving their countrymen through loving their country and, by re-creating themselves, re-creating their nation. That experience I and thousands of others would now be denied. Half of us could continue to drown ourselves in usquebaugh and self-pity ('Here's tae us,/ Wha's like us?/ Damn few/ All deid'), the other half could relax, relieved that the English would be continuing to do our thinking for us.

Fifteen years later I was asked to speak in a St Andrew's Day debate being put out by BBC Television in Edinburgh. The motion was 'That devolution is dead and ought to be laid to rest'. I chose to speak for the motion rather than against, for as a matter of hard fact devolution was dead.

'Where,' I asked, 'is the evidence otherwise?' I went on: 'When I first came back to live here it was a different matter. As a journalist I had seen many countries overseas, all smaller and poorer than ourselves, being granted self-government; and I had hoped that Scotland would not be denied even the limited self-government that was then being dished out to the Cook Islands and the Faeroe Islands and the Cameroons.' But the referendum had killed it. I quoted Shakespeare: ' "Stands Scotland where it did. Alas, poor country, almost afraid to know itself." True in Macbeth's time and true today. For in the matter of self-government, Mr Chairman, we have become, and I am sorry to say it, a nation of political eunuchs.'

There were cheers and boos, but the cheers were uppermost. For there's nothing the Scots enjoy more than the scoring of own goals.

Although I was spending most of my time writing the book on Americans abroad, I see from my records of the late 1960s that I was also presenting several television programmes, both in London and in the north. These included the BBC's *Your Witness*, a courtroom-style debate in which the producer's assistant was a toothy young lady by the name of Esther Rantzen, and two interviews with Prince Philip, once on my own when he came to Edinburgh as Chancellor of the University, the other in Newcastle for Tyne-Tees' *Face the Press*. My last question to him there was what his reaction would be if one of his sons told him he wanted to marry a coloured girl. He smiled, paused, and said it would be really up to them to decide. After the recording he said, 'That was a fast one.'

In the autumn of 1969 the book on the Americans was published in London and New York under the title *Very Lovely People* (from a remark of President Johnson to some White House visitors – 'Mrs Johnson and I are very happy to have you here, and we think you are all very lovely people'). It did well enough, though might have done better if it had covered less ground; also, in the four years that had elapsed since gathering material for it, public interest in the world role that Americans had taken up in the Kennedy years had largely evaporated.

We visited Edinburgh from time to time and one evening were invited by the Queen to a dance at Holyrood House. As we came into the ballroom, I thought the figure on the bandstand, wearing immaculate evening tails and waving a baton, was vaguely familiar. I was right. It was Cam Robbie, whom I had last seen during the war twenty-five years earlier, when he was drummer of a rather tatty three-piece outfit in a night-club in George Street. I used to drop in there occasionally on leave, and sometimes Cam would let me take over the drums when the band was resting. Later, over a dram, Cam would regale me with tales of female conquests. 'Did I ever tell you about wee Sheila?' he'd say, licking his lips. 'Many a romp have I had with her, and boy, could she wriggle.' Or, 'You should have met Jeanie, Ludovic. The most glorious pair of wee titties you ever saw. And okay down below too. Grip like a vice. I'm telling you.' When Moira and I were passing the bandstand, I touched his arm and said, 'Hello, Cam. Remember me?' A flicker of recognition came and as quickly went. 'Oh, aye,' he said, 'seemingly. If there's any particular tune you'd care for, my boys will be very pleased to play it for you.' And he turned his back both on me and on his not-to-be-remembered past.

I also found time to undertake occasional voluntary speaking engagements, one of which in October 1969 was to take part in Lord McLeod of Fuinary's Rectorial debate at Glasgow University. Among others there was the Scottish advocate (and future QC and Conservative MP) Nicholas Fairbairn, a sartorial dandy with a razor-sharp mind whom I had met once or twice in the Borders. Nicky had (and for all I know still has) the reputation of being the best criminal defence lawyer at the Scottish bar and had on several occasions persuaded juries to acquit those whom he had every reason to believe were guilty. But now, as we travelled back to Edinburgh in the last train, he had a different problem. 'Tomorrow morning,' he said, 'I have to make my closing speech in defence of a man who is on a murder charge, and whom I know for certain to be innocent.'

His name, said Nicky, was Patrick Meehan, and he was a well-known and rather incompetent safe-blower, but with no record of violence. The victim was Rachel Ross, who with her husband Abraham, a bingo hall owner, lived in a bungalow in the seaside town of Ayr. On a Saturday night in July they were woken by two burglars who hit Mr Ross repeatedly on the head and body, tied them both up and demanded the keys of the safe. In it they found and pocketed several thousand pounds, the takings of the bingo hall, then left. The Rosses remained tied up over the weekend until discovered by their daily on Monday. They were taken to hospital where Mrs Ross died. All Mr Ross could remember of the burglars was that they both had Glasgow voices and called each other Pat and Jim. He never saw their faces.

How did Meehan come into it, I asked?

The police, said Nicky, had no idea who was responsible, so made routine inquiries of Glasgow's known villains. When it was

Meehan's turn and they asked him what he had been doing that night, he said he had driven to Stranraer (to case the motor taxation office, he admitted later) with an Englishman called Jim Griffiths; and they had come back via the outskirts of Ayr in the early hours of the morning. The police were looking for a Pat and Jim, said Nicky, and here was Pat admitting that he and his friend Jim were in the general area of the crime at roughly the time it was committed. If they needed further proof of their belief that they were on the right track, they were given it when they went to arrest Griffiths and were met by a hail of bullets; after a chase in which Griffiths killed one man and wounded others, he was shot dead while resisting arrest. By now certain that Meehan and Griffiths were the murderers of Mrs Ross, the Crown Office in Edinburgh issued a statement that with Griffiths's death and Meehan's arrest, they were not looking for any other suspects in connection with the Ayr murder – thus, said Nicky, prejudging the very issue that was to come to trial.

I said, 'Even if it was circumstantial, that's quite persuasive evidence.'

'Wait till I tell you what happened then. At an identification parade Meehan was asked to say something Mr Ross had heard one of the burglars say, and when Meehan said it, Mr Ross collapsed, shouting, "That's the voice, I'd know it anywhere." On this flimsy evidence (for no one else on the parade was asked to say the words) they charged him. And the forensic people gave evidence that pieces of brown paper and pieces of white paper they found in Griffiths's overcoat pocket exactly matched pieces of brown and white paper found in Mr Ross's safe.'

'So?'

'The identification parade was rigged and the pieces of paper were planted. And as it was July Griffiths wasn't wearing an overcoat.'

'You're sure?'

'I'm certain. There are many things in Meehan's favour. Ross said both burglars had Glasgow accents. Griffiths came from Lancashire and had an English accent. And if they really were the murderers, would they have been so foolish, after leaving Ayr and with Ross's money in the car, to have picked up as they did two girls who had been stranded by their boy friends, and taken them to their homes in Kilmarnock? The girls said it was still dark when they reached Kilmarnock; but Mr Ross said that when the burglars left it was light. And finally we impeached a man called Waddell who's been boasting to everyone in Barlinnie Jail that he and another man did it.'

Two or three days later I read in the *Scotsman* that the jury of fifteen had found Meehan guilty by a majority verdict. When the judge told him the only sentence he could pass was that of life imprisonment, Meehan said loudly and clearly, 'I want to say this, sir. I am innocent of this crime and so is James Griffiths. You have made a terrible mistake.'

Between the date of Meehan's conviction and his appeal a month later, Nicky told me, he had an astonishing piece of luck in that there had come into his possession a tape-recording of an interview with Griffiths taken some time previously for a programme the BBC had made at Gartree prison. Not only, said Nicky, was this proof positive of the Englishness – indeed the Lancashireness – of Griffiths's voice, but Griffiths had also said that if cornered in future he would shoot his way out rather than submit to arrest – exactly what he did do. At Meehan's appeal Nicky asked the presiding judge, Lord Clyde, if he could call Mr Ross to the witness box to have him listen to the recording. 'If Ross says the man with that voice was not in his house that night, then Meehan was not there either.' Nicky also wanted to call a witness who had knowledge of Waddell's part in the crime, but on both counts Lord Clyde turned him down.

Some time after this Mrs Meehan wrote to me that her husband was innocent, and asked for assistance in having his case re-viewed. But I was occupied with other things and in any event not then wholly convinced of Meehan's innocence. However, she continued to write and then Meehan himself sent the first of many letters, beginning, 'Dear Mr Kennedy, I am serving a Life imprisonment for a horrible murder in which I was never involved.' A year later Mrs Meehan wrote, 'As I say again, Paddy or Jim had never heard of Mr Ross until after this crime, and I know if not this week or this year, he will clear himself one day. Meantime it's a living hell for all of us, and I need all the help we can get to shorten the time he will be in prison.' Such an appeal was not to be resisted, but first I had to tell Meehan that if I did look into his case, I must feel myself free to come to whatever conclusions my investigations led me, 'whether in your favour or not'. His reply was unequivocal. 'I am certainly willing to give you a free hand . . . and to express whatever conclusions you come to as to guilt or innocence. If there are any questions you wish to put to me, then do not hesitate to do so.' This persuaded me it was unlikely I was dealing with a guilty man.

When investigating an alleged miscarriage of justice, I have always made it a rule first to talk to the convicted man's trial solicitor as he is likely to be the last man his client would wish to con, or would succeed in conning if he tried. Meehan, at the time I took up his case, had had three solicitors, all from Glasgow: Joseph Beltrami for his trial, then Ross Harper and later Leonard Murray. All three were convinced of his innocence. From one or other of them I obtained the papers on the case, and these, together with the letters I myself had received from Meehan, were enough to dispel any lingering doubts. For confirmation I visited him in prison, where in protest against his incarceration he had put himself in solitary confinement, and found him to be sandy-haired, bullet-headed and verbose, yet with a redeeming sense of humour; his passionate denials of having played any part in the Ayr murder were too convincing to have been invented. Further confirmation came from the governor of Peterhead, Alexander Angus, after his retirement. 'It would have been a crime completely out of character,' he told me, 'and it was the way he spoke about it that convinced me.' I also visited the scene of the crime at Ayr, and had several lunches and dinners with the diminutive, widowed but friendly Mr Ross; while an interview with the horrible Waddell in a Glasgow pub left me in no doubt that he was his attacker. The alternative, that he was a brilliant actor, was simply not credible.

Mr Angus had said to me *à propos* Meehan, 'Guilty men when they reach prison don't go on insisting on their innocence.' Yet from time to time law officers, judges and others in high places speak disparagingly of letters that they and others receive from prisoners asserting just that. 'Oh, we all know about those,' they say, 'smart fellows trying to have one on.' Indeed, as I write this, I have just been watching on television Lord Denning declaring with self-satisfaction that he puts all such letters straight into the wastepaper basket. My experience, like that of Mr Angus, has been the opposite. The majority of prison letters that I receive have the ring of truth; the reason being that it is not in human nature (of which the law is profoundly ignorant) for guilty men to go on proclaiming their innocence month after month, year after year, when they do not have the evidence, the impetus, or the skills to do so, at least with any show of conviction. As my friend David Jessel has pointed out, even if 99 per cent of all criminal convictions are correct, that still leaves in a prison population of 40,000 some 400 who have no business being there; and I cannot imagine any experience more demoralizing than to be locked up for years for a crime one didn't commit. It is from some of these 400 that the letters come protesting innocence – and if they often ramble and are poorly expressed, that is indicative of a lack of education which made them vulnerable to manipulation in the first place.

Among the papers sent to me by Mr Beltrami were letters from Meehan, written to him almost daily when he was on remand in Barlinnie Prison, Glasgow, awaiting trial. He had heard from other prisoners (he told Beltrami) that a man called Ian Waddell had been boasting that he had taken part in the Ayr crime, and then, on a quite different charge, Waddell was sent to Barlinnie himself. Meehan lost no time in seeking him out and asking him if what he had heard was true. Waddell did not deny it.

> I told him it was important to my defence to know if the old man had been blindfolded. Waddell is most emphatic that the old man was neither blindfolded nor gagged. Waddell says a blanket was thrown over the old man and several times the old man knocked it off and it had to be replaced. Waddell says the old man must have known it was daylight when they left, as the house lights were turned off by Waddell at dawn . . .

Meehan talked to Waddell on several further occasions. 'Waddell says that the names Pat and Jimmy were used during the attack . . . it is no wonder the police were convinced that Griffiths and I were responsible.'

So Nicky Fairbairn, Jo Beltrami and Paddy Meehan travelled to Edinburgh, and to the court where Oscar Slater had been wrongly convicted nearly fifty years before, all of them knowing that when the charge was read and Meehan formally pleaded Not Guilty, he was speaking no less than the truth. They realized there would be difficulties in discrediting the evidence of Mr Ross's false identification of Meehan's voice and of that of the planted pieces of paper, but nonetheless remained optimistic. What they had not bargained for was the prejudice of the trial judge, Lord Grant, who, as Nicky relates in his recently published memoirs,[1] made it plain from the outset that he believed, as the police believed, that Meehan was guilty. Whenever an opportunity arose for him to spike evidence or arguments favourable to the defence, he did not hesitate to do so, even at one choleric moment telling Nicky not to be stupider than he was; and his summing-up was a summing-up for the prosecution. Before it, the talk in the High Court corridors was that Meehan would be acquitted for lack of evidence, but it was a view that few held by the time it was finished. Even so, six of the fifteen jurors resisted Lord Grant's prejudices by voting to acquit.

The story of how Meehan and his advisors tried and failed during the next seven years to obtain justice for him in the light of increasing evidence of his innocence and Waddell's guilt makes sorry reading. Time and time again petitions, requests for a free pardon, Bills of Criminal Letters were lodged with the Lord Advocate or the Secretary of State for Scotland; time and time again they were rejected. Early in 1971 Waddell was found guilty of committing perjury at Meehan's trial[2] and in sentencing him to three years' imprisonment Lord Cameron suggested that had he told the truth there, the Meehan jury might well have arrived at a different verdict. The next year Meehan wrote to Beltrami that he had heard on the prison grapevine that Waddell's accomplice at Ayr was a well-known Glasgow villain named William ('Tank') McGuinness, a vicious little man with a long record that included violence. Later that year, when Beltrami was acting for McGuinness in another matter, McGuinness admitted his involvement at Ayr – information that Mr Beltrami was unable to divulge because of the confidentiality of the client-solicitor relationship. In 1973 Waddell admitted to two BBC reporters that he had taken part in the Ayr murder, unaware that one of them was carrying a concealed tape-recorder; and a programme that included his confession was subsequently broadcast. This, and other information, was laid before the Scottish Office. In 1974 the Secretary of State, Mr Gordon Campbell, announced that after discussions with the Lord Advocate, he proposed to take no further action and a year later, after a change of government, his Labour successor Mr William Ross said he

---

[1] *A Life is Too Short* (Quartet Books, 1987)

[2] He had denied on oath that he had given a solicitor £200 in cash to act for him if he was charged with the Ayr murder. The solicitor on oath said he had.

wasn't going to act either. It was then that with Nicky Fairbairn, Meehan's solicitors (including the latest, David Burnside) and an MP Frank McElhone, I formed the Patrick Meehan Committee, committed to campaigning on his behalf until justice was done.

Overjoyed by the decision of the Lord Advocate not to take action against him, and thinking himself now immune, Waddell confessed again, and in much greater detail. Whether his object in doing this was because of guilt in relation to Meehan or a continued desire for notoriety is impossible to say. But in a two-hour interview with reporters of the Scottish *Daily Record* he listed some fifteen details of the layout of the Ross bungalow and what was in it, information not mentioned at Meehan's trial or in the newspapers, and which he could only have known if he had been there, all of which Mr Ross confirmed ('Colour of bedroom quilts was pink', 'A light tan suit was in the bedroom wardrobe', 'An alarm clock with black face and luminous hands stood in the hatchway to the kitchen', etc.). Not even this could persuade Mr Ronald King-Murray, the new Lord Advocate, to move; presumably because the thought of having to admit that Meehan's wrongful conviction and five years of imprisonment (so far) were due partly to the blunders of his office was too painful to contemplate. In September 1974 Meehan brought a Bill of Criminal Letters against the detectives who, he claimed, had rigged the identification parade. Inevitably it was rejected. During the next year I completed my book, and all our hearts rose when I received a request from Mr William Ross's office to see the manuscript. They fell as quickly four months later. 'The Secretary of State after discussions with the Lord Advocate, finds there are no grounds, etc., etc., etc.'

Early in 1976 my book was published under the title of *A Presumption of Innocence* and the reviews were unanimous in calling for action. The distinguished former judge Lord Devlin sent an unsolicited letter that the case for Meehan's innocence I had put forward was very disturbing and needed to be answered. In the *Financial Times* Lord Snow agreed with him. Louis Blom-Cooper, QC in the *Listener*, Bernard Levin in the *Observer*, Leo Abse, MP in the *Spectator* all called for an immediate inquiry, while Julian Symons in the *Sunday Times,* C. H. Rolph in the *Times Literary Supplement,* Mervyn Jones in the *New Statesman* all declared categorically that Meehan was innocent and should be granted a free pardon under the Royal Prerogative of Mercy.

Always an optimist, I sent copies of these reviews to Mr William Ross and to Mr King-Murray. I should have known better. From the Secretary of State's office came a brief acknowledgement, from King-Murray's office nothing. The longer they had delayed acting, the more difficult it had become for them to act. To have released Meehan from seven years of wrongful imprisonment, recommended a free pardon for him, and then to have arrested and charged Waddell for the same crime would have required a greater degree of resolution than either of them possessed. It seemed that so far as they were concerned Meehan, guilty or innocent, could stay in Peterhead for ever. It was Rillington Place all over again.

And there, as they say, the matter rested, for there was now nothing further we could do; and Meehan might have had to serve many more years in prison had not a further and quite unexpected twist come to this most tangled of cases. On 12 March that year William McGuinness was found dying of head injuries in a Glasgow street. His death enabled Mr Beltrami to apply to the Scottish Law Society for a waiver of the confidentiality he had observed in relation to McGuinness's admissions to the Ayr crime; and he enclosed a statement from Mrs McGuinness that her husband had also admitted the crime and Waddell's participation in it, to her. The waiver having been granted, the papers then went to the Crown Office.

Meehan should have been released immediately, but instead the authorities offered him parole, that is release on licence, which he properly and courageously rejected, knowing it could not be long before he was released unconditionally. Three weeks later his long ordeal came to an end when the new Secretary of State for Scotland, Bruce Millan, announced to the House of Commons that he had decided to exercise the Royal Prerogative of Mercy, i.e. recommend to the Queen the granting of a free pardon. It would have been agreeable if Mr William Ross, who was also in the House, could have been generous enough to admit his own past errors and congratulate his successor on his decision. But all he could manage was, 'Was this the only action open to you?' That afternoon Meehan was released from Peterhead and given an interim compensation payment of £2500 with a promise of more to come.

Now attention shifted away from Meehan and on to Waddell, then back in Barlinnie for stabbing a man with a knife and a saw; and after six months of investigations by two senior police officers, he was arrested, brought to Edinburgh and charged with the murder of Mrs Ross. The opening day of the trial was to be devoted to legal arguments and Mr Beltrami, Moira, Meehan and myself turned up at the Courts of Justice to hear them. Although neither prosecution nor defence lodged any objection to our presence, the presiding judge, Lord Robertson, barred us from attending. As we walked away to a coffee-shop in the Royal Mile, Meehan said, 'That's the first court in my life I've been turned away from.' It was, had we but realized it, an omen of things to come.

As Meehan's main defence at his trial had been an impeachment of Waddell, so Waddell's main defence was an impeachment of Meehan. This meant that despite Meehan's pardon, the proceedings to some extent would be a retrial of Meehan as well as a trial of Waddell; and one of its more lunatic aspects was hearing Mr King-Murray as prosecuting counsel, who for two years had strenuously refused to entertain the notion of Meehan's innocence and Waddell's guilt, now deploying arguments to show that very thing (although unlike Griffith-Jones at Ward's trial, he did not seem to have his heart in it); and conversely to hear Waddell's counsel echoing the arguments of the prosecutor at Meehan's trial to demonstrate Meehan's guilt and Waddell's innocence.

Despite Mr King-Murray's diffident approach, the evidence against Waddell was devastating. First Mrs Agnes McGuinness: 'My husband went out on the Saturday and I didn't see him again until the Sunday morning. He told me he had done a job at Ayr ... he said that Ian Waddell was with him.' Then Waddell's alibi, Donald Carmichael, who had said at Meehan's trial that Waddell had been staying with him on the night of the murder, now admitted this was a lie. Several women friends of Waddell said that he had given them within days of the murder large sums of money; and a barman to whom Waddell had given £1000 for safe keeping said Waddell had told him he had won a packet on the horses. And finally two Ayr police officers said that a shelved 1969 report showed they had picked up a man 'of slight build and a Glasgow accent who said his name was McGuigan or McGuinness' some 600 yards from the Ross bungalow in the early hours of the morning of the murder and dropped him at the bus station; and they now declared from photographs recently shown to them that the man was William McGuinness.

I do not think it had occurred to anybody in court at this time that Waddell's conviction would be anything but a foregone conclusion. But they had not reckoned with Lord Robertson. Lord Robertson is a large man with a Morningside accent and a florid face which in court he used continually to rub with his hand. He is also a keen golfer and a past captain of the Honourable Company of Edinburgh Golfers at Muirfield, to whom he presented a photograph of himself wearing a wig. But the most important thing about Lord Robertson was that in this particular case he was even more prejudiced than Lord Grant, although in the light of all that had recently occurred, with far less excuse. It was evident, as the trial went on, that Lord Robertson had held for many years a belief amounting to an article of faith that Meehan and Griffiths had committed the Ayr murder, and that so paltry a matter as overwhelming evidence to show that they hadn't and that Waddell and McGuinness had, was in no way going to sway him.

The first indication of the direction his mind (or what passed for it) was moving had come at the beginning of the trial when he called in two other judges to help determine whether the free pardon that Meehan had been granted quashed his conviction. This was a peculiar thing to do, because in 1963 in the House of Lords the Lord Chancellor had ruled that a free pardon wiped out a conviction and all its consequences, and the accused was to be regarded as having been acquitted. Now the three Scottish judges ruled that they could not decide on the matter, a decision, as they must have realized, that was profoundly to affect the trial. For had they ruled that a free pardon *did* quash a conviction, then Waddell's defence of impeachment, i.e. that Meehan and not he had committed the crime, would have collapsed; as it was it was greatly strengthened.

Lord Robertson gave a further hand to the defence when the time came for Mr Beltrami to give evidence. Mr Beltrami would tell the jury that on several occasions during the past four years McGuinness had spoken to him in detail about his part in the Ayr murder; and as he has a commanding presence and deep, authoritative voice, his evidence would have gone far to confirm in the minds of the jury what they had already heard from Mrs McGuinness. But Lord Robertson disallowed his evidence, firstly because of the confidentiality of the client-solicitor relationship (though Mr Beltrami had already been issued with a waiver for this from the Scottish Law Society), secondly because evidence against McGuinness could not be competent as evidence against Waddell. But at Meehan's trial this same argument – that evidence against Griffiths in the matter of the planted bits of paper should not be considered competent as evidence against Meehan – was rejected by Lord Grant (Lord Grant being as keen to see Meehan convicted as Robertson was to see Waddell acquitted). One ruling at one trial, the opposite at another.

But it was when he came to his summing-up or, as they say in Scotland, charge to the jury, that Lord Robertson abandoned all attempts at judicial impartiality. A fuller description of this can be found in the paperback edition of *A Presumption of Innocence*, so here I will confine myself to the main points.

He began by saying that seven years earlier Meehan had been found guilty by a jury 'on evidence which was amply justified', and then went on: 'Some public support was whipped up over the years for reasons which were not entirely clear and for motives which might be imagined.' I could hardly believe my ears. What possible reasons and motives could the Patrick Meehan Committee, consisting of a Queen's Counsel, an MP, four solicitors and myself, have had other than a belief in Meehan's innocence and a wish therefore to clear his name? Lord Robertson lacked the courage to tell us.

For a long time, he continued, the Crown authorities had paid no attention to 'this clamour' but then a decision had been taken to recommend a free pardon. 'The reasons for this decision have not become apparent at this trial' (they had but he had chosen to ignore them) and he then attacked the Secretary of State for what he called 'usurping the functions of the judiciary', apparently ignorant that recommendations for free pardons have always been vested in the executive.

Turning to the evidence, he stressed those aspects of it which told against Meehan and in favour of Waddell. He said there was no evidence of Waddell's fingerprints at Ayr, but didn't add the same was true of Meehan. He explained away the list of things that Waddell had seen in the Ross's house as having been published at the trial or in the newspapers, which was not the case. He said that all Waddell's confessions had been made 'for drink or money' but didn't add that the clandestine confession given to the two BBC reporters had been made for neither. He suggested that Abraham Ross might have been mistaken in thinking both burglars had Scottish accents. He gave the jury a list of Meehan's past convictions, knowing that he was prevented by the rules of evidence from telling them that Waddell was at that moment serving a sentence in Barlinnie for wounding or that he had served a previous sentence for perjury at Meehan's trial. 'There is no legal justification whatever', he thundered, 'in saying that Meehan was wrongly convicted, and having heard all the evidence in this case, you might well have come to the clear conclusion that he was in fact rightly convicted.'

At some point during all this nonsense Meehan stormed out of the court, shouting that his free pardon wasn't worth the paper it was printed on. I too had a strong urge to rise up and say, 'My lord, this trial has been a farce, and you are the chief clown!' but, I think wisely, refrained. And I wasn't at all surprised when the jury took only an hour to find Waddell not guilty.

The rest of the story can be told quite briefly. Instead of being handed the life sentence he so richly deserved, Waddell was released from Barlinnie the following year and gave yet another confession to the Ayr murder to the *Evening News*: 'It was me all right.' A few months later he was back in court charged with being in possession of a gun with intent to commit a robbery. And a few years after that his sticky career came to an end when he and a friend called Gentle (who was anything but) murdered a woman called Josephine Chipperfield at her home in Easterhouse and wounded several of her family. They went into hiding immediately after, but when they heard that a warrant had been issued for their arrest, Waddell told Gentle he was going to give himself up. To prevent this Gentle strangled him, put his body in the bathroom for a day or two and then was spotted trying to bury it. At his trial for acting with Waddell in the murder of Mrs Chipperfield, Gentle was found guilty and sentenced to life imprisonment. Had Waddell's trial in Edinburgh not been the farce it was, had he been found guilty of the murder of Mrs Ross as he should have been and sentenced by Lord Robertson to life imprisonment, as he should have been, it would seem likely that Mrs Chipperfield would be alive today. Has Lord Robertson ever had the death of Mrs Chipperfield on his conscience? Somehow one doubts it.

The Meehan case had caused such lengthy controversy that in March 1977 Bruce Millan invited a Scottish judge, Lord Hunter, to chair an independent inquiry into it. Its terms were so depressingly restrictive – it was not to consider the guilt or innocence of

Meehan or Waddell – that the Meehan Committee and Meehan himself debated whether to give evidence to it or not. In the end, and because Lord Hunter was presented to us as a man of independent judgement, we decided to do so, and advised Meehan to do the same. Until the report was published, the question of the balance of Meehan's compensation for seven years' wrongful imprisonment was to remain in abeyance.

In the end, and to add to the injustices he had already suffered, Meehan was obliged to wait five years, which was the time it took Lord Hunter to complete and publish his report. It was an enormously thorough and comprehensive review of the case, running to four volumes and more than 1200 pages, yet it would have been better if it had been half the length and taken half the time. In his preamble to the report Lord Hunter quoted Lord Denning's preamble to the Profumo affair report about the importance of justice to the individual and not condemning on suspicion, and he also promised to avoid what he called wild speculation. Unfortunately by the time he reached his conclusions he had forgotten both these things.

Stated baldly, and cheerfully ignoring the Secretary of State's admonition not to impute guilt to either Meehan or Waddell, his conclusions were that while Waddell and McGuinness probably carried out what he called the initial assault, 'it cannot be disproved that Meehan and Griffiths were not a follow-up team with the role of dealing with the safe or safes believed to be in the bungalow'. Aside from the worthlessness of double negatives, aside from the fact that McGuinness was a far more accomplished safe-breaker than Meehan (he had earned his nickname 'Tank' because it was said he could penetrate even one of those), and aside from the fact that in all the verbiage spilled out by Meehan, Waddell and McGuinness to lawyers, journalists and others for over thirteen years, none of them had so much as hinted at the idea of a quartet, there was not a scrap of worthwhile evidence to support it: it was speculation with a vengeance and extraordinary to find in a report by a judge of his standing.

But it was when I came to ask myself the *reason* for such a wild suggestion that I received a greater shock. All British judges in my experience have a completely blind spot when confronted by evidence which indicates police corruption, and Lord Hunter was no exception. ('Reliance is rightly placed', he wrote, 'on the integrity and competence of police officers.') While this attitude is understandable – for our whole system of criminal justice depends on mutual trust between those who administer the law and those who enforce it – it is nonetheless deplorable. When Lord Hunter asked those officers who could have planted the incriminating pieces of paper in the pocket of Griffiths's overcoat (which he wasn't wearing that night) and all of them, as one would expect, denied it, he could then delude himself into believing that no planting had taken place.

So an alternative explanation had to be found, hence the idea of Meehan and Griffiths as a follow-up team. Claiming that although in the end 'their services had not been required', he thought that nevertheless 'they would have expected and received some share of the proceeds' and it was presumably while Griffiths was being handed his share of the proceeds from Mr Ross's safe that bits of brown paper and bits of white paper could have found their way into his overcoat pocket. Lord Hunter had been unable to free himself from the idea of Meehan as a participant any more than Sir Daniel Brabin had been able to free himself from the assumption of Timothy Evans's guilt; neither could bring himself to admit, perhaps for the sake of the reputation of their profession, that the miscarriage of justice had been total, that Meehan as much as Evans had played no part whatever in the crime with which he had been charged. Fortunately Lord Hunter's Alice-in-Wonderland conclusions had no bearing on the question of compensation for Meehan, and after negotiations between Mr Beltrami and an assessor, he was awarded a total of £50,000.

For me personally there was an epilogue to the story which came about when we bought a house in Edinburgh a year or two later. For twelve years I had greatly enjoyed being a guest of some of the members of the Honourable Company of Edinburgh Golfers on their championship links of Muirfield on the coast of East Lothian, where once or twice as a boy I had played with my grandfather. The members were a blend of middle-class Edinburgh professional people – lawyers, solicitors, doctors, accountants, etc. – and Anglo-Scottish gentry. While not having the sea views of nearby Gullane or Kilspindie, the course was a great challenge to one's golf, and I found the lunches the best of any club-house in Britain. Some time previously and after a wait of five years my name had been proposed and seconded for membership, but when my proposer heard that two members were of a mind to blackball me in the ballot, he (without telling me) withdrew my candidature. After a further six years' wait (during which my original proposer and seconder had died and their nominations had been taken up by two ex-captains), my name came up for election again, and this time, I was told, the opposition from members, particularly those in the legal profession who were friends of Lord Robertson, was fiercer. I was asked if I wished my name to be withdrawn a second time but I declined, feeling it would be wrong to have to continue to rely on the goodwill and hospitality of friends in order to continue playing. So I told my proposer to let my name stand, and said I would accept whatever the ballot box decided, but would not play there again if the vote went against me. In the event there were a gratifying number of white balls but too many black ones to see me through (I was told later by a mole the names of some of those who had cast them, and I can't say I was surprised). I was sad about this because I am a clubbable person by nature, and have never regarded a game of golf as anything but an occasion of pleasurable social exchange; but an end to Muirfield was the price I had to pay for the championing of Meehan's cause.

And not the only price. For at about the same time I was approached by the secretary of Edinburgh's New Club which as a member of Brooks's Club[1] in London I was entitled to use on a reciprocal basis, and which I did use for lunch perhaps a dozen times a year. It was felt by some members, the secretary told me, that as I now had a residence in Edinburgh, I ought to become a fully paid-up member. I can't say I was enamoured of the prospect of paying £150 entrance fee and about the same in annual subscription, but keen to do the right thing, I asked Robert Balfour, then Chairman of the Scottish Arts Council and Dawyck Haig to propose and second me. I could have saved myself the trouble. They do not have black balls at the New Club, but they have even more members in the legal profession than Muirfield; and word reached me that the election committee had received objections to my membership too strong to ignore. On this occasion I was more relieved than sorry, yet couldn't help but smile at the ingenious way they had managed to ease me out.

---

[1] The St James's Club to which I had belonged for many years had closed down, and its members had been accepted by Brooks's.

Sadly, that was not even the last of the clubs to deny me membership. A few years earlier a friend and fellow member of Brooks's, Cyril Salmon, a former Lord Justice of Appeal, had put my name down for election to the Seniors Golfing Society, an English-based club for golfers over the age of fifty-five who met from time to time at a variety of attractive courses. Not now belonging to any particular golf club, joining the Seniors was something I greatly looked forward to. I thought it right to apprise Cyril of what had happened at Muirfield, but having corresponded with the Seniors secretary, he assured me I was on course for election. All the more disappointing therefore to learn later that some Seniors members who had blackballed me for Muirfield had now put in an objection to my joining this club too. As a result Cyril was informed that my application for membership would be turned down. 'I am very sad,' he wrote to me, 'about the disgraceful way you have been treated by the Seniors, and because of it I have informed the captain I am resigning.' I implored him not to, but he was adamant, thus following Rear Admiral Poland who had resigned from Muirfield in consequence of my being blackballed there ('it makes no sense at all', he wrote to the secretary, 'that he can be accepted as a guest but blackballed as a member'): both were sacrifices for which I felt a personal responsibility and which caused me much distress.

19

Admiral Dönitz and the German Navy

The reader who has survived so far may recall that during my wartime service in the Navy I had nursed a great curiosity about the enemy we rarely saw, and that I had promised myself that at some time in the future I would find out more about them, the ships they had fought in and the sort of people they were. Thus began a series of documentary films and books about the conflict with the German Navy in the Second World War.

The first project was a film on Scapa Flow made with a director whose talent in obtaining striking images of light on water, cloud formation, or reeds bending in the wind I had greatly admired in his previous work. I had wanted to return to Scapa for some time, to refresh my memories of that extraordinary and beautiful place and of the strange life I had lived there for nearly three years. The director, the crew and I stayed at Stromness on the Orkney mainland, in wartime too far to visit because of being at short notice for steam; and it was an odd feeling crossing over to Hoy in the ferry, then motoring in a taxi down its eastern side to the once familiar anchorage of Gutter Sound. The oil storage tanks were still there, so was the big, now empty hall which had housed the ENSA concert parties, and a few pre-fabricated administration bungalows, some windowless and with doors creaking in the wind.

But the anchorage where the destroyer headquarters ship with its rear admiral's flag once lay, and where up to a dozen destroyers might be swinging with the tide at their buoys, was now empty water. Looking at it and the bleak shore of Flotta beyond, the memories came flooding back: pink gins before Sunday lunch at twopence a throw; dressing up as Tartars and Eskimos and Bedouins for Tribal parties; cinema shows where the reels were laced up in the wrong order; darts competitions in the wardroom flat; early winter morning torpedo firings in the Flow, very dark and cold; walks to Longhope for fresh eggs, or fishing for sea-trout in the bay; piping the admiral as we passed the headquarters ship and eased our way down to Switha Gate bound for distant waters, the captain on the compass platform with cap at an angle, elbows on hips and gloved hands turned upwards, Spider beside him puffing smoke through a black holder and advising courses to steer; and then, as the ship adjusted herself to the roll and rhythm of the sea, a last flashing message from the signal station at Hoxa Head (now vandalized and abandoned), as it would be the first on our return, days or weeks later. Those years had an intensity, a singularity and a sense of joy about them that I have not known before or since.

On Orkney's west coast cliffs we filmed the memorial to Lord Kitchener and the men of the *Hampshire* which had struck a mine near the shore in 1916 and gone down with all but a handful of survivors; in the Flow we spoke to divers still bringing up steel and copper from the Kaiser's sunken High Seas Fleet; and on the island of Lamb Holm on the eastern side we filmed a sequence of the little Catholic chapel, fashioned out of a Nissen hut by Italian prisoners-of-war who had built a causeway linking the islands after Prien's successful foray in *U.47* against the *Royal Oak*. Prien himself and most of his crew had been killed later in the war, but we managed to track down and invite over from Germany his engineer officer on that famous trip. He had had a long and tiring journey, flights from Frankfurt, Heathrow and Glasgow all having been delayed or cancelled. When he finally arrived, a long, gangling slice of a man, and we commiserated with him on the waywardness of British Airways, he exploded with laughter, saying, 'I tell you this, I got here quicker in U.47!' Over dinner he gave an enthralling account of the entire mission, their excitement at penetrating the Flow undetected, matched only by their relief at finding the way out, and of how on reaching home waters they had been cheered into Wilhelmshaven by the rest of the German fleet and flown to Berlin for a celebratory banquet with Hitler. After dinner, it being light at that time until midnight, we took our friend into the hotel garden and, for possible use in the film, recorded him shouting German wheel and engine-room orders such as would have been used by Prien during the mission. On my way into the hotel, one of the guests said to me, 'What on earth was going on out there?' But it was too difficult to explain. I answered lamely, 'Oh, just a game.'

I also made a documentary about the U-boat campaign which in two world wars had nearly brought us to our knees; and I have always regretted that after the last war, when we sank so many of them in deep water, we did not keep one as a trophy and bring it up the Thames into the heart of London: it would have been a perennial attraction for every schoolboy in the country. As far as I know, there are only two still in existence: one, the U.505, was captured by an American task force towards the end of the war, towed up the St Lawrence and through the Great Lakes to Chicago where a special cradle was built for it to cross the Lake Shore Drive and then set up in a little house of its own in the Museum of Science and Industry. There it rests today with all its wartime equipment on display, and every year thousands of visitors come to see it and the twenty-minute film that was made of its capture.

The other U-boat, brought from Norway, rests on the sands of Kiel Roads, close to the gloomy German naval museum; and Chicago being rather far, we used it extensively in the making of our film. Seeing the cramped, coffin-like quarters in which fifty men had to live, eat, sleep and fight, often in appalling weather for up to six weeks at a time and knowing how marginal were their chances of survival, I couldn't help but admire the resolution that had kept them fighting, their morale undimmed, until the very end. During the war I had felt the same about those they were attacking, the brave men of the Allied merchant fleets.

In Hamburg and elsewhere I talked to several former U-boat captains and instead of the brash abrasive characters I had expected, I found them on the whole to be men of sensibility and humour. There was the gentle, bearded Hans Jenisch who told me of his hesitancy before giving the orders to fire torpedoes. 'I wouldn't know if you could understand it, but it is a strange feeling for a sailor to sink a ship – for a split second you have the idea, should I or shouldn't I? Then you do it.' Peter Cremer gave a graphic account of being depth-charged, with the protective glass on the gauges shattering all round them and cables falling from the roof. 'We have only emergency light and very little air and after two or three hours everybody gets very nervous. Then the crew look at the commander to see if he is afraid or not afraid. If I told you I was not afraid, it would be a lie. But to give the impression I am not afraid, I tell jokey stories to calm them, though I don't feel jokey at all.' Big, burly Ernest von Witzendorff sat at the foot of the conning-tower and laughed when he remembered how tough it had been in 1944 when Allied planes with radar covered the Atlantic. 'They found us everywhere so we had to stay under water nearly twenty-three hours a day, and the air was so bad you had to lie down and sleep so you didn't use too much of it.' And little, twinkly Claus Korth, captain of *U.93* with a crew of forty-four, described poetically how he picked up the forty-nine survivors of a *Bismarck* supply ship, the *Belchen*, and brought his heavily overloaded boat back to France. 'We have not bunks enough and we have only two toilets. So the bunks get very warm all the day, more than a week, more than eight days, and also the seats of the toilets are all the time warm too.'

And then there was the greatest ace of them all, Otto Kretschmer, whose record of having sunk a quarter of a million tons of Allied shipping was never beaten, Kretschmer who had perfected the night tactics, taught him by Dönitz, of letting a convoy pass over him, surfacing between the lines, loosing off torpedoes at ships either side of him, then diving again to get clear. Kretschmer's end had come in the spring of 1941 at almost the same time as his great rivals Schepke and Prien, when his

U.99 was sunk by a destroyer commanded by Captain Donald Macintyre, and he had spent the rest of the war as a prisoner. Afterwards, rehabilitated in the German Navy, he had been an admiral in NATO's northern naval command. Now he had a job in the dockyards at Emden where he lived with his wife.

We arrived at his house and knocked at the door. A friendly but severe-looking woman answered it. Before any of us had time to speak, she said, 'You are from the BBC?' We said we were. 'You want Otto?' We said we did. 'Come in, come in,' she said. 'Welcome.' We followed her to the foot of the stairs and she bawled up it, 'Otto? The BBC are here. Come on down. The BBC don't like to be kept waiting.' She smiled. 'Otto is sometimes slow.' Presently a handsome, lean figure with greying hair came down the stairs. 'This is Otto,' said his wife, in case we had doubts. He shook hands all round. 'Now go in there,' said his wife, pushing Otto and the rest of us into a front room. 'I get coffee for everybody, yes? How many? *Sieben?* You are many people for Otto!' She laughed. '*Gut!*'

Otto turned out to have measureless charm and the most courteous manner, and in slow, correct English told us of how he had perfected his tactics in Baltic exercises before the war, how he had put them into practice in the Atlantic, and how, on the night after his capture, he had played bridge in the day-cabin of Captain Macintyre with one of the ship's lieutenants and the captains of two merchant ships he had sunk, and then slept (for Captain Macintyre was in his sea-cabin) in Captain Macintyre's bunk. After the war captor and captive became friends, and Otto showed us the Zeiss binoculars which Macintyre had taken off him as a trophy of war, but had recently handed back. As we went away to the sounds of Mrs Otto's profuse good-byes, I reflected on the nature of the relationship between her and Otto, almost the opposite to what one might have expected: the gallant captain going off to sea where his authority was absolute and his orders brooked no delay, and returning to a wife whom he clearly adored but where the roles were reversed. It was a syndrome I had observed in other service marriages, not least in that of my own parents, and I have sometimes thought what a good subject it might make for a novel or play. (A week later the director and crew went to Captain Macintyre's house in the country to obtain his side of the story. The door was opened by a woman wearing a tweed skirt and smoking a pipe.)

And finally we went to see Karl Dönitz, the admiral who throughout the war had epitomized the U-boat service and been its inspired leader, who in 1943 had relieved Admiral Raeder as Germany's naval commander-in-chief, and finally for a very brief period before arrest and ten years' imprisonment in Spandau had succeeded Hitler as Chancellor. Unlike Raeder, who was a-political, he was and remained a fervent admirer of Hitler. His crews adored him. 'He was the greatest military leader I ever met,' Otto Kretschmer had said, and Jenisch spoke of him as 'the father of us all'. At eighty-one now he had outlived his family except for his daughter and her children: his wife had died, so had his son-in-law, and both sons had been killed in the war.

He lived in the ground floor flat of a large ugly villa in Auhmühle, thirty miles south of Hamburg, convenient for naval reunions there and for walks in the adjacent forest. A brass plate beside the door said 'Eingang Dönitz' and an arrow pointed the way. We rang the bell which made musical chimes, and the admiral answered it. It was strange to see in the flesh a man whose name and face had since 1939 been almost as familiar to me as those of Churchill or Hitler. 'So!' he said, 'Dönitz!', and shook hands with us all. He had always been small but now seemed quite shrunken, though still erect in bearing and in neatly pressed charcoal-grey suit and shining shoes dapper in his dress; but there was no mistaking the ferret-like face, the money-box slit of a mouth and the blue, commanding eyes.

He helped the crew hang up their coats, said, 'So!' again, and led us into the living-room, a modest affair with a bookcase of mainly naval books, a desk with photographs of his dead family, a crucifix, and, on a separate table, a model of a U-boat. Through our interpreter, Christine, he said, 'I used to have many more mementoes from my naval career, but the British' – he seemed to speak not of us but of some distant tribe – 'looted them.' As if to show that bygones were bygones, he produced a bottle of Sandeman's sherry from a cupboard and, though it was three in the afternoon, poured out glasses for all. Christine said, 'He says he's sorry about his deafness, it's because he's so old.' To me, he said in a quavering voice, 'When I was a young man, people lived to be fifty-five or sixty. Later they lived to be sixty-five or seventy.' He took my arm in a fatherly way and said, 'I am eighty-one. You will live to be ninety or a hundred.' Christine said, 'He's using "*Du*" to address us, as though he's known us all a long time.'

Before leaving London I had sent him, as requested, two questions about the U-boat war which I wanted him to answer for the programme. Seated at his desk, he opened a file, then said in English, 'There is a figure I need which I do not have. Five years ago I had it at my fingertips. I must speak to Rohwer.' I knew Rohwer was a German naval historian. He picked up the telephone, spoke, and then said, 'Rohwer is not there.' He seemed hugely disappointed. He muttered to Christine who said, 'He's very sorry about not having the figure. If he finds it, he will send it to you.' Then he said to me in English, 'I have written answers to the two questions you sent me,' and opened the file. I saw it contained fifteen or twenty pages, and thought, my God, this is like the interview I did with Adenauer twenty years ago all over again!

The director said 'Action', the sound recordist said 'Running', the assistant cameraman said 'One forty-five take one', and I put the first question – how did he think the war would have gone if he'd started it with the 300 U-boats he'd asked for in 1938? Dönitz adjusted his glasses, took the first sheet of paper from the file, opened his mouth and bawled at the microphone as though it was the furthest sailor on the longest parade ground in the Third Reich. Twice the director stopped him to urge restraint, but television was too new a trick for this old sea-dog and he rampaged on, regardless. After ten minutes I heard the camera motor stop as the film ran out, but the director, knowing by now we couldn't use a foot of it, let the old boy run on until he had finished. For the second question and answer we didn't even bother to load the camera, though as a matter of courtesy, we let him carry on bawling. This took another eight minutes. Then the two of us were filmed walking round the garden, and back at the BBC to cover these shots I narrated a commentary which was a distillation of what Dönitz had said. Afterwards he gave me signed copies of two of his books, 'Write your name clearly on this piece of paper. So many people in Germany have names that are impossible to read.' Before I left, he said, 'I will endeavour to send the figure I mentioned.' Whatever it was, he never did.

A year later I went back to Auhmühle to conduct an interview with the admiral for the *Telegraph* colour magazine. He had aged noticeably, his voice was higher-pitched and more quavery, but he was still alert mentally and willing to range over the whole of the naval war and his relationship with Hitler. Before I left Britain one of the best-kept secrets of the war had at last been revealed – the breaking by the Bletchley Park mathematicians of the ciphers encoded by the German Enigma machine: this priceless intelligence had enabled us to sink all the *Bismarck*'s supply ships, monitor the movements of *Tirpitz* so that attacks could be launched on her (see page 144) and destroy many U-boats at the height of the Battle of the Atlantic. Captain Stephen Roskill, the official naval historian, had told me that Dönitz had informed him in 1959 that he had no reason to think that the German naval codes had been broken. Armed with contrary information, I asked the admiral if he would accept my word for it. He looked uneasy, shifted a little in his chair. His answer, when it came, was vague: he had heard rumours, but knew nothing for certain; there had been talk of treachery. I knew then that what I was telling him he was hearing for the first time. Was he too old, I wondered, to console himself after I had gone, with the knowledge that without our penetration of Enigma, he might still have won the U-boat war?

I also made documentaries on the battleships *Bismarck* and *Tirpitz*, with both of which, as the reader may recall, I had had distant brushes, and the battlecruiser or fast battleship *Scharnhorst* which had sunk my father's *Rawalpindi*. The *Bismarck* film was the most difficult because apart from newsreel sequences of her launching and on exercises in the Baltic, there was no historical material. However, I was lucky in the quality of eye-witness contributors. The actor Esmond Knight who was an RNVR officer in the new battleship *Prince of Wales* gave a dramatic account of the arrival of the *Bismarck*'s salvo that had blinded him (though he continued to act after the war and performed in *The Red Shoes* with Moira). On the German side I interviewed Baron von Mullenheim-Rechberg, the *Bismarck*'s fourth gunnery officer and senior surviving officer, a former assistant naval attaché at the German Embassy in London without whose fluent and colloquial English it would have been impossible to give the film the necessary balance.

I also spoke to two other former German naval officers. One was Herbert Wohlfarth, one-time captain of the U-boat *U.556*. In 1940 *U.556* had been fitting out at Hamburg at the same quay as the *Bismarck* and in return for borrowing *Bismarck*'s band for her commissioning ceremony, Wohlfarth, who was a skilled cartoonist, prepared a document, charred at the edges to show its age, whereby *U.556* would 'adopt' *Bismarck* (as towns in Germany and England then were adopting warships) and protect her from harm in all the oceans, seas, lakes, ponds, puddles of the world. Strangely this pledge was nearly fulfilled, for when the crippled *Bismarck* was making for the shelter of Brest, the *U.556*, returning from patrol, came within torpedo firing range of the aircraft carrier *Ark Royal*, then hurrying north to intercept the German battleship. But Wohlfarth had expended all his torpedoes and had to watch in anguish as the huge aircraft carrier, without a protective destroyer screen, slid past him. It was late that evening that the torpedo from one of *Ark Royal*'s Swordfish planes smashed *Bismarck*'s rudder, thus ensuring her destruction by the British fleet.

The other officer was Gerhard Junack of the *Bismarck*'s engineering staff, who helped dispel a myth which had gained some credence in the Royal Navy that it was British torpedoes and shells exclusively that had sent the allegedly unsinkable *Bismarck* to the bottom. Junack told me that he personally had received orders from Commander Lehmann to scuttle the ship by placing explosive charges in the cooling water intakes and to open the seacocks, and that he and others had done this; and this was confirmed by an engine-room rating named Werner Lust who stayed on in England after his release as a prisoner-of-war.

My *Tirpitz* film also produced some outstanding contributors, among them two Norwegian resistance men and Rear Admiral Godfrey Place, VC. I interviewed Place in a midget submarine in Portsmouth dockyard similar to the one in which he and two other men had travelled up the long fjord in northern Norway at the head of which *Tirpitz* lay, cut their way through the nets surrounding her and laid charges beneath her hull which, when they exploded an hour later and Place was a prisoner-of-war on board her, put the ship out of action for six months. If I had found the cramped interior of the U-boat at Kiel oppressive, it was nothing to the claustrophobia I felt inside the midget submarine, and I marvelled again at the courage and calm that had enabled Place and his crew to live a daily life in such surroundings, far less undertake and brilliantly accomplish their mission.

But the interview about which I was most apprehensive came

in making the film on the *Scharnhorst*. The fact that she had been the ship that had sunk the *Rawalpindi* and killed my father did not seem to me to be a valid reason for omitting her from the series, for apart from the utter impersonality of a modern sea battle, she was by far the most successful of all the major German surface ships as well as being the happiest. This was due in large measure to the character of her captain, Kurt-Cesar Hoffmann, much admired by the naval high command, much loved by his officers and crew, a sailor of sunny temperament and ready wit. All the same I felt a twinge of unease as he came to greet me in the bar of the Atlantic Hotel in Hamburg, an admiral now and much older, hobbling a little and holding a stick. He put out a hand, and I took it. 'I know you must be thinking very much of your father at this moment,' he said. Then he smiled and said, 'And now I buy you a drink.' I said, 'No, the BBC will buy us both drinks,' and after that it was fine.

There was a curious sequel to the *Scharnhorst* film. Years later Moira and I were on board the *Queen Elizabeth II* as guest lecturers when she sailed from Hong Kong to Acapulco in Mexico as part of that year's world cruise. Among the films I brought was that of the *Scharnhorst* and when its showing time was listed in the ship's paper, I was informed that one of the passengers, a Captain Danckwerts, had been the *Scharnhorst*'s wartime assistant navigating officer. With an interpreter we met for a drink and he told me that because his home was in East Germany he had been forbidden to travel abroad until quite recently when he became an old-age pensioner; this voyage was his first taste of freedom. That afternoon in the big, empty cinema, I gave him a private showing of the film, and there were many pictures of Danckwerts's shipmates of thirty years earlier, including an interview I had had with his immediate superior, Captain Helmuth Giessler, the ship's navigating officer, who told me of the secret preparations he had made for the midnight departure from Brest in February 1942 of the *Scharnhorst, Gneisenau* and *Prinz Eugen* on the eve of their audacious dash through the English Channel to Germany. When the lights came up and I turned to ask his reactions, I found him sitting speechless, tears coursing down his cheeks. 'When I introduce the film this evening you must say a few words too,' I said, and he agreed. If only he had! Like Dönitz, he didn't know when to stop, and in the end I had to prod the interpreter to bring him to a close. But it was understandable, and I think the audience appreciated the gesture.

With so much archive material from the *Bismarck* and *Tirpitz* researches left over I was able to incorporate much of it in two successful books, *Pursuit* on the *Bismarck*, and *Menace* on the *Tirpitz*. In the course of researching extra material for *Pursuit* in the Public Records Office I made one lucky and quite unexpected find. In a memo (signature illegible) to the assistant chief of naval staff dated two months after the sinking of the *Bismarck*, the writer said that it had 'unofficially' come to his notice that an Ensign Smith of the US Navy was in the Catalina aircraft that had resighted the *Bismarck*, then *en route* to Brest, two days after British naval forces had lost contact with her; and that an Ensign Rinehart was in another searching Catalina. 'I am not quite sure,' the writer said, 'why these American officers were in the Catalinas', and he went on to say that if they did play a valuable part in the operation, the Admiralty might care to recognize their services. He added, in typically British fashion: 'Perhaps "silver salvers" suitably inscribed would be a good way of doing this.'

Intrigued, I wrote to the US Navy Department and received in reply a copy of Ensign Smith's report on the operation. This showed that he had not only been in the Catalina that had sighted the *Bismarck* but was actually piloting it and had taken avoiding action when the *Bismarck* opened fire. Further inquiries revealed that in 1941 President Roosevelt had authorized the secondment of a score of US Navy Catalina pilots to the RAF to gain wartime experience with the pilots of Coastal Command. But as America and Germany were still at peace, and the leasing of the pilots was a clear breach of the US Neutrality Act which Hitler, had he come to know of it, might have used as an excuse for sinking American ships, the news had to be kept strictly secret. And it was. When the British columnist Godfrey Winn travelled to Northern Ireland in June 1941 to interview the crew of Smith's Catalina and found that he had the scoop of a lifetime, he was not able to use it, and based his article instead on Smith's co-pilot, Flight-Lieutenant Briggs of the RAF.

In the summer of 1973 when *Pursuit* was on its way to the printers, the BBC sent me to Washington to cover the Senate Watergate hearings. This meant staying in my room in the Georgetown Inn to watch the proceedings on the three networks during the day, and presenting a programme with extracts and interviews at night. During a lull my thoughts turned to Ensign

Smith and the possibility that he might still be alive, and on an impulse I dialled the Navy Department.

'Navy Department.'

'You may think this an impossible request,' I said, 'but I'm trying to trace a man called Smith. All I can tell you about him is that he was an ensign flying a Catalina aircraft in England thirty-two years ago.'

'One moment, sir.'

Pause; sounds of an extension ringing.

'Officers' Locator.'

I repeated the story.

'Does this Ensign Smith have any initials?'

'L.B.'

'One moment, sir.'

Another pause; this time a little longer, but not much.

'Sir?'

'Yes.'

'Do you have a pen or pencil there?'

'Yes.'

'Take this down, please. Captain L. B. Smith, 1709 West 39th Street, Kearney, Nebraska.'

'Well, thank you very much.'

'You're welcome, sir. Have a nice day.'

In London, I thought, a request of that sort would not have produced an answer in under a week, if at all. I dialled long distance, and within five minutes of my original call to the Navy Department, heard a voice in Kearney saying, 'Smith speaking.'

So, with a day to spare after Watergate, I flew out to Kearney and over an eggs and hash brown breakfast at Captain Smith's, heard the story of his life and how he came to be piloting the Catalina that sighted the *Bismarck*. He gave me a photograph of himself and two other ensigns at their base at Lough Erne in Northern Ireland and other information which I was able to use in my book. Nothing seemed to have come of the silver salver idea, no doubt because of the continuing need for secrecy. As we drove back to the airport Smith said that at the end of the war he had been executive officer at a naval air base in California, and that one of the officers there had been a certain Lieutenant Richard Milhous Nixon. He remembered him as 'a brown bagger', that is a man who to save money brought a sandwich lunch in a brown bag rather than waste time and money eating in the mess. Smith called him 'one of the most conscientious and hard-working officers I've ever met'.

Published in 1974, *Pursuit* was an instant success and was subsequently translated into thirteen foreign languages.[1] The *Tirpitz* book, *Menace*, also did well, and was illustrated with more than a hundred photographs and copies of relevant Ultra signals decrypted from the Enigma machines and now in the Public Records Office at Kew: to my surprise it has brought in more royalties from the Public Lending Right scheme than any other book I have written, including *10 Rillington Place*.

Yet the most welcome consequence of the making of those documentaries and books was quite unexpected. One who had given me invaluable help in tracking down German sources and participants was a sixty-year-old cultural attaché at the German Embassy by the name of Herbert Sulzbach. He was a member of a well-known Jewish banking family in Frankfurt, and had the unique distinction of having served in the trenches in the Kaiser's uniform in the First World War and then, having sought shelter here from the Nazi persecutions of the 1930s, having served as a British officer in King George's uniform in the Second. Posted to a large prisoner-of-war camp in Northumberland, his job was to de-Nazify the most fanatical of Hitler's supporters. He was a dear, lively little man with the bluest of blue eyes who had himself become a fanatical Anglophile, devoting his life until well into his eighties to the furtherance of Anglo-German relations; and I was proud to be asked to give one of the brief tributes to him at his memorial service at the German Embassy.

Herbert told me that his government, saddened by so many post-war feature films in which heroic Allies and horrid Nazis went on refighting old battles (to me no more than the modern equivalent of cowboys and Indians) was much impressed by the non-partisan nature of my films and books, and intended to give public expression of their approval. Some time later I was informed that I had been awarded the *Verdienstkreuz* or West German Order of Merit, First Class, which their ambassador pinned on me in a charming family ceremony at the Embassy in Grosvenor Square. The cross itself, red in colour, is similar in shape to the Iron Cross given to U-boat commanders and is worn, as they wore it, on the left breast. Most people who notice it at parties are too polite to ask what it is and why I am wearing

[1] *Pursuit* is to be reissued as a Fontana paperback in 1989.

it, but to the few who do I say (because I find it embarrassing to explain) that it is concerned with the story of the sinking of the *Bismarck*; and then relish the look of puzzlement on their faces.

I have mentioned Captain Stephen Roskill, the official naval historian and the most charming of scholars, who was of great assistance to me in researches for my naval documentaries and books. A Sephardic Jew, he was a tall, spare man of high moral principles and the most courteous manners and an odd habit when listening of purring like a cat. I valued his judgement highly, and look back with pleasure to the several visits I made to him and his equally delightful wife Elizabeth at their cottage in Cambridge where he was a fellow of Churchill College.

When engaged in writing the naval history of the war, he had of course accumulated more material, both British and German, than he was ever able to use; and one day over coffee at Cambridge I asked if he knew of any naval occasion of the Second World War which had not yet been told and which, in his view, ought to be.

He thought for a moment. 'There's one.'

'What is it about?'

'A submarine atrocity.'

I knew that on the whole the U-boat commanders had fought the submarine war cleanly, the only major exception being the murders committed by the *U.852* and her captain, Lieutenant-Commander Eck. In March 1944 the *U.852* was on patrol off the west coast of Africa: she was the fifth U-boat to have been given this area of patrol, the previous four, commanded by aces such as Wuppisch and Schultz, having all been sunk by aircraft. On the night of 13 March the *U.852* sank a steamer called the *Peleus* and then cruised round the area shining a searchlight on wreckage and survivors while the ship's first lieutenant, doctor and engineer officer with two ratings picked up guns and grenades and by indiscriminate firing endeavoured to destroy all traces of the sinking before the patrolling aircraft arrived in the morning. They were not entirely successful. Twenty-five days later three survivors, all wounded, were picked up from a raft and taken to Capetown. The U-boat, having itself rounded the Cape, ran aground on the coast of Kenya and the crew were taken prisoner. They did not have time to destroy the ship's logbook and this, combined with the testimony of the survivors, was evidence enough for Eck and those of the crew who had carried out the shooting to be arrested and tried by court-martial. This took place in Hamburg in October 1945. Eck's defence was that of 'operational necessity', i.e. that if he did not destroy all traces of the sinking, his boat would be in grave danger of itself being sunk by Allied aircraft in the morning, as had happened to his four predecessors. But this was nonsense. The *Peleus* had been sunk at 7.30 p.m.; Eck therefore had a whole night's steaming to put himself a hundred miles from the sinking before submerging at dawn. And one of the most experienced U-boat commanders, Adalbert Schnee, who had been on sixteen patrols and later became a member of Dönitz's staff, gave evidence that it was contrary to orders to kill survivors and that there could be no excuse for what Eck had done. As a result Eck, the doctor and the engineer were found guilty, sentenced to death and executed by firing squad on Luneberg Heath.

Intrigued by the story, I had approached the late Mr Justice Melford Stevenson who, as Deputy Judge Advocate, had conducted Eck's trial. Over some excellent claret at the judge's lodgings in St Albans, he said, 'What I remember most about the trial – and I hadn't expected it – was the character of Eck. He impressed all of us. He had courage, dignity and class, which was more than could be said of some of his judges. The trouble was, he'd lost his head.'

'Was yours another Eck?' I asked Stephen Roskill.

'It wasn't one of theirs. It was one of ours. And it was disgraceful.'

He told me the story. A British submarine on patrol off Crete had come across several Greek *caiques* or schooners of around 100 tons and known to be carrying German troops, petrol and ammunition. The captain of the submarine surfaced and took his craft alongside one of the schooners. There was a brief battle in which two German soldiers were shot and the remainder, seven men from an Alpine regiment, were forced to get into a rubber dinghy while demolition charges were laid and lit. As the submarine pulled away, the captain ordered one of two soldiers he was carrying on board to open fire with his Lewis gun on the survivors in the dinghy. The soldier refused and went below. The first lieutenant also refused and also went below. The order was then carried out by a seaman, and all seven survivors were killed. It was, said Stephen, as appalling an atrocity as you could find.

When Stephen told me the name of the submarine captain, I recognized it. He was a much-decorated officer who had risen to high rank before an honourable retirement. His courage and

exploits were legendary, and his crews were said to have un-
bounded faith in him. 'Whatever scrapes he'd get you into,' one
of them had once said, 'you always knew he'd get you out.'

I made a few inquiries. First, at the Public Records Office, I
inspected the submarine captain's report of proceedings of the
patrol in question. It seemed that there were two incidents, and
he had made no attempt to gloss over either. The first, which
Stephen had not mentioned, concerned a small ship flying the
Nazi flag. 'Surfaced and sank the enemy with gunfire, *using both
Lewis guns to destroy the boats and personnel.*' The second,
concerning the Alpine soldiers, took place five days later: 'Submarine cast off and *with the Lewis gun accounted for the soldiers
in the rubber raft*' [my italics]. I also tracked down the first
lieutenant of the submarine and one of the two soldiers carried
on board and they confirmed the killings. Other papers in the
Public Records Office showed the misgivings of the naval staff
about the two incidents, for by now the Germans had found the
dead soldiers, and there were fears of reprisals against any British
submarine crews subsequently captured – indeed it may be that
these events had some bearing on the subsequent shootings of
British commandos captured in that area.

Then I wrote to the captain himself. Would he care to have lunch
with me to discuss certain aspects of the naval war? He replied
guardedly, what aspects? I came clean: the incidents of the survivors of two schooners sunk by his submarine near Crete in 1941.
'Is your view about them today the same as it was then or do
you now feel you might have acted differently?' I received a dusty
answer. His work for various public bodies left him little spare
time. 'I would really not find research into events that took place
some thirty-five years ago any relaxation whatever.' I replied that
I was sorry to hear it but that I might return to him later, and
enclosed a copy of *Pursuit*. This time a secretary answered, saying
that as her employer 'has a large backlog of books to read, he found
the addition of another one rather an embarrassment . . . he has
passed it to a friend in a London hospital.'

For a long time I had it in mind to write a story contrasting
the fates of Eck and his British counterpart. There had been little
enough to choose between the two killings, yet all the difference
in the world between the fates of those responsible: the one
retired with honours, the other shot by firing squad at the age of
twenty-eight. In the end I decided against it. The courage the

British captain had shown on numerous dangerous patrols into enemy waters and the havoc he had wrought against shipping there was something I could never match in a hundred years. What right had I to tarnish the reputation of an acknowledged war hero and needlessly distress his family? Time enough to think about resuscitating the idea after he was dead.

Today he has been dead for several years, and still I haven't told the story. And I don't know which has nagged at me most, the lack of courage shown by this brave man in fending me off and declining to discuss what he had done, or my lack of courage in declining to write about it. Maybe I will write about it one day. Maybe not.[1]

20

Cardinal Hume, Albert Speer and the Queen Mother

For most of the 1970s while living in the Borders I was commuting to London by air for three nights a week to present late-night current affairs programmes – 24 *Hours*, *Midweek*, *Tonight*, *Newsday*. Of the thousand-plus programmes I must have taken part in during those years I remember very little, and those mostly trivial things: Thor Heyerdahl the Norwegian explorer arriving half an hour late from Broadcasting House because the taxi driver sent to fetch him understood he had been told to pick up *four airedales* (a reasonable enough request, he reckoned, from the BBC); the maverick film director Ken Russell whacking Alexander Walker, the *Evening Standard* film critic, over the head with a copy of his own paper; Norman St John Stevas, MP (now Lord St John of Fawsley) winking at a cameraman who had had the stars and stripes sewn on to the bottom of his jeans; Enoch Powell's eyes filling with tears when I asked if he was an emotional man; A. J. P. Taylor on his seventy-fifth birthday admitting he had never been offered an honour and when I asked him which he would like if given the choice, his replying, 'A baronetcy,

---

[1] Since this book was first published, the *Daily Telegraph*, after making its own investigations, revealed that the officer in question was Commander, later Rear-Admiral, Sir Anthony Miers, VC, DSO.

because it would make my elder son so dreadfully annoyed.'

But there were some characters who, for one reason or another, I have cause to remember. The novelist Rebecca West, for instance. We were due to record a longish interview with her one afternoon, and over lunch at her favourite restaurant in Basil Street my producer Anthony Rouse and I both asked if there was any subject in her long life that she did not want touched upon. She said none: 'Ask what you like.' This clearance was important because I did intend to ask one or two questions about a matter which had already been aired in several books and articles, her love affair with H. G. Wells and the child of that union, the writer Anthony West. There had been conflicting stories as to whether Anthony had been intended, Wells having gone on record as saying he had been conceived in a moment of carelessness, Professor Gordon Ray, who edited the West-Wells correspondence, as saying it was a deliberate attempt by Wells to keep Rebecca with him, and Rebecca herself as saying, 'Wells cheated me of all but one child.' Was the child intended? I asked, and she answered firmly, 'The child was not intended.'

A day or two later Anthony Rouse and I were astonished to hear that her agents were demanding the interview be withdrawn because, as she complained in a letter to the BBC's Director General, Hugh Carleton-Greene, *we had given her a solemn undertaking over lunch not to mention the matter of Wells and their son at all*. I suppose she thought that Greene would not ask us to confirm what she had said, but chide us for impropriety on the strength of her word alone. Whatever her reasoning, I was greatly shocked that a woman of her achievements and reputation should stoop to such shabby fibbing.

A good example of how upset people could be in those days by the questioning of their religious beliefs occurred in my interview with Basil Hume soon after he had received his cardinal's hat. Before the interview we talked over coffee in his study next door to Westminster Cathedral. A long, lean man with an ascetic face, he looked the celibate monk he had always been, but in private conversation he was unpompous, outgoing, witty. When he told me that he had inherited the cardinal's robes of his predecessor, Cardinal Heenan, and I asked if they fitted, he said, 'No. But I have a gem of a nun who's a wizard with a needle, and after she'd taken a tuck in the waist and put two inches on the hem, they looked almost tailor-made.' He also spoke of an occasion when, dressed in his archbishop's robes after some function, he had hailed a taxi to go home and realized he had no money. 'I thought, if I tell the driver I'm a real archbishop and I'll pay him the other end he'll just say, "Oh, stuff it, mate!" Luckily Reggie Bosanquet was standing nearby, so I borrowed a quid off him.'

When it came to the interview he was somewhat nervous and on the defensive (not being an old hand at it), and while I did my best to make him feel at ease, I felt it incumbent to put questions about the Roman Catholic Church's teachings on divorce, homosexuality, abortion, celibacy, etc., the answers to which I believed would be of interest to Catholics and non-Catholics alike. Being an honest man, he tried to answer honestly; and there were times when he clearly found it difficult to reconcile the absolutism of his Church's dogma with the dictate of his own conscience. Noting and regretting his discomfiture, the public subsequently turned on the questioner. 'By his assurance, condescension, ease of posture and conversational initiative,' said a *Times* editorial, 'Mr Kennedy might just as well have been a bishop testing a candidate for ordination.' Those looking for a sign of grace or spiritual solace from the Cardinal had to make do with what *The Times* called 'exemplary patience and meekness' and writers to the letters column taxed me with shallowness and poor taste. But I had my supporters. Claiming that millions of people had had their lives damaged by the teachings of Roman Catholicism, one correspondent wrote, 'There should be no restraint in asking the most searching questions of a man . . . who aspires to bring people and their children into the Catholic fold.' As with the comments of Heald, Shawcross and others after my documentary on the police, I do not believe that such an interview would attract that sort of attention today. But then today that kind of interview rarely happens.

I also interviewed two healers. One was the famous Harry Edwards whom I visited with Anthony Rouse at his home and healing centre in Surrey. After the interview I mentioned as casually as I could that as a result of blocked sinuses I had lost my sense of smell (with the exceptions of petrol, laundry and excrement) for years, and could he think of any way of restoring it? He leaned towards me, put the middle finger of each hand on either side of my nose and with a look of intense concentration rubbed each one gently up and down. Within a few minutes I not only felt *but heard* the tissue in the sinuses beginning to break up, and by the time he had finished both were completely clear. They remained clear, and my sense of smell returned, for two years.

Bruce Macmanaway's achievements were even more remarkable. I had known Bruce for some years as he often ministered to friends, and on two or three occasions when he had laid his hands on my back, the heat emanating from them was like a blowtorch. He had discovered his gift for healing quite by chance. Attending on the battlefield to a wounded soldier who was crying out with pain, he took the soldier's hand in his. At once the soldier stopped crying, the pain having disappeared; but as soon as Bruce removed his hand, it returned.

Bruce had a simple pendulum of the kind people employ to locate water, and which he used for diagnosis. To show how it worked, he ran it lightly around my producer while we were discussing the shape of the interview. When he reached his right thigh, the pendulum became quite agitated. 'Something not quite right there,' said Bruce. The producer looked stunned. 'I had an operation there last month,' he said. Bruce said, 'I can use the pendulum to do more than that. If you were to write down on a sheet of paper half a dozen simple statements of fact which were either true or false and then turn the questions face down, the pendulum will come up with which are which.'

I made no comment on this at the time (though privately I thought it a brash boast) but when we met for the interview I asked if he had brought the pendulum with him. He said he had. Half-way through the interview I reminded him of his claim, pulled out a sheet of paper on which I had written three true statements and three false ones, and putting it face down on the table, invited him to use the pendulum to indicate the correct answers. He got the first one right, the second one right, the third one right, the fourth one right, the fifth one wrong, the sixth one right. I thought it was a *tour de force*, but he seemed far more concerned about getting one wrong ('It could have been the studio lights') than pleased at getting five right.

At this time still a regular smoker, I made one film which made me drastically change my views about it. This was a documentary on cancer research. One distressing sequence we filmed in the laboratories portrayed mice with their little noses pushed into holes in a plastic tube along which was passed tobacco smoke equivalent to that inhaled by a human on twenty cigarettes a day. I forget now what the simulated time factor was – I think twenty years – but the upshot was that three-quarters of the mice developed lung cancer and died. More disturbing was this statistic: that while seven out of eight of those who died of lung cancer were heavy smokers, only one heavy smoker in eight died of lung cancer. This may have brought comfort to some but statistically it was as risky as playing Russian roulette, and I laid off smoking for the next seven years.

One film which, sadly, was never made was a documentary proposed by Alasdair Milne, then Controller of BBC Scotland, to celebrate the seventy-fifth birthday of the Queen Mother. She had not yet been interviewed on television or radio, but we thought it worthwhile approaching her private secretary to see if she might consider it. As a result I was bidden to Clarence House for a pre-lunch gin and tonic with her and Princess Margaret. She asked what I had in mind, and I said an informal conversation about the principal events of her life from her girlhood at Glamis Castle to the present day. She seemed to consider the proposal favourably and Princess Margaret, who I knew was keen on the idea, was supportive. Then the Queen Mother said, 'I'm sure you'll understand there is one subject I couldn't possibly talk about.' I was pretty certain what it was, but I wanted to hear her say it. 'The abdication.' 'Not at all, not even briefly?' I said. She was adamant. 'I'm afraid not.' She gave me a winning smile. 'I'm so sorry.'

For the next week I thought long and hard about undertaking an interview with the Queen Mother which would cover every aspect of her life but the great historical event which had changed it for ever; which had propelled her and her husband to the throne, had made happy and glorious a reign which might otherwise have been disastrous, yet which was tragically cut short by illness and death, and which in the long run had made her far and away the most loved of all the members of the Royal Family. I was not proposing to ask her about her relationship, or lack of it, with Edward VIII and Mrs Simpson, or to what degree she blamed them for the unexpected and, at the time, unwelcome change in her life. But not to have mentioned the subject at all, to leave a void which demanded to be filled – that, it seemed to me, would have been Hamlet without the Prince (or, more accurately, Queen Mother). And so, with regrets, the project lapsed.

Ten years later however the BBC asked me at very short

notice to compile a programme to celebrate the Queen Mother's eighty-fifth birthday. This was really no more than a collage of bits and pieces of archive film, intercut with brief interviews, for which I wrote and narrated a restrained but admiring commentary. I had no idea of course how she had received it, and was therefore pleased to receive a letter a week later from her private secretary, Sir Martin Gilliat. 'Queen Elizabeth the Queen Mother has asked me to tell you how appreciative she is of your splendid BBC TV programme last Friday evening . . . knows what trouble you went to in the very limited time at your disposal . . . your wonderfully successful endeavour clear for all to see', etc., etc. Reading this, I could have been forgiven for conjuring up a picture of the Queen Mother settling down comfortably by a television set at Sandringham, perhaps a daughter at her side, a corgi at feet and refreshment to hand, basking in the glow of my birthday tribute to her, and making a mental note to instruct the private secretary in the morning to send a line of thanks to those concerned. But later, finding myself sharing a sofa with her at a friend's dinner-party, I mentioned the film and that I understood she had approved of it. 'I'm afraid,' she said with admirable honesty, 'I missed it. It was *so* disappointing, but we had to go to something in King's Lynn.' Walking back to the club that night and recalling old Martin's letter, I began to understand some of the qualities that make a successful courtier.

I also made a number of foreign trips. One was to Germany to film a documentary on the wretched William Joyce, nicknamed Lord Haw-Haw, whose wartime broadcasts from Berlin had led to his trial and execution for treason after the war. En route to the exquisite *fin de siècle* Baden-Baden, my producer Chris Olgiati and I stopped our car on a main road short of a T-junction to read the signposts and study the map. Sitting in the car we heard a distant rumbling sound which slowly grew louder. We took our eyes off the map to look at each other, at first in surprise and then, as the rumbling grew to a roar, in terror. When it seemed that the sound and whatever it emanated from was about to overwhelm us, the engine and coaches of an express train appeared in the left-hand window and whizzed past a few feet from the front bumper. There was no level-crossing gate and we had not seen the rails, which were sunk deep into the tarmac, nor a red light winking on top of a very high pole. We sat shaking for some minutes before regaining sufficient composure to drive on.

In Tel Aviv I interviewed the Israeli Prime Minister, Golda Meir, and in Amman King Hussein of Jordan, one of Harrow's most distinguished sons. The interview took place on a Friday afternoon in the Royal Palace and was as bad as any I can remember: the king was bad, I was bad, the room was gloomy, nothing went right. That night over a pretentious dinner ('delicate strips of milk-fed veal on a bed of herbs and accompanied by a tangy aromatic sauce specially prepared by our chefs') in a pretentious modern hotel and fortified by a bottle of local plonk, my producer John Reynolds and I resolved to telephone the Palace Chamberlain in the morning, say that owing to a technical fault the film was not usable, and did the king have a spare hour in which we might shoot the interview again? Not only did the king have a spare hour for what turned out to be an excellent interview in the palace gardens, but on learning that there was now no plane to take us home until Monday, laid on two helicopters to take us all on a Sunday outing to Petra (the 'rose red city half as old as time'), then on to Aqaba on the Red Sea for lunch and a swim, and home across the desert and the black tents of the Bedouins in the evening. It was an extraordinarily considerate gesture.

I returned to Germany, to Heidelberg, to interview Albert Speer, Hitler's architect and later brilliant organizer of the German wartime industrial economy, on the occasion of the publication of his book *Spandau: The Secret Diaries*. Written on pieces of lavatory paper and smuggled out weekly by one of the guards, this was a fascinating account of the prison lives and conversations of those Nazi leaders – Hess, von Schirach, Funk, von Neurath, Raeder, Dönitz – who, like Speer, had escaped the war crimes gallows. How greatly had the mighty fallen: 'Monday is washday. Dönitz and Schirach wash our socks, Hess and I do underclothes and bedding.' Speer had served every day of his twenty-year sentence – from the age of forty to sixty – and seemed to have emerged unscathed. Unlike Dönitz, he was a highly cultivated man who had much charm, spoke fluent, conversational English and was quite at home with the microphone. One of the difficulties in taxing Speer about his Nazi past was that he, alone among his colleagues, freely admitted and was repentant for his share of guilt – though how much this was assumed and how much genuine it was hard to tell. His wife lunched with us, and I was much struck by her character.

Although allowed to visit her husband only rarely during his twenty years in Spandau, she and her six children had never ceased to support him, and I was not surprised to hear that during their father's absence all six had obtained university degrees.

At Frankfurt Airport I found I had just missed one plane to London and there was not another for three hours. Wandering round this huge complex, I came to a kind of crossroads where signs pointing in four directions said things like 'Chaplain's Office', 'VIP Lounge', 'Flight Information'. One also said, to my amazement, 'Porno Film', and having time to kill I made my way there. There was a bar at the entrance where one paid a few marks for a drink, and behind a curtain an auditorium of perhaps twenty or thirty comfortable seats. The film in progress when I arrived showed a football match between a team of nuns and a team of soldiers, and every time the referee blew his whistle for a penalty (which was every few seconds) the player concerned had to lose a garment. Before long football had given way to a different sport, and a surreal Bosch-like survey of the entire field showed all kinds of what my mother called hanky-panky in full swing. Later, both teams adjourned to the changing rooms to continue their frolics, and there were close-ups in technicolour of all sorts of couplings and triplings. This was followed by a film of a mediaeval banquet at which the guests, after much lusty eating and drinking, undressed one another at a leisurely pace, then climbed on to the refectory table for a general post, to the accompaniment on the sound track of much wheezing and grunting. A third film, embellished with live dialogue, showed one couple making friends with another at a restaurant, returning to an apartment and there engaging in a quartet.

I had seen only one other porno film before, a miserable five-minute affair in grainy black and white in Tangiers, and what surprised me about two of the three films was the quality of the finished product. The women were young and not unattractive, the sets handsome, the costumes (what little we saw of them) pleasing, the camerawork professional and the dialogue or sub-titles not without humour. All this made me wonder what class of people were involved in the production. Did the camera and sound and lighting technicians peck their wives on the cheek each morning before dropping the children at school, spend the day recording erections and ejaculations, then return to family supper and games with the children? Did the wives say, 'Had a good day, dear?' and did the husbands reply, 'Not bad except that poor Fred couldn't get it up at all. Said he thought it was something he ate. And Daphne had to lay off because of her period. Better luck tomorrow.' Were the technicians indifferent to what they were recording or did they sometimes become aroused too, and if so, were there rules against them joining in? And how did the performers feel about performing in semi-public and for posterity? What sort of relationships did they all have outside performing hours? What did they talk about at lunch? When dressed, did they observe the normal courtesies? Was anybody ever inhibited? *Was no one ever embarrassed*?

Another thing that struck me was the difference in sexual attitudes between Germany and Britain. I had already observed it in hotel saunas and swimming-pools in Germany, where men and women sat and swam together in the nude and thought nothing of it. If that was unacceptable in Britain, how much more so would be a proposal to set up a porno cinema at Heathrow or Gatwick? One could hear the cries of outrage from the likes of Mrs Whitehouse and Mrs Thatcher. And yet had it ever been suggested that Germany (or France, or any other country which had a more open public attitude to sex) was somehow less moral than us? Was not the German or French family unit as strong as that of the British?

It was the same with brothels. In some countries they consider the regulation of prostitution to be pleasanter for the girls, more agreeable for their customers and, with medical checks, safer for public health. But in Britain we equate *acknowledging* man's need for instant sex with *approving* of it, and rather than have that levelled at us, we reject the idea of licensed brothels. We prefer that prostitutes should stand in the streets to be picked up by passing cars (not the roomiest place for sex), in constant danger of being beaten up and even murdered, and that valuable police and court time be wasted in arresting, convicting and imposing heavy fines on girls who, unable to pay, return to soliciting even harder, that pimps should come into being to batten off the girls, and that women who are not prostitutes should be harassed by cruising motorists who will not take no for an answer. It is British hypocrisy at its very worst.

At this time, and like most public or semi-public figures, I was receiving a fair amount of mail from strangers. Most letters asked for autographs or photographs, some complained of or praised a person interviewed or view expressed, and there was always a sprinkling of old dears short of correspondents who rambled on about the old days. I destroyed most after answering them, but three I do remember. One began, chillingly, 'Did I ever tell you about the day we found the nurse's body in the cellar?' What a multitude of questions that begged. What nurse? How had she got there? Were the police informed? And why *Did I ever tell you*, as though I were an old friend? The second was a gem:

> Dear Mr Kennedy,
> Please could you give me some information on being an INTERLECTUAL. I'm nearly twelve and my mind is messy with O level results and general problems.
> I think I'm an unknown interlectual ... Please, please, send me some information.

The third, from a young man in Birmingham, was altogether more disturbing. I seem to have lost it now, but it ran something like this:

> Dear Father,
> It is a great pleasure to write to my father as my mother has often told me about him, and I hope to be allowed to get to know him better ...

At first I thought this must have been intended for someone else and began grubbing about in the wastepaper basket to find the envelope. No, there it was, as large as life in capital letters: TO MR LUDOVIC KENNEDY, BBC TELEVISION STUDIOS. Cripes, I thought, and although as certain as I could be that the lad was not mine, who can be totally positive about any putative event of twenty years earlier? The first thing to discover was the date of his birth. This took a little time during which I pondered uneasily on the possibility, however remote, of having to recognize the existence of additional progeny, and all that it would entail. Given the date, it was then a question of working backwards and consulting an old diary; and I found that during the period in question I was in India for *Panorama*.

But if I was going to have to disillusion the boy, I thought it kinder to do it personally than by letter, and I invited him to come to the studios to see the programme and have a drink. He was a very nice young man and did bear some small resemblance to me which I supposed was why his mother, perhaps not knowing who his father was, or knowing but having been abandoned by him, had woven this fantasy about a familiar figure from the television screen. I hoped, as we said goodbye, that he would suffer no psychological ill-effects from the deception, and that my exposure of it would not impair his relationship with his mother.

Another unexpected and disturbing event, though of quite a different order, occurred one evening in 1973 when I was preparing the late night showing of 24 *Hours*. Peter Pagnamenta, the editor, came into my room to say there was a message for me to ring the Hawick police: there had been an accident involving my family but he did not know the details. The Hawick policeman told me it was a very serious accident in which Moira, Rachel, Fiona and Alastair had all been involved: they had been taken to different hospitals but he did not know the extent of their injuries or any other details.

Peter arranged a taxi to Victoria for me to catch a train to Gatwick and the last flight to Edinburgh. Halfway between Victoria and Gatwick there was a power failure, the lights went out and the train ground to a halt. I was alone in the darkness in one of those old-fashioned six seater compartments, and I neither knew nor had any means of knowing whether my family was alive or dead. I felt as if I was in limbo. After a few minutes I unexpectedly found myself singing a song which I was sure I had not sung since Eton days forty years before. I sang it very loudly and (as always) very out of tune.

> Abide with me, fast falls the eventide,
> The darkness deepens, Lord with me abide.
> When other helpers fail and comforts flee,
> Help of the helpless, O, abide with me.
>
> Hold thou thy Cross before my closing eyes.
> Shine through the storm and point me to the skies.
> Heaven's morning breaks and earth's vain shadows flee,
> In life, in death, O Lord, abide with me.

To my astonishment the words came flooding back, and for some ten minutes, while the train lay cocooned in a web of silence and darkness, I continued my singing, grateful that I had the compartment to myself. I cannot describe the solace it gave me.

Later, I asked myself whether in my extremity I, the helpless, had been seeking, as the hymn said, the help of God, and that in the act of seeking it, I had been granted it (he who seeks God, said Pascal, has already found him); or whether this spontaneous welling-up of emotion from the depths of my being was no more than the expression of a statement to myself. Was I, and am I, just juggling with words? I did not know the answer then, and I do not know it now.

At the barrier at Gatwick, I was met by a friendly policeman who told me that the injuries were not as bad as had at first been thought, and that none of my family was in danger – news which immediately reduced me to tears. That night in the Edinburgh Royal Infirmary I saw Moira, with five cracked ribs and cuts over her eye and on her leg, and she told me what had happened. A driver going north along the A68 through the village of Earlston had mistaken an access road to his right for the southward lane of a dual carriageway. Thinking it safe to pull out to pass a lorry he ran head-on into Moira and the children coming south. Of the children Rachel was the worst injured, with tiny pieces of glass from the windscreen in her eyes, but in time she recovered. Fiona had a cut and Alastair and the labrador, Glyn, were unharmed; so was the driver of the other car. My car was a total write-off.

In 1979 I interviewed for the first (and last) time the newly elected Prime Minister, Margaret Thatcher. The occasion was a documentary film I was making on the life of Airey Neave, the MP who had masterminded her election to the Tory leadership and, as Shadow Secretary of State for Northern Ireland, been killed by an IRA car bomb when leaving the Palace of Westminster.

We were informed that the Prime Minister had set aside an hour for us, and she arrived on the dot, nicely accoutred and coiffeured and saying she was ready to go when we were. It was as satisfactory an interview as I have conducted in that, it being entirely non-controversial, question and answer flowed without interruption or the need for retakes; and in her assessment of Airey Neave both as friend and politician she seemed entirely relaxed. Indeed so professional was her performance that halfway through the time allotted to us, we found we had finished. We expected handshakes all round, the departure of the PM to affairs of state, and an aide leading us to an ante-room for ginger snaps and coffee. We had not expected the Prime Minister to look at her watch and say, 'I see it's only eleven, so we have half an hour in hand. Would you like me to show you round the house?'

It was as thoughtful and generous an invitation as King Hussein sending us down to Petra and Aqaba. Although the PM had only recently arrived in Downing Street, she had already boned up on its history and as she led us round she spoke of Pitt and Walpole, Disraeli and Gladstone, and of their connection with this tapestry or picture or that room. Then we came to the state dining-room with its long mahogany table and rows of high-backed chairs. 'You know I had Giscard d'Estaing here the other day,' she said. 'Where do you think I placed him?' We said we had no idea. 'Here,' she said, smacking a chair. 'And why here?' We looked puzzled. 'Look up,' she said, and we did, to see on the opposite wall full-length portraits of Nelson and the Duke of Wellington. When we spilled out into the street a few minutes later, it was in a kind of glow.

Looking back on that visit, as I sometimes do, I find it difficult to reconcile the warm, charming and amusing hostess who spared the time to entertain us that day with the latter-day basso profundo screecher of the House of Commons and the earnest, ingratiating gusher of numerous television interviews (performances which make me dream wistfully of the old saw, 'In the ideal society politics should be as unobtrusive as drains'). Nor can I forgive her for having blocked Moira's appointment as BBC Governor for the Arts after it had been cleared by the Home Office. It could not have been for lack of qualifications, for Moira had served seven years on the BBC's General Advisory Council and four years as a director of Border Television; so one can only assume it was because of my Liberal Party connections. I have heard of other appointments which she has blocked for similar reasons, and in my lifetime can recall no other Prime Minister, Labour or Conservative, who felt the need to exercise such petty partisanship.

When I was in London during the early years of this period I often stayed with my mother in Hampton Court. The dog Ben and the cat Wolsey had died, but another cat called Mingo had taken his place. My eldest daughter Ailsa was staying there part of the time, studying art at the Byam Shaw College of Art, and falling in love with her tutor, whom she later married. One vacation she was given a holiday job in the palace gardens, pricking out marigolds. For this task she was required to sign the Official Secrets Act – in case, I was told, confidential papers from the National Physical Laboratory in Bushey Park were borne by the wind on to her marigold patch. I wrote a letter to *The Times* about this lunacy, and it was picked up and ridiculed by all the national papers.

Advanced age had by now somewhat mellowed my mother, with the result that I enjoyed my visits to the palace, for when the subject was other than myself she could be stimulating and amusing company. But she never abandoned her attempts to plumb my innermost emotions, always asking, 'What do you *feel* about X, Y, or Z?', never 'What do you *think*?' Fending off these assaults was always taxing. When she was eighty and no longer able to cope with running her apartment (it was in fact a house of four storeys) she moved into a nursing home at Sunbury-on-Thames. I and my sisters visited her there when we could, she was always ready to join one in what she called 'a dry mart' before lunch or in the evening, and for a time seemed content enough. But as time went on, the quality of her life deteriorated. She suffered severely from arthritis, was unable to read for more than short periods of time, was bored and confused by television, and for long periods lay inert, half dozing, half listening to the radio.

When she had been there a couple of years and I asked her how she was, she said, 'Pretty mouldy.' While I was thinking how to respond, she said, 'Oh, how I long to be gathered' (a Scottish euphemism for death). During the course of the next year, she expressed the same view each time I saw her. 'I've had a marvellous life and enjoyed every minute of it, but it's over and now I want to move on.' She was, I am sure, less motivated by dreams of Elysian fields than a longing to shuffle off her mortal coil and be freed both from the arthritis and the meaninglessness of what her life had become. She was expressing much the same sentiments as Bob Boothby had expressed in his last letter to me, and which I have heard other old people express too. But there was nothing that I or anyone else could do about it; she, and we, had to wait another six months before she was finally gathered.

I had long been a believer in voluntary euthanasia, and my mother's experience strengthened it; for to me what matters most is not the length of a person's life but its quality, and that death, when it comes, should have dignity. I have always been nervous of dying, but not of death. The poets, mankind's unacknowledged legislators, have shown death to be what Anne Lindbergh, after the murder of her kidnapped child, saw as a *little* door. 'O, Death, where is thy sting?' (Corinthians). 'Death in itself is nothing' (Dryden). 'Half in love with easeful death' (Keats). 'After the first death, there is no other' (Dylan Thomas). But dying is something else. I have a dread of reaching a state when I lie inert and incontinent in bed, tubes in the nose and a drip-feed in the vein, all love of living gone and yet still forbidden final release.

It is true that my mother was not in that state, but she too had lost the will to live; and she too was denied the balm of curtailment. It is ironic, I think, that the release which out of the compassion of our hearts we give to old, sick animals, we deny to old, sick human beings. It is the life force within us that is the cause of that denial, which makes it impossible for the healthy to imagine a time when it will have faded, which makes them tremble at the thought that, were voluntary euthanasia ever legalized, abuse would inevitably follow, and when *they* became old and ill, they would be at risk of being put away. This is an understandable fear and must be met by the provision of cast-iron safeguards, such as they have in Holland where, under the beneficent tutelage of Dr Admiraal, voluntary euthanasia has been legalized and practised with considerable success for several years. In time and with an increasingly ageing population, I foresee the same thing happening here; that when people feel the time has come for release, they will gather the family round them to say farewell and then with those they love most beside them, they will ask for and be handed, as their right, the means of self-deliverance. If we are not yet ready for such a grave ceremony, sooner or later we will be; and if anyone thinks it macabre or mawkish, let them first read Derek Humphry's moving account in his book *Jean's Way* of how, when his wife had entered the terminal stage of bone cancer, he and she sat together over coffee and she took the pill which, with her full approval, he had obtained and kept safe for the occasion, and how she died peacefully in his arms. Such occasions will inevitably involve grief and the shedding of tears, but there is much to be said for that. Too often now death comes to one alone and unprepared and the news of it is broken to others, perhaps at night, by an impersonal voice on the telephone. Better surely to embrace it in the company of those one has loved, and as one slips away, to know from their tears how much they have loved one too.

21

The Luton Post Office Murder

We stayed at Makerstoun from 1966 to 1978 and then, while keeping Makerstoun for weekends, bought a property in Edinburgh; a neat terraced Regency house in Upper Dean Terrace on the Water of Leith, just around the corner from Raeburn's lovely Ann Street and a few hundred yards downstream from the house in Belgrave Crescent where I was born. This move had three objects: to complete the education of our two younger children, Fiona at Fettes (where my old Highfield playmate Inky Chenevix-Trench was now headmaster) and Alastair at the Edinburgh Academy; to have Moira's mother who was living alone in an Edinburgh flat and becoming increasingly tottery to live with us; and to own property once again and so benefit from its ever-increasing rise in value. Our second daughter Rachel had gone off to a finishing school near Florence, while Ailsa and her painter husband had bought a house in the country near Bury St Edmunds in Suffolk. A regular visitor to Upper Dean Terrace was my grandmother's old cook, Bessie, whose chicken cream and queen of puddings had been such a highlight of Nairn holidays, and who was now living in retirement in nearby Learmonth Terrace. In 1934 when my grandfather died, my grandmother had given her his silver-handled walking stick, and just fifty years later, in 1984, she gave it to me. It has been my constant companion ever since.

Looking back to the latter half of our time in Scotland, I seem to have been engaged in a variety of activities: was twice part of a consortium to bid (unsuccessfully) for the franchise for Scottish Television; was appointed chairman of the board of Edinburgh's Royal Lyceum Theatre Company, a post I held for seven years; was persuaded to stand as a candidate for Lord Rector of Edinburgh University and (mercifully) was defeated by its former Roman Catholic chaplain; gave poetry recitals with Moira at Edinburgh Festivals and elsewhere; attacked in a lecture to the Royal Society of Arts the moronic language of disc jockeys whom I referred to as 'the Anyway Boys' (the word 'anyway' being their standard linking passage) — but singled out for praise a comparative unknown by the name of Terry Wogan; rejoined the Liberal Party; took part in a shoot where in the gloaming I brought down what I thought was a woodcock but turned out to be a parrot, escaped recently from its cage a mile away; fished for salmon in Spain where my guide was called Jesus (and enjoyed bawling for him down the river bank) and on the way home visited the marvellous cave paintings of Altamira and Lascaux; proposed the health of Prince Philip at a Variety Club luncheon and of London's Lord Mayor at his midsummer banquet (he was also chairman of the London Rubber Company to which I made some fruity references); and for a year was resident British columnist of the American weekly magazine, *Newsweek International*.

I also kept in touch with the Navy by accepting, every October, invitations from a variety of naval establishments all over the country to propose the toast of the Immortal Memory of Lord Nelson at their Trafalgar Night dinners. To me the Navy has always been unrivalled for the style in which it clothes ceremonial occasions, and these dinners, from the entry of the President's party heralded by nautical airs from the marine band, to the ritual procession of the baron of beef through to the (sometimes seated) loyal toast, are no exception. It is style that is the Navy's hallmark, and nowhere in its long history has it been more evident than in those laconic naval signals in which the maximum humorous or dramatic impact is made in the minimum number of words.

A good example of the former occurred during the passage of the British submarine *H.50*, which in 1941 was being escorted by the destroyer *Worcester* off the north Norfolk coast in waters where German E-boats often used to attack. At dusk the *H.50*'s captain, Lieutenant-Commander Mervyn Wingfield, signalled the *Worcester*'s captain, Lieutenant-Commander Ian Maitland-Magill-Crichton, 'In the event of enemy attack I intend to remain on surface.' Maitland-Magill-Crichton at once replied, 'So do I.' Examples of more dramatic moments excel by their simplicity. Nelson before Trafalgar: 'The order of sailing is to be the order of battle.' Beatty on the surrender of the German High Seas Fleet in 1918: 'The German flag is to be hauled down at sunset and is not to be hoisted again without permission.' Cunningham to the

Secretary of the Admiralty on the surrender of the Italian fleet in 1943: 'Be pleased to inform their Lordships that the Italian battlefleet now lies at anchor under the guns of the fortress of Malta.' And in 1949 Commander Kerans on bringing the damaged *Amethyst*, bottled up the Yangtse for two months by the communists, to the safety of the open sea: 'Have rejoined the fleet south of Woosung. No damage or casualties. God Save the King.'

One summer I was invited to chair a Brains Trust at the Scottish Lawyers' annual conference at Aviemore. I was told before leaving that the chief guest was to be the Lord Chief Justice of England, Lord Lane. I had met only one other Lord Chief Justice and that was Lord Goddard. The occasion was a small dinner-party given by Arthur Bryant and his wife at which Moira and I were the only other guests. I had greatly looked forward to the meeting, hoping to hear words of wit and wisdom about the law, and perhaps a few good legal anecdotes. But all Goddard did was to tell a succession of *risqué* and not at all funny stories more suited to the smoking-room than to a dinner in mixed company. I was never more disappointed in anyone.

I hoped that Lord Lane would not prove of similar kidney. I had not met him socially before, but we had once clashed in court when he was counsel representing the police at the Brabin Inquiry into the Timothy Evans case. The first question he shot at me after the midday adjournment was, 'Mr Kennedy, have you been discussing the case with your counsel during the luncheon break?' It was delivered with a grim face and a tone of undisguised hostility. 'Yes,' I said, for it had never occurred to me not to. Later I was told that in criminal trials counsel are not permitted to talk to their witnesses during adjournments. Yet this was not a criminal trial but a judicial inquiry, and even if Lane wanted to chance his arm by putting the question, Brabin might have come to my rescue by explaining it. I think Lane was attempting to intimidate me in relation to his further questions, answers to which might otherwise be critical of the police, and in this he partly succeeded. Here was another example of the capriciousness and artificiality of our adversarial system of justice, geared as much to stifling the truth as to revealing it. Indeed an inquiry of this sort should not, in my view, have been conducted on adversarial lines at all.

But the Lord Lane I met at Aviemore could hardly have been more different — affable, witty and without a trace of self-awareness of his office; and if I call him Geoffrey here, it is only because after Aviemore we became friends, played the odd round of golf together, exchanged letters and met on several social occasions. Once I asked him what he thought of the French system of criminal justice and he replied that during his career he had no time left over from practising our own system to study any other (which I think is representative of the Bar as a whole). On another occasion, and because I felt he was a remote figure of whom the public knew nothing, I asked if he would be guest at an off-the-record private dinner-party to which I would invite half a dozen senior media people such as Robin Day, Perry Worsthorne of the *Sunday Telegraph*, and Tony Howard of the *Observer* for an exchange of views. Sadly he declined, saying in a charmingly self-deprecatory way that he doubted he had any views worth hearing.

On our second day at Aviemore a curious thing happened. After an admirable talk by Geoffrey in the morning, we were all given the afternoon off before reassembling for a hula-hula party in the evening (when off duty, staid Scottish lawyers are inclined to let their hair down even further than their English counterparts). Geoffrey and others went off to play golf, while Moira and I paid a visit to Mr Campbell's celebrated tweed shop at Beauly. At seven we gathered for the party, most of us in summer trousers or Bermuda shorts and garlanded with home-made *lei* (the Lord Chief Justice no exception). 'How did you enjoy your golf this afternoon?' he asked me. I said I hadn't been playing. He looked unbelieving and said, 'But surely you remember when we were going down the eighth, you were coming up the ninth, and I waved and your wife waved back, and then you waved.' I said, 'I'm sorry, but we spent the afternoon in Beauly.' He said, 'That's extraordinary. *I could have sworn* it was you.' Too late I thought of adding, 'On oath, my lord?', for I have never seen a more striking example of the perils of what the law calls 'fleeting identification', and this from a witness to whom I was not a total stranger and who himself, both as counsel and judge, had had long experience in assessing the worth of ID witnesses in court.

Oddly enough, in the next murder case I found myself investigating, Geoffrey was to play a small, terminal part, the effects of which were slightly to take the gilt from my findings. This was the Luton Post Office murder, and although, in view of my long labours on the Meehan case, I had resolved not to take up any more cases, this was one that I did not see how I could refuse.

One morning a letter arrived from my literary agent, Michael Sissons, enclosing a handwritten manuscript of some 100,000 words written by a prisoner named David Cooper who, ten years earlier, had been sentenced to life imprisonment for his part in the Luton murder. Michael had been sent this manuscript by another of his clients, the writer and broadcaster Bryan Magee, who also happened to be Cooper's MP. It was not publishable as it stood, said Michael, but might it be of interest to me?

All I knew then of the Luton case was what I had read in the papers and seen on television. Its bare outlines were that in a Luton car park a gang of four men had shot dead a sub-postmaster while trying to obtain from him the post office keys. The gang then fled. One of them, an ageing villain named Alfred Mathews, was subsequently found and arrested, and in exchange ·for not being prosecuted, agreed to turn Queen's evidence and name his accomplices: David Cooper, Michael McMahon and Patrick Murphy, all petty thieves from the East End but with no record of violence. At their trial, in which Mathews was the principal prosecution witness, they were all sentenced to life imprisonment with a recommendation they serve not less than twenty years. Patrick Murphy was later released when his conviction was quashed on appeal.

That left Michael McMahon, and when I wrote to his solicitors I was astonished to hear that he too had written a 100,000-word manuscript. It was better written than Cooper's and, thankfully, in typescript, but its theme was the same: a passionate denial of having played any part in the Luton murder at all. Having read both manuscripts carefully I had no doubts at all that both men were speaking the truth. Indeed it was one of the most shocking stories of police corruption and legal incompetence I had ever read, and believing that I had the ability to rectify it, I decided, whatever my other commitments, that I must bring it to public notice as soon as possible.

My initial reasons for believing in the men's innocence were ones of which the law takes no cognisance at all. Firstly, there was the bare fact that two London East Enders, both of whom had left school at fifteen and were quite untutored in writing, had felt so passionately about their situation that, in different prisons and unknown to each other, they had each set themselves the daunting task of writing the equivalent of full-length books. Would they have done this in the knowledge that they were guilty? I thought it beyond the bounds of credibility. Secondly, the bitterness and resentment with which the two expressed themselves could not, in my view, have been simulated. Thirdly, it was not just the bald declarations of innocence that impressed me, but the nature and quality of those declarations: there were passages in both books which, as in Meehan's letters to me, had the sharp ring of truth. Having been segregated in different prisons after arrest, the three men came together in Brixton prison just before their trial. Cooper was pleased by the move because he badly wanted to find out where the others stood in the affair.

> I did not give much thought to the possibility of their innocence and in fact thought that they were both involved with Mathews in the crime. This of course was a quite natural reaction, and perhaps subconsciously I was hoping they were guilty, in which case they would vindicate me.
> Soon after speaking to McMahon and Murphy, it became clear that they were as bewildered and anxious as I was. Unless they were very good actors, they sounded very convincing to me when they said they were innocent.

Then McMahon:

> If the air needed clearing, then our first conversation did exactly that, for it saw each man strongly protesting his innocence and strenuously denying any involvement in the murder. Given my own predicament, I was left in no doubt that Cooper and Murphy had also been fitted up. Cooper was in a state of disbelief, tempered only by his reluctance to believe he could possibly be convicted.

Nine years later both men were completing their books. Cooper again:

> I shall be vindicated. I am more certain of that than I am of anything in my life, and although it is a slow and at times agonizing road I tread, the time will come when I shall be heard and cleared of the indictment held against me.

And McMahon:

> For the past ten years I have been keeping vigil in a nocturnal maze, and will continue to do so until daybreak. I am

sometimes weary, sometimes depressed, sometimes afraid of being struck down by illness, but throughout even these moments, the driving force created by the injustice never deserts me . . . In or out of prison I will relentlessly fight my case until my conviction for the murder of Reginald Stevens is finally quashed.

Were these two men both callous thugs who, as part of a gang, had shot a helpless postmaster in cold blood, and at the same time brilliant actors trying to con the world into believing they hadn't? I couldn't bring myself to believe it, and after I had visited Cooper in Maidstone Prison and McMahon in Long Lartin Prison and spoken to their two solicitors, Gareth Peirce for Cooper and Wendy Mantle for McMahon, as well as to Tom Sargant, the secretary of JUSTICE, who had also taken up the case, I was convinced that they were as innocent of the Luton murder as I was.

During the course of the next few months I uncovered a tale of wickedness and depravity hard to credit. Until then I had always held the view that police officers do not fabricate evidence against men they know to be innocent, but rather against those whom they genuinely, if mistakenly, believe to be guilty. But in the Luton case there was no question of the officer in charge, Commander Kenneth Drury of Scotland Yard's Flying Squad, believing that Cooper, McMahon and Murphy were guilty. *He knew for a fact that they were innocent.* A brilliant officer with more than twenty commendations, he had grown to believe he was omnipotent; and when Mathews refused to tell him the names of his accomplices, saying it was more than his life was worth, Drury, obsessed with clearing up another case, offered him a deal: make a statement that three men whose names I will give you were your accomplices, testify against them in the witness-box, and in return no charges will be brought against you, and we'll come to an arrangement about the reward money offered by the Post Office. Mathews, who otherwise faced the prospect of life imprisonment, had no option but to accept.

In addition Drury persuaded one witness to amend his evidence so as to incriminate Cooper, arranged for another to be shown a photograph of McMahon so as to pick him out in an identification parade, omitted to tell the defence of two witnesses crucial to their case, cited another as prosecution witness to prevent the defence from calling him, and bribed two prisoners in Leicester Prison, where McMahon was on remand, to say that McMahon had admitted to them his part in the crime. In his summing-up to the jury Mr Justice Cusack said that the nub of the case was Mathews's evidence, and suggested that for him to have implicated three quite innocent men, as the defence claimed, would be 'wicked beyond belief'. That is what the jury thought too, and after an absence of two and a half hours returned guilty verdicts against all three. Soon after a list was published of how the Post Office reward money of £5000, authorized by the Postmaster General, Mr John Stonehouse, was, on Drury's recommendations, to be distributed. Astonishingly Mathews, the only member of the murder gang to be apprehended, was given £2000, half of which he passed to Drury. The remaining £3000 was distributed among those other witnesses I have mentioned and whom Drury had coerced into bolstering the prosecution's case: there is evidence that Drury took a whack of some of that money too.

If the success of Drury's frame-up was breathtaking in its audacity, the failure of the Appeal Court to expose it during the next ten years was no less so in its crassness. The Appeal Court heard or reheard aspects of the case an unprecedented five times, three times on referral back by the Home Secretary. At the first appeal the court rejected vital evidence earlier suppressed by Drury of the two witnesses whose description of the driver of the getaway van, whom Mathews had declared was the 26-year-old Murphy, exactly fitted the 53-year-old Mathews. At the second appeal Murphy's conviction was quashed, a new witness coming forward to say that at the time of the murder in Luton he had seen Murphy in a London street. Because this alibi showed Mathews to have lied in identifying Murphy, Roy Jenkins, the Home Secretary, asked the Appeal Court to consider whether this did not raise suspicions about Mathews's identification of McMahon and Cooper. Incredibly the Appeal Court ruled that Mathews was *not necessarily lying* in saying that Murphy was the driver of the getaway van *but could have been mistaken*; and this third appeal was dismissed. A ruling so contrary to common sense caused a flurry of critical comment in the press and on television. Cooper and McMahon, who had imagined they would be walking from the court as free men, were shattered. When McMahon received a letter from the Archbishop of Canterbury in answer to one of his to the effect that God Almighty still loved him, he replied that a certain quotation always stayed with him: 'I rage, I melt, I burn. The feeble God has stabbed me to the heart.'

After the two men had served more than six years in prison, there came a new twist to the case. A man called Slade made a statement that he had seen Cooper twice in London on the day of the murder, indeed had had a cup of tea with him in a café. This was enough for the Home Secretary to send the case back for a fourth hearing to the Court of Appeal, with the recommendation that they summon Mathews as a witness to test his credibility. This they did. At times rambling incoherently (one observer in court thought him demented) Mathews repeated all the lies he had told at the original trial and added several more. But Lord Justice Roskill, Lord Justice Lawton and Mr Justice Wien, who were hearing the appeal, took a different view: 'Each of us watched him closely while he was giving his evidence. The conclusion which each of us independently has reached in this court on the vital part of his story is that he was clearly telling the truth ... we see no justification for disturbing the verdicts which in our view were entirely correct.' Bryan Magee, Cooper's MP, was also in court: 'The judges did not watch Mathews closely while he was giving evidence. I watched both them and Mathews closely throughout both days while he was giving evidence, and for most of the time all three of the judges had their heads and eyes down on the notes they were keeping.'

Cooper was not in court to hear the judgement, but the effect on McMahon was explosive: 'One moment I was sitting bent over in the dock in utter despair, the next I was on my feet with arms outstretched, screaming at the judges. "I am fucking innocent – *innocent*. Can't you understand that?" ... I was immediately dragged from the dock by the screws and led to the cell downstairs.' *The Times*, more restrained, came to the same conclusions: 'To most sensible, rational people, a verdict which depends on the evidence of a man like Mathews, in the circumstances in which he gave that evidence, cannot be safe.'

In 1977 yet another alibi witness surfaced, one Richard Hurn, who knew nothing of the case or of McMahon's imprisonment but told a friend that he remembered seeing McMahon in London on the afternoon of the murder, a date which for other reasons he had cause to remember. The Home Secretary again referred the matter to the Court of Appeal who considered it in private and then rejected it. McMahon hardly considered it would do anything else: 'I sit here in my cell writing this, having served almost nine years of a life sentence for a murder I did not commit . . . I also know that I sit here, not because of any evidence against me but because of the legal establishment's concerns for its own pretensions to infallibility. Is this the statement of an embittered, biased man? I do not think so.'

Throughout 1979 I was busy preparing my book on the case which I decided to call (*pace* Mr Justice Cusack) *Wicked Beyond Belief*. The object of the book being to bring about the release of Cooper and McMahon as soon as possible, I also decided to forgo a hardback publisher, whom I knew could not publish in under ten months, and contracted instead for an original paperback. I was fortunate to be able to include in addition to my own account a lecture by the former Lord Justice Devlin in which he took the fourth Appeal Court severely to task for the illogicality of its reasoning and for usurping the functions of the jury, and a chapter by Bryan Magee about his efforts over the years to try to persuade the Home Office to reopen Cooper's case. He had some harsh things to say about Roskill, Lawton and Wien, the judges of the fourth Appeal Court:

> Their general demeanour was like that of elderly clubmen determined that it should be clearly understood that they were men of the world, fully alive to all the tricks of your Tom, Dick and Harry; yet their actual questions and comments revealed that they had not the remotest notion what sort of a world it was that these East End people they were listening to actually lived in, or how to evaluate their characters and the plausibility of what they said.

I also included contributions from Tom Sargant of JUSTICE and the men's two solicitors, all three of whom unequivocally asserted their innocence.

From my own experience and that of others, I knew that books about miscarriages of justice were always published in a kind of limbo where they remained for months if not years, totally ignored by those authorities whose business it was to evaluate and act on them. I had had to wait seven years for Evans's pardon and another seven years for Meehan's, and, knowing the reluctance of the Home Office even to consider whether a mistake has been made, far less admit it, I had little hopes of any quick remedial action.

But this time, and quite fortuitously, I was in luck – or rather, as will be seen, partly in luck. Among those to whom I sent a copy of the book on publication was Quintin Hailsham, then Lord Chancellor, with whom, despite our differences of opinion on many matters, I had been friendly over the years. His Permanent Secretary at that time was my cousin Wilfrid Bourne, and this is what he later wrote to me:

> Your book landed up with a pile of others on the desk of Hailsham's private secretary. He did not know what to do with it, Hailsham being far too busy to read it at the time. I happened to look in on the Private Office before going home in order to see whether there was anything I ought to take account of. Your book caught my eye. I had, for once, no official papers to read and picked it up to read in the train. I was so disquieted by it that I finished it that evening.

Next day Wilfrid spoke of his disquiet to an old friend, Dick Thompson, the Registrar of Criminal Appeals, and he, having read the book, felt a similar concern. Approaches were then made to Brian Cubbon, the Permanent Under Secretary at the Home Office responsible for criminal matters, with the result that within three weeks of publication the Home Secretary Willie Whitelaw announced to the House of Commons that because of continued unease about the case and after discussions with the Lord Chief Justice, he had ordered the release of Cooper and McMahon from prison. He added that this was not a case for a free pardon because – wait for it – *there was no proof that Cooper and McMahon were innocent.*

As the reader now knows, and as Willie's advisers should have told him, there was massive proof that Cooper and McMahon were innocent and should never have been put on trial, let alone convicted. So why was a free pardon not granted? I did not obtain the answer to this until several years later when, meeting Willie on holiday, I tackled him on it. 'I was all in favour of a free pardon,' he said, 'but Geoffrey Lane objected.'

I had known Willie since childhood days at Nairn, Geoffrey I had come to know later; and while I greatly admired them both, and still do, I found this closing of establishment ranks deeply shocking. Willie should have ignored Geoffrey's protests, and

Geoffrey (presumably hoping to protect the wretched judges of the Appeal Court from further criticism) should never have made them. It was not justice these two were dispensing but the semblance of justice. And so, without a pardon or any monetary compensation for ten years of wrongful imprisonment, Cooper and McMahon were shuffled discreetly out of prison to rejoin society, branded for the rest of their lives as convicted murderers.

What was it Bryan Magee had written in his chapter in the book? 'We ought none of us to lose sight of the fact that human beings count far more than institutions or procedures or precedents, and we ought always to be willing, given justification, to sacrifice the latter to the former.' But that is not a view held by those who lack the imagination to enter into the hearts and minds of others, and to do to them as they would be done by; among them the then Home Secretary and the then Lord Chief Justice.

There is a tailpiece to the Luton case. While Cooper and McMahon were still serving their sentences, the Postmaster General who had announced the £5000 Post Office reward money, John Stonehouse, MP, and the detective who had arranged its distribution, Commander Kenneth Drury, were themselves convicted of criminal charges and also sent to prison. I have sometimes wondered if they, Cooper and McMahon ever managed to get together for a rubber of whist or bridge.

I now turn to the professional encounters I had in the late 1970s and early 1980s with two senior but very different public figures, Lord Mountbatten and Harold Macmillan (later Earl of Stockton).

Lord Mountbatten first swam into my ken in 1940 when his destroyer, the *Kelly* and mine, the *Tartar*, found themselves in company with the fleet the day after the German invasion of Norway; and from then on, throughout the war and after, I viewed his various exploits with admiration. I interviewed him when he became First Sea Lord and on one or two other occasions, and I always slightly regretted that my commitment to current affairs had prevented me from taking up Associated Rediffusion's offer to spend two years with him, at home and abroad, researching and scripting the thirteen programmes they were planning on his *Life and Times* – a task subsequently and admirably performed by John Terraine.

I did not meet him socially until 1975 when we were both invited as guest speakers to the annual dinner of the Newcastle-upon-Tyne division of the Royal Naval Reserves. This was to take place in the headquarters ship, HMS *Calliope* in the dockyard. Mountbatten was to propose the toast to the Navy, I to the guests.

The day before the dinner I received word from the admiral's ADC that if I were to present myself at 6.55 p.m. at his suite in the Gosforth Park Hotel, where we were both staying, he would give me a lift to the dockyard. I turned up a couple of minutes early, found the door into the suite ajar and the sitting-room in darkness. Had I made a mistake? Was it the lobby where we were to meet, and were the two of them waiting there now? I was about to head for the lift when I noticed a chink of light at the end of the corridor. A new set of questions arose. Were they still dressing or had the ADC forgotten to switch off the lights?

There was only one way to find out. I tiptoed along the corridor and put my head gingerly round the semi-open door. There I saw an unusual sight: the admiral in shirtsleeves and braces sitting astride a very low dressing-table stool and gazing keenly at his reflection in the mirror, the ADC on his knees behind him brushing the curls at the back of his head. Clearly this was no place for me, and having tiptoed back to the sitting-room, I switched on a light and picked up the evening paper. Presently the admiral breezed in, his uniform ablaze with orders and medals. 'Ah, there you are, Kennedy. All ready? Shall we go?'

During the twenty-minute drive to the dockyard the admiral chattered away without pause about his naval career and royal relations. For a time I didn't know quite how to respond. Remarks like, 'Good heavens!' or 'You don't say!' seemed somehow inadequate. Then I realized that he *didn't want* one to respond, that a response of almost any kind would have interrupted his flow, and the politest thing to do was follow the ADC's example and just listen. This was no hardship, for he was marvellously outspoken and indiscreet about many things.

As every after-dinner speaker knows, a toast to the guests requires a gentle ribbing of the guests. But how to rib Mountbatten? In preparing my speech I recalled (as the reader also may) the occasion during my first watch in *Tartar* when the first lieutenant had shown me the various instruments on the bridge, and that when I asked why one had a canvas cover, he had said, 'Oh, that's the Mountbatten station-keeping gear, and we keep it covered because the captain finds it quite useless.' So I related this tale and, while the audience responded warmly, stole a glance to my left. Not a flicker of a smile disturbed that noble face, nor even an acknowledgement that he had heard. Nothing I invent, it seemed to say, is useless; and we are not amused. But he bore no malice, and on the way back to the hotel gave me quite a run-down on his cousin Ena, who he said had once been Queen of Spain.

A couple of years later I was telephoned by a BBC producer called Ron Webster, who said he wanted to talk to me about Mountbatten's obituary programme. A cheerful, boozy chain-smoker, who had started his career as a film editor, Ron had a cough that seemed to rise from the soles of his shoes, and a propensity for laughing hugely at his own, often very filthy, jokes.

Ron said that he'd been preparing an obituary of Lord Mountbatten for some time, that Mountbatten had somehow got wind of it and had approached the BBC with a view to taking part. 'In what way?' I asked. 'He'd like to be interviewed about his life, and talk about the kind of funeral he wants to have. And because of your naval connections, we thought you might do the interviewing.'

So Ron and I went down to Broadlands, the country house on the Test at Romsey which had once belonged to Lord Palmerston and was later left to Edwina Mountbatten, the admiral's wife. Mountbatten looked much older than when we had last met, still handsome and alert, but with deaf-aids in both ears, wearing a blazer that now hung loosely on him, and in his walk the beginnings of old man's shuffle. He had kindly invited us to what he called a light lunch, which consisted of an egg dish, lamb cutlets, a pudding, cheese and a dessert of frosted redcurrants, all served by a bearded butler and two footmen in naval battledress.

After lunch we retired to the drawing-room where the camera crew had already set up, and I sat on one sofa and he on another. After taking us through his life and times, he moved on to the matter of his death which he hoped would be quick and peaceful. For his funeral he had made a list of people he wanted invited (they did not include any Japanese), the lessons he wanted read, the hymns he wanted sung. Was all this, I wondered, an act of consideration to pre-empt family arguments, or yet another example of his abiding vanity?

We completed the film during the early summer of 1979 and in August Mountbatten was granted the quick but not peaceful death he had asked for when his boat was blown up by an IRA bomb off the west coast of Ireland. That night the BBC ran the obituary twice – the first time they had ever done so for anyone, and the first television obituary to consist of a filmed interview with the deceased. After this I put my name forward as a candidate for the official biography and so informed my editor at Collins, Philip Ziegler. Some time later Philip wrote to say that, although he had not put his own name forward for consideration, he himself had been invited to be the official biographer and had accepted. And a wise choice it turned out to be.

The BBC planned to give the film a third airing on what would have been the admiral's eightieth birthday, and when this became known we were approached by Lord Brabourne, Mountbatten's son-in-law, to say that his cousin Prince Charles who, as everyone knew, adored his uncle, wanted to pay him a personal tribute. Ron and I thought that the best way to arrange this would be for me to interview the Prince about his uncle, and to tack the result on to the end of the obituary programme. We were summoned to Buckingham Palace to discuss this, and as we approached the gates in my car, I remembered that I had a case of 250 cartridges in the boot. So, imagining we would have problems with security, I turned round, dumped the cartridges at Brooks's and returned to the Palace. The policemen, without looking in the boot, waved us through.

It was agreed with the Prince that the interview would take place at Broadlands where he would be staying with the Brabournes in a few weeks' time. The night before the interview Ron and I motored down to Romsey, and after an excellent dinner punctuated by more of Ron's awful stories and a good night's sleep, set out for Broadlands next day. In view of the presence of the Prince there, and especially in the light of some critical remarks he had made recently about the IRA, I had expected a posse of police to be guarding the entrance gates. There were none. We drove up the drive and came to the back door; there were no police there either. The door was open, and as there was no reply to our knocking, we walked in and along the corridor which I knew led to the main living quarters. In a room at a corner of the house a man fiddling with coffee cups looked up briefly, said good morning, and carried on fiddling. We continued unimpeded until I saw ahead of me the drawing-room where I had interviewed Mountbatten, and sitting on one of the sofas with his back to us the unmistakable profile and balding head of Prince Charles. Had I been an IRA man, I could have pulled out my little Luger and shot him dead – a thought so unnerving that the next day I wrote to his private secretary to suggest improved security.

It was strange to see the Prince occupying the same segment of sofa where only the year before I had talked to his uncle. I found his blend of assurance, diffidence and wit beguiling, and I have often wondered what he might have done had he been born free. He spoke of the affection he and his uncle had had for each other and what a marvellous counsellor he had been. He related some good anecdotes about him and told us that although the admiral had been killed in August, he had already chosen and wrapped up the Royal Family's Christmas presents and – even more remarkable – had already chosen and wrapped up Prince Edward's twenty-first birthday present, then six years away. No vanity there – only an amazing thoughtfulness for others and, who knows?, a premonition of death. The interview was duly shown at the end of the third broadcast of the obituary pro-gramme and was very well received.

Before this, however, Ron and I had had an offer from Lord Brabourne of further Mountbatten film. Film had always played an important part in the admiral's career (he had founded the Royal Naval Film Corporation), and rather than write his autobi-ography, he had recorded, with John Terraine as questioner, some seven hours of reflection on his life and personal relation-ships, and had left instructions that none of it was to be shown publicly until after his death. It took Ron and myself two days to view it, and compulsive viewing most of it was. A working title for it might have been 'How I Got my Way, and Was Proved Right in Everything I Did'. Then I remembered Stephen Roskill telling me not to believe a word Mountbatten said or claimed unless it was corroborated from other sources.

Ron and I came to call it 'Firm Friends'. This was because of a minor theme on which the admiral wove several variations which went something like this: 'I said to So-and-So [often a general, minister or other senior official]: "Are you refusing to do what I ask?" And he said, "Yes, I am." So I said, "Well, if that's the case, I'm going straight to the President/Prime Minister/

Foreign Secretary/First Lord, etc., to say So-and-So won't do what I ask, so I'm not prepared to carry on and here's my resignation." "Oh," said So-and-So, "you wouldn't do a thing like that." So I said, "Yes, I damn well would." Then So-and-So had to climb down. But afterwards, when it was all over, *we became firm friends.*'

We divided the material into six programmes which we then had to clear with the Cabinet Office under an agreement that had been made with the Broadlands Archives Trust. Although we did not foresee any difficulties, we were astonished to hear that the Secretary of the Cabinet, Sir Robert Armstrong, had asked for the programme on the Suez operation of 1956, in which Mountbatten had been First Sea Lord, to be deferred 'possibly for some months'. He gave two reasons: over-critical remarks of Hailsham and Macmillan and – the main reason – 'It is judged that the showing of the Suez programme could have untoward consequences while the situation in the Arab world is as critical as it is at present.'

Aside from the situation in the Arab world then *not* being critical, this was an incomprehensible decision. Had Mountbatten been lambasting the Arabs, there might well have been grounds for constraint. But the bulk of the programme was Mountbatten's account of how he had done everything in his power, both professionally and privately, to dissuade his old friend, Anthony Eden, *from attacking* the Arabs. What 'untoward' consequences could derive from that? And why, after all the other chief participants in the affair had had their say, should Mountbatten be denied his? I had an uneasy feeling that Sir Robert Armstrong had other reasons for wanting the programme postponed, but would not say what they were.

This feeling was greatly strengthened when, six months later, Sir Robert was again approached about the Suez programme and again asked for it not to be shown. This time he had shifted his ground; not a word about the criticisms of Hailsham and Macmillan which we had agreed to delete, nor about untoward consequences in the Arab world: this time it was 'breach of confidential relationships' contrary to what was laid down in the Report of the Privy Council on Ministerial Memoirs. With great difficulty I obtained a copy of this document and while it stated that 'public servants should not reveal the opinions and attitudes of colleagues as to the government business with which they have been concerned', another section said quite clearly that a reasonable timescale for a public servant's silence would be 'fifteen years or for the service life of the adviser, whichever is the longer'. As Suez had occurred twenty-four years earlier and as both Eden and Mountbatten were dead, it seemed to me that Sir Robert's arguments were nonsensical. But leaned on in this way, Lord Brabourne and the Broadlands Trust felt they had no option but to accept his advice, and permission to show the Suez film was withheld.

Exasperated with all this pussy-footing, and knowing of Mountbatten's wishes that what he had said should be known, I saw to it that a transcript of the Suez programme reached my friend Bernard Levin at *The Times*, and he published the core of it in two long articles. Needless to say there was not a whisper of dissent from the Arab world. But I was not surprised when, several years later, I read that Sir Robert Armstrong, appearing for the government in the *Spycatcher* trial in Sydney, had admitted to cross-examining counsel that he had been what he called 'economical with the truth'. It seemed to be in his blood.

There are few people who came to know Harold Macmillan who do not have some anecdote about him, and I am fortunate in that having interviewed him at length twice, as well as running into him on a number of other occasions, I have garnered quite a few. When he was Prime Minister he made little personal impact on television, bared his teeth at the cameras like an old dog, and was generally aloof and buffer-like. But after his retirement, in interviews with Robert Mackenzie, and on many private occasions, he revealed a quite different side – avuncular, anecdotal, witty, an old trouper who could, when he was in the mood, move you to tears or laughter. Who will ever forget his touching description of President Kennedy's visit to Birch Grove, his country house in Sussex, and his remark, delivered with a catch in his throat, 'Before the leaves had turned, he was gone.'

I first met him when, after retirement, he took part in some current affairs programme about Britain and the Common Market. We had been advised that if we laid on a couple of bottles of champagne he might stay and chat for a while after the show. This he did, and it was then that I experienced for the first time his unexpected propensity for one-liners, conjured out of thin air. There were two that evening. 'Sweden's a poor little country, don't you think?' was the first. Nobody felt they knew enough about Sweden to agree or disagree. 'No good murders since they did away with capital punishment' was the second, coming from nowhere and an equally effective conversation-stopper. Yet it was true: knowing the defendant was to swing concentrated one's own mind, as well as his, wonderfully.

Some time later I found myself next to him at a dining-club. 'I've had a most interesting day,' he said, 'I've been to the Balcombe Street siege.' This was a house where four IRA men, surrounded by the police, had been holed up for a number of days.

'Oh?' I said, somewhat surprised.

'I used to go everywhere by bus or tube, but my son Maurice – do you know my son Maurice?'

'We were at Eton together.'

'He thought the time had come for me to have a car, and very kindly provided me with one. Well, I had lunch today with Diana Cooper – do you know Diana Cooper?'

'A little.'

'And after lunch she said, why don't we take the car and go and look at this siege in Balcombe Street? And we did. The first man I saw was a *Daily Mirror* photographer and he said, "I'm surprised to see you here," and I said, "I'm quite surprised myself." Then we met the officer in charge, a most interesting man. Said he remembered me in North Africa. He told us they'd cut off the water supply to the house, and as no one can carry on long without water, he thinks they'll surrender quite soon. A most instructive day.'

Another time in the same club he turned to me and said, 'The fellow on my other side went up the Irrawaddy in 1943 and he's been taking me back there with him. How do I get downstream?' A few minutes later he rose and I heard him say, 'Goodnight and thank you for giving me your interesting reminiscences.' If I hadn't known otherwise I would have said that he meant every word of it.

One Christmas when Macmillan was in his eighties his grandson Alexander (Maurice's son and the present Lord Stockton), who looked after the old boy in many ways, asked me if I would read the eighth of nine lessons at a carol service in a London church in aid of dependants of the Publishers Association. Other people in the public eye would be reading the first seven, and his grandfather the ninth. 'Be sure,' said Alexander before the service started, 'to turn over the page to my grandfather's lesson when you have finished yours.' I duly did so, and returned to my seat. Halfway through the next carol, the old boy rose slowly to his feet and with the help of his stick, made his way to the lectern. There, equally slowly and, it seemed to me, deliberately, he closed the Bible.

What would happen now? Had I perhaps misinterpreted Alexander's instructions? For the remainder of the carol I was on tenterhooks, not daring to take my eyes from the lectern. The carol ended. The congregation sat down. Then, as slowly and deliberately as before, Macmillan drew from an inside pocket of his coat a smallish piece of paper and raised it to within a couple of inches of his right eye. He paused. We waited spellbound. Then he spoke. 'In the beginning was the word.' A half glance at the congregation, then back to eyeing the piece of paper. 'And the word was God.' Another glance. 'And God was the word.' It was like that all the way, the timing impeccable, a theatrical *tour de force*. As he tottered back to his seat it was as much as I could do not to applaud.

Both my television interviews with him took place at Birch Grove, the first on the occasion of the publication of a picture book about his life and times, the second on the publication of his Middle East diaries. On each he was in excellent form. 'Where did you stay last night?' he asked while we waited for the cameras to be set up. 'A place called Gravetye,' I said, 'about twenty miles from here. I don't suppose you know it.' 'Know it well,' he said. 'Used to be owned by a fellow named Robinson who invented the herbaceous border.' After the first morning's filming we assembled by the front door to go to Alexander's house, half a mile away, for lunch. 'Which car are we going in?' he asked Alexander. 'Are we going in Mrs Thatcher?' He must have seen my expression, for he said, 'This car makes a noise if you don't fasten your seat-belt, and a light starts flashing if you haven't closed the door. It's a *very bossy* car.'

At first I found him a difficult subject to interview because, to paraphrase Donne, when he had done he had not done, he still had more; and I had to learn to give him at least five seconds' grace before moving on, because his afterthoughts were often gems. He spoke movingly of his time in the trenches in the First War and of how a whole generation, many of them his friends, had been wiped out, of the effect that the unemployment of the 1930s had on his political thinking, of how being Prime Minister was less demanding than being an ordinary Minister, of (and this with tears in his eyes) his devotion to his late wife, who had fallen dead of a heart attack close to where we were sitting, of his belief in God. And he had some good two-liners, too. 'The vocabulary of broadcasters today gets smaller and smaller. Now it's down to about a hundred words.' And, 'When I was a boy it was always considered bad form to talk about food or money. Now no one talks of anything else.'

The only moment when he seemed ill at ease was when I raised the question of the forced repatriation to Russia at the end of the war of thousands of White Russian and Cossack soldiers from camps in northern Italy and Yugoslavia. Controversy about this event had been raised by Count Tolstoy in a book in which he – and later many others – said it should never have been permitted to happen, for on their arrival in Russia the soldiers were massacred. As Macmillan at the time was political adviser to General Alexander whose army occupied that area, many felt that he bore some responsibility. Indeed he had not tried to disguise in his Middle East diaries what he knew would happen to the soldiers. They were being sent back, he said, 'to torture, slavery and death'. Why had he not excised this passage? Was it because he hadn't spotted it, or because he felt it would be dishonest to do so, or because he never expected criticism? As I listened to him fumbling for words of explanation, I wished he could have said boldly that what was thought to be so heinous today was not thought to be so then, but that looking back now, he deeply regretted what had happened.

On one of the last occasions I saw him, I mentioned my dealings with Mountbatten and asked what he thought of him. 'Very good at his job, but very vain.' He paused a moment. 'After Winston had retired, he used to give lunch parties every two weeks or so in the basement of his house in Hyde Park Gate. One day there were about a dozen of us there, including Dickie and myself; I was Prime Minister at the time. Winston wasn't in a very good mood. Dickie bored him all through the first course with stories of the Navy in the First World War, and all through the second course with stories of the Navy in the Second World War, and then he got up and said, "I've got to go now to a meeting of the Chiefs of Staff, but the Prime Minister will keep you amused." Winston was furious. He waited until Dickie had reached the foot of the stairs and then said in a very loud voice, "*Who is that fellow? Ought I to know him?*"'

My father taught me that there is only one thing more boring in life than listening to other people's dreams and that is listening to stories about their operations; and I only tell mine now because those I had during the early 1980s are as good an example as any of how modern medicine has helped to prolong life; without them it is unlikely that I would be sitting here writing this. Two were routine, one richly comic, one quite serious; and in none did I experience the slightest pain or discomfort.

Two were also products of what one might call the orifice revolution, i.e. gaining entry to the inside of the body other than by cutting into it from the outside. Like getting at the prostate, for instance. In the old days the surgeon made an incision in the lower portion of the tummy and reached the enlarged gland that way, but before the coming of antibiotics it was quite common for infections to develop or for the prostate to turn cancerous. That happened, as the reader may remember, in my grandfather's case; for the last two years of his life he was bedridden, often in acute discomfort, before finally succumbing.

But today the prostate operation is routine, as I discovered when I visited the operating theatre a few days after I had had mine. From a sort of mobile console a thin tube containing a fibre-optic light and a wire-cutter is uncoiled and inserted into the penis. When it reaches the bladder the surgeon, like a submarine commander, applies his eyes to the other end of the fibre-optic and sees the area of tissue that needs to be cut away. He then, with a foot pedal, activates the wire-cutter. It is as simple as that (though I guess the skills required are far from simple). I asked my own surgeon how many of these prostate operations he did in a year, and he said around four hundred. I also asked if it affected sexual performance. He said only to the degree that when you came, you did not come, i.e. there was orgasm without emission; a change which on several grounds has much to recommend it.

Throughout my life my tummy has been, as it were, my Achilles heel; and around this same time the condition of my colon, which for the latter part of my life has had a habit of tying itself in knots, became particularly acute. So I went to see a man in

Devonshire Place and he sent me down the road for a barium meal X-ray. When it was over the doctor there said, 'We've found four polyps in your colon, and I'm happy to tell you that none are cancerous.' Not knowing then what a polyp was, I still found my eyes welling up with tears of relief. 'Are they often cancerous?' I asked. 'They're apt to grow cancerous,' he said, 'if they're not found and taken out. But we've found yours in time.'

The Devonshire Place man said, 'The sooner you have them out the better. I'll arrange for you to go into the London Clinic. They have a first-class man there.' I envisaged two or three weeks in hospital, missing several television programmes and having to cancel various writing commitments. 'How long for?' I said.

'Oh, about a couple of hours,' he said. 'No anaesthetic, and you'll feel as right as rain afterwards.'

And so I became a beneficiary again of the orifice revolution. Last time the fibre-optic and wire-cutter had gone in by the front door; this time they were to enter by the back.

Instructions (entitled *Having a Colonoscopy* and illustrated with a picture of a cheery-looking doctor waving a piece of paper) reached home a few days later. I was to starve for thirty-six hours beforehand, take a powerful laxative and drink plenty of clear fluids 'including alcohol if you wish'. I did wish, and spent a happy preparatory period in a haze of vodka and tonic.

The rest of the instructions were immensely reassuring. 'When the tube is in place, air will be passed through it to distend the colon and give a clearer view of the lining ... you may pass some wind, but although you may find this embarrassing, remember that staff do understand what is causing it.' All my life I had done my best not to sound off in company. Yet here was express permission to do so; what might be called a farter's charter. By nature an exhibitionist, I greatly looked forward to it.

At the agreed hour I reported to the Endoscopy Unit of the London Clinic, was shown into a small room, told to undress and put on a blue shift, then lie down on a mobile bed. A nurse came in and asked for my X-rays and I remembered I had forgotten them. 'Not to worry,' said the nurse, but I did, for how else could they find the polyps? Presently a man with greying hair and specs came in and said he was the doctor who was going to remove the polyps. I noticed he said *doctor* not *surgeon*, which made me wonder if he was really up to it. He seemed full of beans though, and after he had given me a rundown on the life cycle of the polyp, three nurses wheeled me across the corridor and into another room.

In the far corner of this room stood a man in a white coat who looked like President Mubarak. 'This is a colleague of mine from Cairo,' said the doctor. 'You don't mind if he watches, do you?' I said I'd be delighted. 'You don't have many polyps in Egypt, do you?' said the doctor, and the man from Cairo said, 'Not in the colon,' though without adding where they did have them.

The nurses turned me on my side and the doctor put a needle into a vein behind my knuckle to make me relax. While doing this he gave a wonderful imitation of his coal merchant and his wife. I couldn't decide whether he was doing this to make me even more relaxed, like a television warm-up man, or because he was over-excited at the prospect of getting at my polyps.

The nurses meanwhile had put the tube in, and now they blew in some air as well. One put her hand on my tummy and the doctor said, 'Try and do a pooper.' I couldn't: it was terribly disappointing. 'Never mind,' said the doctor, 'now we'll look for the polyps. You can see what happens if you like.'

He handed me an eyepiece attached to a long lead and there, through a series of prisms, were my lower intestines in glorious technicolour. We seemed to be travelling down a sort of miniature, pinkish Channel Tunnel.

'Ah!' said the doctor gleefully. 'Here's the first one now.' There was no mistaking it: bright red, like a little cherry, on the end of a long white stalk and swaying gently in the breeze. 'Now watch,' said the doctor, and suddenly the wire came out of the tube in a kind of loop and the doctor lassoed the polyp as if it were a steer. Then he drew the wire tight, applied some heat and polyp and stalk parted company. 'Like to see it?' he asked, and there was the polyp on a tin tray in front of me, looking very battered and sorry for itself. 'That was Father polyp,' said the doctor, and soon afterwards we located Mother polyp and two baby polyps. One of the baby polyps proved intractable, appearing in the eyepiece one moment, vanishing the next. 'What a coy little polyp you are, to be sure,' said the doctor, but he eventually lassoed and dispatched it too. With only one to go, I asked the doctor from Cairo if he'd like a dekko down the eyepiece, but he declined, which I found surprising in view of the scarcity of polyps in Egypt.

Ten minutes later I was back in the changing-room on my

mobile bed wolfing tea and sandwiches, parts of which would eventually find their way into my now polypless colon. And an hour after that I was back in the club sipping a whisky and soda and pondering what to have for dinner. One way and another it had been a thoroughly enjoyable afternoon.

The third and fourth operations were of a rather different order. For seven or eight years I had been aware of a growing numbness, first in the muscles of my right leg and later in those of my left, for which no doctor or specialist could find any adequate explanation. Finally I was sent to a neurological specialist who said it would be necessary to examine the top half of my spinal cord, which houses the motor for the body's muscles. To do this he sent me to another sort of specialist who inserted through my neck a needle containing blue dye, guided it with the help of a television screen into the top of my spinal cord and then watched its progress as it trickled down. After a bit he said, 'I think we've located the cause of your trouble. You have a misplaced disc which is pressing hard on the top of your spinal cord.'

When the distinguished surgeon who had agreed to operate if necessary was told this, he said he doubted if that was the cause, as there was no numbness in my arms, and he would like to see the effect of the blue dye on the lower half of the spinal cord. So I went along to his hospital, lay down beneath a huge X-ray machine and the process was repeated. Everything went smoothly so long as I lay on my tummy, but when they turned me on to my back I was assailed with a searing pain there. The surgeon's face appeared on a level with my own: 'We've found a tumour in your spinal cord which we think is the cause of your troubles.' I found the word *tumour* chilling, and he must have sensed it. 'There's no reason at the moment to suppose it's not benign, but if we don't take it out, it could turn nasty. So you won't be going home this afternoon. We'll give you a room here, do some tests on you over the weekend and take you to the theatre on Tuesday.' And that's just what they did.

Those three operations then are the measure of modern medical practice: cancers which might have developed from an enlarged prostate, some rogue polyps and a spinal tumour, any one of which could have proved fatal, were all pre-empted by discovery and cure; and I cannot be other than deeply grateful for this additional lease of life.

The end of the story is anti-climactic. The removal of the tumour made no difference to my legs, so thinking the misplaced disc might after all be the cause, they decided to have a go at that. 'What exactly are you going to do?' I asked, and they said, 'Remove the disc and replace it with a piece of bone which we'll take from your hip.' They added, almost as an aside, 'By the way, we go in from the front of your neck, and you may find a tiny scar there afterwards.' 'The *front* of my neck?' I said. 'But my spine is at the *back*.' They said, 'Yes, we know that, but it's easier to get at from the front.' I said, 'But what about all that gunge that's in the way, like the back of my tongue and Adam's apple and so on?' They said, 'Oh, we just push it all to one side.' When I mentioned this to my GP he smiled. 'It's a routine operation now,' he said.

For them I'm sure it was. But for me, soon after the operation, there occurred something so removed from anything I had ever experienced that I have never forgotten it. The operation took place at midday and I was taken to the recovery room in the course of the afternoon. I was conscious soon after, and for the next few hours was in a state of half-sleeping, half-waking, yet aware of the presence of a pretty young nurse, perhaps Thai or Korean, who alternated between giving me sips of water and jabbing a needle in my bum. By nine in the evening I was fully conscious and observed out of the big window at the end of the room the light beginning to drain from a violet sky. At that moment, and perhaps for an hour afterwards, I was on Cloud Nine – in a state of happiness, contentment, euphoria, joy and utter peace such as I have never experienced before or since: everything is all right, an inner voice said, and everything from now on will always be all right; how wonderful to know that life can be like this. At the time I thought little more about it, but later I realized that it must have been caused by some powerful pain-killing drug. But what – heroin? cocaine? I never dared to ask, but I understand now what it is that drives addicts back to the needle time and time again whatever the cost to their health and sanity; I understand now what the mystics lay claim to when they speak of the peace that passeth all understanding.

Disappointingly, the operation did nothing for my legs.

22

The Lindbergh Baby Kidnapping Case

On 3 November 1979 I celebrated my sixtieth birthday with a dinner with my camera crew in the railroad station of Ogden, Utah; and later on the platform some very tipsy Mormons plied us with lukewarm white wine out of paper cups while we awaited the arrival of the *San Francisco Zephyr*. I was then in the middle of filming *Coast to Coast*, my contribution to the BBC series, *Great Railway Journeys of the World*; this included a re-enactment of the ceremony of the Golden Spike at a spot in the desert forty miles north of Ogden where the Union Pacific and Central Pacific lines had joined hands in 1869. At midnight the *Zephyr* pulled in and we all climbed aboard.

Among the camera crew was a lighting man called Ray, a quiet, stocky, dark-haired fellow aged around fifty. When we were in Denver Ray bought himself a ten-gallon stetson and showed it to us all with pride. But we noticed he never wore it. 'When are you going to wear your stetson, Ray?' I said one day, and he said, 'Oh, I'm not going to wear it here, I'd look so conspicuous. I'm going to wear it when I get home.' Home was Salford and I said, 'But Ray, don't you think you'd look more conspicuous in Salford?' Ray shook his head, 'They know me there,' he said.

Fate, however, had decreed that Ray would never wear his stetson, for in the middle of that night, as the *San Francisco Zephyr* snaked its way across the Humboldt desert, Ray was found dead in one of the washrooms. At a place called Winnemucca his body was disembarked and taken by the cameraman and sound recordist to the local hospital. There a certificate of death was made out, and a day or two later our executive producer Roger Laughton arrived to accompany the hearse that would take Ray's coffin to Las Vegas airport for onward shipment to New York, Manchester and Salford. On top of the coffin was strapped a large hat box containing Ray's stetson. It sat there proudly, a kind of personal standard, a talisman, a sentinel to keep watch over Ray on his long journey home. And as a final surreal touch the hearse, as it bowled along the inter-state highway, was pulled up by the cops for speeding.

The next year I was back in America, this time in New York, to do a couple of interviews for a new programme I had been asked to present called *Did You See?*, a weekly review of television, and it was here, without the slightest warning, that I found myself caught up once more in an investigation into a major miscarriage of justice.

The place was my hotel bedroom, the time around 8 a.m. As one often does in New York at that time of day, I was flicking idly through the television channels while awaiting the arrival of orange juice and coffee. I did not even know which channel I was tuned to when there swam into my vision a very old lady proclaiming with vehemence that her husband was innocent of the crime of which he had been convicted. I sat up and paid attention for this was, as it were, my territory. As the interview unfolded I recognized the questioner as Tom Brokaw, so knew I was switched to the NBC *Today* show; then slowly it dawned on me – for the scene had been set before I had tuned in – that the old lady was none other than Anna Hauptmann, the widow of Richard Hauptmann, the German immigrant who had been executed by the State of New Jersey in 1936 for the kidnapping and murder of the baby son of Charles Lindbergh, the man whose solo flight from New York to Paris in 1927 in a tiny monoplane had stunned the world by its daring and in some ways determined the shape of things to come. And then I remembered from Eton days a picture that would be seared on my mind for ever, a full-page photograph of the haunted unshaven face of Richard Hauptmann as it first appeared after his arrest and then again, on the day of his electrocution two years later.

And now, nearly half a century on, here was his widow not only proclaiming his innocence but telling Tom Brokaw (and this was the peg for the interview) that as a result of new information about the case, she was taking out a suit against the State of New Jersey for her husband's wrongful conviction and execution. And once again, as when I was about to embark on *10 Rillington Place* and the Meehan case and the Luton Post Office murder, I felt the old adrenalin surging through me and a sense of heady exhilaration; for I thought it improbable in the extreme that an old lady in her eighties would have agreed, forty-four years after her husband's death, to have travelled all the way to New York to appear on an early morning television show to assert her husband's innocence and launch a suit against a powerful state if she knew (and she would have known) that her husband was guilty; not unless she was out of her mind, and she did not seem to me to be that.

So, through NBC, I lost no time in contacting her lawyer, a Mr Robert Bryan from California, and from him learnt that under the Freedom of Information Act, he had had access to the FBI documents on the case, and that following this the New Jersey State police had also opened their files, and that a combined study of these provided overwhelming evidence that the case against Hauptmann had been rigged. Mr Bryan also referred me to a book by the American journalist Anthony Scaduto, *Scapegoat*, in which after extensive inquiries and getting access to the files of the Bronx District Attorney and the New York City Police, he explained how he had come to the same conclusion.

With archive film of the period and of the case available, my first plan was to make an hour-long television documentary, and to this end I telephoned the BBC in London and spoke to Will Wyatt, head of Documentary and Features. He told me he had already taken note of the case and was in broad agreement with my proposal; and in 1981 I returned to the United States with director Sue Crowther and a camera team.

The background to the case was this. On the stormy night of 1 March 1932 the twenty-month-old baby son of Charles Lindbergh was kidnapped from his crib in the nursery of their recently completed country house at Hopewell, New Jersey, and taken down a makeshift ladder which the kidnappers abandoned on leaving. Because Lindbergh was America's great national hero, the American press and public were outraged by the news, which also made banner headlines throughout the world. A series of ransom notes were delivered and acted on, and on 2 April an intermediary acting for Lindbergh called Dr Condon handed over $50,000 to one of the kidnap gang in a cemetery in the Bronx. On 12 May the baby's body was found in woods not six miles from the Lindberghs' house. He was already dead when the ransom money was handed over. Despite a nationwide hunt for the kidnap gang, not a trace of them was found.

Two and a half years passed, then some of the marked ransom notes began circulating in the Bronx. They were actually traced to a German immigrant and carpenter named Richard Hauptmann who lived in the Bronx with his wife Anna and their baby son

Manfred. Questioned by the police he denied possessing any Lindbergh ransom money, but when the police dug up the floor of his garage they found some $14,000 of marked ransom bills. Hauptmann said he had been given them for safekeeping by a business partner named Isidor Fisch just before Fisch had left for Germany where, unfortunately, he had recently died. He, Hauptmann, had no idea that the money was Lindbergh ransom money, and the reason he had secreted it was (a) because the money was in gold certificate notes which had become illegal tender since America had gone off the gold standard and (b) because the money belonged not to him but to Fisch's estate. He added that as he had recently discovered that Fisch was a crook who had tricked him out of several thousand dollars, he considered he was only paying back to himself what he was owed.

The American public had almost despaired of the Lindbergh baby's murderers ever being caught, and now here was one of them found with the loot in his possession. There was not a man or woman in America who did not regard Hauptmann's explanation of how he had obtained the money as preposterous, and I have no doubts at all that had I or anyone reading this book been in America at that time, we would have felt the same. 'LINDBERGH KIDNAPPER JAILED' screamed the two-inch banner headlines of the next day's *New York Daily News*, and most other papers followed suit.

It was generally assumed that it would be only a matter of time before Hauptmann confessed to the crime and named the other members of the gang. But despite a severe and prolonged beating-up by the New York City police, he continued to assert his innocence and went on asserting it until the day of his death. The American people found these persistent denials of Hauptmann, whom everyone knew to be guilty, puzzling.

During the next four years, at first in the making of the BBC documentary on the case and then for a long book about it which I called *The Airman and the Carpenter*, I made as thorough an investigation into the case as half a century's time lapse would allow. I spoke at length to Anna Hauptmann and her late husband's two best friends, Hans Kloppenburg and Henry Uhlig (an hour with either of them was enough to sow doubts about Hauptmann's guilt among even the most sceptical), to Lewis Bornmann, one of the principal detectives in the case, to Betty Gow, the baby's nurse and the first to find him missing, and to

Ethel Stockton, the only surviving member of Hauptmann's trial jury. I went through the files of the FBI in Washington and those in the Lindbergh room of the New Jersey State police headquarters at Trenton, New Jersey. I visited the former nursery in the Lindbergh house (now a delinquent boys' home) at Hopewell from which the baby had been snatched and the area of the woods where his body had been found; the rented apartment in the Bronx where Hauptmann and his family had lived, especially the attic there from which the prosecution had claimed that he had taken a length of his landlord's flooring to fashion one of the sections of the now famous kidnap ladder; the courtroom in the sleepy town of Flemington where he had been tried and the cell he had occupied there; and his cell and the execution chamber on Death Row in Trenton. I then went through the back editions of the *New York Times* from 1932 to 1936 and studied, page by page, the 4000 pages of transcript of a trial that had lasted more than six weeks. At every stage I was prepared, as I had been in all my previous cases, to find some piece of evidence that would confirm beyond argument the convicted man's guilt. At no stage did I find it; and by the time I was through I knew for certain that he was innocent.

For a detailed analysis of the falsity of the charge against Hauptmann and of the evidence that was led to support it, the reader is referred to *The Airman and the Carpenter* and to Anthony Scaduto's book *Scapegoat*. Here I will restrict myself to the main heads of the State's evidence: the identification of Hauptmann near Hopewell and in the Bronx cemetery when the ransom was handed over; the alleged similarity of Hauptmann's handwriting to that of the writer of the ransom notes; evidence that a section of the kidnap ladder had come from Hauptmann's attic; and the claim that he had no alibi for the day of the kidnapping.

Lacking a confession, the New Jersey State police had no witnesses to place Hauptmann in New Jersey at the time of the kidnapping, and without one they were unable to secure his extradition from New York. So they fabricated one: a poverty-stricken hillbilly and well-known local liar named Millard Whited. Interviewed within weeks of the kidnapping Whited had told the police he had seen nobody suspicious near the Lindbergh estate. But two and a half years later, in return for $150, $35-a-day expenses and a promise of reward money, he travelled to the

Bronx to declare in court that he had twice had a fleeting glimpse of Hauptmann near the scene of the crime. After Hauptmann's death he admitted he had been bribed. To reinforce Whited's evidence at Hauptmann's trial the police produced a half-blind 87-year-old Prussian war veteran who, having been shown pictures of Hauptmann, said that he too recalled having had a fleeting glimpse of him two and a half years earlier driving past his house; and he too was promised and received reward money.

Yet the most damning identification evidence came from Colonel Charles Lindbergh who had accompanied his intermediary, Dr Condon, to the Bronx cemetery for the handing over of the $50,000 reward money. Sitting in his car in the dark some hundred yards from the cemetery Lindbergh heard one of the kidnap gang shout out, 'Hey, Doc' to indicate to Condon where he was. After his arrest two years later, Hauptmann was brought into a room in the Bronx District Attorney's office where Lindbergh was sitting in disguise; and on the DA's instructions, Hauptmann shouted out 'Hey, Doc' in a variety of voices. Pressurized by the New Jersey State police who were desperate for evidence to convict, and assured by them that there was not the slightest scintilla of doubt that Hauptmann was guilty, Lindbergh agreed to testify that the voice he had heard in the cemetery was that of Hauptmann. Coming from him that must have carried great weight with the jury, although the *New York Law Journal* and other authorities suggested that to claim recognition of a voice from two words said in the dark at a hundred yards' distance two and a half years earlier was carrying identification to the point of absurdity. Meanwhile Dr Condon, who had spoken to one of the kidnap gang on two occasions (both in the dark) and declared that it was not Hauptmann, changed his mind when told that if he didn't testify to the contrary, he himself would be put under arrest.

When Hauptmann's handwriting was first studied after his arrest by two of America's leading handwriting experts, they declared categorically that there was no similarity between it and the writing in the ransom notes; and only changed their minds when told of the $14,000 ransom money having been discovered in his garage. Later, the New York police dictated to Hauptmann a composite statement which included words that had been mis-spelled in the ransom notes. After Hauptmann had taken the dictation correctly several times, the police instructed him to take it again, but this time writing the mis-spellings ('ouer' for 'our', 'note' for 'not', 'bee' for 'be', etc.). Believing that this would help clear his name, Hauptmann readily agreed. At the trial *the dictated statement with the mis-spelled words and not the ones spelled correctly was tendered as state's evidence*; so that the prosecution handwriting experts could say with confidence that Hauptmann was the author of the ransom notes. 'I just can't believe', said one of them naively, 'that this is just a coincidence.' 'Nor can I,' said one of Hauptmann's attorneys, though for a rather different reason; and when he suggested to a handwriting man called Cassidy that Hauptmann had mis-spelled the words because he had been told to, Cassidy said, 'I have got a certain amount of faith in humanity and I just can't think those officers would do a trick like that.' I illustrated in my book a copy in Hauptmann's hand of the dictated statement spelt correctly and, also in his hand, a copy of it with words mis-spelled as in the ransom notes.

But if the identification and handwriting evidence went far towards convincing the jury of Hauptmann's guilt, the evidence about the wood used in the ladder must have sealed it. It was something that the State of New Jersey, fearful that what had passed for evidence so far might not be believed, did not produce until the very end of the prosecution's case. Then a government wood expert by the name of Koehler, believing like everyone else in Hauptmann's guilt, testified that one of the seventeen sections that made up the kidnap ladder had originally been part of the flooring in the attic of Hauptmann's apartment. The state needed this evidence badly, for without it they had nothing to connect Hauptmann with the actual kidnapping and murder; without it they might be denied the death penalty that they – and all America – were seeking.

There were technical arguments to disprove this claim (the knots didn't match, the saw marks were different, one was thinner than the others, etc.) and two wood experts for the defence did refute it (though to no avail) in the witness-box. Aside from this, it does not seem to have occurred to the defence team to discredit by ridicule a claim so utterly inconsistent with the norm of human behaviour. Hauptmann was a professional carpenter, his counsel might have reminded the jury, and the state did not deny that he always kept a stock of ready timber on his premises which he would replenish from a timber merchant a couple of blocks away.

So if he had made sixteen of the ladder's seventeen sections from this timber, why on earth would he want to steal the remaining section from his landlord's flooring up in the attic? Did the jury know what a journey to the attic involved? At that time the only entrance to it was through a trapdoor in the ceiling of the corridor. There was no step-ladder in the apartment high enough to reach it so that to gain entrance you had to remove all the linen from the linen closet in the corridor, climb up the cleats, push open the trapdoor from below, then hoist yourself upwards by the arms; a difficult task at the best of times but doubly so if encumbered with saw, chisel and hammer. The flooring was firmly nailed down, so it would have required a considerable effort on Hauptmann's part to lever up and saw off a section. Having brought it downstairs, he would have then needed to plane off two inches to make it fit into the 1 by 4 standard strips that made up the rest of the ladder's vertical sections. What human being and especially what sort of carpenter would do something so crazy? When I visited the cramped little attic in the course of my researches (a folding ladder has since been installed) I couldn't help but smile at the lunacy of the prosecution's claim; and maybe Hauptmann's defence team would have recognized the lunacy of it too had not the State of New Jersey, who had taken possession of the apartment, incredibly (or perhaps not so incredibly) denied them all access to it.

Yet what could still have saved Hauptmann, if the evidence for it had not been suppressed, was his claim that on the day of the kidnapping he was working as a carpenter on a Manhattan building project until 5 or 6 p.m. – insufficient time to travel back to his apartment in the Bronx, load up the car with the ladder, pick up any accomplices and reach Hopewell in time to abduct the baby by 9.30 p.m. A newspaper reporter tracked the records of the employment agency which confirmed that he did work a full day; and in my researches into back numbers of the *New York Times* I found a paragraph saying that when these records were shown to Mr Foley, the Bronx District Attorney, and to Mr Wilentz, the New Jersey Attorney General, they had been forced to admit that Hauptmann *had* worked that day. They added however, and without a shred of evidence to support it, 'We know he quit work early.' The employment agency records and the timesheets that confirmed that Hauptmann had worked a full day were then 'lost' by the New York City police, and others were doctored to show that Hauptmann did not start work on the building project until three weeks after he actually did, and quit the day after the handing over of the ransom money. In my book I included photographs of both the police receipt for the 1 March timesheets and of the doctored timesheets.

On the positive side there were two reasons for believing Hauptmann to be entirely innocent. The first was the evidence of those who had come into close contact with him in prison. They included the Governor of New Jersey, Harold Hoffman, who had had a long conversation with him in his Death Row cell. Hoffman had expected to see what he called 'a cringing criminal pitifully begging for mercy' and was astonished to find instead 'a man making a vehement claim of innocence, bitter in his denunciation of the police and the prosecution and their methods'. (When I read this I recalled what the Governor of Peterhead prison had said about Meehan – 'It was the way he spoke that convinced me'.) Hauptmann's steadfast Flemington lawyer Lloyd Fisher never wavered in his belief in Hauptmann's innocence, nor did the two prison chaplains, Reverend Werner and Reverend Matthiesen, who ministered to him daily on Death Row. They both declared their belief publicly, which so enraged their parishioners that Werner, although a pastor for thirty years, was declared unfrocked and deprived of his pension and Matthiesen was publicly rebuked by his parish council. There were others too, such as the famous criminal lawyer Clarence Darrow, the writer H. L. Mencken and Eleanor Roosevelt, who believed that Hauptmann had been railroaded, and that with a competent chief counsel instead of the alcoholic wreck Edward Reilly (whose fees were paid by the anti-Hauptmann Hearst Press), he should have been acquitted.

But for me the clinching argument was this. Shortly before Hauptmann's execution Governor Hoffman made a deal with Attorney General Wilentz that Hauptmann's life should be spared if he would agree to making a full account of his participation in the crime. To this offer Hauptmann said, 'If I had taken part in the crime, I would have admitted to it long ago. But as I am quite innocent of it, there is nothing I can say.' Then the *New York Evening Journal* offered to pay his widow $90,000 if he would deliver to them a full account of his role in the affair, to be published after his execution. Knowing that he was going to leave his beloved Anna penniless, Hauptmann must have been sorely tempted to invent a story to give her and his son Manfred financial security; and it says much for his integrity that, although facing death, he refused even to consider it.

Those who try and explain away those two refusals of Hauptmann to 'confess' before he died do so by saying that he was so ashamed of what he had done that he only wanted to die. There is not an iota of evidence to support this: indeed the opposite is true, that he fought for his life and to establish his innocence right up to the eve of his execution. 'HAUPTMANN REMAINS SILENT TO THE END' said the *New York Times* the day after, unable to believe in anything but his guilt. Far from being silent, he had, ever since his arrest and with every breath in his body, asserted his innocence to anyone who would listen.

The documentary that Sue Crowther and I made on the case, *Who Killed the Lindbergh Baby?* was well received on both sides of the Atlantic. But a fifty- or sixty-minute film with a commentary of around seven thousand words could not do justice to such a difficult and complex case, and it was on the publication of my book, *The Airman and the Carpenter*, that I pinned my hopes of a re-assessment of the case by the New Jersey authorities and of Anna Hauptmann seeing her husband's name cleared before she died. In this I was sorely disappointed. Not a single critic of the book in America or Britain disagreed fundamentally with my findings; many said that the case I had made out for Hauptmann's innocence was overwhelming, and hundreds of private letters from people anxious to see the record corrected said the same. But the State of New Jersey would not budge.

There were, I think, two reasons. The first was that Anna Hauptmann's suits against the State for her husband's wrongful conviction and execution were hardly calculated to make the State's officials well disposed towards reassessment; and the suits having failed (as they were bound to after such a lapse of time), they were content to let things rest. Also, although the case was now more than fifty years old, it had been at the time so traumatic, such a *cause célèbre*, that echoes from it still lingered in the public mind. Hauptmann's arrest and conviction had been hailed as a triumph for Jersey justice and a feather in the cap of the New Jersey police; such an achievement was not to be relinquished easily. There was also the personal factor. The longer a person clings to a belief, however flawed, the more difficult it becomes to wean him from it, especially when he knows that millions of others believe the same; and there are private citizens in New Jersey and throughout America today who become (as I can confirm from personal conversations) quite enraged at any suggestion that their lifelong beliefs have been a delusion.

Indeed so concerned were the New Jersey authorities by Mrs Hauptmann's suits and the books by Tony Scaduto and myself that they gave their backing to a recent book on the affair, *The Lindbergh Case* by Jim Fisher (1987); and the police officer in charge of the Lindbergh archive room at police headquarters became consultant to the project. Mr Fisher is described as an associate professor of Criminal Justice at Edinboro University in Pennsylvania, and if that is so, I shudder to think of the standards of scholarship prevailing there. Nor will it enhance the reputation of the Rutgers University Press who published it; for in reaffirming the *status quo ante*, that Hauptmann was rightly convicted and executed, Mr Fisher has, unbelievably, omitted almost all the information made available in recent years and used by Mrs Hauptmann's lawyer, Tony Scaduto and myself to prove the exact opposite. His object doubtless was to pull the wool over the eyes of all those beginning to be awakened to the fact of an injustice as great if not greater than those suffered by Dreyfus or Sacco and Vanzetti, and because the case is so complex that only those who have spent years studying it are familiar with all its ramifications, it may well have partly succeeded. The critics of the *New York Times* and the *New York Review of Books* were clearly baffled by it, and although Tony Scaduto and I wrote corrective letters in their correspondence columns, the bafflement was not entirely dispelled. I was also disappointed to hear that a treatment based on my book and submitted by the independent Hollywood producer Bill Self to all three American networks had been turned down. Professionally, I was told, they all thought it a fascinating story that would make a gripping screenplay, but as network producers they did not feel they could support a programme whose conclusions were contrary to those arrived at by the American courts, and not yet reversed by them. The New Jersey establishment had triumphed again!

That one day, when memories and prejudices have faded, the record will finally be corrected, I have no doubts. The good name of American justice as much as the wrong done to Richard Hauptmann deserves it. I trust it will not take another fifty years.

*

394

Although I had looked on each miscarriage of justice that I had studied as a unique aberration, I was increasingly disturbed by the common denominator that seemed to exist between them – police falsification of evidence in order to secure a conviction. The Lindbergh case had shown that this was not a defect peculiar to Britain, but one that could be expected wherever the adversary system of justice was practised.[1] In the Evans case the police had browbeaten Evans into signing a false confession to murder and persuaded witnesses to alter statements that might have cleared him, in the Meehan case they had planted incriminating pieces of paper in the pocket of the co-accused, while in the Ward case, the Luton Post Office murder and the Lindbergh case they had bribed or blackmailed witnesses into giving false evidence as well as giving false evidence themselves. In other cases which had been brought to my notice, such as Hanratty, Confait, Fellowes, the Mcdonagh brothers, Long, etc., their evidence had been less than satisfactory; while their methods in obtaining 'confessions' from those convicted of the IRA Birmingham and Guildford pub bombings fifteen years ago, whom many believe to be entirely innocent, are at this moment of writing still a matter of debate. In only one of the above cases (the Luton Post Office murder) did the police deliberately frame innocent men. In the others they had deluded themselves into thinking the accused were guilty but, lacking proof, had egged the pudding to ensure, as they saw it, that justice was done. It never seems to have occurred to them that one reason they lacked evidence to convict was because the accused were not guilty but innocent.

One day in conversation with Tom Sargant, for twenty-five years the much-admired secretary of the lawyers organization JUSTICE, he mentioned the inquisitorial system of justice as practised in France and elsewhere on the continent, and said that not only did he think that miscarriages of justice in the most serious cases there (murder, manslaughter, rape, etc.) were less likely to occur, but that in other ways it was a superior system. So I went over to France to study it, spoke to a number of advocates and officials, and attended several courts, including

[1] Writing in the *Stanford Law Review* of November 1987 the American Professors Hugo Bedau and Michael Radelet claimed that since the beginning of this century in America 350 accused were wrongly found guilty in capital cases and of these twenty five (including Hauptmann) were wrongly executed. In the majority of cases dubious police evidence was crucial to conviction.

the Tribunal Correctionel where justice is dispensed by three judges sitting alone whose verdict has to be unanimous, and the highest criminal court of all, the Cours d'Assise, where three judges and nine jurors sit on the bench together.

In the lower courts where the gathering of evidence is left entirely to the police, I saw no evidence to suggest that justice miscarried any more or less than in Britain. But miscarriages arising from verdicts in the Cours d'Assise were, I was told, extremely rare. And there is good reason for it. In the very serious cases with which the Cours d'Assise deals, the preliminary investigations are not in the hands of the police but of an examining magistrate called the *juge d'instruction*. He *directs* the police in their inquiries, and interrogates any suspects or witnesses for as long and as often as he may wish, including the bringing together of witnesses whose evidence conflicts. There is nothing like the pressure on him, as there is on the police in Britain, to get results. When, after months of painstaking investigation, he finally commits an accused to the Cours d'Assise for trial, the likelihood is that he is guilty (hence the British misconception that in French courts you are assumed to be guilty until proved innocent), and this is reflected in a conviction rate of more than 90 per cent. Unlike the police in Britain the *juge d'instruction* will never chuck a name into the ring on the off-chance it will stick; and had such an official been conducting preliminary investigations into the cases of Evans, Meehan, Ward, Cooper and McMahon and Hauptmann, I think it improbable that any of them would have gone forward for trial, let alone have been convicted.

But it is in the trial procedure that the difference between the adversary and inquisitorial systems are most marked. The adversary system is a comparatively late development in English law and essentially artificial; is in no way a search for the truth but a contest to determine the narrow issue of whether the defendant can be proved guilty. It is a system in which the defendant, who probably knows more about the crime than anyone present, is not obliged to say what he knows; in which a spurious sense of drama is created which encourages counsel, who are the dominant figures in court, to strike postures and attitudes and often indulge in sarcasm (as with Mr Christmas Humphreys and the wretched Timothy Evans); in which some questions which could provide a short cut to the truth are not allowed to be asked, and others which are asked are not allowed to be answered; in which the evidence of witnesses is shaped by what they think prosecuting and defence counsel want them to say; in which other witnesses whose evidence might reveal the truth and influence the verdict are not called for fear of saying the wrong thing; in which police evidence given or suppressed can and often does convict an innocent man, and the skills of counsel can and sometimes do set free a guilty one. I cannot imagine that anyone sitting down today to devise a system of justice would, in a hundred years, come up with anything so childishly idiotic as this.

By contrast the inquisitorial form of trial is deliberately low-key and undramatic (and quite unsuited for adaptation to third-rate courtroom dramas as happens in Britain and America). In the Cours d'Assise the questioning is done by the presiding judge, counsels' role being limited to opening and closing speeches and sometimes suggesting to the presiding judge questions he may have omitted to put. Questioning by the judge saves the time taken up in British courts by prosecution and defence counsel covering the same ground, often at tedious length, and is less confusing for the jury; and questions put in a quiet, non-partisan but forceful way can often produce a more truthful response than a more aggressive approach. This is particularly true when it comes to the examination of the accused, whose failure to answer questions will be held by the court (as it cannot be in Britain) as indicative of guilt. Expert witnesses such as pathologists and psychiatrists are also treated intelligently, the court endeavouring to find a consensus; whereas in the adversary system each side chooses its own expert witnesses and opposing counsel try and make them contradict each other – humiliating for them and again confusing for the jury. And lastly, the trial itself does not come grinding to a halt, as so often happens in Britain, when the jury have to leave the court while the judge gives a ruling on admissible evidence. In a system whose object is to find the truth, there is no evidence, so long as it is relevant, that is not admissible.

There are some who think that judges and jurors sitting together on the bench makes the jurors susceptible to judicial influence, but I have also heard it said that they are made to feel less the detached observers they are in Britain and more a responsible and integral part of the trial process. When it comes to reaching a verdict, judges and jurors confer together on both verdict and sentence. Of the twelve votes cast there must be at least an eight to four majority for verdict and a simple majority of seven to five for sentence.

When a miscarriage of justice *has* occurred, when an accused has been wrongly tried, convicted and sentenced to a long term of imprisonment, what are the chances of having the miscarriage rectified? Depressingly, very few. The Home Office is deeply reluctant to reopen a case unless forced to – Tom Sargant once told me that he did not know of a single case which, on petition by a prisoner alone, had been referred back to the courts. The Court of Appeal too, although given greater latitude in recent years to hear fresh evidence and order re-trials, prefers on the whole to confine itself to matters of legal procedure. One cannot entirely blame them because with their heavy workload of case following case, restricting them to a day or two's reading of the relevant papers, their review of any case must inevitably be superficial. They can have no real grasp of the background to it nor of the characters of those involved, and in their unwillingness to disturb the verdict of the trial jury they give scant attention to the possibility of it having reached a false verdict, not because it was contrary to the evidence, but because the evidence tendered to it (including police evidence) was false.

But the greatest barrier to the rectification of miscarriages of justice, and particularly where the miscarriage has come about as a result of police malpractice, lies in the attitudes of the judges themselves. I have already mentioned the failure of Mr Scott-Henderson and later Sir Daniel Brabin in the Evans case and of Lord Hunter in the Meehan case to face up to police malpractice; the same can be said of Mr Lewis Hawser, QC, in his report rejecting any miscarriage in the Hanratty case, while Sir Henry Fisher's report on the Confait case was also flawed. A similar attitude persists in the Court of Appeal, where judges will invariably dismiss an appeal if the alternative is to admit to police malpractice. One of the worst malpractices is the obtaining of false 'confessions' from suspects by duress. This has been reported as having happened in many cases apart from that of Timothy Evans; among them those convicted of the IRA bombings of pubs in Guildford and Birmingham, who remain in prison to this day. Appeals in both these cases were dismissed, but this has not dissuaded those who have studied them in depth from continuing to believe that those convicted are innocent. Yet rather than face up to police malpractice, this is what Lord Denning said when refusing legal aid to the six men convicted of the Birmingham bombings, who were bringing an action against the police for injuries inflicted on them when in police custody:

> Just consider the course of events if this action is allowed to proceed to trial. If the six men fail, it will mean that much time and money will have been expended by many people for no good purpose. If the six men win, it will mean that the police were guilty of perjury, that they were guilty of violence and threats, that the confessions were involuntary and were improperly admitted in evidence and that the convictions were erroneous. That would mean the Home Secretary would either have to recommend they be pardoned or he would have to remit the case to the Court of Appeal. *This is such an appalling vista that every sensible person in the land would say: 'It cannot be right that these actions should go any further.'* [author's italics]

If this does not mean that it is better that six possibly innocent men should continue to rot in prison rather than run the risk of a number of police officers being found guilty of perjury, violence and threats, it is difficult to know what it does mean. And if it does mean that, then it seems to me that judges who refuse to entertain the idea of police corruption when it is the most likely explanation of the case, or part of the case, against the accused become no less corrupt themselves. It is moreover a vicious circle, for the police, relying on the judges' support, are encouraged to continue their malpractices.

Judges are the only senior members of any profession that I know who still live and perform largely in a world of their own making. I say this without personal rancour, for several are my friends and those of us who have been privileged to have been entertained at one of the Inns of Court guest nights know what entertaining company they are. For years however judges were cocooned from the rough and tumble of public life by being forbidden to utter publicly except in court; as Lord Chancellor Kilmuir, a man of very limited vision, said in his guidelines to judges in 1955, 'So long as a judge keeps silent, his reputation for wisdom and impartiality remains unassailable', which might be thought to have been pushing it a bit. Recently, under a new

Lord Chancellor, they have been encouraged to dip a cautious toe into the waters of public debate. The walls of Jericho have not come tumbling down; and refreshingly informative it has been for the rest of us.

Yet judges still enjoy a reputation for wisdom which has been inflated out of all proportion to their talents. The Scottish judge Lord McCluskey has told me how astonished he was on becoming a member of the House of Lords by the deference paid to members who were lawyers. 'The utterances of judges in particular', he wrote to me, 'seemed to be treated with something approaching reverence.' The attitude that most people have of judges being beyond criticism is bad for them, bad for us, and bad for justice. It would be a step in the right direction if they could be made to abandon those ridiculous wigs (put aside by gentlemen in the eighteenth century and by bishops in the nineteenth). If they can be discarded in child abuse cases, they should be discarded in adult cases too, for fear must always be an enemy to communication and understanding; a plain gown with white bands is all that is needed for the dignity of the court and the dispensation of justice.

And, as I wrote after the Ward case, judges might care to think again about the preservation of their archaic language ('As your ·lordship pleases', 'resiling', '*ex parte*', 'avocation', 'pray in aid', etc.), so unsettling for the layman. The Bar Association is currently considering whether to allow some trials to be televised, the adversarial system with its pseudo-dramatic basis being tailor-made for it (I doubt if the question would ever be raised in France). There would be problems (such as who would be responsible for the editing, all trials being full of *longueurs* and repetitions) but even if only a few trials were thought suitable for television, the arrival of the cameras would, I believe, do more than anything else (as they may do in the House of Commons) to encourage the modernization of communication and procedure.

The public's reluctance to criticize judicial practices springs from two things: the belief of the average citizen that he (or she) knows so little about them that he is not in a position to criticize, that there is a mystique about the operations of the law which are beyond his ken (and, one might add, which is how the judges want to keep it); and secondly because until some major injustice befalls him personally, he really couldn't care less. As Tom Wolfe says in *The Bonfire of the Vanities*, 'A liberal is a conservative who has been arrested.'

Can therefore nothing be done to review those cases like Evans and Hanratty in their day, like the Guildford four and the Birmingham six at the time of writing, which have outrun every appeal available, yet still continue to trouble the public mind? A few years ago a parliamentary committee was set up to examine the whole question of miscarriages of justice. They recommended the establishment of a kind of court of last resort which would have no official basis but could re-examine a case at leisure and free of the normal constricting rules of evidence. It was in fact to be an *inquisitorial* court whose brief would be to reach the truth, so far as it was able.

Inevitably the Home Office turned the idea down, no doubt fearful of what a can of worms it might unloose. But it is my earnest hope that one day, until such time as we review the whole system, a court of last resort will come about; that while it should be chaired by a judge or senior barrister to lend tone and order to the proceedings, he should be assisted by two lay assessors, who would inquire rigorously into the circumstances of how statements came to be made, and give to police evidence the same scrutiny as to any other evidence. There is nothing very radical in this. Every judge in his summing-up tells every jury that while he will explain to them the law, it is for them as laymen to come to a verdict on the facts.

For a layman like myself, untrained in the law, to fight what has been virtually a one-man campaign in favour of the inquisitorial system they practise on the continent rather than the adversary one we employ here may be thought by some to be spitting in the wind. But two years ago, and after I had written many articles and letters in the press, came a tiny breakthrough. My old friend Jeremy Hutchinson, QC, one of the most successful criminal advocates of his day, invited me to expound my ideas to the first conference of the English Bar Association at the Connaught Rooms in London. I was pleased by the reception both in the hall and in the press: several barristers told me that I had made them think of criminal law procedure in a way they had never thought of it before. And stemming from this I received a further invitation in 1987 from the organizers of the three-yearly New Zealand Bar Conference attended by 2000 delegates from those countries that practise the adversarial system (mostly the Commonwealth and America) to repeat the address there. And so I took my place – and felt greatly honoured – on a panel with a past chairman of the American Bar Association, the Law Lord, Lord Griffiths, and a New Zealand High Court judge, with Robert Alexander, QC, one of England's most prominent silks, in the chair. Both Lord Griffiths and the New Zealand judge admitted, perhaps for the first time publicly, that the inquisitorial system did have some advantages over our own.

British lawyers are so conservative by nature that I doubt if I will see any major changes to our present procedures in my lifetime; although the simple yet radical reform of appointing a corps of examining magistrates to interview suspects in all serious cases would have two great advantages: bringing to an end the suspect's right to silence and helping to bring to an end some of the worst of police malpractices. I see no reason either why the accused should not be called to answer the charges against him at his trial; although so long as we maintain the adversary system, this would have to be conducted by the presiding judge rather than partisan counsel.

That further changes in the direction of an inquisitorial system will come in time, I feel certain; and I would like to think that in my speeches to the English and New Zealand Bar conferences, I had made the first, tentative steps towards them.[1]

23

Reflections on Television and the Almighty

I turn now to television in which I have participated since the beginning of the commercial network in 1955, and about which a very great deal of nonsense has been written. One particular nonsense is that most of what it produces is rubbish. Well, most plays, books, films, magazines and newspapers are rubbish, so why pick on television? In fact, as anyone who watches regularly will tell you, both BBC and ITV consistently produce good programmes which may have taken six months or a year to make, occupy perhaps an hour's screen time and are then forgotten as though they had never been.

[1] A breakthrough came in the summer of 1988 when I found an unexpected ally in the shape of Sir Peter Imbert, Commissioner of the Metropolitan Police. In the course of interviewing him for *The Times*, he told me: 'The adversary system is a game that prevents us from discovering the truth. I think the time has come to look at our whole criminal justice system afresh.'

When *Did You See?* came to an end in 1988 and I said goodbye after its eight-year run, some people thought I was retiring for good; they included Richard Ingrams who sent me an E. J. Thribb (17) poem beginning 'So, farewell Ludovic Kennedy'! But with a few shots still in the locker I aim to go on for a little while yet. One or two projects have recently fallen through. I was hoping to interview the Archbishop of Canterbury on the subject of 'What (or perhaps Who) is a Christian?', but after laying on a delightful lunch at Lambeth Palace, he wrote a charming letter in his own hand declining on the grounds that if he said what he really wanted to say, he could be in trouble with the Evangelicals (not a pop group but a band of religious fundamentalists). I then tried York, but he talked in such densely, indeed incomprehensibly, theological terms that that had to be abandoned too. I also had an opportunity of interviewing a retired SS officer by the name of Schulze-Cossens who had been Hitler's ADC between 1941 and 1944; and when this tall, still handsome man showed me in a locked room up a stair in his Dusseldorf flat his Aladdin's cave of Hitler memorabilia, a gold watch inscribed with Hitler's signature, cufflinks from Hitler, medals, flags and many photographs of him with Hitler at the Wolf's Lair in the forests of East Prussia, I looked forward to arranging a revealing interview. But to my surprise, he had almost nothing to say. At first I thought that this reticence could have been the quality that made him a good ADC. Then I realized it was probably Hitler who had had nothing to say – or at any rate very little worth hearing or remembering. For the paradox of Hitler was that while his influence on crowds was magnetic, in private, as accounts of his table talk reveal, he seems to have been one of the most boring as well as one of the most deeply unattractive leaders who ever lived.

During my thirty-four years in television I have, as the reader will be aware, taken part in a very great number of studio programmes and documentaries; and I have done my best to fulfil the terms of the BBC charter to educate, inform and entertain. Because I believe television to be a great educator in that it has introduced us to people, places, situations and events we would not otherwise have seen, and is also a fount of information, I believe my career has been well spent.

At least that is my view from the business end of the camera. From the other end I see it rather differently. As a viewer I think of television as being comparable to a long train journey. As one gazes vacantly out of the window a succession of ever-changing images passes by. Occasionally something – the look of a house, a cricketer bowling, flowers in a garden – momentarily diverts the attention until another image takes its place, then it too vanishes and is forgotten, and presently, as with the television, we look away or pick up a newspaper or magazine. For the essence of television is its ephemerality: it is a world of flickering images, each dying at the moment it is born. In the years that I have been involved in it, it has become part of the furniture of almost every household in the country. Like the water tap or the electric light switch, we can take it for granted, turning it on or off at will, shifting from this channel to that, seeing a horse being born, survivors being pulled from wreckage, Miss World being crowned, one fish gobbling up another. Unlike the cinema, which involves leaving our homes to share an experience, paying money to sit in silence together before a large screen, television has its constant distractions: the telephone, other people's chit-chat, the need to feed the dog/cat/baby, someone at the door, and above all perhaps sleep: I know of no other agency except alcohol which can so rapidly and effortlessly bring the head to the chest, and the two combined are as good as any sleeping pill.

But that, to my astonishment, is not how some people see it. Mrs Whitehouse: '*The power of television to reshape our morals.*' Lord Deedes: '*This explosive influence over the human mind.*' Mr Paul Johnson: '*A dangerous medium which must be effectively supervised.*' Mr Peregrine Worsthorne, Mr Peter Ackroyd, Mr Norman Tebbit (the only politician in my lifetime who has made me understand how civil wars start), and others have all come out with similar views. With respect to the lot of them, they are talking bilge. For a start they are confusing influence with size, imagining that a thing said simultaneously to ten or fifteen million people will carry more influence than something said privately at a pub or dinner-party or picked up elsewhere in the course of the day. In fact a thing said or done on television is no more or less likely to influence one to a belief or course of action than things said or done anywhere else. Secondly they either forget or do not realize that the tendency to reject a given view on television is no less great than the tendency to accept it. If you disbelieve this, observe the reactions of Labour Party supporters in a Gorbals pub listening to a Conservative Party broadcast, or those of a

Conservative Party audience in South Bucks listening to Mr Hattersley or Mr Kinnock. These critics assume most viewers to be, unlike themselves, mindless morons (they themselves of course are immune from influence). I think they also deeply resent the fact that they have no control over what is offered to them.

Mrs Thatcher talks of the necessity of not giving terrorists the 'oxygen of publicity'. Her assumption is that the more coverage they are given, the more favourably will people regard their cause. I have never seen evidence of this. No one but the most extreme Israelis would deny that the PLO has a substantive case, but what reason is there to suppose that blowing up airliners in the desert, hijacking others and killing the passengers has in any way advanced its cause? Indeed in view of the fanaticism and brutality it has displayed there are many who consider its actions to have been counterproductive.

In Britain it is programmes that touch on Northern Ireland and the IRA that drive politicians, and particularly Conservative politicians, into near hysteria, as a few examples will show. In 1971 the BBC decided to put on a major discussion programme about Northern Ireland with representatives of various factions there (though not the IRA) participating, with three wise men, Lords Devlin and Caradon and Sir John Foster, as a sort of tribunal. A few days before the programme was due to go out, the Home Secretary, Reggie Maudling, asked the BBC to drop it on the grounds that it could be 'potentially dangerous' and could do 'serious harm', though without spelling out the nature of the danger or the harm. The Chairman of the BBC board, Lord Hill, himself a former Conservative politician, had the courage to reject the request, but Robin Day who, for all his gifts, is essentially an establishment man, withdrew as presenter, and I took his place. All this of course made banner headlines and a running story in the newspapers, which cannot have been what Reggie had in mind. In the event the programme went off perfectly amicably, as most of us knew it would, and within a few days and like everything else on television, it was forgotten. Far from being dangerous or causing harm, it was, as one BBC executive wrote 'responsible to the point of dullness'.

Then in 1985 came the *Real Lives* controversy, another BBC programme, showing filmed profiles of a Loyalist extremist and an IRA extremist, the idea being to show the kind of men they were and how, in their attitudes and lives, they compared. Once again and without even having seen the programme the Home Secretary, now Leon Brittan, asked the BBC to ban it. The board of governors, against all tradition, then demanded to see it themselves and led by Sir William Rees-Mogg, the nanny-like vice-chairman, decided to bow to Leon Brittan's request. This led to a strike by National Union of Journalist members at both the BBC and ITN, and voices all over the world ridiculing the BBC's much vaunted claims to be independent of government. But Alasdair Milne, then Director General, was determined the programme should go out, and it did go out in the autumn. Neither of the two men profiled were up to much; and again people wondered what on earth the fuss had been about.

And then in the spring of 1988 came the furore following the shooting by SAS men in Gibraltar of three IRA terrorists who were planning to plant a large bomb there – an incident which again led to controversy both at home and abroad. Believing that the government wanted the incident to be disposed of with the minimum of publicity, Thames Television and the BBC launched separate inquiries into the shootings and interviewed two people in Gibraltar who said they had seen the soldiers shoot the terrorists without giving them the opportunity to surrender. Once again, led by the Prime Minister and with the support of Conservative opinion in Parliament and the press, there were shouts of protest. 'Trial by television,' cried Mrs Thatcher. 'Prejudicial to the coroner's inquiry,' claimed others. To call the programme a trial was nonsense because no one was on trial or likely to be, and the coroner and his jury would be perfectly capable of assessing the witnesses' evidence for themselves. What the two programmes did ensure was that two witnesses who by accident or design might not have been called, would be called. Of course the root of the matter was not that the witnesses had been approached but what they had actually said. Had they said they had seen the terrorists reaching for their guns and that was why the SAS men had shot them, I doubt if we would have heard a single protest. What made the Prime Minister and her supporters so enraged was the assertion that the sporty fair play British had shot people in cold blood without giving them the chance to surrender; yet they might have added to their advantage that there was a case to be made out for getting rid of the terrorists *without* allowing them to surrender, given the hideous nature of the enterprise they were embarked on.

It is surely less an imperative to deprive the terrorists of 'the oxygen of publicity' that leads the government to keep the IRA off our screens, than something much more fundamental and personal – the resentment of many at their intrusion by television into the nation's homes. If that is so, and I think it so, then it would be more honest of the government to admit it and forget all about the imaginary 'oxygen of publicity'.

All governments expect the broadcasting organizations of their countries to support them, and in dictatorships they differ at their peril. In democracies the position is trickier, for there are some issues on which the broadcasters can back the government and others where they cannot. For instance when Mrs Thatcher asks the BBC if they are for or against terrorism, they can say they are against those acts of bloodshed and violence that constitute terrorism. What they cannot say is that they are for or against the terrorists' long-term aims – in the case of the IRA the ejection of the British administration from Northern Ireland – for there are some people in Britain who think that option desirable, and it is the duty of broadcasters to reflect all shades of opinion.

It is the refusal of the broadcasting media to support the government as it would often wish, combined with their own readiness to mount programmes critical of it, that our present leaders find so galling. The longer a government remains in power, the more it thinks itself beyond criticism, and that to be captious of it is a kind of *lèse majesté*. It was much the same in the years of Labour rule, and it is the reason why this government after nearly ten years of office, and with the help of allies in the press, recently mounted a smear campaign against the BBC with the object of drawing its teeth. And because the government believes that those who are not for it must necessarily be against it, any critics are at once labelled left-wing, just as critics of the Labour government were labelled right-wing, and critics of the South African government are labelled communists.

Of course the BBC, like all publishers, has had its excesses, but they have not been serious enough to justify such vilification. And the vilification has, to some degree, succeeded. Whether the BBC will ever regain its nerve, it is impossible to say, but at the time of writing it has become a shadow of itself and its whole future as a non-commercial and effective public service broadcasting organization would seem to be in the balance. Still regarded overseas as a fount of truth and one of the brightest jewels in the British crown, it would be a tragedy if it was allowed to wither on the vine for no other reason than that a prickly government could not see that it constituted as much a part of democracy as itself.

We remained in Edinburgh seven years, then moved back south. All the children were now in the south or overseas, I was finding the weekly commuting to Heathrow for television increasingly irksome and both of us missed our friends in Fleet Street and television, the theatre and the law, politics and publishing. Beautiful though Edinburgh is and happy as my childhood days there had been, it has its social limitations. It was not that people were not hospitable or gregarious, but that conversation at most dinner-parties seldom became airborne. There was a sort of inbred formality about social relationships that I found deeply depressing, a reluctance to say or do anything that might remotely provoke or offend; and if anyone did ever go out on a limb, as people occasionally did when primed, their sallies were apt to wither in the air. It might be asked what else you would expect from a solid *bourgeoisie* of lawyers and accountants, doctors, dentists and businessmen. But in bawdy, earthy, warm-hearted Glasgow, only forty miles away, its professional people are a different breed. ('Here,' they claim, 'if you arrive unexpectedly at a friend's house, the first thing they'll say is, "You'll stay to tea?" But across in Edinburgh the first thing they'll say is, "You'll have *had* your tea."') In business affairs the canniness and caution of the Edinburgh Scot has been his strength; socially it is less attractive.

After eighteen months of house-hunting from London, we found what I hope will be our last, a small Georgian house in a Wiltshire village set among the Downs, with a large and lovely garden at the back, an old church opposite and a village shop and post office at the head of the street. Here Moira and I now live on our own, as we did at Clabon Mews when we were first married nearly forty years ago. Fiona and Alastair are at present in Hong Kong, she in the Hong Kong and Shanghai Bank, he as an officer in the Gurkhas. Recently our second daughter Rachel was married in the village church and we gave 150 guests lunch in a marquee in the garden afterwards. Her husband Bill Hall landed in the best man's helicopter in a field behind the church, and he and Rachel went away in an aeroplane which had landed on one of Jeremy Tree's gallops. Two of the bridesmaids were our flaxen-haired grandchildren, Ailsa's Saskia and Cait. I am immensely proud of all our darling children, of who they are and of what they have become.

Looking back over the last fifty years, I suppose I can say that I have managed to achieve what I set out to achieve, though not quite in the manner I had intended. I planned to become a writer and a broadcaster and I have been a writer and a broadcaster with some success (though those in the television world and the literary world each think I belong to the other). What I did not foresee was what I would principally write about. Why the Navy, and why miscarriages of justice? I suppose it could be said that my love for the Navy was a reflection of my love for my father, and my absorption with the criminal law was a reflection of my love for my grandfather in whose library I was first introduced to the subject. But why so keen *to correct injustices*? Was it that my own feelings as a boy of being tossed about by an uncaring fate, made me want to identify with others likewise tossed about, to speak for those unable to speak for themselves? I do not know, and in any case I do not think it much matters.

Certainly I have travelled a long way from being unduly deferential to authority as a boy to being freely critical of it in later years. Perhaps the reader may feel that at times I have been over-critical, but when I see what the exercise of power can do to people, when I am made aware of deceit, deviousness, prejudice, blindness, pomposity and cant in high places, I feel an overpowering urge to reach for hatchet and scalpel. And yet if power does corrupt some, I can think of others quite unsullied by it – public figures like Devlin and Scarman in the law, Hume and Runcie in the Church, Peter Carrington and John Biffen, Jo Grimond and Michael Foot in politics; there are many others who all share an inner integrity which, I think, has something to do with that particular brand of humour that confers on those who have it a sense of balance and perspective.

Regrets I have a few, as the song says. I'd like to have had a lower handicap at golf and been a better shot and learnt to cook a little and play the clarinet like Benny Goodman, and had a tumble with one or two girls I didn't have a tumble with (as Maugham said, it's the temptations one has resisted that one remembers and regrets, not those one has succumbed to). I wish

I hadn't had such a hang-up about money, having earned a fair amount of the stuff but never having known quite how to cope with it. I only visit the City when I have to, and cannot get away from it quick enough; and, like reaching for the switch when one hears the approach of *The Archers* or *Neighbours*, I skip as fast as I can through the financial pages of the newspapers with their queer jargon about rights issues and bear markets and pictures of entrepreneurial gents and yobboes growing richer by the hour, whom I view with a mixture of envy, wonder and horror. And although a feature of advancing age is that the things that worried you as a youth (turning up for a dinner-party in the wrong gear) no longer do so, I am more conscious than ever of occasions when I have said or done the wrong thing, usually when drunk, and later have acutely regretted it. When I happen to recall those occasions, I am often so embarrassed that I find myself saying '*Arseholes!*' out loud. It brings some relief. I said it in a lift the other day, forgetting where I was, and got some very rum looks.

I have never been offered any British honour (though I was delighted when Strathclyde University made me an Honorary Doctor of Laws as a rejoinder to the Scottish legal establishment's entrenched view of the Meehan case), nor have I ever coveted any except, as a clubman, membership of that exclusive club which demands no entrance fee and pays you attendance money when you grace it with your presence: I mean the House of Lords, with its excellent and enviable debates. I am not attracted by becoming a peer *as such* (though it might come in handy in making reservations), indeed I find the whole concept of creaking politicians, trade union leaders and others put out to grass becoming *lords* as ludicrous as the continued statutory right of hereditary peers to have any say in the country's legislation. But I am a great believer in a revisionary and on occasions originating second chamber, and I hope a time will come when instead of *lords*, with all that implies of elitism and snobbery, there will be a second house of elected and appointed senators.

I have in fact twice had the opportunity of embracing the ermine and twice had to decline it. When I left the Liberal party on the Scottish issue in 1966, Jeremy Thorpe, then staying with David Steel in the Borders, came over to Makerstoun to sound me out about joining the Liberal benches in the Lords; but in the circumstances it was not a time to consider it. I had a second bite of the cherry a few years ago when, before chairing a meeting at which David Steel was speaking in the Fulham by-election, he invited me to fight the seemingly winnable seat of Edinburgh Central in the coming general election, with the generous promise that if I wasn't elected, he would recommend me for the Lords. But the prospect of returning to a constituency which I had but recently left and entering Parliament for the first time at the age of sixty-seven to the detriment of writing and broadcasting activities in which I was immersed was not appealing, and regretfully I had to turn the offer down. With even greater regret I observed the Alliance candidate in Edinburgh Central come bottom of the poll; and, turning things on their head, consoled myself with the unlikely proposition that had *I* been standing, I might have won!

I have left to the very end the question of the Almighty, and there can be no better place to put down my confused thoughts about him (or, if you like, Him) than this quiet corner in the library of my club. I have dined and slept in this club and its predecessor, played backgammon, read the papers, entertained people to drinks or lunch for the past forty-seven years; when I have clocked up fifty, my annual subscription will be waived. I am fond of the place; it has been a very present help in time of trouble.

The reader may remember what an impression Tom Paine's book *The Age of Reason* had made on me when I was in Newfoundland during the war, releasing me from the bondage to Christian dogma that had held me, however unwillingly, through ten years of school services and evening prayer and readings from the Bible; and that I couldn't help but feel some resentment at the huge confidence trick that had been played on me by teachers and others who instilled in me as *historical fact* what many if not most must have known that at best was an exaggeration and at worst pure invention. Yet if it had taken Paine to convince me that Christ, inasmuch as we knew anything about him, was no more than human (attributions of divinity being man-made, how could it be otherwise?) and that the various supernatural events attributed to him were beyond credibility, I was still left with puzzlement as to the existence or non-existence of God. And in order to try and find a solution to the puzzlement, I invested for many years in books that I thought might throw some light. They fill two shelves of my study today and have titles like *The Biology of God, The New Theologian, A History of Christianity, Myths and Gods, The Sea of Faith, The Nature of Belief*, and so on.

Now what I had never been able to embrace, any more than the miraculous events pertaining to the life of Christ, was the idea of an external, universal, transcendent god, the one whom Milton called 'The Eternal King who rules all Heaven and Earth, Angels and Sons of Man', which seemed to me to have all the texture of wet cement; and just as the idea of the devil or Satan, until recently also believed in as an external, universal reality, had now crumbled, so I had seen in my lifetime the idea of God Almighty begin to crumble too. But if I did not believe in *that* sort of god, did I believe in *any* sort of god? Was I an atheist? Or an agnostic? The words were and to some degree still are pejorative, for they posit Christian belief as the norm and any divergence from it a personal and moral lapse. But to be an atheist was by definition to *assert* the non-existence of an external god, and I didn't feel assertive about the thing at all: like millions of others I just couldn't go along with it.

In any case one of the difficulties in distancing oneself from the concept of God altogether was that whatever else he was, he still existed as an idea in the mind. The idea of the devil, with horns and tail, once so vivid and frightening, had ceased to be part of current parlance: people no longer told others to go to the devil or the devil take them. But the idea of God persists. We all know what the word means: printers print his name with a capital G, people invoke his name and swear by him every minute of the day, pictorial images of him still have a reality which those of the devil do not. So if he exists as an idea in the mind, then surely the gap between acknowledging that and the additional idea that he exists externally is very narrow.

I sustained this not very original or satisfying belief for many years, and then in time the revelation came to me – and I cannot think why it had not come before – that the mind was the *only place* where God or gods had ever existed, and that anything else was a projection of the human imagination; in short that men created gods, not gods men. The Greeks and Romans, Egyptians and Scandinavians, had all believed in the external existence of their numerous gods, but no one today saw these as anything more than myth. Why then should future historians regard the Christian (or Jewish or Muslim) God as other than myth? And when I read that the German theologian Dietrich Bonhoeffer had said that the last refuge of God today was in the individual human being, I felt the excitement of recognition. Kant and Kierkegaard had encouraged the same viewpoint, that the idea of a transcendent, external god was now outmoded, and that the only true gods were those that existed within. It was quite unrealistic too to say that there was only one God: there were as many gods as there were people to conceive of them. 'Every individual', said Kierkegaard, 'must form his own idea of God as the unifying symbol of the life-aim to which he is committed.' The corporate worship which the present Archbishop of York wishes to rescue from decline is no longer meaningful for, as Don Cupitt says in *The Sea of Faith*, religions which used to be collectivist now preach self-realization.

Thus it was that I came to know and cherish the concept of the I and Thou relationship, of the still, small voice that speaks at unexpected times and in unexpected places. And nowhere, it seems to me, is this concept more tellingly and movingly expressed than in the lines of metaphysical poets like John Donne:

> Since I am coming to that Holy Room,
> Where with thy choir of saints for evermore,
> I shall be made thy music; As I come
> I tune the instrument here at the door,
> And what I must do then, think here before.

and George Herbert:

> But as I raved and grew more fierce and wild,
> At every word,
> Methought I heard one calling *Child*,
> And I replied, *My Lord*.

The last line of Somerset Maugham's *A Writer's Notebook*, published in his seventies, says 'I am on the wing', though in fact the old codger lived for another sixteen years. I am not yet on the wing, though I cannot deny that Donne's Holy Room and the Pearly Gates that lead to it have now begun to swim over my horizon. Do they exist other than in my imagination? I rather hope so, and as I write these final lines here in my earthly club, would count it as an added blessing to find a heavenly one with a candidates' book and no blackballs, awaiting my arrival.

Index

n before a number denotes a footnote

Abse, Leo 318
achievements 59, 60, 409, 410
    English Festival of Spoken Poetry
        competition 228
    Rockefeller Foundation Atlantic
        Award in Literature 195
    Verdienstkreuz 339–40
Admiraal, Dr 357
Admiral Graf Spee 97–8
Admiral Hipper 122
Admiral Scheer 122, 144
Adventurers' Club 209
Agar, Bill 61
Age of Reason, The 162, 411
Aherne, Brian 221
Airman and the Carpenter, The 387,
    388, 393
Aldershot Repertory Company
    Theatre 233–4
Alexander, General 378
Altrincham, Lord *see* John Grigg
Alvarez, Al 179
Al-Wahhabi, Sheikh 281
Amateur Emigrant, The n152
America 200–9, 384, 385, 386
    elections 203
        Macarthy hearings 202–3
        Sadler's Wells Ballet 200, 202, 203
Amethyst, HMS 360
Ammon, Charles 159
Ampthill House 97
And Quiet Flows the Don 55
Anderson, Sub-Lieutenant 99
L'Angelier, Pierre 63
Angora, HMS 19
Angus, Alexander 315
Ann 49
Archer-Shee, Tiny 107, 172
Ark Royal, HMS 116–18, 127, 132,
    335

Armstrong, Sir Robert 374, 375
Arnold, Tom 234
Asdic 25, 104
Ashdown, Rose 67, 179–82
Ashridge Adult Education College
    184–7, 191–2, 194–5
Ashridge Quarterly 186
Ashton, Freddie 205, 222
Astor, Lord 291, 292
Astor, Michael 280
Atlantis 113
atomic bomb test explosion 223
attitudes
    to the Arts 174
    to authority 409
    to capital punishment 232–3
    to corporal punishment 54–5
    to judicial system 39, 63, 297–8,
        360, 361, 395–8, 401–2
    to judiciary 237–8, 279, 280,
        295–6, 297–8, 317, 368–9,
        393–4, 398–400
    to killing 232
    to police behaviour 276, 297
    to pornographic films 350–1
    to prisoners 39
    to prisoners of war 124–5
    to prostitution 351
    to punishment 63
    to religion *see* Kennedy, Ludovic
        religious beliefs
    to Scottish independence 64,
        305–11
    to television 402–4
Aunt Alice 16, 48
Aunt Ju 87
Aunt Mab 65
Aunt Moggie 18
Aunt Susan 87, 88
Australia 17

Bacon, Lieutenant 137
Baddeley, Hermione 189
Baird, Roger 304
de Bajza, Aladar 88
Balanchine, George 204
Baldwin, Stanley 154, 185
Balfour, Robert 326
Balmoral, invitation to 183
Bar Association 400
Barfleur, HMS 19
Barrett, Vicky 292, 293, 295
Bartholomew 43
Batsford, B. T. 151
Beatty, Admiral of the Fleet Lord
    David 19, 21, 111, 167, 259
Beatty, Peter 94
Bedford 34, 39, 97
Bedouin, HMS 137
Beechwood 68
Beerbohm, Max 215, 217–18
Belgrave Crescent (Edinburgh) 22, 23,
    63
Beltrami, Joseph 315, 316, 317, 319,
    321, 325
Ben (dog) 70, 139, 188
Ben Hur 34
Benthall, Michael 234
Bentley, Derek 230, 231–2
Bessie 24, 46, 62, 358
Betjeman, John 178
Biggleswade Chronicle 102
Birkett, Lord 277
Birmingham bombings 399
Bisley 75
Bismarck 125, 126–9, 130–2
    documentary 334
Black, Peter 242–3, 254, 280
Black Arrow 60
Black Police of Queensland 17
Blackwood's Magazine 23, n86
Blair, David 46
Bletchley Park codebreakers 138, 144,
    334
Blom-Cooper, Louis 293, 318
Board of Admiralty 103
Bombay 266–7, 271
Bonfire of the Vanities, The 400
Bonham-Carter, Mark 249
Bonhoeffer, Dietrich 413
Boothby, Bob 20, 46, 65–7, 90, 187,
    195, 356
Free Speech 238, 239
    Hitler story 66
Boothby, Mabel (nee Dundas) 20, 64,
    65
Boothby, Sir Robert (Tom) 20, 21, 64,
    67
Boothby family 46, 62, 63, 65
Bootle, Lord 66
Bornmann, Lewis 387
Bourne, Wilfred 368
Bowen, Elizabeth 178
Bowra, Maurice n67
Boxer rebels 19
Brabourne, Lord 373, 375
Brew, Dr Macalister 186
Brien, Alan 179
Brighton Yacht Club 94
Britannic 125, 126
British Broadcasting Corporation
    (BBC) 61, 241, 266, 344, 407
    BBC2 285
    elections 247
    First Reading 228–9
    Gibraltar killings 406
    News 97, 101, 239, 243
    Northern Ireland 405–6
    Panorama 254–5, 256–74, 280
British criminal justice 63
Brittan, Leon 406
broadcasting career 61, 228, 238,
    343–53
    Coast to Coast 384
    Democratic Convention (1960)
        258–60
    Did You See? 385, 403
    Disunited Kingdom, The 307
    Face the Press 311
    First Reading 228–9
    gaffes 243
    Lord Jim 285
    Mountbatten, Lord 371–2, 373–5
    Neave, Airey 354
    newsreader for ITN 240–3
    Panorama 254–5, 256–74
    Profile 238
    reflections on 403–4
    reviews 229, 243, 256, 280–1, 285,
        286, 301, 302, 345, 393
    Television Reporters International

280–5 *see also* Television Reporters International
This Week 249, 253, 254, 300–1
Watergate hearings 337
Who Killed the Lindbergh Baby? 393
World War II series 327–36
Your Witness 311
Broadlands 371, 372–3
Trust 375
Brokaw, Tom 385
Brooke, Rupert 120
Broughton, Urban 185
Brown, Bill 238
Brown, Hamish M. n86
Brown, Jeremy Murray 262, 263, 264, 280
Bryan, Robert 386
Bryant, Dr Arthur 184, 360
Buckingham Palace 372
Bug, the 40, 42, 43, 45
Burge, James 292
Burials at Sea, Inc. 289
Burnside, David 318
Butler 73
Butler, R. A. 277
Buxton, Maurice 75–6, n80
Bynner, Witter 221

Calliope, HMS 370
Calvocoressi, Ion 192, 286
Cambridge Theatre 234
Cameron, Alan 46
Cameron, Lord 317
Campbell, Gordon 317
Campbell, Harold 95
Can Europe Keep the Peace? 60
Canadian Pacific 225
Cannes 216
Cape, Charles 233
capital punishment 232–3, 234, 376
Carey, Peter 48
Carey, Simon n67
Carls, Admiral 144, 145, 146
Carter, Crummy 39
Cassandra, HMS 19, 21
Cassels, Billy 55–6, 59, 73–4
Cecil, David 175–6, n176, 178, 217
Chamberlain, Neville 101

Chaplin, Charlie 203, 224, 225
Chataway, Chris 239, 240
Chenevix-Trench, Tony 40, 358
Chipperfield, Josephine 323
Chitral, HMS 101, 102
Christ Church, Oxford 75, 87–8, 174–9
Christie, John 235, 236, 275
Christie, Mrs 236, 275
Christmas Garland, A 218
Church, Richard 228
Church Row, Hampstead 226
Churchill, Randolph 239, 302
Churchill, Winston 66, 218, 378–9
Ciliax, Vice-Admiral 145, 146, 147
Clabon Mews, London 195, 196, 199, 220, 226
Clark, Jane 219, 220
Clark, Sir Kenneth 218, 219, 220
Clifford, Arthur 241, 242
Clifton, Talbot 70
Clyde, Lord 314
CND 196
Collins, Canon 196
Combined Operations 124
Condon, Dr 386, 389
Connolly, Cyril 178, 179
Conservative Party 247, 405
Constance, HMS 22, 25
Cooper, David 362–9
Cooper, Duff 220
Corbett, Mr 227
corporal punishment 36, 41–2, 53–5
Courageous, HMS 25, 27, 30
Coward, Noël 66, 154, 160
Cowichan, Lake 225
Cowper 177
Cox, Geoffrey 241
Craig, Christopher 230, 231
Cranston, Maurice 178
Crawley, Aidan 239, 241
Cremer, Peter 330
Croft, Michael 178
Crowther, Sue 386, 393
Croydon rooftop murder 230–1
Cruel Sea, The 168
Crump, Miss 104
Cubbon, Brian 368
Culloden Moor 47
Cupitt, Don 413

Culzean 15
Cunningham 359
Cusack, Mr Justice 365

Daily Mail 210, 243, 254, 280, 302
Daily Mirror 76, 247, 302, 376
Daily Record 318
Daily Telegraph 246
Dal Lake 272
Dance with Me 61
Danckwerts, Captain 336
Davenport, John 228
David, Dick 171
Davos 59
Day, Robin 239, 240, 241, 242, 253,
    254, 405
  Panorama 256, 258, 259, 262, 263
Day Lewis, Cecil 228
Deanyers 17–18, 29, 32
Deedes, Lord 404
Denison, Philip 76, 80, n80
Denning, Lord 295, 296, 315, 399
  Profumo affair report 295–6
Dent, Admiral 29, 31
Deutschland 97–8, 99
Devlin, Lord Justice 279, 318, 367
Dilhorne, Lord 300
Dimbleby, Richard 251, 262
Dobree, Bonamy 229
Dobson, Zuleika 218
Dönitz, Admiral 55, 330, 332–3
Dolin, Pat 284
Douglas, Lord Alfred 226
Douglas, Mrs Helen 203
Drury, Commander Kenneth 364,
    365, 369
Dudgeon, Brigadier General 233
Dudley, Lord 154
Duncan, Mrs 167
Dundas, Anne 20, 48
Dundas, Cecil 20, 67
Dundas, Henry 20, 90
Dundas, Neville 20, 64, 67
Dundas family 63
Dunston 41
Durrell, Henry 107, 169
Durschmied, Eric 280

Eck, Lieutenant-Commander 340–1,
    342

Eddowes, Michael 234, 237, 278
Ede, James Chuter 277, 278
Eden, Anthony 244, 374
Edinburgh 24, 90, 101, 139, 358, 408
  Festivals 358
  Grants 22–5, 62–3
  University 22
Edward, Prince 19
Edwards, Captain 26, 29, 31
Eliot, T. S. 187, 220
Elizabeth II, Queen 182, 311
Elliott, Claud 81, 83–6
Elsewhere 216
Elvin, Violetta 201, 202
Emberglow 61
Empire Cinema, Leicester Square 56
End of the Affair, The 219, 220
Enemy Within, The 178
English Bar Association 401
English Story 179
Enigma machine 138, 144, 334, 339
Eskimo, HMS 125, 126
Eton 52–62, 73–4
  flight to France 74–80
Europe, invasion of 168–71
Eustace and Hilda 177
Eutaw 201–2
euthanasia 67, 356–8
Evans, Beryl 235
Evans, Geraldine 235
Evans, Harold 278
Evans, Michael 76, n80
Evans, Timothy 235–7, 251, 275,
    276–7
  asserts innocence 275–6
  Brabin Inquiry 279, 360
  debate in House of Commons 277
  investigation by Ludovic Kennedy
    274–6
  struggle for pardon 276–80
  Timothy Evans Committee 279
Evening News 323

Fairbairn, Nicholas 312–14, 316, 318
Fairey 42–3
Farebrother, Mike 60–1
Farnham Common 52, 167
Fearn, Charlie 246, 251
Fegen, Captain Fogarty 102
Ferrier, Susan 23

Fighter Pilot 151
Financial Times 318
Findlater, Richard 234
Finkelstein, Miss 259, 260
Firebrace, Brigadier 166
Fisch, Isidor 387
Fisher, Jim 394
Fisher, Lloyd 392
Flarepath 177
Fleming, Ian 227
Foley, Mr 391
Foot, Michael 239
Fonteyn, Margot 201, 226
Fortescue 55
Fox, Paul 260, 269, 280
Franklin 206
Free Speech 238, 239
Freedom of Information Act (USA) 386
French Fleet 115
Fry, Charles 151
Fry, Christopher 228
Fyfe, Sir David Maxwell (Lord
    Chancellor Kilmuir) 231, 232,
    236, 237

Gabrielianz, Dr 209
Galumbo, Dr 259-60
Garbo, Greta 203
general election (1959) 252-3
George VI, King 95, 182
German Fleet 21, 111, 119, 328
Giessler, Captain Helmuth 336
Gilliat, Sir Martin 348
Gilmour, Ian 237, 246, 278
Gladstone, Mr 19
Gloag, Commander 30
Glorious, HMS 114
Gneisenau 98, 100, 101, 113, 119,
    122, 123
Goa 270-1
Goddard, Lord 231, 360
Goldwyn, Sam 203-4, 207-8, 221
    Hans Christian Andersen 203-4,
    208, 221
    Wuthering Heights 204
Gollancz, Victor 292, 297
Goodman, Lord 295
Gonzenheim 95
Gordon, Sir John Watson 23
Gow, Betty 387

Grade, Lew 280, 285-6
Graham, Harry 50
Graham of Skelmorlie, John 63-4
Grand Fleet 21
Grandy, Flight-lieutenant John 75
Grant, Lord 316
Grant family 20, 22, 45
Great Dictator, The 224
Greatorex, Admiral 25, 27, 30, 32
Greene, Graham 219, 220
Greene, Hugh 266
Greenock 91, 104
Grenville, Sir Richard 100
Grey, Beryl 201
Griffith-Jones, Mervyn 292, 293, 297
Griffiths, Jim 313, 314
Griffiths, Lord 402
Grigg, John (formerly Lord
    Altrincham) 237, 240, 278, 286
Grimond, Jo 244, 245, 247, 253, 301,
    307
Guardian 246
Guild of Television Producers 302
Gunston, Sir Derrick 159

Haddon, Peter 233
Hailsham, Quintin (Lord) 247, 248,
    249, 252, 368, 374
Hall, Bill 408
Hall, Henry 34
Hamburg 123
Hampshire, HMS 328
Hampton Court Palace 103, 165,
    179-82, 187-8, 192, 243,
    355-6
Handley, Tommy 114
Hangover Club 209
Happy Three, The 41
Harper, Ross 315
Harris, Kenneth 178
Hartley, L. P. 177
Hauptmann, Anna 385, 387, 393
Hauptmann, Richard 385-94
    case against 387-91
    case for 392-3
    investigation by Ludovic Kennedy
    387-8
Hayworth, Rita 221
Heald, Sir Lionel 300
Hearn 79

Helen 24
Helpmann, Bobby 234
Herbert, A. P. 159
Herbert, David 254
Herbert, John 178
Hicks, Sir Seymour 216
High Wycombe Parish Church 103
Higham, David 359
Highfield Preparatory School 39–43,
   n43
  fiftieth anniversary 43–4
  friends 40–1, 43
  homosexuality 40
  staff 40
Highland Burn Water 288
Hipper 103
His Excellency 179
Hitler, Adolf 66, 88, 111, 124, 138,
   144, 148, 329, 334, 403
Hodge, William 63
Hodges, Admiral Sir Michael 30, 31
Hodson, Harry 200
Hoffman, Harold 392
Hoffman, Kurt Cesar 98, 336
Holland-Martin, Pinky 107
Holyrood Palace 182, 311
Home Secretaries 231, 232, 236,
   277–8, 279, 291, 365, 366, 368,
   405, 406
Honourable Company of Edinburgh
  Golfers 326–7
Hood, HMS 126, 131, 132, n132
Hopwood, Rear Admiral Ronald 50
Horizon 179, 184
Hornblow, Arthur 204
Horse and Hound 102
Horton, Sir Max 102
House of Lords 66, 400
Hove 92–3
Howard, Anthony 301
Humphrey, Derek 357
Hunter, Lord 323–5
Hurn, Richard 366
Hurok, Sol 200, 203
Hurrah for the Life of a Sailor 15
Hussein of Jordan, King 349, 355
Hutchinson QC, Lord 401
Huxley, Aldous 223

I, of All People 303

Illustrated London News 41, 137
In Memoriam 68
In Which We Serve 154
Independent Broadcasting Authority
  (IBA) 93
Independent Television network 238
  Associated Rediffusion 252
  elections 247, 248
  Granada 247, 249
  News (ITN) 239–43, 406
  Thames 406
India 266–74
  bureaucracy 266
  Indian Defence Academy 269
  taxi incident 267–8
Ingrams, Richard 403
interviews 240, 252, 257
  Adenauer, Chancellor Konrad 250
  Bakshi Ghulam Mohammed 272
  Bevan, Aneurin 252
  Butler, R. A. 252–3
  Charles, Prince 372–3
  Dalai Lama 272–4
  Denning, Lord 295
  Dönitz, Karl 332–3, 333–4
  Edwards, Harry 345
  Gaitskell, Hugh 252
  Gardner, Antoinette 257
  Grigg, John 240
  Hailsham, Quintin (Lord) 252
  Hume, Basil 344–5
  Imbert, Sir Peter n402
  Kennedy, John F. 260–2
  Kretschmer, Otto 331
  Kurschid, Mr 272
  Lloyd, Selwyn 250
  Macmanaway, Bruce 346
  Macmillan, Harold 377–8
  Meir, Golda 349
  Mountbatten, Lord Louis 369, 371
  Nehru 272
  Pandit, Mrs 257
  Philip, Prince 311
  Ramsay, Michael 255
  Sellers, Peter 250–1
  Soustelle, Jacques 253
  Speer, Albert 349
  Thatcher, Margaret 354–5
  Toynbee, Arnold 257
  Trevelyan, Sir Humphrey 266

West, Rebecca 344
Invergordon 47–8
IRA 395, 398–9
  Gibraltar killings 406
  media coverage 405, 407
Irwin, John 238
Isherwood, Christopher 205
Isis
  literary editor 177
  short story competition 179
Isis, HMS 169
Islay 69–72, 81, 89
It was Good While it Lasted 150
Ivanov, Captain 291, 296

James, Henry 193
Jan Mayen Island 137
Jaques, Dr 187
Jeanmaire, Zizi 222
Jean's Way 357
Jellicoe, Admiral 111
Jenisch, Hans 330, 332
Jenkins, Roy 279, 365
Jervis Bay, HMS 103
Jessel, David 316
John Bull 32
Johnson, Paul 404
Jones, Mervyn 318
Joyce, William (Lord Haw-Haw) 348
judicial systems 395–8
Junack, Gerhard 335
Juncker 107
Jungmann, Elizabeth 217
JUSTICE 364, 367, 395

Kashmir 272
Kaye, Danny 220, 221
Keaton, Buster 224, 225
Kee, Robert 256, 280, 281, 283
Keeler, Christine 291, 292, 294
Kenderdine, Commander 168, 171
Kennedy, Ailsa (daughter) 226, 227,
  355–6, 358
Kennedy, Alastair (son) 281, 304,
  358, 408
Kennedy, Captain Edward Coverley
  (father)
  Admiralty 31
  coal miners' strike 25–9
  Conservative Party constituency
    agent 33, 34

  death 97–102
  diaries 50
  health 19
  interests 49–50
  letter to Ludovic 95
  marriage 20–1
  naval career 19–22, 25–33 *see also*
    naval career (Kennedy, Captain
    Edward Coverley)
Kennedy, Edward (grandfather) 15,
  17, 23, 63
Kennedy, Fiona (daughter) 281, 304,
  358, 408
Kennedy, John F. 258, 259, 260–2, 375
Kennedy, Katherine (sister) 45,
  165–6, 167, 192
Kennedy, Ludovic
  accident to family 353–4
  acting 75, 160, 177
  ambitions 48, 59–60, 228, 409–10
  America with Moira Shearer
    200–9, 220–5
  ancestry 47, 88
  anxieties 34–5, 41, 42, 54, 57, 71,
    183, 212–15
  barred from clubs 325–7
  birth 22
  Boothby, Bob 66–7
  broadcasting *see* broadcasting
    career
  business ideas 287–90
  childhood 18, 22–5, 34–9, 45–7
  confirmation 81
  creative arts 61–2
  diaries 223
  drowning officer 135
  education 39–43, 52–62, 73–5,
    87–8, 174–9, 184
  electric shock therapy 214
  family 15–25, 48, 52, 63–4
  and father 37, 39, 49–50, 51, 58,
    91, 182
  favourite authors 41, 174
  favourite smells 46
  fishing 70, 137, 161, 304
  friendships 40–1, 55–6, 94, 209
  and grandfather 23–4
  and grandmother 64–5
  holidays 45–50, 69–72, 192–4,
    225, 254, 286–7

Kennedy, Ludovic – *cont.*
  letters to 351–2
  love affairs 71–4, 87, 162, 173,
    174, 189–91
  medical history 34, 58–9, 345–6,
    379–83
  and Moira Shearer 190, 191–4,
    195–6
  and mother 35–8, 51–2, 57–8, 62,
    174, 213, 356
  music 60, 61–2
  naval career *see* naval career
    (Ludovic Kennedy)
  nightmares 90
  poetry, love of 68–9, 229, 230, 413
  politics *see* political career
  psychological problems 57, 212–3
  psychotherapy 213–15
  public speaking 160, 312
  reading 174
  reflections 409–13
  relationships in wartime 139–40
  religious beliefs 80–1, 162–5, 229,
    345, 411–13
  sexual education 39, 40, 43, 45, 56,
    71
  sexual initiation 74
  sport 41, 62, 68, 70, 75, 82–6, 137,
    161, 286–7, 304–5
  television and radio career 160
  thoughts on German sailors 119,
    138, 327
  writing *see* writing career
  youth 35, 52–86
Kennedy, Morar (sister) 21, 22, 45,
  165–6, 167
Kennedy, Rachel (daughter) 243, 358,
  408, 409
Kennedy, Rosalind (née Grant)
  (mother) 20–1, 70, 90, 174,
  179–80, 356
  behaviour towards Katherine
    165–6
  behaviour towards Ludovic 35–8
  behaviour towards Morar 165–6
  children's theatricals 187
  clichés 188
  Drown Box 166
  Hampton Court 165–6, 187–8
  hygiene 38

Naval Officers Leave Bureau, The
  139
spiritualism 166–8
Kennedy, William (Great-Uncle
  William) 15–16, 49, 92, 94, 161
Kerans, Commander 360
Keyes, Admiral 41
Kidnapped 174
Kimmins, Commander Anthony 168,
  171
King, Francis 178
King Alfred, HMS 92–4, 96
King George V, HMS 136
  search for *Bismarck* 126–30
  battle with *Bismarck* 131
King-Murray, Ronald 318, 319, 320
Kirkup, James 303
Kloppenburg, Hans 387
Knight, Esmond 334
Korda, Alex 216, 227
Korean War 202
Korth, Claus 330
Krebs 138
Kretschmer, Otto 330, 331, 332
Kripalani, Acharya 267

Lady Chatterley's Lover 221
Lamarr, Hedy 81, 207
Lancaster, Margaret 63
Landverk 16–17, 48–50
Lane, Lord 360–1, 368
Largs, HMS 169
Lauenberg 137–8
Laver, James 304
Lawrence, Frieda 221, 222
Lawton, Lord Justice 366, 367
Laye, Evelyn 136
League of Empire Loyalists, The 240
Leggett, D. 229
Lehmann, Commander 335
Lehmann, John 178
Levin, Bernard 318, 375
Liberal Party 244, 245, 247, 249, 253
  party political broadcasts 301–2
  Scottish Liberal Party's Council
    305–7
Liberalism 39, 244, 307
Lieutenant 179
Life of Nelson 184
Life is Too Short, A n317

Limelight 224
Lindbergh, Charles 385, 389
  kidnap of son case 386–94
Lindbergh Case, The 394
de Lisle, General 28
Listener 318
Little, Admiral Sir Charles 89, 102
Loesser, Frank 204, 221
London 139, 171
London Clinic 380
London School of Journalism 59
Longhurst, Henry 150
Longman, Mark 220
Lonsdale, Frederick 216
Lorne, Tommy 62
Los Angeles 221
Lust, Werner 335
Luton Post Office murder case 362–9
Luvaglio, Michael 298
Lynn, Vera 114
Lyttleton, Humphrey 61

Mabane, William 199
Macbeth, George 179, 228
McCann, Jack 246, 247, 248
MacCarthy, Desmond 200
McElhone, Frank 318
McEwen, Robin 304, 305
McGrath, John 179
MacGregor, Mr 65
McGuiness, William 317, 319, 321–2
Macintyre, Captain Donald 331
Mackenzie 375
McCluskey, Lord 400
McMahon, Michael 362–9
Macmillan, Harold 249, 258, 260,
  295, 369, 374, 375–7
MacNiece, Louis 228
Magee, Bryan 362, 366, 367, 369
Maitland-Magill-Crichton,
  Lieutenant-Commander Ian
  359
Makerstoun 304, 358
Malibu 205
Man on Your Conscience, The 234
Mantle, Wendy 364
Margadale, Lord 70
Margaret, Princess 347
Marschall, Vice-Admiral 98, 101
Marshall, Sir Archibald 292

Mashona, HMS 125, 127, 132
  sinking of 134–5
Mason, Gully 76
Mason, James 222
Massigli, Rene 220
Matabele, HMS 144
Mathews, Alfred 362, 366
Matthiesen, Reverend 392
Maudling, Reggie 405
Maugham, Robin 40
Maugham, W. Somerset 193, 219,
  220, 413
May, Derwent 179
Meehan, Mrs 314
Meehan, Patrick 312–25
  appeal 314
  attempts to obtain justice 317–19
  Committee 318, 322
  independent enquiry 323–5
  questioning 313
  release 319
  verdict 314

Melford-Stevenson, Mr Justice 341
Melody Maker 59
Memories n67
Menace 337, 339
Menon, Krishna 267, 269
messman's menu incident 141–2
Meyer, Michael 178
MGM 204
Miall, Leonard 254
Miles, PC 230, 231, 232
Millan, Bruce 319, 323
Milne, Alasdair 299, 347, 406
miscarriages of justice 300, 315, 317,
  367, 395–6, 398
  appeals 398, 401
  attitudes of judges 398–9
  Cooper, David 362–9
  Evans, Timothy 236–7, 274–9
  Hanratty case 398
  Hauptmann, Richard 385–94
  McMahon, Michael 362–9
  Meehan, Patrick 312–19
  Ward, Stephen 291–8
Mitchell-Innes 39
MI5 296
Modern Boy 34
Modern Times 224
Moncreiffe, Iain 88

Monsarrat, Nicholas 168
Monsieur Verdoux 224
Moore, Henry 220
Moore, John 168
Moorehead, Agnes 222, 225–6
Morgan, Charles 106, 178
Morris, Malcolm 275
Moscow 262–5
   churches 263
   Kremlin Museum 265
   Moscow State Television 262, 263,
     264
Mossman, James 256, 280
Mountbatten, Edwina 371
Mountbatten, Lord Louis 110, 245,
     369, 370–1, 372, 378
   obituary programme 371–2
Muggeridge, Malcolm 256, 280, 283
von Mullenheim-Rechberg, Baron 334
München 138
Murder Story 233–4
Murphy, Patrick 362
Murray, Leonard 315
Myra 71–3

Nairn 45–6, 48
Nanny-Noo *see* Rose Ashdown
Nasser, Colonel 244
National Association of Youth Clubs
   186
National Institute of Industrial
   Psychology 62
National Maritime Museum 103
National Union of Journalists 406
National Youth Theatre 178
naval career (Kennedy, Captain
   Edward Coverley) 19–22, 25–33
   China 19
   court-martial 30–1, 89, 102
   honour 102–3
   Newport mutiny 27–30, 102
   Rawalpindi, HMS 90, 91, 95, 97
   reinstatement 89
   World War I 19
naval career (Kennedy, Ludovic)
   ADC to Governor of
     Newfoundland 156–62
   Admiralty Press Division 168–71
   Cardington, RAF 96–7, 103
   cat incident 117–18

correspondence officer 119
demobilization 173
entry 90–2
escorting Russian convoys 140–4
Europe, invasion of 168–71
fancy dress 143
fecklessness 121–2
health 59
King Alfred, HMS 92–4
navigator 172
night watches 120
Osprey, HMS 104
Press Liaison Officer 168
promotion 152
Tartar, HMS 104–22, 122–38,
   138–50
Watchman, HMS 152–6
Wheatland, HMS 172–3
Zebra, HMS 171–2
Nehru 271
   invasion of Goa 271
Nelson, HMS 48, 98
Nelson, Lord 58
Nelson's Band of Brothers 184, 196,
   199, 201
Nelson's Captains see *Nelson's Band
   of Brothers*
New Club 326–7
New Statesman 179, 184, 227, 229,
   301, 318
New York City police 387
New York Daily News 387
New York Evening Journal 392
New York Review of Books 394
New York Times 388, 391, 393, 394
New Yorker 179, 261
New Zealand, HMS 19
New Zealand Bar Conference 401
Newcastle, HMS 100
Newfoundland 156, 158–62
Newport, Monmouthshire 26–9
Nieuw Amsterdam 225–6
Nixon, Richard 203, 338
No Admittance Except on Business 61
Nobel, Admiral Sir Percy 29
Nore, HMS 94
Norfolk, HMS 126
North, Christopher 22–3
Northern Echo 278
Northern Patrol 91

Norway 49–50
  German Fleet 144–8
  Norwegian Campaign 113, 123,
    124
Notable British Trials 63
Novello, Ivor 218

Oberon, Merle 204
O'Brian, R. Barry 295
Observer 178, 277, 318
Odhams 184
Officers Training Corps 75
Official Secrets Act 356
Old Amersham 243, 302
Old Curiosity Shop, The 174
Olgiati, Chris 348
Olivier, Sir Laurence 193, 204
One Man's Meat 227
Orama 113
Orbell, Dorothea 172
Orion, HMS 29
Orr-Ewing, Robert n80
Osprey, HMS 104
Owen, Gwil 179
Oxford University Dramatic Society
    177
Oxford University Writers' Club
    177–9

Paget, General Sir Bernard 185
Paine, Thomas 162, 411
Panorama 251
Parker, Lord 296
Parkinson, John 246, 247, 248
Paul, Leslie 187
Peacock, Michael 259, 285
Pearson, Signalman 125
Peirce, Gareth 364
Peleus 340–1
Pelham, John 76, n80
Pelly, Captain 96
Philips, Miss 44–5
Philips, Morgan 247
Phillimore, Admiral 29
Physical Training School 104
Pickersgill, Lieutenant 99, 100
Pinnacle Ridge 82–3, 86, n86, 89
Pitt-Rivers, Pauline 189
Place VC, Rear Admiral Godfrey 335
Plowden, Lady 93

Poland, invasion of 89
Poland, Rear Admiral 327
police malpractice 300, 324, 362, 364,
    385, 398
  confessions 274, 276, 293–4, 398
  false evidence 293–4, 313, 325,
    364, 388–92, 395, n395
  harassing witnesses 274–5, 294
  identification 313, 318, 389–90
  violence 387
Policeman, the 84–6
political career 254
  general election (1959) 253
  Liberalism 244
  party political broadcasts 301–2
  Rochdale by-election (1957) 245–9
  Scottish independence movement
    305–11
  Scottish Liberal Party's Council
    305–7
Polyarnyy 44, 142
Poona 269–70
Portsmouth 103
Portsmouth Evening Echo 32
President, HMS 243
Presumption of Innocence, A 318, 322
Prien, Gunther 95, 111, 328, 329
Prince of Wales, HMS 126, 131
Pringle, Miss 205
Prinz Eugen 125, 132, n132, 144
Pritchett, V. S. 178
Private Eye 242
Profumo, Jack 291
Profumo affair 291–8
Public Lending Right scheme 339
Puke 115
Punch 290
Purser, Philip, 286
Pursuit 60, n127, 177, 337, 339
Pym, Roland 215, 218

Queen Elizabeth II 336
Queen Mary 209
Queen Mother 347, 348
*Queen Victoria's Tour of the
    Highlands* 217

Radziwill, Stas 258, 260, 261, 262
Raeder, Admiral Erich 97, 332
Rambert, Marie 284, 285

Rantzen, Esther 311
Rassine, Alexis 205
Rattigan, Terence 177
Rawalpindi, HMS 90, 91–2, 168, 336
  press coverage 102, 115–16
  sinking of 98–100
  survivors 102
Ray, Professor Gordon 344
Ray, Ted 114
Razzle 56
Real Lives controversy 405–6
Red Shoes, The see Shearer, Moira
Redfern Gallery 178
Rees-Mogg, Sir William 406
Reilly, Edward 392
Reinhardt, Gottfried 222, 225
Repulse, HMS 126
von Reuter, Admiral 111
Reynolds, John 349
Ricardo, Ronna 292, 294, 295
Rice-Davies, Mandy 292, 293, 294
Richardson, Maurice 227
Richey, Paul 151
Richmond, Bill 93, 104, 150–1, 173,
    174, 177, 184
  best man at wedding 195
  death 211–12
  friendship with 209–11
Rights of Man, The 162
Rillington Place, 10 235, 236, 237
Rinehart, Ensign 337
Robbie, Cam 311–12
Robertson, Lord 320, 321–3
Robinson, Edward G. 206
Robinson, Mrs Edward G. 206
Rodney, HMS 98, 125
  search for *Bismarck* 126–30
  battle with *Bismarck* 131
Rogers, Millicent 221
Rolph, C. H. 318
Roosevelt, Dirk 175
Roskill, Captain Stephen 334, 340,
    341, 373
Roskill, Lord Justice 366, 367
Ross, Abraham 312, 314, 315, 318
Ross, Rachel 312
Ross, William 317–18, 319
Rothenstein, Sir William 226
Roughhead, William 63
Rouse, Anthony 344, 345

Rowse, A. L. 184
Royal Air Force 75
Royal Courts of Justice 296
Royal Family 182–3, 347
Royal Lyceum Theatre Company 358
Royal Naval Film Corporation 373
Royal Naval Volunteer force 92
Royal Navy 15, 48, 97, 101, 127,
    359–60
  Home Fleet 47, 98, 101, 105, 112,
    144
  tradition 99–100, 101
Royal Oak, HMS 95, 111, 328, 329
Rubenstein, Arthur 203
Ruge, General 113
Runcorn Courier 154
Russian convoys 140–4, 149
  PQ17 148, 359
Ruxton, Dr Buck 63
R.101 18, 57

Sadler's Wells Ballet 200, 202, 203
St Clair, HMS 135
St James's Club 209, 211
St John's Players 160, 177
St Leonards School 87
Salmon, Lord 327
San Francisco Zephyr 384
Sargant, Tom 364, 367, 395
Saudi Arabia 281–3
Scaduto, Anthony 386, 387, 394
Scannell, Vernon 228
Scapa Flow 95, 105, 111–12, 116,
    122, 171, 327–8
Scapegoat 386, 387
Scharnhorst 98–101, 113, 119,
    122–3, 168
  documentary 334, 336
  sinking 172
Schnee, Adalbert 341
Schulze-Cossens 403
Scotsman 314
Scott, George 175, 178, 227, 235
Scott, Sir Walter 23
  Sir Walter Scott Club speech 308–9
Scott-Henderson, QC, John 237, 277
Scottish National Party 307
Scottish independence 64, 305–11
Scottish Rugby Union 308
Sea of Faith, The 413

Seawolf, HMS 144
Secret Battle, The 159
Self, Bill 394
Seniors Golfing Society 327
Separate Tables 92
Shaw, George Bernard 204, 218
Shawcross, Lord 300
Shearer, Moira
   America 200–9, 220–5
   Ballet de Paris 199
   Border Television 355
   Bristol Old Vic 303
   British Broadcasting Corporation
    (BBC) 355
   Carmen 199
   children 222
   courted by Ludovic 190–5
   film-making 222, 225, 303
   Giselle 201
   Hans Christian Andersen 203–4,
    208, 220, 221–2
   Happy Hypocrite, The 215, 218
   holidays with Ludovic 192–4
   marriage to Ludovic 195–6
   Maugham, Somerset 219
   Profile 238
   Red Shoes, The 189, 196, 201, 204,
    303
   reviews 201, 209, 303
   Rochdale by-election 246, 248
   Sleeping Beauty 196, 201, 203, 208
   Story of Three Loves, A 222, 303
   Swan Lake 201
   Tales of Hoffman, The 199, 216,
    303
Sheffield, HMS 128, 131
Singer, Burns 228
Sigurd Jarl 49, 113
Sissons, Michael 362
Sitwell, Sachie 220, 221, 226
Skelton, Red 204
Skipwith, Commander Kim 107,
   148–9
Skye 81, 89
Slade 366
Slater, Sam 52, 55
Smith, Cyril 246, 253
Smith, Ensign 337–9
Smith, Godfrey 179
Smith, Madeleine 63

Smith-Calthorpe 56
Snow, Lord 318
socialism 39
Society of Authors 154
Somali, HMS 125
Somerville, Admiral 115, 127
Soskice, Frank 277, 278, 279
Spandau: The Secret Diaries 349
Spannier, Muggsy 208
Spectator 227, 246, 278, 297, 302,
   318
Spessivtzeva, Olga 284–5
Sport in the Navy and Naval Yarns 15
Sport, Travel and Adventure 15
Spycatcher trial 375
Standard 302
Stanford Law Review n395
Star 227
Steel, David 301, 305, 411
Stevens, Reginald 364
Stevenson, Adlai 258
Stevenson, Robert Louis 152, n152
Stockton, Ethel 388
Stonehouse, John 365, 369
Storr, Anthony 40
Strand 179
Stravinsky, Igor 222–3
Stravinsky, Vera 223
Sub-Lieutenant 154
Suez, invasion of 242, 244–5, 374
Suffolk, HMS 126
Sulzbach, Herbert 339
Summing Up, The 193
Sunday Afternoon 238, 239
Sunday Dispatch 245
Sunday Telegraph 286
Sunday Times, The 199, 200, 202,
   223, 227, 278, 318
Svenner 169–70
Symons, Julian 318
Synge, John 178

Tablet 227
Taranto 168, 173
Tarland 45–6, 48
Tartar, HMS
   assignment to 104
   damaged 149–50
   escorting Russian convoys 140–4
   first watch on 108–11

Tartar, HMS – cont.
  interception of Tirpitz 147
  joins 105–7
  leaves 150
  life on board 111
  Lofoten Islands 123–4, 137
  records achieved 137
  search for Bismarck 126–9
  search for Lauenberg 137
  taking Swedish destroyers 114–16
  under air attack 133–6
Taylor, A. J. P. 239
Tebbit, Norman 404
Telegraph 102, 295, 333
television
  power of 404–5
  pressure from governments 404–8
Television Reporters International
    280–5
  'Arab Ferment, The' 281–3
  'Jew in the World, The' 283–4
  Sleeping Ballerina, The 285
  10 Rillington Place 60, 251, 254,
    n261, 274, 276, 280, 359
  reaction to 276–9, 290
Terra Nova 158–9, 162
Terraine, John 373
Thatcher, Margaret 354–5, 377, 405,
    406
Thirty Seasons in Scandinavia 17
Thomas, Huw 243
Thompson, Dick 368
Thorpe, Jeremy 301, 410
Thwaite, Anthony 179
Tiller, Terence 228
Times, The 102, 201, 234, 300, 307,
    345, 356, 366, 375, n402
Times crossword 70, 88
Times Literary Supplement 318
Tirpitz 144, 145, 172
  attack on 146–8
  documentary 334, 335
  search for 146–7
  sinking 148
Tovey, Admiral 126, 128, 131, 136
  search for Tirpitz 146
Townsend, Group Captain Peter 183
Tracy, Spencer 204
'Transport Song, A' 229
Trewin, J. C. 234

Trial of Stephen Ward, The 297
Trials of Evans and Christie 276
Tribune 301
Trident, HMS 14
Trout Inn 178
Truth 32, 175, 227, 234
Tudor-Price, David 295
Two Quiet Lives 176–7
Tyser, Alan 76

U-boats 25, 111, 155, 172, 329–31,
    333
  U.47   95, 328
  U.93   330
  U.99   331
  U.110 138
  U.505 329
  U.556 334–5
  U.852 340
'Uckers' (nickname) 107
Uhlig, Henry 387
Ukraine Hotel 262, 264
Ultra 138, 144, 145, 146, 148
US Neutrality Act 337

de Valois, Ninette 204
Vass, Chief Petty Officer 93, 152
VE Day 172
Vernon, HMS 169
Very Lovely People 311
Victorious, HMS 144, 145, 146, 148
Victory, HMS 30, 103
Vidor, Charles 221
Volkoff 73

Waddell 314, 315, 316, 317, 318,
    319, 320
  trial 320–3
Wain, John 228, 229
Wallfisch, Anita 283–4
Walsh, Leslie 238
Ward, Stephen 291, 292, 293, 294,
    296
Wardroom 160
Warre, Philip 20, 21
Warspite, HMS 106
Watchman, HMS 152–7
Watkins, Vernon 228
Watney, John 178
Waugh, Evelyn 177, 178, n179, 184

Webster, David 216, 218
Webster, Ron 371
Weekly Intelligence Report 119
Werner, Reverend 392
West, Anthony 344
West, Rebecca 344
West Highland Gazette 154
West Indies Station 25
Whalley, George 107, 131
Wheatland, HMS 172
Whited, Millard 388–9
Whitehouse, Mrs 404
Whitelaw, Willie 46, 368
Whitfield, Brian 55, 78
Wicked Beyond Belief 367
Wien, Mr Justice 366, 367
Wilentz, Mr 391, 392
Williams, Francis 280
Willis, Dave 68
Willis, Mr 274
Wilson, Harold 301–2
Wilson, John 22–3
Wilson, Spider 107, 115, 126, 133,
    137, 146, 169
Wiltshire 408
Wingfield, Lieutenant-Commander
    Mervyn, 359
Winn, Godfrey 178, 337
von Witzendorff, Ernest 330
Wogan, Terry 359
Wohlfarth, Herbert 334–5
Wolfe, Billy 307
Wolfe, Herbert 278
Wolfe, Tom 400
Wolsey (cat) 188
Woolf, Gabriel 228
World War I 19, 21, 41
World War II 327–43
    Atlantic convoys 152–6
    atrocities 340–3
    Battle of the Atlantic 155, 334
    code-breaking 138
    end 172–3
    Europe, invasion of 168–71
    evacuation from Dunkirk 114
    Norwegian Campaign 113, 123,
        124

radar 153
reprisals n124
Russian convoys 140–4, 148, 149,
    359
Sweden 114–16
U-boats *see* U-boats
Writer's Notebook, A 413
writing career 61, 151, 174
    Airman and the Carpenter, The
        387, 388, 393
    Americans abroad 298–9, 311
    Ashridge Quarterly 186
    first article published 59–60
    first book published 151–2, 153
    history of Home Fleet 171
    journalist 200, 227, 251
    Menace 337, 339
    mentions idea to family 59
    Murder Story 233–4
    and music 61–2
    Newsweek International 359
    One Man's Meat 227
    Presumption of Innocence, A 318,
        322
    Pursuit 60, n127, 177, 337, 339
    reviews 154, 184, 200, 220, 227–8,
        234, 277, 297
    Rockefeller Foundation Atlantic
        Award in Literature 195
    short stories 179
    Star 251
    Sub-Lieutenant 154
    Sunday Times, The 199, 200, 223,
        227
    10 Rillington Place 60, 251, 254,
        n261, 274, 276–9, 280, 290, 359
    'Time for Decision, A' 200, 202
    Trial of Stephen Ward, The 297
    Very Lovely People 311
    Wicked Beyond Belief 367
Wyatt, Will 386
Wyndham, John (Lord Egremont) 76,
    78, n80

Zanzibar 16
Zebra, HMS 171
Ziegler, Philip 372